CRITICAL INSIGHTS

Mark Twain

CRITICAL
INSIGHTS

Mark Twain

Editor
R. Kent Rasmussen

Salem Press
Pasadena, California   Hackensack, New Jersey

Cover photo: The Granger Collection, New York

Published by Salem Press

© 2011 by EBSCO Publishing
Editor's text © 2011 by R. Kent Rasmussen
"The *Paris Review* Perspective" © 2011 by Sasha Weiss for *The Paris Review*

∞ The paper used in these volumes conforms to the American National Standard for Permanence of Paper for Printed Library Materials, Z39.48-1992 (R1997).

Library of Congress Cataloging-in-Publication Data
Mark Twain / editor, R. Kent Rasmussen.
  p. cm. — (Critical insights)
Includes bibliographical references and index.
ISBN 978-1-58765-689-7 (alk. paper)
  1. Twain, Mark, 1835-1910—Criticism and interpretation. I. Rasmussen, R. Kent
PS1338.M2727 2010
818'.409—dc22
                                                              2010029143

PRINTED IN CANADA

Contents

Career, Life, and Influence

Critical Contexts

Critical Readings

Resources

About This Volume _____

R. Kent Rasmussen

The essays in this volume offer a cross section of provocative interpretations of Mark Twain's writings that have been selected to encourage readers to adopt new perspectives on one of America's greatest writers. Twain wrote on such diverse subjects in so many different genres it is impossible to cover every facet of his writing adequately in a single volume of this size. For that reason, this collection focuses mostly on the long works by Twain that modern students most frequently encounter and on the issues with which they are most concerned.

This introductory section opens with my overview of Mark Twain's significance as a writer and what I see as the most important and interesting aspects of his work, particularly as they relate to the essays within this volume. This is followed by a biography of Twain that outlines the main events in his long and active life, showing, wherever possible, how closely his life story is tied to his writings. The final piece in this section is a perspective on Twain's writings from Sasha Weiss, writing for *The Paris Review.*

The second section of the volume, "Critical Contexts," contains newly commissioned essays by four leading scholars in the field of Twain studies. In "Mark Twain and His Times," Stephen Railton—who teaches literature and administers the Mark Twain in His Times Web site at the University of Virginia—surveys the full breadth of Twain's writings within the context of the periods in which he wrote them. After carefully identifying links among the events of Twain's life, his writings, and the historical changes through which he lived, Railton concludes that Twain was as closely tied to his times as were the famous so-called Siamese twins about which Twain enjoyed writing.

In "Mark Twain's Critical Reception," Alan Gribben surveys Twain's writing career from the perspective of what literary critics and reviewers have said about his work, starting with Twain's earliest major books and continuing up to the present day. Gribben shows how re-markable Twain's present exalted reputation as a writer is, given the obstacles that long stood between him and literary respectability. The first of these was Twain's early reputation as a travel writer, which con-fused readers and critics alike when he started writing the novels for which he is now most famous. He also confused his contemporaries by getting deeply involved in public business ventures, including owner-ship of his own—ultimately unsuccessful—publishing firm. Of greater relevance to his reputation as a writer, however, has been his huge and sustained popularity among readers. Unfortunately, during his time, as during our own, critics tended to be suspicious of the literary merits of best-selling authors. Many of them assumed that any writer as popular as Twain need not be taken seriously—an assumption that few Ameri-can writers contemporary to Twain shared. (On the other side of the At-lantic, however, Sir Walter Scott and Charles Dickens were notable ex-ceptions to this bias.) Twain's literary status was also long questioned because of his reputation as a humorist. If being wildly popular were not cause enough for suspicion, his ability to make people laugh—and laugh hard—provided an even greater cause for doubting his literary merits. Even now, Twain's continuing popularity and renown as a hu-morist cloud some judgments of his literary merits, though not as much as in the past. Of greater ongoing concern is the fifth obstacle Gribben identifies—questions about his literary craftsmanship. Virtually every book Twain wrote has some kind of serious flaw. Whether these flaws should ultimately detract from his reputation, however, is a question still being debated.

One of the predominant subjects in modern Twain scholarship has been Twain's treatment of gender issues. A curious aspect of his writ-ing career is the contrast between the importance of strong women in his life and the relative scarcity of strong female characters in his fic-tion. This contrast has inspired a number of penetrating studies of the role of women in Twain's writing, but until recently, little attention had been paid to his depictions of men as men. In "'Pluck Enough to Lynch a Man': Mark Twain and Manhood," Hilton Obenzinger presents a highly original take on Twain's view of masculinity. After analyzing the leading male characters in Twain's most important works, Obenzinger arrives at Twain's definition of a "whole man." Perhaps surprisingly, he finds only one character in Twain's fiction who fits that definition. The identity of that character may knock some readers off their chairs.

The last new essay in this section, Lawrence I. Berkove's "Kindred Rivals: Mark Twain and Ambrose Bierce," offers another highly original perspective on Twain's writing. One of the best ways to gain insight into a particular author is to compare that author's life and works with the life and works of another writer; the similarities and contrasts that one finds almost inevitably turn up surprises that illuminate both writers. Here, Berkove compares Twain with one of his contemporaries whose name has for too long been known far better than his actual writings. Most famous for *The Devil's Dictionary* (1911), a collection of typically cynical but often brilliant aphorisms, Bierce was also the author of a large body of fiction that has only recently been made fully available to modern readers. As an established expert on both Twain and Bierce, Berkove is well placed to compare them, and what he finds is almost startling. In addition to making a case for elevating Bierce's reputation, he finds so many parallels between Twain's and Bierce's work that there is good reason to believe that they borrowed from each other. Berkove is careful to separate fact from conjecture, but he points out that if his conjectures about Twain's apparent borrowings from Bierce can be substantiated, Twain may not have been as original a writer as he is generally believed to be. However, Berkove adds, even if this proves to be true, it does not necessarily diminish Twain's greatness.

The "Critical Readings" section of this volume reprints a selection of outstanding essays that present challenging views on Twain's major works. As Twain first established his authorial reputation as a travel writer, it is appropriate that this section opens with a lengthy excerpt on his travel writings from Larzer Ziff's *Return Passages: Great American Travel Writing, 1780-1910* (2000). In the selection titled here "Mark Twain as a Travel Writer," Ziff analyzes the first two of Twain's five travel books, *The Innocents Abroad* and *Roughing It*, which also happen to be the Twain travel books that are still most widely read and studied.

Cynthia Griffin Wolff's essay *"The Adventures of Tom Sawyer*: A Nightmare Vision of American Boyhood" provides a sharp change of direction, as Wolff examines the first novel that Twain wrote entirely on his own. *Tom Sawyer* is the first introduction to Twain for many readers, who typically regard the book as a pleasantly nostalgic depiction of American boyhood during a simpler time. Wolff reveals the novel's menacing and often frightening undercurrents and shows that the dark themes and pessimism for which Twain's late writings are well known can also be found in his early fiction.

Beyond any question, *Adventures of Huckleberry Finn* is both Twain's most important book and one of the most frequently assigned novels in American classrooms. For these reasons, it deserves special attention. Substantial discussions of the novel can be found in several of the new articles in the "Critical Contexts" section, and within "Critical Readings" three more articles focus specifically on *Huckleberry Finn*. After opening with an intriguing comparison of *Huckleberry Finn* and Herman Melville's *Moby Dick* (1851) to introduce the subject of literary realism, Tom Quirk's "The Realism of *Huckleberry Finn*" examines the overall structure of the novel and touches on a variety of its themes. Everett Carter's "'Huckleberry Fun'" offers a concise overview of the novel that relates its humor to the very serious issues it addresses. Finally, in a wide-ranging discussion of race, David L. Smith addresses the novel's most controversial aspect—the modern charge that it is a "racist" book—in "Huck, Jim, and American Racial Discourse." Since the first publication of Smith's essay in 1984, a great deal has been written about the subject of race in both *Huckleberry Finn* and Twain's writings generally, but Smith's article remains important for its pioneering contribution to raising the issue of racism in the novel to the level of reasoned, scholarly debate.

In "*Connecticut Yankee*: Twain's Other Masterpiece," Lawrence I. Berkove makes a persuasive case for regarding *A Connecticut Yankee in King Arthur's Court* as a novel in the same class as *Huckleberry Finn*. Although long popular among readers, *Connecticut Yankee* has been widely regarded as fundamentally flawed because of its apparent unevenness in tone. The first part of the novel is filled with humor, which most first-time readers expect to continue, only to be shocked by the book's nightmarish climax. Many critics have seen this unexpected shift in tone as evidence that Twain lost control over his material, but Berkove persuasively argues that the book's shift in tone actually reflects such a brilliantly subtle design that one must take a different approach to reading the novel to appreciate its greatness.

The time-travel theme of *Connecticut Yankee* ties in with the next article in this section, David Ketterer's "Mark Twain as a Science-Fiction Writer," originally published as his introduction to *The Science Fiction of Mark Twain* (1984). Ketterer's book, later reissued as *Tales of Wonder* (2003), is a collection of Twain's short pieces and extracts from his longer works, including *Connecticut Yankee*, that employ science-fiction themes and devices. Because many of these stories were not published until well after Twain died, many readers may be surprised by the breadth of their themes and their sheer inventiveness. Ketterer argues that, had more of these writings been completed and published during Twain's lifetime, Twain might now be ranked alongside Jules Verne and H. G. Wells as one of the great pioneers of science fiction.

The final selection in this section, Michael J. Kiskis's "Mark Twain and the Tradition of Literary Domesticity," offers another fascinating shift in direction—an examination of family issues in Twain's life and writings within the larger context of nineteenth-century literature. Through all the complexities of Twain's long life and diverse works, he remained, at heart, a family man, and family issues permeate his writings. Kiskis makes his case by focusing on *Huckleberry Finn*, Twain's complex autobiographical writings, and the moving tribute to his daughter Jean that he wrote immediately after she died.

In addition to the essays presented in this volume, readers will find a concise chronology of Mark Twain's life, a list of his major published works, and a bibliography listing a selection of useful general works on him. Also provided are biographical sketches of the contributors to this volume and its editor as well as a detailed index.

CAREER, LIFE, AND INFLUENCE

On Mark Twain

R. Kent Rasmussen

Is Mark Twain the greatest writer America has yet produced? Many people would answer that question in the affirmative, but perhaps such a question should not be asked in the first place. Leaving aside the matter of whether it is even possible to answer such a question, it should be enough to say that Twain *is* a great writer. Proof in support of this assertion lies in the fact that fully a century after his death people continue to read his books avidly—even when they are not assigned in school—and scholars continue to offer new and often exciting interpretations of his life and work.

In 1906, four years before Twain died, he observed that over the course of the preceding century, 220,000 books had been published in the United States, but "not a bathtub-full of them are still alive and marketable." That statement may contain some exaggeration, but Twain's essential point is as true now as it was then: few books outlive their authors. Indeed, this may have been especially true for nineteenth-century American novelists, most of whom are utterly forgotten today. There are exceptions, of course, and of these, Twain is clearly the most outstanding example. In the year 2010—a full century after Twain died—not only were most of his books still in print, some had never gone out of print, even briefly, since they were first published during the nineteenth century. There may not be another American author from his time for whom the same can be said. This fact raises questions about what accounts for Twain's enduring popularity and whether his popularity says anything about his greatness as a writer.

A simple but incomplete answer to the question of why Twain's popularity has endured is that at least three of his books have entered the realm of acknowledged classics. The title characters and basic story lines of *The Adventures of Tom Sawyer* (1876), *Adventures of Huckleberry Finn* (1884), and *The Prince and the Pauper* (1881) have become so deeply ingrained in American culture that many people aware of these titles may not even know that Twain wrote them. Indeed, when the Disney Company used "The Prince and the Pauper" as the title for an animated Mickey Mouse film in 1990, it did not even bother to include Twain's name in the film's credits—an omission that seems to suggest that Twain's story has passed beyond the realm of a mere classic to become a timeless and anonymously created fairy tale. However, this sort of popularity does not account for why a book such as *Huckleberry Finn* is assigned reading in thousands of high school and college classes every year and is the subject of a seemingly endless outpouring of scholarly theses, articles, and books.

Among scholars, the difference between literary works worthy of study and those that are not lies in the matter of their "interpretability"— or, in simpler terms, how much can be read into them. Whereas a book such as Herman Melville's *Moby Dick* (1851) lends itself to nearly endless interpretations of its themes, symbols, and multiple levels, an intelligent, witty, beautifully crafted, and immensely entertaining modern novel may reveal all that it has to say on its first reading, with nothing remaining to be interpreted. I submit that Mark Twain is a great writer because many of his books can be read both as high entertainment and as hefty literary works of almost endless interpretability.

Twain's writings are repeatedly read, analyzed, deconstructed, and reinterpreted because they continue to have something fresh to say to each new generation. In his essay on Twain and Ambrose Bierce written for this volume, Lawrence I. Berkove states that Twain "remains an unaccountable literary genius, a giant for the ages." Berkove's phrase "unaccountable literary genius" is an apt one, as it reflects the growing view that Twain has depths that can never fully be plumbed, that we can go on forever reading and studying him and never fully explain him. This is a view with which I concur. Throughout the nearly twenty years I have studied and written about Twain, I have never come close to growing bored with the man. Every time I reread one of his books, I notice things I do not recall having noticed before. Every time I am satisfied I have answered one of my questions about him, I find one or two new questions emerging to take its place. Every year sees the publication of at least a half dozen new books about him, and each time I read one of them, I feel like I am finally beginning to understand him fully for the first time—until, that is, the next new book comes along.

If all this makes studying Twain sound like it should be wearing, it is not. In fact, it is exactly the opposite. Every person I have met who has spent years reading and studying Twain—both scholars and "buffs"— relishes sharing in the thrill of making new discoveries, and I do not recall ever meeting anyone who has lost interest in Twain because reading his works and studying him had become boring. Indeed, I wonder how it would even be possible to find Twain boring.

Some years ago, when Shelley Fisher Fishkin and I were conducting almost daily e-mail conversations about our work on Twain, we asked each other why we never get bored with him. I have not forgotten the little epiphany that Shelley shared with me on one occasion: we do not get bored with Twain because he connects with *everything*. Like Twain's bathtub anecdote, this remark may be a bit of an exaggeration, but it also expresses an important truth. Mark Twain really does connect with almost everything. During his nearly seventy-five years on our planet, he lived through one of the greatest periods of social, political, and technological change in human history.

As Stephen Railton discusses in "Mark Twain and His Times" within this volume, when Twain was born in 1835, fewer than thirteen million Americans were living in the nation's twenty-four states. By the time he died, in 1910, more than ninety-two million Americans were living in forty-six states, and the percentage of them living in cities had more than doubled. Moreover, at the time of Twain's birth, slavery was flourishing, steam-powered trains and vessels were still in rudimentary stages of development, medical practices had scarcely advanced since the Middle Ages, and inventions such as photography, telegraphy, and even typewriters still lay in the future. By the time of his death, tens of thousands of miles of railroad tracks were moving high-speed trains around the country, iron-hulled steamships were plying the world's oceans, gas-powered automobiles were on the roads, and airplanes were taking to the skies. Photography had advanced to color pictures and motion pictures, telegraphy was already giving way to telephones and wireless radio, medicine was on the threshold of its modern era, and slavery had long since been abolished.

Mark Twain was not the only American to live through all these and other changes, but he was unusual in closely observing and commenting on them. Moreover, he was also exceptionally well traveled; he lived for at least a few months in every region of the United States. He also spent nearly twelve years abroad and visited every inhabited continent. During his widespread travels, he met many of the world's leading cultural, political, and scientific figures and had close relationships with more than a few of them. The essays in this volume are concerned primarily with Twain as a writer, but all aspects of his life are so fascinating that he has attracted almost as much attention from biographers as he has from literary scholars.

Twain's interests were so broad and diverse that it is difficult to find a subject on which his writings do not touch, at least briefly. He also had a rich imagination and incredibly inventive mind that allowed him to project into the future technologies and political and social developments that had not yet occurred. As David Ketterer discusses in "Mark Twain as a Science-Fiction Writer" in this volume, Twain even wrote about a device similar to television decades before it was invented. For all these reasons and more, saying that Twain connects with everything may not be as great an exaggeration as one might suspect.

There are, of course, other important dimensions to Mark Twain that keep readers and scholars coming back to him. One of the most important of these is his remarkable ability to make readers laugh. Whatever else one thinks about his writing, he is frequently very funny and often in unexpected ways. A major part of his "unaccountable genius" is his knack for investing his writing with an unforced humor. His writing style grew out of the American Southwest's tradition of frontier humor, which was built on such devices as eccentric characters, outrageous exaggeration, and colorful dialects. Like many nineteenth-century humorists, Twain used these devices and others; however, he quickly distanced himself from his contemporaries by investing in his work qualities other writers could not match. One of the chief among these was the naturalness of his dialogue. He was always an excellent observer, and he had a particularly good ear for language. Whereas many of the humorists of his time strove for laughs by inventing fractured idioms and using cacography—the deliberate misspelling of words—to exaggerate the ignorance of their characters, Twain strove to emulate natural human speech and looked for humor in other devices. One of the most popular American humorists of the mid-nineteenth century, and an important influence on Twain himself, was Artemus Ward. This passage from Ward's sketch titled "Women's Rights" is an extreme example of cacography:

> I pitcht my tent in a small town in Injianny one day last seeson, & while I was standing at the dore takin money, a deppytashun of ladies came up & sed they wos members of the Bunkumville Female Reformin & Wimin's Rite's Associashun, and thay axed me if thay cood go in without payin.

Can there be any doubt about why few people still read this sort of thing? Passages such as these reek of artificiality; no living human could ever have spoken such words. Compare Ward's passage with the opening lines of Twain's *Huckleberry Finn*:

> You don't know about me, without you have read a book by the name of "The Adventures of Tom Sawyer," but that ain't no matter. That book was made by Mr. Mark Twain, and he told the truth, mainly. There was things which he stretched, but mainly he told the truth. That is nothing. I never seen anybody but lied, one time or another, without it was Aunt Polly, or the widow, or maybe Mary.

Expressed in the narrative voice of the youthful and largely unschooled Huck, this passage resembles Ward's in that it is permeated with grammatical errors, but at the same time it feels authentic. When we read it, we can believe we are hearing the unaffected voice of an ignorant backwoods boy, not an artificial creation. Almost amazingly, Twain was able to sustain that voice throughout the entire novel.

One of the reasons *Huckleberry Finn* is considered a great novel is the contribution it made to American literature by helping to liberate it from the shackles of stiffly formal narrative techniques. Twain's use of the ignorant Huck as his novel's narrator was a bold experiment. Some contemporary critics damned the book as coarse because of Huck's grammatical errors and occasional vulgarities, but this same voice would influence many great twentieth-century American writers, and it is now considered one of *Huckleberry Finn*'s primary strengths.

A large part of the academic and scholarly attention given to Mark Twain has long been lavished on *Huckleberry Finn*, which is arguably his greatest book. At the Sixth International Conference on the State of Mark Twain Studies in Elmira, New York, in August 2009, Louis J. Budd, the dean of Twain studies, exhorted fellow scholars not to focus so much on one Twain work that they neglect his many other writings. Not every book that Twain wrote is great, or even important, certainly, but almost everything he wrote is of interest for one reason or another. A good example is *Tom Sawyer*, which is the subject of an essay by Cynthia Griffin Wolff in this volume. Although *Huckleberry Finn* is clearly the superior book and the one that garners the most serious attention, *Tom Sawyer* has probably been read by more people, and Tom may be an even more familiar American icon than Huck. Nevertheless, as Alan Gribben points out in "Mark Twain's Critical Reception" in this volume, *Tom Sawyer* has yet to receive a book-length scholarly analysis. This oversight seems remarkable in view of the book's enduring popularity. However, it can probably be at least partly accounted for by the long-standing perception of the novel as a simple "boy book"—a juvenile work not worthy of serious adult attention.

I was mesmerized by *Tom Sawyer* the first time I read it at the age of nine, and most children who read it like it as much as I did as a child. However, Twain wrote the novel not merely for children but also for adults. As he explains in the book's preface, "Part of my plan has been to try to pleasantly remind adults of what they once were themselves, and of how they felt and thought and talked, and what queer enterprises they sometimes engaged in." Because he was thinking of his adult readers when he composed the book, much of what happens in *Tom Sawyer* goes over the heads of its younger readers, as it conveys what Wolff calls a "nightmare vision of boyhood." Although *Tom Sawyer* does not deal with themes as weighty as slavery and social degrada- tion, as *Huckleberry Finn* does, it presents a dark and often frightening depiction of life in a frontier village during the mid-nineteenth century that is in sharp contrast to the pleasantly nostalgic vision the novel is generally perceived as conveying. *Tom Sawyer* is clearly a novel that requires careful reading.

Another popular book by Twain that merits a more careful reading is *A Connecticut Yankee in King Arthur's Court* (1889). In this novel, a late-nineteenth-century American suddenly finds himself in sixth- century England, which he tries to transform into a modern democratic republic. One of the first novels to use time travel as a plot device, this sprawling story has long delighted readers with its many humorous scenes pitting the past against the nineteenth-century present, such as armored knights playing baseball and wearing sandwich boards to ad- vertise soap, the modern Yankee using a lasso to best the finest knights in a jousting tournament, and the meek surrender of six belligerent knights at the sight of ersatz tobacco smoke shooting through the bars of the Yankee's metal helmet. However, the novel's playful humor eventually gives way to almost unimaginable violence and destruction, turning the Yankee's dream of creating an egalitarian republic into an- other kind of nightmare vision. As they do with the flaws in other Twain stories, many readers are inclined to dismiss this jarring shift in the novel's tone as mere carelessness on Twain's part. However, as

Lawrence Berkove argues in his essay on *Connecticut Yankee* reprinted in this volume, the problem lies more in our misreading of the novel than in Twain's design. While explaining how the novel should be read, Berkove argues that Twain may be an even greater writer than is generally acknowledged—another example of how Twain's works are constantly being reinterpreted.

A buzzword that arose on American high school and college campuses during the late twentieth century was "relevance." Increasingly dissatisfied with traditional academic course work, students began demanding that what they studied have more relevance to their real lives and the challenges they would face as working adults. They were also reacting against what they perceived as overly narrow perspectives on history and culture and demanded broader representation of nonwhite and feminist points of view. If relevance is what readers are looking for in literature, they are likely to find more of it in Mark Twain's writings than in the works of other American writers of his time. The kinds of issues that Twain addresses and the style in which he writes have a kind of timelessness that make his works as relevant today as their were in his own time.

Biography of Mark Twain_____

R. Kent Rasmussen

Mark Twain's life was sufficiently complex and full of incident to be of great interest for its own sake. His life is of particular interest to students of his writing, however, because of the large amount of autobiographical material on which his writings draw. Many plot elements that Twain used were inspired by incidents he experienced or observed; many of his fictional characters are clearly modeled on his relatives, friends, and acquaintances; and the principal setting of his most famous novels, *The Adventures of Tom Sawyer* (1876) and *Adventures of Huckleberry Finn* (1884), is closely modeled on the Missouri town in which he grew up. Moreover, the travel books that made him famous during his lifetime constitute important parts of his autobiography. Consequently, any examination of Twain's life will reveal much about his literary work.

The man destined to find fame as Mark Twain was born Samuel Langhorne Clemens on November 30, 1835, in the tiny northeastern Missouri village of Florida, about thirty miles west of the Mississippi River. Known as Clemens throughout his entire life, he would not adopt the pen name Mark Twain until he was twenty-seven, and even though he would publish all his most important writings under that name, he never made a secret of the fact that his real name was Samuel Clemens.

Early Boyhood

The sixth of his parents' seven children, Sam Clemens was one of only four who would reach adulthood. Several years before his birth, his Virginia-born father, John Marshall Clemens, had moved the family to Missouri in the hope of finding the prosperity that had eluded him in eastern Tennessee. His failure to realize that goal would leave a lasting imprint on Twain, who went through his entire life fearing he would duplicate his father's financial failure—which, in a sense, he eventually did. Like many of his boyhood experiences, Twain's family's futile quest for prosperity would figure into his future writings. In fact, the eleven chapters that open *The Gilded Age* (1873), his first novel, which he cowrote with Charles Dudley Warner, is essentially a retelling of his family's migration from Tennessee and their struggle to succeed in Missouri. "Squire" Si Hawkins, the patriarch of the novel's fictional family, closely resembles Twain's father in taking an immense pride in his aristocratic pretensions as a southerner, in his naive faith in unsound business speculations, and in leaving his family impoverished upon his death. John Clemens would also appear in slightly different guises in some of Twain's other writings, most notably in *Pudd'nhead Wilson* (1894), in which he appears as Judge York Leicester Driscoll, a justice of the peace who is "very proud of his old Virginian ancestry."

Because Twain's father died when Twain himself was a little over eleven years old, his greatest influence on his son's life may have been as a role model not to be emulated. In contrast, Twain's mother, Jane Lampton Clemens, would play a more seminal role in his life. This was partly the result of her outliving her husband by more than forty years, during which she was always in close communication with Twain (although they never lived close to each other after the 1850s), but her influence on him owed primarily to the force of her personality. In contrast to her husband, she was cheerful, demonstrably affectionate, and fun loving. She was also an excellent storyteller who doubtless helped inspire Twain to become one. Her main appearance in her son's fiction is as Tom Sawyer's loving Aunt Polly, but she had a much stronger personality than Polly ever exhibits.

Another family member who played an important role in Twain's life and writings was his older brother, Orion Clemens, who lived until 1897. After their father's 1847 death, Orion became the titular head of the family and was also Sam's on-again, off-again employer for several years while he published small-town newspapers and ran a print shop.

Although Orion and Sam would always remain close, their relationship was never easy. Sam rebelled early against Orion's attempts to control what he wrote in his brother's newspapers, and he resented Orion's failure to pay him his meager salaries. Sam never had great respect for Orion. Although Orion was intelligent, principled, and industrious, he inherited his father's gift for failure and had a mercurial temperament that caused him constantly to change direction and rarely finish anything he started. Sam would never tire of ridiculing him, especially after he himself began achieving success as an author. Eventually, his relationship with Orion would become inverted, and he would be Orion's principal means of support. He would also use Orion as the model for some of his most eccentric characters. In an 1879 letter, Twain said that he did not "believe that a character exists in literature in so well-developed a condition as it exists in Orion's person. . . . Orion is as good and ridiculous a soul as ever was" (*Letters* [Paine] 1: 347). In a later comment on Orion's desperate eagerness to win the approval of others in matters of religious and political opinions, Sam remarked that Orion "never acquired a conviction that could survive a disapproving remark from a cat" (*Autobiography* [Paine] 2: 272).

The other two siblings of Twain who survived to adulthood were his older sister, Pamela Clemens Moffett, and his younger brother, Henry Clemens, who would die from injuries received in a steamboat accident when he was not quite twenty years old. Like Orion, Pamela would stay in close communication with Sam until she died, in 1904. Her principal appearance in her brother's fiction is as Tom Sawyer's gentle cousin Mary. Henry appears as Tom's priggish and somewhat detestable half brother, Sid, but Twain himself later said of Henry, "He is Sid in *Tom Sawyer*. But Sid was not Henry. Henry was a very much finer and better boy than ever Sid was" (*Autobiography* [Paine] 2:92-93). Whatever Twain had actually thought of Henry when they were growing up together, he went through most of his later life feeling guilty for having gotten Henry the steamboat job that would lead to his death.

A curious aspect of Twain's use of his family members in *Tom Sawyer* is the little changes he made in their interrelationships. Although he claims in the book's preface that Tom himself "is a combination of the characteristics of three boys whom I knew, and therefore belongs to the composite order of architecture," it is clear that Tom is principally modeled on the young Sam Clemens himself. It seems a little odd, therefore, that he made Tom an orphan who is living with his deceased mother's sister Polly, whom he modeled on his real mother. Mary, whom Twain modeled on his sister Pamela, is Tom's cousin in the novel (her relationship to Polly is not explained), and Sid, whom Twain modeled on his brother Henry, is Tom's half brother. In *Huckleberry Finn*, Sid's surname is explicitly identified as "Sawyer," seemingly suggesting that he and Tom had the same father and different mothers. If so, this would imply that Tom lost not only his father and mother but also a stepmother before coming to live with Polly. Twain was often careless about details concerning his fictional characters, so it may be a mistake to try to read too much into these matters, but one wonders what his use of his family members in *Tom Sawyer* reveals about his actual childhood.

In 1839, when Twain was less than four years old, his father gave up on seeking his fortune in Florida, Missouri, and moved the family to nearby Hannibal, a larger, riverfront town that showed promise of becoming a major transportation hub, which to some extent it eventually did. In Hannibal, John Clemens would achieve some prestige as a justice of the peace and civic leader (like *Pudd'nhead Wilson*'s Judge Driscoll), but he still failed to prosper. Meanwhile, his children, including Sam, grew up in a town very much like the fictional St. Petersburg of *Tom Sawyer*. Sam resided in Hannibal until 1853, when he was in his eighteenth year. Through those years, he lived in houses only a few blocks away from the Mississippi River and received all the formal schooling he would ever have in one-room schoolhouses. Around the age of thirteen, he was apprenticed to a local printer, and he later worked for his brother Orion in the same capacity. (Other nineteenth-century writers who began their careers as printers include William Dean Howells and Joel Chandler Harris, both of whom would later become Twain's friends.) Although Twain's formal schooling ended early, he was ever a prodigious reader, and he began writing occasional articles for his brother's newspaper at an early age. He would eventually become one of the great self-educated figures of his time.

Although the Clemens family always lived close to the poverty line—especially after John Clemens died—Twain's parents owned a few slaves. One of these was a young boy named Sandy, who would find his way into *Tom Sawyer* as the carefree "small colored boy" named Jim (no relation to the Jim of *Huckleberry Finn*). Twain never became an abolitionist, but during his later life he would become fiercely critical of slavery in all its forms. In 1899, he wrote, "It would not be possible for a humane and intelligent person to invent a rational excuse for slavery" (*Collected Tales* 440), which he had earlier called a "bald, grotesque, and unwarrantable usurpation" (*Autobiography* [Paine] 1: 123) for which white Americans should atone. However, despite the strength of his antislavery views, he tended to look back on the slavery of the Hannibal of his youth unrealistically, calling it the "mild domestic slavery, not the brutal plantation article" (*Autobiography* [Paine] 1: 124). The reality was that slavery was probably as brutal in Hannibal as anywhere else in the American South, and Twain's own father was not above beating his slaves. The literary consequence of Twain's almost apologetic view of Missouri slavery is that slaves are almost invisible in *Tom Sawyer*, and a central theme in both *Huckleberry Finn* and *Pudd'nhead Wilson* is the fear of Missouri slaves that they might be "sold down the river," where slavery was supposedly more brutal than in Missouri. Although slavery figures into all of Twain's Mississippi writings, the books in which he attacks slavery most directly are *The Prince and the Pauper* (1881), which is set in sixteenth-century England, and *A Connecticut Yankee in King Arthur's Court* (1889), which is set in sixth-century England. In both these novels, all the slaves are white.

The first novel that Twain wrote entirely on his own, *Tom Sawyer*, is the most thoroughly autobiographical of his fictional works. The principal physical features of the novel's riverfront village of St. Petersburg closely resemble those of the real Hannibal. However, the fictional town seems somewhat smaller and has more of a rural flavor than the Hannibal of Twain's youth. One reason for this is that Twain invested in St. Petersburg elements of his natal village of Florida, where during his youth his family spent many summers on the farm of his uncle John Quarles. The fictional St. Petersburg might therefore be considered a composite of Hannibal and Florida. St. Petersburg was not the only fictional town that Twain would model on Hannibal. Elements of it can also be found other riverfront towns in *Huckleberry Finn*, in the Dawson's Landing of *Pudd'nhead Wilson*, and in the titular location of "The Man That Corrupted Hadleyville" (1899), one of Twain's most famous short stories.

Twain's autobiographical writings display his fond memories of summers on his uncle's farm, which he recalls as a "heavenly place for a boy" (*Autobiography* [Paine] 1: 96). The Quarles home would provide the model for the Grangerfords' "double log house" in *Huckleberry Finn*. More important, however, the Quarles farm had fifteen to twenty African American slaves with whom Twain became intimately acquainted. He developed a warm feeling for African Americans that he would carry throughout his life, and he had especially fond memories of a man known as

"Uncle Dan'l," a middle-aged slave whose head was the best one in the negro quarter, whose sympathies were wide and warm, and whose heart was honest and simple and knew no guile. He has served me well these many, many years. I have not seen him for more than half a century, and yet spiritually I have had his welcome company a good part of that time, and have staged him in books under his own name and as "Jim," and carted him all around—to Hannibal, down the Mississippi on a raft, and even across the Desert of Sahara in a balloon—and he has endured it all with the patience and friendliness and loyalty which were his birthright. It was on the farm that I got my strong liking for his race and my appreciation of certain of its fine qualities. This feeling and this estimate have stood the test of sixty years and more, and have suffered no impairment. The black face is as welcome to me now as it was then. (*Autobiography* [Paine] 1: 100)

Itinerant Printer and Steamboatman

During the summer of 1853, when he was only seventeen and one-half years old, Twain left Hannibal and struck out on his own. He would revisit Hannibal in later years but would never again live there. Over the next several years, he essentially led the life of an itinerant printer. After living with his sister Pamela's family while he worked for a St. Louis newspaper for several months, he moved on to the East and worked for newspapers in Philadelphia and New York City, where he resided at the time the city hosted a great world's fair. A long letter that he wrote to his family from New York during this visit is the earliest surviving example of his correspondence. He would eventually write tens of thousands of letters. Meanwhile, during this same trip, he paid his first visit to Washington, D.C.

In early 1854, Twain returned to the Midwest and rejoined his mother and brothers Orion and Henry, who by then were living in Muscatine, Iowa. Over the next several years, he shifted his residences between Muscatine and Keokuk, Iowa, and St. Louis, Missouri, and spent much of this period doing printing work for his brother's unprofitable enterprises. By late 1856, he had moved on to Cincinnati, Ohio, where he continued to work as printer. While he was in Cincinnati, he wrote several letters under the pen name Thomas Jefferson Snodgrass that were published in a Keokuk newspaper, anticipating what would later become his brief career in travel-letter writing.

A curious aspect of Twain's later writing career is the limited use he made of his printing experience in his fiction. The only story he wrote in which printers figure prominently was a novel he started in 1902 and left unfinished at the time of his death. In 1982, that story was published for the first time as *No. 44, The Mysterious Stranger*. Although it is set in medieval Austria, the print shop it depicts is so much like the mid-nineteenth-century shops in which Twain worked that it provides glimpses into his own printing experiences that cannot be found elsewhere. A character in the story known by the nickname "Doangivadam" is a swashbuckling journeyman printer who may be the kind of carefree itinerant printer that Twain imagined himself to be when he was young.

The next phase of Twain's life brought a major change that would influence his future writing career as much as his youth in Missouri was to do. Exactly how he made this transition is clouded by the romanticized account that he later wrote in articles serialized in *The Atlantic Monthly* as "Old Times on the Mississippi" in 1875. In one of the most overtly autobiographical works that he published during his lifetime, he told of how he took a steamboat down the Ohio and Mississippi rivers with the intention of making his way to South America, where he wanted to explore the Amazon. After reaching New Orleans, from which he found it would be almost impossible to continue on to South America, he instead decided to fulfill his boyhood ambition of becoming a steamboat pilot.

Twain's story about wanting to reach the Amazon seems unlikely, but it is undeniable that he did, in fact, become a steamboat pilot. By the time he reached New Orleans in early 1857, he had persuaded the master pilot Horace Bixby to take him on as an apprentice, or "cub," in return for a payment of $500—$100 in advance, the balance to be paid later from his wages. After borrowing the advance money from his brother-in-law in St. Louis, Twain began an apprenticeship that lasted two years. On April 9, 1859, he received his piloting license. He then worked as a pilot another two years, only to abandon the profession in April 1861, when the outbreak of the Civil War ended commercial traffic on the Lower Mississippi River.

Becoming a fully licensed steamboat pilot was a significant accomplishment, and one for which Twain earned $250 a month—almost a princely sum during the mid-nineteenth century. Through his four years as an apprentice and a licensed pilot, he steered steamboats up and down the Lower Mississippi, between St. Louis and New Orleans. The articles he later wrote for *The Atlantic Monthly* provide a colorfully embellished and highly detailed account of his experiences through his cub piloting years but say almost nothing about his years as a licensed pilot. Like some of his other travel writings, these articles make his unnamed narrator seem much younger and more naive Twain himself actually was during the period they describe. Nevertheless, they offer a generally accurate account of the incredible amount of information that pilots had to learn and also demonstrate the extent of Twain's familiarity with the river that he would later use as the backdrop for his masterpiece, *Huckleberry Finn*. When Twain published *Life on the Mississippi* in 1883, he expanded the "Old Times" articles for his book, to which he added chapters on the history of the river and a lengthy account of his return visit to the Mississippi in 1882.

From the Civil War to Hawaii

Twain happened to be in New Orleans in April 1861, at the moment Civil War hostilities began. The war would stop commercial steamboat traffic on the Lower Mississippi, but he managed to get back to St. Louis on the last passenger boat out of Louisiana. After visiting his sister's family there in St. Louis, he returned to Hannibal, where he and some of his boyhood friends briefly joined a militia unit called up by the state's governor. In late 1885, Twain would publish a magazine article titled "The Private History of a Campaign That Failed," which recounts a two-week period during which he claimed to have served in a "Confederate" military unit called the "Marion Rangers." However, there is no other evidence that such a unit ever existed. Because Missouri was never part of the Confederacy, it seems clear that Twain's magazine article was largely fiction, and he was never a Confederate soldier.

Meanwhile, Abraham Lincoln's election to the U.S. presidency brought Orion Clemens an appointment to the most important position he would ever hold—secretary to the government of the newly created Nevada Territory. This appointment was a reward for Orion's service during Lincoln's election campaign. Out of a job and not eager to get involved in the Civil War, Twain decided to accompany Orion to Nevada, where he proposed to serve as his brother's private secretary. Thanks to the money he had saved during his piloting years, he was able to pay both his and his brother's hefty travel expenses to take a steamboat up the Missouri River to St. Joseph, Missouri, from which they rode a stagecoach to Carson City, Nevada. The brothers' eventful cross-country journey would become the subject of the first twenty chapters of Twain's *Roughing It* (1872).

After Twain reached Carson City, Nevada, in August 1861, his position as his brother's private secretary quickly evaporated. Subsidized by his brother's substantial new income, he took off on his own to prospect in the region's rapidly developing silver and gold fields. He first tried the Humboldt district to the northeast of Carson City and then spent about five months in the Esmeralda district to the south. Fortunately for American literature, all of Twain's prospecting efforts came to nothing, otherwise he might have been content to retire early. Meanwhile, he was beginning to become a serious writer. While he was prospecting in Esmeralda, he sent travel letters under the pen name "Josh" to Nevada's most important newspaper, the *Virginia City Territorial Enterprise*. When Joseph Goodman, the paper's editor, offered him a staff job in September 1862, he abandoned his unpromising prospecting career and walked 130 miles to Virginia City to become a newspaper reporter. Under Goodman's imaginative and permissive tutelage, Twain developed into one of the most popular writers in the Far West. In addition to doing ordinary "beat" reporting, he published occasional hoaxes and sharpened his skills as a humorist and satirist. In February 1863, he signed the name "Mark Twain" to one of his stories for the first time and afterward made that pen name his regular byline.

During his years in Nevada, Twain occasionally visited California's chief city, San Francisco. In May 1864, he permanently left Virginia City for San Francisco and became a reporter for the *San Francisco Call*. This job did not offer him the freedom he had enjoyed in Nevada, and he soon got into trouble with the San Francisco police, whom he severely criticized in his articles. He and his friend Steve Gillis—who was having troubles of his own in the city—took refuge at a Tuolumne County mining camp in the foothills of the Sierras. Two of Gillis's brothers lived there with another prospector named Dick Stoker, whom Twain would later immortalize as "Dick Baker," the narrator of the blue jay yarn in *A Tramp Abroad* (1880).

During a brief prospecting foray into neighboring Calaveras County, Twain heard a yarn about a jumping frog involved in a wager that he would afterward recast in his own words. First published as "Jim Smiley and His Jumping Frog," his story appeared in an eastern magazine in November 1865 and brought him his first national recognition as a writer. Meanwhile, he returned to San Francisco and busied himself with writing sketches for local publications, such as Bret Harte's *Overland Monthly* and travel letters for the *Territorial Enterprise*.

In early 1866, Twain sailed to the Hawaiian Islands, then known as the Sandwich Islands, with a commission to write travel letters about the islands for the *Sacramento Union*. He liked the islands so much that he remained there for six months. Before returning to California, he had the good fortune of becoming the first writer to deliver to the mainland a story on the sinking of the clipper ship *Hornet*. When he got back to San Francisco in August, he discovered that his travel letters and his story on the *Hornet* had greatly enhanced his reputation, and he used his newfound celebrity to launch a new career as a public lecturer. His first lecture, on the Sandwich Islands, was such a success that he organized a small lecture tour through Northern California and western Nevada.

In December, Twain departed for the East Coast, which he reached by sailing down the Pacific Coast and crossing Nicaragua. He left San Francisco with a new commission, to write travel letters for the city's *Alta California* newspaper. These letters would later be collected in *Mark Twain's Travels with Mr. Brown* (1940). A fictitious traveling companion Twain had invented in his Hawaii letters, the "Mr. Brown" persona allowed him to express opinions he did not want to attribute to himself. Other fictitious companions would appear in some of his later travel writings, including *A Tramp Abroad*, which is enlivened by the largely imaginary Mr. Harris.

World Traveler

While sailing down the Pacific coast on the SS *America*, Twain befriended the ship's captain, an old salt named Ned Wakeman, whom he would meet a second time during his return trip to California in 1868. Despite the brevity of their encounters, Wakeman made an indelible impression on Twain, who would later model at least a half dozen of his most colorful characters on him. However, what seems to have impressed Twain most about Wakeman was the latter's account of a vivid dream he had had. Forty years later, Twain would adapt Wakeman's dream to fiction in *Extract from Captain Stormfield's Visit to Heaven* (1909), in which the old seaman finds the real Heaven to be nothing like the dreary place he learned about in Sunday school.

After a seven-week stay in New York City, Twain returned to the Midwest, where he visited relatives and old friends and delivered lectures on Hawaii. One of the newspaper reporters who attended his second lecture in St. Louis was Henry Morton Stanley, a Welshman who would later become an explorer in Africa. Stanley angered Twain by publishing such a detailed description of Twain's lecture in a local paper that Twain could not reuse the same lecture material in the region; however, the two men later became close friends.

Before Twain returned to New York City, he learned of a tourist cruise to Europe and the Holy Land on a steamship called the *Quaker*

City that was to be led by the famous Brooklyn preacher Henry Ward Beecher. After persuading the editors of the *Alta California* to pay for his passage and to give him twenty dollars for each of fifty travel letters he proposed to write during the voyage, he signed on for the cruise. In June of 1867, the *Quaker City* set sail from New York for Europe. It turned out that neither Beecher nor the person who was to be the cruise's principal celebrity passenger, Civil War hero General William T. Sherman, made the trip, and Twain found himself the most famous passenger aboard the ship.

The five months that Twain spent on the *Quaker City* excursion constituted another significant turning point in his life. In addition to taking him on the first of the twenty-five transatlantic crossings that he would eventually make and introducing to him to several people who would become influential, lifelong friends, the cruise gave him a platform on which he would build not only national but also international fame as a writer. Highlights of the voyage included visits to the Azores, Gibraltar, France, Italy, Greece, Turkey, Russia, Palestine, and Egypt. The trip gave Twain his first deep exposure to foreign cultures and sharpened his ideas about what it meant to be an American. The lively and often irreverent letters that he wrote during the trip repeatedly returned to the theme of differences between the Old World and New World culture, with the latter almost invariably made to look superior. Twain's unrelenting, often satirical, and generally humorous digs at the Old World—and especially the Holy Land—made his letters unlike anything Americans had ever read. As his letters were copied and reprinted in newspapers throughout the United States, his fame grew rapidly even while he was still traveling.

Becoming an Author

When the *Quaker City* returned to New York in November 1867, Twain found that he was genuinely famous. Moreover, within days of his arrival, the Hartford, Connecticut, publisher Elisha Bliss invited him to write a book about the voyage for the American Publishing Company, which specialized in "subscription books," which canvassers sold door-to-door. Although Twain had already arranged to publish a small collection of sketches he had written in the West, he did not yet think of himself as an author of books and did not immediately accept Bliss's offer. Instead, he went to Washington, D.C., to serve as private secretary to one of the senators of the new state of Nevada, William Morris Stewart, whom he had known in Nevada. A member of the U.S. Senate's influential post-Civil War Radical Republican faction, Stewart would distinguish himself by helping to draft the Fifteenth Amendment, the ratification of which in 1870 guaranteed male African Americans the right to vote.

While living and working with Stewart in Washington, Twain got a close look at how the federal government functions and collected ideas for future sketches and stories with political themes. His experience in Washington left him with a decidedly negative attitude toward politicians, and he would later frequently ridicule the intelligence and integrity of members of Congress.

In October 1868, nearly a year after completing the *Quaker City* cruise, Twain finally signed a contract with the American Publishing Company to write the travel book that would be published as *The Innocents Abroad, or The New Pilgrims' Progress; Being Some Account of the Steamship Quaker City's Pleasure Excursion to Europe and the Holy Land* (1869). By this time, he had already begun working on the book. His initial plan was simply to make minor revisions in the travel letters he had written for the *Alta California* and other newspapers, but he ended up making much more substantial changes and adding wholly new material to compensate for gaps in his letters.

While Twain was working on his book in early 1868, he learned that the *Alta California*'s editors were planning to publish their collection of his letters, so he sped to California to stop them. He succeeded in that effort, and while he was in San Francisco, he finished writing *The Innocents Abroad* with the help of fellow writer Bret Harte. Twain later credited Harte with having helped transform him into a real writer, but he eventually became bitterly resentful of Harte for personal reasons and criticized his writing severely. Meanwhile, from the West Coast he traveled to Nevada during a brief lecture tour. Then, after delivering a farewell lecture in San Francisco in July 1868, he again left California, to which he would never return.

Finally published in July 1869, *The Innocents Abroad* was an immediate and enduring success. Not only would it sell the most copies of all Twain's books during his lifetime, it would also become the best-selling American travel book of the nineteenth century. However, its very success and that of Twain's next book, *Roughing It*, raised Twain's expectations to such a high level that he would measure the success of his later books by comparing their sales to those of his first two major books.

Family Man

Another indirect but important consequence of Twain's *Quaker City* trip was his meeting his future wife, Olivia "Livy" Langdon, just over a month after completing the trip. The sister of one of Twain's fellow passengers on the voyage, Livy was a member of a prosperous and genteel family of Elmira, New York, where her father built a fortune in the coal industry and other enterprises. During their first meeting, Twain and Livy attended a public reading presented by the English novelist Charles Dickens in New York City. (At that time, Dickens was as popular in the United States as Twain would later become in England.) After delivering his *Innocents Abroad* manuscript to Elisha Bliss during the following summer, Twain went to Elmira to court Livy seriously. Both Livy and her parents were leery of Twain's rough western manners and uncertain financial prospects, but by early 1869, Livy had accepted his marriage proposal. Her father gave his approval, although the letters of reference that he had received from Twain's acquaintances in the West were mostly unsatisfactory.

During this period, Twain undertook the first of what would become several long lecture tours, through the Midwest and upstate New York. He was a superb public speaker who delighted audiences by making them laugh at the same time they felt they were learning solid facts, and just as his popularity as an author enhanced his popularity as a lecturer, his lecture tours helped his books' sales. Nevertheless, he could probably have made a prosperous career solely as a lecturer, even if he had never published any books. In any case, he soon came to loathe lecture tours because of the heavy physical demands that constant travel made and because he wearied of the dreary sameness of the towns through which he passed.

While Twain was making plans for his coming marriage, he still thought that his future career was in journalism, so he looked for a newspaper in which to invest. With the help of a substantial loan from his future father-in-law, he purchased a one-third interest in the *Buffalo Express* in the fall of 1869 and took up residence in a Buffalo, New York, boardinghouse. In November, he began his second long lecture tour, this time through New England and other eastern states.

On February 2, 1870, Twain married Livy in the Langdon family's Elmira home. The ceremony was conducted by two Congregationalist ministers, Thomas K. Beecher of Elmira, the brother of Henry Ward Beecher and Harriet Beecher Stowe, and Joseph Twichell of Hartford, Connecticut, whom Twain had met while visiting Elisha Bliss the previous year. Although Twain never fully accepted Christian beliefs, Twichell would become one of his most intimate friends and be present at most of the important family events, including funerals, through the remaining thirty-five years of Twain's life.

The day after the wedding, Twain, Livy, and most of the members of the wedding party rode a train to Buffalo, where Twain had asked a friend to secure rooms in a boardinghouse for him and his new wife. After arriving in Buffalo and enduring an agonizingly long carriage ride to his new abode, he was astonished to learn that his father-in-law had purchased, furnished, and staffed with servants a grand house, the deed to which he gave to Twain. The unexpectedly large income that Twain was about to receive from the sales of *The Innocents Abroad* and other books and the inheritance that Livy brought to the marriage ensured that Twain could continue to live mostly in high style through the remainder of his life.

Although Twain remained deeply in love with Livy through the rest of his life, his eventful first year of married life was almost unimaginably difficult. The success of *The Innocents Abroad* was making him so marketable as a writer that he began taking on additional writing work, including a monthly column for *Galaxy* magazine. In July, he accepted Elisha Bliss's invitation to write another big travel book. He was soon hard at work on the book about his years in the Far West that would be published as *Roughing It* in 1872. Meanwhile, family matters were making increasing demands on his time. After his father-in-law, Jervis Langdon, became ill with stomach cancer, he and Livy spent a great deal of time in Elmira helping with the nursing. By the time his father-in-law died in August, Livy was pregnant and in poor health herself. One of Livy's old Elmira College friends, Emmy Nye, happened to pass through Buffalo and stayed to help nurse Livy. In September, however, Nye contracted typhoid fever and died in Twain's house. On November 7, Livy prematurely delivered Twain's first child and only son, Langdon. Afterward, she was still so ill and her baby was so weak that Twain feared they both might die.

In March 1871, after Livy and Langdon had survived their crises, Twain put his interest in the *Buffalo Express* and his Buffalo home up for sale and took his family to the Quarry Farm home of Livy's sister, Susan Crane, outside Elmira, to rest. Over the next two decades, Quarry Farm would serve as a regular summer refuge for Twain's family, much as his uncle John Quarles's farm had been a summer refuge for his parents' family when he was growing up in Hannibal, Missouri. All three of Twain's daughters would be born at Quarry Farm. In 1874, his sister-in-law had a detached study built for him, and he would use it to do much of his most important writing. Meanwhile, however, he moved his family to Hartford, Connecticut, which would be his permanent residence over the next two decades.

Connecticut Yankee

In September 1871, Twain rented a house in West Hartford's Nook Farm community. A year later, he purchased property on West Hartford's Farmington Avenue, where he and Livy commissioned the construction of a nineteen-room mansion (during the late twentieth century, this home would become a public museum known as the Mark Twain House). Meanwhile, to help pay for this new home, Twain embarked on another long lecture tour through the eastern states.

In June 1872, Twain's nineteen-month-old son Langdon died, effectively ending the male line of Clemenses. (The only other son of John Marshall Clemens to have a child was Orion, but Orion's only child was a daughter who died at the age of eight.) By the time of Langdon's death, Sam and Livy had had their first daughter, Susy, who was born on March 19, 1872. Their second daughter, Clara, would follow on June 8, 1874, and their third, Jean, on July 26, 1880. Of Twain's four children, only Clara would outlive him.

The decade of the 1870s was an important period for foreign travel in Twain's life. In August 1872, he went by himself to England, which he had not visited during his 1867 *Quaker City* trip. He arrived there with the notion of gathering material for a satirical travel book but quickly abandoned the idea and instead spent his time sightseeing and making arrangements for future visits. The following year he returned to Great Britain with his family. Among the many literary figures whom he met on this trip were Robert Browning, Ivan Turgenev, Herbert Spencer, Anthony Trollope, Wilkie Collins, and Lewis Carroll. He also began what would be a long friendship with the Scottish physician and writer John Brown. While he was in Britain, Twain delivered several lectures on Hawaii. After taking his family back to New York in

November 1873, he almost immediately turned around and went back to England by himself to undertake a longer lecture tour. Five years later, he would return to Europe with his family for a much longer stay in Germany, Switzerland, Italy, and France.

Budding Novelist

Between his first two trips to England, Twain made his first foray into long fiction by coauthoring *The Gilded Age* with his Hartford neighbor Charles Dudley Warner. Until then, the bulk of the fiction he had written took the form of sketches, most of which he published in California periodicals. In May 1867, shortly before he left on the *Quaker City* cruise, he published his first book, *The Celebrated Jumping Frog of Calaveras County, and Other Sketches*, a collection of twenty-six of his sketches. His travel books *The Innocents Abroad* and *Roughing It* contain many fictional elements, and the latter is sometimes classified as a novel, but neither book can rightfully be called such.

A complex multifamily saga whose pieces do not fit together completely satisfactorily, *The Gilded Age* is a sprawling novel that gave its name to an entire era of American history; the work satirizes the corporate greed and government corruption of the late nineteenth century. As noted earlier, the novel opens with eleven chapters based on Twain's own family history. Twain himself can be seen within the novel as the Hawkins family's adopted son, Clay, the most sensible member of the family who eventually becomes the primary support of his financially foolish relatives. Clay has a dreamy, impractical brother, Washington Hawkins, who is another of Twain's characters inspired by his brother Orion. One of the novel's central story lines concerns the Hawkins family's long and ultimately unsuccessful struggle to sell a huge tract of land that Si Hawkins purchased in Tennessee to provide for the family's future. This plot element comes directly from Twain's family history. Before Twain was born, his father purchased for his family's future seventy thousand acres of Tennessee land that would eventually prove to be far more of a bane than a blessing, thanks largely to Orion's mismanagement. Around 1870—well before he cowrote *The Gilded Age*—Twain wrote a commentary on the Tennessee land in which he lamented his father's laying on his heirs "the heavy curse of prospective wealth" (*Autobiography* [Paine] 1: 3). More than three decades later, he was doubtless thinking of his father's legacy when he wrote, "It is good to begin life poor; it is good to begin life rich—these are wholesome; but to begin it *prospectively* rich! The man who has not experienced it cannot imagine the curse of it" (*Autobiography* [Paine] 1: 94).

One of the first novels to be marketed as a subscription book, *The Gilded Age* was moderately successful, but it inspired a play that was even more successful. In early 1874, Gilbert B. Densmore adapted parts of the novel to the stage in San Francisco, making one of Twain's characters, Colonel Sellers, the central figure. Because the production was unauthorized, Twain had it stopped. He then bought out its owner and made an arrangement with Warner that gave each of them sole rights to any works adapted from his own portions of the original novel. After rewriting the play, Twain opened it in New York as *Colonel Sellers*. With the popular actor John T. Raymond in the title role, the play toured the United States for twelve years and made Twain a fortune.

The unexpected success of *Colonel Sellers* encouraged Twain to write other plays, but none of them succeeded until his long-unproduced and nearly forgotten drama *Is He Dead?*—about a struggling artist—enjoyed a brief run on Broadway in 2007-2008. Meanwhile, in 1884, he collaborated with his friend William Dean Howells on a play titled "Colonel Sellers as a Scientist." Twain hoped that Raymond would again play Sellers, but Raymond was not interested, and no other actor would consider playing the character he had made famous. The play was never produced, but Twain salvaged some of its material in a short novel called *The American Claimant* (1892). An eternal optimist whose faith in grandiose financial schemes never flags, Sellers was originally modeled principally on a cousin of Twain's mother named James Lampton. The Sellers character in *The American Claimant*, however—like Washington Hawkins, who also reappears in the novel—contains elements of Orion Clemens, most notably the volatility of his religious affiliations and his tinkering with impractical inventions.

After returning from his third trip to Britain in early 1874, Twain began writing some of the works for which he is now best known, including his first solo novel, *Tom Sawyer*. Later that same year, he published his first contribution to the prestigious *Atlantic Monthly*, "A True Story," a brief tale narrated by a former slave woman. *The Atlantic* was edited by the novelist William Dean Howells, who had become one of Twain's closest friends after publishing a favorable review of *The Innocents Abroad* in his magazine. Thereafter, Howells reviewed most of Twain's books and encouraged him in his writing work. In fact, it was partly through Howells's encouragement that Twain wrote "Old Times on the Mississippi" for *The Atlantic*. This embellished memoir of his experiences as an apprentice steamboat pilot helped motivate him to begin writing his greatest work, *Huckleberry Finn*.

Twain finished *Tom Sawyer* during the summer of 1875, but the book was not published in the United States until the following year, by which time publishers in England, Germany, and Canada had already issued their own editions. Twain was livid at the freedom with which Canadian publishers could ignore his American copyrights and issue pirated editions of his books, thousands of which found their way into the United States. His unpleasant experience with pirate editions of *Tom Sawyer* drew him into a long struggle to secure copyrights of his books in Canada. In later years, he would become a champion of increasing copyright protection of authors in American law.

After finishing *Tom Sawyer*, Twain began writing *Huckleberry Finn* as a direct sequel, but this new book took unexpected turns that would cause him to set it aside and delay its completion for nearly eight years.

The next few years were a comparatively fallow period during which he wrote mostly short works. In 1877, his best-selling work was his self-pasting scrapbook, an invention he patented and had manufactured by a company owned by one of his old *Quaker City* buddies, Daniel Slote. That same year ended on a sour note when Twain delivered a poorly received speech at a Boston banquet honoring John Greenleaf Whittier's seventieth birthday. One of the many unanswered questions about Twain's life is whether the embarrassment of that speech motivated his decision to leave the country the following year. Between April 1878 and August 1879, he traveled in western Europe with his family while gathering material for his third travel book, *A Tramp Abroad*, which focuses mostly on his time in Germany and Switzerland. A few months after returning to the United States, he delivered a speech that was an unqualified personal triumph at a banquet honoring the Civil War hero and former U.S. president Ulysses S. Grant in Chicago.

Twain's 1878-1879 trip was his last foreign travel until the 1890s. After finishing *A Tramp Abroad* in early 1880, he started a new novel, *The Prince and the Pauper.* This historical novel set in sixteenth-century England represented a major departure in his writing, but it contains elements of the boy stories he set in nineteenth-century Missouri. Around this same time, he also began working on what he hoped would become a "standard book" on the Mississippi River. In order to write such a book, he had to return to the river, so in early 1882 he went west with his new publisher, James Osgood, and a secretary, Roswell H. Phelps. In St. Louis, Missouri, they boarded a packet steamboat on which they sailed down the Mississippi River to Vicksburg, Mississippi, from which a second steamboat took them to New Orleans. After returning home, Twain combined a new account of his recent journey with an expanded version of his "Old Times on the Mississippi" articles to produce *Life on the Mississippi.*

Business Ventures

Twain's return to the Mississippi River doubtless helped prompt him to finish *Huckleberry Finn*. That book was published by Charles L. Webster & Co., a new firm that Twain formed in early 1884 in the hope of increasing the profits from his books. He made his sister Pamela's son-in-law, Charles L. Webster, his junior partner and president of his company, but he played an active role in its operations until it went bankrupt in 1894. *Huckleberry Finn* was Webster's inaugural publication in February 1885, but English and Canadian editions had appeared in late 1884. Over the next several years Clemens focused much of his energy on business matters, particularly those of his publishing firm. Webster's biggest success was the two-volume *Personal Memoirs of U. S. Grant*, which came out in 1885-1886.

While Twain was trying to develop his publishing firm, he was also investing large amounts of money in the development of an automatic typesetting machine by the Hartford inventor James W. Paige. Impressed by how fast Paige's compositor could set type in comparison with the speed of human typesetters, Twain was confident that after Paige finished perfecting his machine, every newspaper in the world would buy at least one, and he would become fabulously rich. Paige's machine was, indeed, a marvel. However, it was so complicated and had so many moving parts that Paige could never get it to run for any length of time without breaking down. Meanwhile, the German inventor Ottmar Mergenthaler developed the linotype machine, which would capture the market that Twain had dreamed of cornering.

Twain's only major work of the late 1880s was *A Connecticut Yankee in King Arthur's Court*, which his own firm published in 1889. In this pioneering time-travel story, an inventive late-nineteenth-century American named Hank Morgan is mysteriously thrown back to sixth-century England, which he tries to make over in the image of modern America. Twain's most overtly sociological and political novel, this book can be read as a satire on both medieval England and the modern United States.

Years of Exile

After enjoying nearly twenty years of comfortable life in Hartford, Connecticut, Twain experienced a financial crisis during the early 1890s. His vast household expenses were becoming unmanageable, his publishing firm was sinking, and his huge investments in the Paige compositor were bringing no return. In June 1891, he closed down his big Hartford house and took his family to Europe in the hope of lowering his living expenses. The family would never again live in the Hartford house—which Twain would eventually sell in 1903—and would not have another fixed American abode until 1900.

Over the ensuing year, Twain and his family moved around in western Europe, dividing their time between big cities and health spas, such as Aix-les-Bains in France and Marienbad in Bohemia. Twain meanwhile kept busying writing articles for magazines, finishing *The American Claimant,* and keeping up with his correspondence with Frederick J. Hall, who had replaced Charles Webster as president of his publishing firm in 1888. Twain's growing concerns over the condition of his firm and his investment in the Paige compositor kept him shuttling back and forth across the Atlantic, while his family remained in Europe. In June 1892, Twain returned to the United States on the first of four round-trips he would make before 1895. When he rejoined his family in Italy in September, he rented a villa near Florence.

While in Italy, Twain wrote *Pudd'nhead Wilson*, a short novel set in antebellum Missouri. In contrast to *Tom Sawyer* and *Huckleberry Finn*, this book offers a more explicit treatment of slavery, racial identity, and murder. Long fascinated by the famous "Siamese twins," Chang and Eng Bunker, Twain began this book with the idea of building a story around the comic possibilities of conjoined Italian twins with sharply contrasting personalities. Eventually, however, he dropped that idea and took the book in a radically different direction by having a virtually white slave woman named Roxana switch her own baby with that of her widowed master. The novel then jumps ahead two decades to explore what becomes of the switched children.

After publishing *Tom Sawyer* and *Huckleberry Finn*, Twain began at least five other stories using Tom and Huck as characters but published only two of them during his lifetime. While he was still in Europe, he wrote *Tom Sawyer Abroad* with the idea of making it the first of a series of books in which Tom and Huck have adventures in faraway places, but he evidently lost interest midway through this book, which ends abruptly. After the story appeared as a serial in Mary Mapes Dodge's *Saint Nicholas Magazine* in 1893-1894, Charles L. Webster & Co. made it the last book the firm published before it declared bankruptcy.

After seeing his publishing firm go into bankruptcy in April 1894, Twain still believed that the Paige compositor would make him rich. That dream soon ended, however. By this time, he had enlisted the financial advice of one of the Standard Oil Company's top executives, Henry Huttleston Rogers, an admirer of Twain who would become an intimate and valued friend. In October of 1894, Rogers went to Chicago on Twain's behalf personally to oversee a practical test of Paige's machine at the *Chicago Herald*, which was already using a large number of Mergenthaler linotype machines successfully. Repeated breakdowns caused Paige's compositor to fail its test completely, leaving Twain's entire investment in the machine a dead loss.

Now, not only was Twain's dream of great riches dashed forever, he was also saddled with huge debts from his publishing firm's bankruptcy. With the help of Rogers, he arranged settlement terms that made his wife, Livy, the firm's primary creditor. This was fair, as Livy had invested much of her inheritance in the company. Rogers also arranged to protect Twain's valuable copyrights from other creditors by having them reassigned to Livy. Finally, Rogers laid a foundation for Twain's future writing income by negotiating an agreement that made Harper & Brothers his sole authorized publisher in the United States. This agreement would later pay large royalties to Twain and his estate.

Throughout the period during which Twain was traveling frequently and worrying about his financial problems, he managed to complete the last long novel he would publish during his lifetime—*Personal*

Recollections of Joan of Arc. His third historical novel, *Joan of Arc* has some similarities to *The Prince and the Pauper* and *Connecticut Yankee* but differs in that it is essentially a fictionalized history with little humor or invention. Twain regarded it as his best book—a view shared by few others—and in the hope of having it taken seriously, he insisted on publishing it anonymously when *Harper's Magazine* began serializing it in May 1895. However, when Harper & Brothers published it in book form the following year, his name appeared on the title page.

Meanwhile, to restore his solvency and help pay off his bankruptcy debts, Twain planned what would become a 140-lecture tour that would take him literally around the world. In May 1895, he took his family back to the United States and went directly to Quarry Farm, where they rested before he began his tour in July. Leaving his daughters Jean and Susy with his in-laws in Elmira, Twain began a journey across the northern United States and southern Canada with his wife and daughter Clara and his lecture agent, James B. Pond, making lecture stops along the way. In August, Twain, Livy, and Clara sailed from British Columbia aboard the SS *Warrimoo*. Twain's first lecture stop was to be in Honolulu, Hawaii, which he greatly looked forward to revisiting, but a cholera epidemic prevented his going ashore there.

After crossing the Pacific Ocean to Fiji for a quick stop, the *Warrimoo* reached Australia in mid-September. Twain then spent the rest of the year touring Australia and New Zealand. On New Year's Day of 1896, he and his family left Australia for Ceylon and India, where he toured another two months. After leaving India in late March, they rested on the Indian Ocean island of Mauritius for two weeks before continuing on to South Africa. They arrived in South Africa shortly after Leander Starr Jameson's abortive raid on the South African Republic of the Transvaal increased the tensions between the British Empire and the Afrikaner (Boer) republics that would lead to the South African War three years later. Twain was fascinated by these developments, which he would write about at length in *Following the Equator* (1897), his book about his round-the-world trip. On July 15, 1896, Twain officially ended his lecture tour in Cape Town, from which he sailed to England with Livy and Clara.

After landing in England, Twain rented a house in Guildford, outside London, with the intention of having his daughters Susy and Jean rejoin him as soon as possible. However, when he and Livy received messages reporting that Susy was ill, they became alarmed, and Livy immediately left for the United States with Clara. Before Livy and Clara reached New York, Susy had died from spinal meningitis. Still in Guildford, Twain learned of her death by telegram. After overseeing her burial in Elmira's Woodlawn Cemetery—where all the family members would eventually be interred—Livy returned to England with Clara and Jean. Susy had been Twain's favorite daughter, and neither he nor Livy ever fully recovered from the shock of losing her. The fact that Susy had died in the family's Hartford house, during a visit from Elmira, was one of the reasons the family never lived in the house again. Meanwhile, Twain remained in England for a year, during the first half of which he wrote *Following the Equator*. He would later tell his friend Howells that he wrote the book "in hell," while trying to convey the impression that "it was an excursion through heaven" (*Twain-Howells Letters* 2: 690).

In September 1897, Twain took his family to Switzerland and then to Vienna, Austria, where they lived for twenty months. Afterward, they visited Budapest, Prague, London, and Sanna, Sweden, before returning to London in October 1899 for a longer stay. Through these years, Twain wrote sketches and articles for magazines and frequently spoke at banquets and public occasions. He also began writing many novels that he would never finish; most of these would be published long after his death. Dark themes can be found in Twain's much earlier writings, but many of his late unfinished works are even darker and seem to reflect the despair he must have been feeling after his financial failures and Susy's death. Many of these stories revolve around characters—whom he modeled on himself—undergoing nightmarish experiences in which they cannot differentiate between dreams and reality.

Back in the United States

In October 1900, Twain returned to the United States with his family after having been out of the country continuously for more than five years. By this time, the fact that he had paid off all the debts connected with his firm's bankruptcy was publicly known, and he was received as something of a hero. Over the next two years, while he and his family resided in Manhattan and in a place now part of the Bronx, he kept busy with social engagements and was frequently invited to be a banquet speaker. In the late spring of 1902, he returned to Missouri for the last time to accept an honorary degree from the University of Missouri. While he was on that trip, he also paid his final visits to Hannibal and the Mississippi River.

Livy's health had never been strong, and now it went into such a decline that she was advised to leave the country to find a milder climate. In October 1903, Twain took his family to Italy and, once again, rented a villa outside Florence, where Livy died the following June. When Twain returned to the United States with Clara and Jean, he spent a few months in western Massachusetts and then rented a house in Manhattan that remained his home for four years. Through this period, he continued to write, turning out comparatively minor works such as *A Dog's Tale* (1904), *Extracts from Adam's Diary* (1904), *King Leopold's Soliloquy* (1905), *Eve's Diary* (1906), *What Is Man?* (1906), *A Horse's Tale* (1906), and *Christian Science* (1907).

By the first decade of the twentieth century, Twain ranked as one of the most famous Americans of his time, and he relished his celebrity. Despite his despondency over his wife's death, he stayed active socially and made frequent speaking appearances. He also received many honors, including a big banquet put on by *Harper's Magazine* to honor his seventieth birthday in December 1905. In 1907, he went to England to accept an honorary degree from Oxford University that he regarded as the pinnacle of his success.

After spending the summers of 1905 and 1906 in southern New Hampshire, Twain decided to acquire his own summer home. On the advice of Albert Bigelow Paine, whom he had recently given permission to be his official biographer, he purchased land outside Redding, Connecticut, and commissioned an architect to design an Italianate mansion for him. His daughter Clara and his private secretary, Isabel Lyon, supervised the house's construction and furnishing, and he did not even visit the site until he moved in on June 18, 1908. Although he initially intended the house to be only his summer residence, he liked it so much that he decided to stay there year-round. He later dubbed it Stormfield, for the fictional protagonist of *Extract from Captain Stormfield's Visit to Heaven*, which during the following year would become the last book he published during his lifetime.

Twain's residence in Stormfield was brief but eventful. In October 1909, his daughter Clara married the Russian musician Ossip Gabrilowitsch there before going to Europe to live. On Christmas Eve of that year, his youngest daughter, Jean, died in her bath there after suffering an apparent heart attack during an epileptic seizure. In January 1910, Twain went to Bermuda—one of his favorite vacation spots. By then his own health was rapidly declining. In mid-April, Paine traveled to Bermuda to bring him home. On April 21, 1910—only a week after he was back at Stormfield, Twain died from heart failure. Clara and her husband had returned from Europe in time to be with him when he died. They remained in the house through August, when Clara gave birth to Twain's grandchild, Nina Gabrilowitsch, who would be the last of his line.

Albert Bigelow Paine, who had by the time of Twain's death become his literary executor, served as the editor of the Mark Twain Papers through the remaining twenty-seven years of his own life. In 1912, he published a nearly 500,000-word biography of Twain that would remain a standard authority through two generations. He would also publish collections of Twain's speeches, letters, autobiographical writings, notebooks, and previously unpublished stories and essays.

Bibliography

Baetzhold, Howard G. *Mark Twain and John Bull: The British Connection.* Bloomington: Indiana UP, 1970.

Bridgman, Richard. *Traveling in Mark Twain.* Berkeley: U of California P, 1987.

Burns, Ken, Dayton Duncan, and Geoffrey C. Ward. *Mark Twain: An Illustrated Biography.* New York: Alfred A. Knopf, 2001.

Dempsey, Terrell. *Searching for Jim: Slavery in Sam Clemens's World.* Columbia: U of Missouri P, 2003.

Emerson, Everett. *Mark Twain: A Literary Life.* Philadelphia: U of Pennsylvania P, 2000.

Fanning, Philip Ashley. *Mark Twain and Orion Clemens: Brothers, Partners, Strangers.* Tuscaloosa: U of Alabama P, 2003.

Gold, Charles H. *"Hatching Ruin": Or, Mark Twain's Road to Bankruptcy.* Columbia: U of Missouri P, 2003.

Gribben, Alan. *Mark Twain's Library: A Reconstruction.* 2 vols. Boston: G. K. Hall, 1980.

Hill, Hamlin. *Mark Twain: God's Fool.* New York: Harper & Row, 1973.

Hoffman, Andrew. *Inventing Mark Twain: The Lives of Samuel Langhorne Clemens.* New York: William Morrow, 1997.

Horn, Jason Gary. *Mark Twain: A Descriptive Guide to Biographical Sources.* Lanham, MD: Scarecrow Press, 1999.

Kaplan, Fred. *The Singular Mark Twain: A Biography.* New York: Doubleday, 2003.

Kaplan, Justin. *Mr. Clemens and Mark Twain: A Biography.* New York: Simon & Schuster, 1966.

Lauber, John. *The Inventions of Mark Twain.* New York: Hill & Wang, 1990.

_____. *The Making of Mark Twain: A Biography.* New York: Noonday Press/Farrar, Straus and Giroux, 1988.

LeMaster, J. R., and James D. Wilson, eds. *The Mark Twain Encyclopedia.* New York: Garland, 1993.

Meltzer, Milton. *Mark Twain Himself.* New York: Thomas Y. Crowell, 1960.

Messent, Peter, and Louis J. Budd, eds. *A Companion to Mark Twain.* Malden, MA: Blackwell, 2005.

Obenzinger, Hilton. *American Palestine: Melville, Twain, and the Holy Land Mania.* Princeton, NJ: Princeton UP, 1999.

Paine, Albert Bigelow. *Mark Twain: A Biography—The Personal and Literary Life of Samuel Langhorne Clemens.* 3 vols. New York: Harper & Brothers, 1912.

Powers, Ron. *Dangerous Water: A Biography of the Boy Who Became Mark Twain.* New York: Basic Books, 1999.

_____. *Mark Twain: A Life.* New York: Free Press, 2005.

Railton, Stephen. *Mark Twain: A Short Introduction.* Malden, MA: Blackwell, 2004.

Rasmussen, R. Kent. *Critical Companion to Mark Twain: A Literary Reference to His Life and Work.* 2 vols. New York: Facts On File, 2007.

Twain, Mark. *The Adventures of Tom Sawyer.* Hartford, CT: American Publishing, 1876.

_____. *The Autobiography of Mark Twain: Including Chapters Now Published for the First Time.* Ed. Charles Neider. New York: Harper & Brothers, 1959.

_____. *Collected Tales, Sketches, Speeches, and Essays, 1891-1910.* Ed. Louis J. Budd. New York: Library of America, 1992.

_____. *Mark Twain-Howells Letters: The Correspondence of Samuel L. Clemens and William D. Howells, 1872-1910.* 2 vols. Ed. Henry Nash Smith and William M. Gibson. Cambridge, MA: Harvard UP, 1960.

_____. *Mark Twain in Eruption: Hitherto Unpublished Pages About Men and Events.* Ed. Bernard DeVoto. New York: Capricorn Books, 1968.

_____. *Mark Twain's Autobiography.* 2 vols. Ed. Albert Bigelow Paine. New York: Harper & Brothers, 1924.

_____. *Mark Twain's Letters.* 2 vols. Ed. Albert Bigelow Paine. New York: Harper & Brothers, 1917.

_____. *Mark Twain's Letters,* vol. 1, *1853-1866.* Ed. Edgar Marquess Branch, Michael B. Frank, and Kenneth M. Sanderson. Berkeley: U of California P, 1988.

_____. *Mark Twain's Letters,* vol. 2, *1867-1868.* Ed. Harriet Smith, Richard Bucci, and Lin Salamo. Berkeley: U of California P, 1990.

_____. *Mark Twain's Letters,* vol. 3, *1869.* Ed. Victor Fischer, Michael B. Frank, and Dahlia Armon. Berkeley: U of California P, 1992.

_____. *Mark Twain's Letters,* vol. 4, *1870-1871.* Ed. Victor Fischer and Michael B. Frank. Berkeley: U of California P, 1995.

_____. *Mark Twain's Letters,* vol. 5, *1872-1873.* Ed. Lin Salamo and Harriet Elinor Smith. Berkeley: U of California P, 1997.

_____. *Mark Twain's Letters,* vol. 6, *1874-1875.* Ed. Michael B. Frank and Harriet Elinor Smith. Berkeley: U of California P, 2002.

_____. *Mark Twain's Own Autobiography: The Chapters from the "North American Review."* Ed. Michael J. Kiskis. Madison: U of Wisconsin P, 1990.

_____. *Mark Twain's Travels with Mr. Brown, Being Heretofore Uncollected Sketches.* Ed. Franklin Walker and G. Ezra Dane. New York: Alfred A. Knopf, 1940.

_____. *Traveling with the Innocents Abroad: Mark Twain's Original Reports from Europe and the Holy Land.* Ed. Daniel Morley McKeithan. Norman: U of Oklahoma P, 1958.

Wagenknecht, Edward. *Mark Twain: The Man and His Work.* 3d ed. Norman: U of Oklahoma P, 1967.

Wecter, Dixon. *Sam Clemens of Hannibal.* Boston: Houghton Mifflin, 1952.

Welland, Dennis. *The Life and Times of Mark Twain.* New York: Crescent Books, 1991.

*the*PARIS
REVIEW

The *Paris Review* Perspective

Sasha Weiss for *The Paris Review*

Samuel Clemens was a creature of the Mississippi River. He grew up on its banks, in the town of Hannibal, Missouri, and traveled up and down the river's length, collecting accents, anecdotes, folklore, and rituals like bits of driftwood. He assembled these scraps into a career of newspaper columns, dozens of novels and short stories, books of travelogues, and lecture tours. He became one of the foremost men of American letters by writing about life along the river under the pen name Mark Twain. It is a name chosen to evoke the wet wilderness of his childhood: "Mark twain!" was an expression used on steamboats to indicate when the boats moved into water two fathoms deep, the dividing line between safe and unsafe depths.

Twain is best known for his comedic talents, but he also wrote impassioned polemics against American imperialism, and his fiction at times gave voice to a Manichaean despair about humankind's weakness in the face of an unrelentingly cruel universe. His greatest gift, evident in his work from the very beginning, was in using his raucous sense of humor as a tool to expose all manner of cruelties.

In "Jim Smiley and His Jumping Frog," Twain's first nationally successful story and one of his most popular works, we see many of the defining characteristics of his writing in miniature: his studious ventriloquism of regional dialects, the adaptation of the acrobatic pleasures of oral storytelling to written language, and the potential destructiveness of transactional relationships. The story is told in the form of a letter from Twain to a "Mr. A. Ward" (Artemus Ward was a well-known humorist who had solicited the story for a book he was editing) in which

Twain accuses Ward of playing a trick on him by asking him to inquire in the small mining town of Boomerang about a man by the name of Leonidas W. Smiley. In Boomerang, Twain encounters the garrulous Simon Wheeler and, asking about Leonidas Smiley, accidentally elicits an endless tale of one *Jim* Smiley: "He was the curiosest man about always betting on any thing that turned up you ever see, if he could get any body to bet on the other side; and if he couldn't, he'd change sides." Smiley has trained a frog to jump farther than any other frog in the neighborhood ("Smiley said all a frog wanted was education"). A stranger comes to town and bets Smiley he can find a frog that can jump even farther, but he sabotages Smiley's frog, filling its mouth with buckshot, to win the bet. Smiley is flummoxed until he discovers how he was cheated; then he chases after the stranger but fails to catch him.

Wheeler regales Twain with this tale in a droll, matter-of-fact tone, "which showed me plainly that, so far from his imagining that there was anything ridiculous or funny about his story, he regarded it as a really important matter, and admired its two heroes as men of transcendent genius in finesse." The innocence of Wheeler, his earnestness and candor, underscores the hilarity of his idiosyncratic language. But however tickled we might be, there is something deeper at work in Wheeler's seriousness—a proper sense, perhaps, of the gravity of the story he is telling. It is, after all, a story about human cunning and aggression.

Huckleberry Finn likewise is a more complicated moral being than the vagabond and layabout he imagines himself to be. It is true that he is happiest when he is displaced from the rigidities of "civilized" life, lolling on the bank of the Mississippi River cooking catfish over a pit fire, with a raft close at hand should he need to escape, but Huck is deeply civilized despite his professed wildness. Through his adventures on the river he articulates a code of conduct based on empathy, hatred of misused power, and allegiance to the dispossessed (particularly the escaped slave Jim, who becomes his closest friend).

"Huck does indeed have all the capacities for the simple happiness he says he has," Lionel Trilling wrote in his essay "Huckleberry Finn," "but circumstances and his own moral nature make him the least carefree of boys—he is always 'in a sweat' over the predicament of someone else." Huck may be Twain's most ingenious comic creation, and his speech—hearty, shambolic, but nonetheless intensely expressive—gives delight on every page. But, Trilling points out, he has a great sense of the sadness of human life, drawing our attention to a moment early in the book, when Huck's vision of the world is quietly revealed:

> Well, when Tom and me got to the edge of the hilltop we looked away down into the village and could see three or four lights twinkling where there were sick folks, maybe; and the stars over us was sparkling ever so fine; and down by the village was the river, a whole mile broad, and awful still and grand.

"The identification of the lights as the lamps of sick-watches," Trilling observes, "defines Huck's character." It is through Huck that Twain invented the language with which to express the problems of American life in the wake of the Civil War—a period of national recovery that was quickly swept up in a manic industrial boom. *Adventures of Huckleberry Finn* secured the status of vernacular American English as a literary language, and Huck is its quintessential speaker. He is a kind of idealized figure for the upright American character, with the Mississippi River as the source of his sturdy moral vision and the mellifluous rhythms of his speech.

Bibliography

Trilling, Lionel. *"Huckleberry Finn."* *The Liberal Imagination: Essays on Literature and Society*. 1950. New York: New York Review of Books Classics, 2008.

Twain, Mark. *Adventures of Huckleberry Finn*. 1884. New York: Bantam Classics, 2003.

_____. *The Best Short Stories of Mark Twain*. Ed. Lawrence I. Berkove. New York: Modern Library, 2004.

_____. *Life on the Mississippi*. Ed. James M. Cox. New York: Penguin Classics, 1985.

CRITICAL CONTEXTS

Mark Twain and His Times_____
Stephen Railton

In many respects the time between 1865 and 1910 *was* Mark
Twain's. Mark Twain was "born" in 1863, when Samuel L. Clemens
first used that pseudonym as a byline on newspaper articles in Nevada.
However, it was in 1865 that his story about the jumping frog of
Calaveras County, which was published in New York and reprinted in
papers around the United States, started to make him celebrated too.
The Innocents Abroad, his first book, appeared four years later and immediately became one of the period's best sellers. By the time his novels about Tom Sawyer and Huckleberry Finn came out, his lecture
tours and other live performances had made the "Mark Twain" persona
as famous as any of his fictional characters. One of the earliest and
most enduring American idols, Twain was also among the first to
achieve international fame, as he proved in 1895-1896 during his successful around-the-world lecture tour. Compared to our modern Inter-
net age, mass communication in Twain's time looks primitive; however, Mark Twain was always a media favorite. It has been suggested
that, after Queen Victoria, he was the most frequently photographed
person of the nineteenth century. Often when he made a joke—as when
he told a reporter in London in 1897 that "the report of my death was an
exaggeration"[1]—hundreds of newspapers picked it up from the wire
services, and millions of readers all over the world laughed. When he
really died in 1910, reports of that event made headlines on several
continents.

In his first novel, *The Gilded Age: A Tale of Today* (1873), co-
authored with Charles Dudley Warner, Twain gave his era the name by
which historians still refer to it. Although he missed the Civil War,
probably his generation's most decisive experience, his life otherwise
seems dramatically to embody his cultural time and place. Born into
poverty in the middle of the country, he went west to look for silver in
frontier mining camps and later traveled east to find status in the man-

sions of old cities. He loved the latest inventions, such as the telephone and the typewriter. He could not resist speculative investments. He made a fortune, lost it, made another. However, while he plunged exuberantly into his contemporary world, one of the many paradoxes that define his career is that his most successful books carry American readers away from the Gilded Age to other times and places.

Travel Writing

During his life, Twain was more successful as a travel writer than as a novelist, and the least successful of his travel books, *Life on the Mississippi* (1883), was the one that spent the most time telling about "today." Travel is a central motif in his fiction too, whether Huck and Jim's journey down the Mississippi or Hank Morgan's journey through time. In two of his travel books, Twain takes American readers to modern Europe (*The Innocents Abroad*, 1869, and *A Tramp Abroad*, 1880). In novels he takes them to Tudor England (*The Prince and the Pauper*, 1881), to Arthurian England (*A Connecticut Yankee in King Arthur's Court*, 1889) and to medieval France (*Personal Recollections of Joan of Arc*, 1896). His life and work seem centered on the river that flows through the middle of America, but apart from the second half of *Life on the Mississippi*, his stories about the river—from "Old Times on the Mississippi" (1875) to *Pudd'nhead Wilson* (1894)—also travel through time, back to an antebellum America that was gone before "Mark Twain" came into existence. With few exceptions, notably *Joan of Arc*, contemporary readers were glad to go with Twain's imagination wherever it went. This prompts a question: How did his tales meet the needs of the times he and his American audience shared?

Mark Twain's America was itself on the move. The country into which Sam Clemens was born in 1835 contained fewer than thirteen million people living in twenty-four states, and his native Missouri was then the only state west of the Mississippi. When he died nearly seventy-five years later, more than ninety-two million people lived in forty-six states, and the country had extended its reach as far west as the Philippines. In 1835, fewer than one in six Americans lived in cities, and the largest of these, New York, contained fewer than 300,000 inhabitants. By 1910, more than one-third of the nation's population was urban, and New York City alone contained almost five million people.

Like the sixth-century England to which the Connecticut Yankee travels, the America into which Twain and his contemporaries were born was essentially agrarian; by the end of the century one-quarter of all American jobs—like the job Hank leaves behind in Hartford—were in factories, and that percentage was rapidly growing. By 1920, it was almost one-half. During this same period, the nation's population became much more ethnically diverse than it had ever been. The Statue of Liberty was unveiled in 1886, just in time to greet the millions of non-English-speaking European immigrants who would arrive over the next two decades. Few generations in American history have lived through as much social change as Mark Twain's.

Nostalgia

Amid these transformations and disruptions, *The Adventures of Tom Sawyer* (1876) did not just take readers away from contemporary reality; it gave them a place of refuge from it. While the great river flows beside the fictional St. Petersburg, time seems to stand still in Mark Twain's fantasy about children and summertime in a middle-American village. Though usually regarded as a children's book, the story is told by an adult narrator who looks back on the passions and pleasures of childhood with a nostalgia that kids themselves never feel, and the nostalgic mood suffuses an earlier America with the same glow. Theodore Dreiser, an American novelist born just after the Civil War, came of age amid the new forces of urbanization, industrialization, and immigration and could not share Twain's novel's faith in what it calls "those old simple days." In 1894, Dreiser visited his fiancé's family on a farm in Missouri that was not far from Mark Twain's Hannibal but impass-ably removed from the idyllic world of *Tom Sawyer*. Remembering in his autobiography what he had seen in the harsh light of steel factories, he realized that ideal past was a "sentimental and purely imaginative tradition" he might long for but no longer believe in: "I had seen Pitts-burgh. I had seen Lithuanians and Hungarians in their 'courts' and hov-els. I had seen the girls of that city walking the streets at night" as pros-titutes (354).

While Dreiser and other writers, such as Stephen Crane and Jacob Riis, sought to depict this modern America in such books as *Sister Carrie* (1900), *Maggie: A Girl of the Streets* (1893), and *How the Other Half Lives* (1890), most American adults were willing to collabo-rate with the way Twain's imagination constructs "this old time life" through Tom's adventures. Writing in 1907, Hamilton W. Mabie ob-served, "Society in the Mississippi Valley in Tom Sawyer's time was a pure democracy, in easy circumstances, free from anxiety, charitable of everything except cowardice and meanness, taking life comfortably" (650-51). *Tom Sawyer* was an early example of local-color writing, a regionalist mode that evoked the customs, idioms, and rhythms of life in close-knit communities like New England towns, Tennessee moun-tains, or Louisiana bayous. "Local colorism" was the most popular fic-tional genre among late-nineteenth-century readers, and their favorite locality was clearly Tom's St. Petersburg, with its heavenly sounding name. Americans still cherish the image of a national past that *Tom Sawyer* provides and return to it in various ways. "Tom Sawyer's Cave," just outside the real town of Hannibal, was already a tourist attraction by 1899. Visitors to Disneyland in California and Disney World in Florida have enjoyed adventures on "Tom's Sawyer's Island"—the only theme-park attraction Walt Disney designed personally.

Of course, Tom's world is not really a "pure democracy." His Aunt Polly is a slave owner, and the "half-breed" Injun Joe is a skulking re-minder of the nation's vexed racial history. However, another aspect of the service the novel performs for American readers is to disarm slavery and racism of any power to disturb their collective conscience. Joe, for example, is a melodramatic villain, not a cultural symptom. There may be a significance that Twain's contemporaries never suspected in the fact that the novel's most famous scene describes a whitewashing.

When Twain imaginatively returned to St. Petersburg in the book Huck Finn narrates, he took a more complex and challenging look at the same past that *Tom Sawyer* idealizes. *Adventures of Huckleberry Finn* (1884) has always been more controversial. When it was first published, it was notoriously banned from the Concord Library; in 1904, educators in Denver made the earliest attempt to ban it from public schools. It was not until the 1950s, however, that anyone accused the novel of racism. Among Twain's contemporary readers, it was the best selling of all his novels. For those readers, Huck's good heart was a prophylactic against the narrative's representations of greed, hypocrisy, and violence; the friendship Huck and Jim share on the raft was a defense against racial fears; and the ending, in which Huck announces his intention to "light out for the Territory," was a way to keep alive the idea of going into the West, and with it the American myth of escaping "sivilization." No matter that less than a decade after the novel's publication, historian Frederick Jackson Turner announced that for Americans "the frontier has gone" (60). Huck's readers can always vicariously go with him into that Territory, a space that is even more recuperative than Tom's village.

A National Self-Image

Even a full century after Twain's death, our culture continues to rely on the past he invented as a foundation for our national self-image. During his lifetime, his work was at least equally important in helping contemporaries toward the American future. That is the cultural reason that, of all his books, they liked *The Innocents Abroad* best. It is the record of Twain's adventures in Europe and the Holy Land (as the Middle East was known at the time) as a member of the *Quaker City* excursion in 1867, the first-ever organized American tour group to visit the Old World. As readers of *Daisy Miller* (1878) or any of Henry James's other international tales know, soon after the end of the Civil War, Americans began traveling abroad in unprecedented numbers. For most Americans, then and now, the purpose of going to Europe is the acquisition of culture, a purpose that can make the naves of cathedrals or the rooms of museums pretty solemn places.

What distinguishes Twain's *Innocents Abroad* among the scores of travel books written by pilgrims to these shrines is its humor. Much of this is supplied by the hapless figure Twain creates for himself as the narrator's naive first-person protagonist, but at the same time readers are invited to laugh at, and thus look down on, many of the Old World's claims to cultural superiority. Refusing to learn their preposterously foreign names, for example, the narrator starts calling all the local guides "Ferguson." He treats the sights they show him in places such as Paris and Constantinople with playful contempt, using irreverence to liberate his young American sensibility from all kinds of "Old Masters." "I never felt so fervently thankful," he writes after a few weeks in Italy, "so soothed, so tranquil, so filled with a blessed peace as I did yesterday when I learned that Michael Angelo was dead." Leonardo da Vinci's *Last Supper* probably was a great work of art, once—"but it was three hundred years ago"; now, like so much of the Old World, it is "dimmed with age," "scaled and marred." Europe and the Holy Land may have had a great history, but the future clearly belongs to the New World. Americans, with their colonial heritage, may have been taught to revere the achievements of that Old World, but by making fun of them Twain's account opens up a different kind of territory for his readers: a point of view, both psychic and cultural, a more comfortable place from which they can begin taking possession of the larger world.

The same years in which "Mark Twain" took Samuel Clemens from an obscure village to international stardom were the years in which the United States was moving toward the role of world superpower it would play in the twentieth or "the American Century." Twain's work helped enable that rise too. If we look back at *Tom Sawyer* from this perspective, for instance, the demonization and exorcism of the Indian as "Injun Joe" aligns itself with the nation's first imperialist enterprise, the colonization of the West on the ideological basis of "Manifest Destiny." This doctrine asserted that white America had a God-given and exclusive claim on that same "Indian Territory" that Huck lights out for. We want to absolve Huck himself of any complicity in this agenda, but Twain's early works often endorse it.

Twain's second major book, *Roughing It* (1872), recounts his own travels westward a decade earlier, to the Nevada Territory, then to California, and ultimately to Hawaii. In chapter 19 he meets his first Indians, the Goshoots, whom he calls "the wretchedest type of mankind I have ever seen . . . treacherous, filthy and repulsive." It is probably a mistake to read too much into Twain's spelling here, though the tribe's name is usually written as Goshute. But while he does not say "go shoot Indians," he does say that "wherever one finds an Indian tribe he has only found Goshoots more or less modified by circumstances and surroundings—but Goshoots, after all." And he does implicitly endorse their dispossession: The place Indians occupy in his narratives effectively denies them any place in the national future. One could say that, if *The Innocents Abroad* offers the Old World to his readers, *Roughing It* gives them the West.

American Imperialism

Having "saved the Union" and "won the West," the United States took its first intercontinental step toward becoming an imperial power by declaring war on Spain in 1898. In some respects Twain's fiction anticipated this move. In *The Prince and the Pauper* he colonizes Britain's royal history by interpolating an unmistakably American fable about human equality and aristocratic tyranny into it. The imaginative project of *A Connecticut Yankee in King Arthur's Court* looks even more overtly imperialist: Hank Morgan, "a Yankee of the Yankees," travels across the ocean and through thirteen centuries to plant the flag of America's republican, Protestant, capitalist ideology in Camelot, the very citadel of aristocratic tradition. In comparison with Hank's advanced technological know-how, the sixth-century England of Twain's novel is essentially a Third World country, which makes it a land of opportunity for Hank to "introduce the great and beneficent civilization of the nineteenth century" into its culture and to "peacefully replace the twin despotisms of royalty and aristocratic privilege with a 'Republic on the American plan.'" This is how Mark Twain himself summarizes the novel's plot for readers of a prepublication excerpt in *The Century Magazine*.

Many modern readers are tempted to read *Connecticut Yankee* ironically. For them, behind Hank's self-proclaimed ambition to liberate and enlighten the medieval Britons can be found a will to dominate and exploit them for his own aggrandizement. However, if Twain intended his readers to see through Hank's jingoism to his own version of "the heart of darkness" that the contemporary British novelist Joseph Conrad would use the theme of imperialism to depict, he gave no indication of it. Twain owned the publishing company that brought out *Connecticut Yankee* and so sanctioned the promotional materials that advertised it as "a book that appeals to all true Americans"—the way it was read by his contemporaries. For British reviewers, the novel's flag-waving was a flaw; they found it vulgar rather than egalitarian. To most reviewers in the United States, however, both Hank and his creator were culture heroes: "Mark Twain," wrote one, "has come up from the people. He is American to the backbone."

Six years after publishing *Connecticut Yankee*, Twain went west again, but this time he did not stop at Hawaii. His around-the-world lecture tour in 1895-1896 not only enabled him to convert his international drawing power into a way to work himself out of bankruptcy but also gave him a firsthand look at the effects of British imperialism in Fiji, Australia, New Zealand, India, and South Africa. In the book he wrote about these travels, *Following the Equator* (1897), he takes a much more critical look at the dispossession and exploitation of indigenous peoples, often describing the acts of violence by which "the blessings of Progress" were inflicted on them. In 1900, in the aftermath of the Spanish-American War, Twain publicly declared, "I am an anti-imperialist," and in his essays "To the Person Sitting in Darkness" (1901) and "King Leopold's Soliloquy" (1905) he used his celebrity status as a pulpit from which to denounce European and American brutalities in China, the Philippines, and the Congo Free State.

Twain's late protest pieces are frequently anthologized in our time; the often savagely ironic voice he deploys in them resonates deeply with modern readers. In his time, however, they were never widely popular, but they did increase his status as an advocate for the common people, people like the poor white Huck, the enslaved Jim, the untitled Arthurians, and the aborigines of Australasia. However, it is important to note the limits that Twain imposed on his critique of imperialism. It does not occur to the author of *Following the Equator* to compare British treatment of the Tasmanians, for example, with white America's treatment of Indians, and while Twain attacks President William McKinley for betraying the rights of Filipinos, it is with nothing like the rhetorical force of his exposé of King Leopold's abuse of the Congolese. When he says that McKinley's mistake was to "play the European game" in the Philippines, as opposed to "the usual and regular *American* game" he rightly played against Spain in Cuba, Twain even makes sure not to ride too roughly over his American readers' sentiments. Having won their love throughout his career, Twain was very careful about allowing himself to attack his own culture as opposed to attacks on other times and places. The most emphatic antislavery passages in the works he published are found in *Connecticut Yankee*, in which none of the slave owners or slave drivers are Americans, and the slaves themselves are all white. More and more often in his last years, he censored his own writing, deciding against publishing pieces such as "The United States of Lyncherdom" (written in 1901) and "The War Prayer" (written in 1905). Published posthumously, these too are widely reprinted and esteemed in our time, but in his lifetime, Twain deemed them too dangerous to print. "I shouldn't have even half a friend left down there" in the South, he said about the essay on lynching, "after it issued from the press" (qtd. in Kaplan 365).

Humor

The public in his time saw Mark Twain very differently from the way readers see him in the twenty-first century. Few modern readers are likely to go as far as Ernest Hemingway did when he asserted that "all modern American literature comes from one book by Mark Twain called 'Huckleberry Finn'" (22). However, within scholarly studies, English classes, and media stories Twain is treated as a great author and *Huck Finn* as a national treasure, a masterpiece of world literature. To his contemporaries, Twain was as much an entertainer as an artist, and *Huckleberry Finn*, to quote from the promotional ads Twain's own publishing company produced, "a mine of humor." Twain's contemporaries read *Huckleberry Finn* to laugh, not to think, and doubtless the perception of it as simply a funny book made it possible for them to overlook the darkness that shadows its vision of American society.

It could in fact be argued that for his culture Twain's great gifts as a humorist had something like the same value as his travel writings and historical fictions: Giving readers opportunities to laugh was another way to let them get away from the more unsettling aspects of their everyday reality. Out of the political corruption that was so rampant in the Gilded Age, for example, Twain distilled aphorisms such as "It could probably be shown by facts and figures that there is no distinctly native American criminal class except Congress." Out of the many economic "panics" (as recessions were then called) that ruined thousands of people at regular intervals during the period—including Twain himself in 1894—Twain brought this advice: "There are two times in a man's life when he should not speculate: when he can't afford it and when he can." One-liners such as these from "Pudd'nhead Wilson's Calendar" were reprinted in late-nineteenth-century newspapers next to stories about bribery scandals and rising unemployment.

In an 1884 essay that Twain took very personally, the British critic Matthew Arnold complained that in the United States "the addiction to 'the funny man' is a national misfortune" (283). However, another eminent European contemporary, Sigmund Freud, greatly admired Twain's humor because he understood the therapeutic value of wit as a means to transform the inescapable sources of human pain into occasions for mental pleasure. Certainly when Twain turns the idea of his own death into that joke about exaggeration, he displays a superiority to the gravest of circumstances that can uplift everyone.

Twain also believed that humorous writing can play a serious social role: "Humor must not professedly teach, and it must not professedly preach, but it must do both." His reply to Arnold's complaint that the "funny man" kept the United States from achieving a great civilization was that American humor kept America free; "a discriminating irreverence," he wrote, "is the creator and protector of human liberty." Books such as *The Innocents Abroad* and *Connecticut Yankee* rocked the pedestals on which rested the sacred icons of high culture—such as Michelangelo's art and knightly chivalry—but Twain was not trying merely to smash them. By bringing down these Old World icons, Twain sought to lift up the idea of ordinary people in a new world. The statue of Arthur that Hank intends someday to put up in Camelot would not show a king clad in armor, slaying a giant or a dragon; it would instead depict him in commoner's garb, helping a poor woman with smallpox.

By mocking the superannuated, the false, the sentimental, Twain sought to exorcise the spell that conventionality, under the name of genteel refinement, had cast over the American mind. To some of his contemporaries this was heresy. When, for example, Twain's after-dinner speech at the birthday dinner *The Atlantic Monthly* held for John Greenleaf Whittier in 1877 juxtaposed the formal elegancies of Ralph Waldo Emerson's, Oliver Wendell Holmes's, and Henry Wadsworth

Longfellow's poetry with such realities of life on the Pacific frontier as whiskey drinking, gambling, and knife fighting, newspaper editorials accused the humorist of insulting the country's true artists. The Concord Library Committee proclaimed that Huck's bad grammar was as dangerous to the well-being of young readers as his habit of lying. There was even one American reviewer of *Connecticut Yankee* who refused to find anything enjoyable in Hank's "contemptible tricks" or Twain's "sheer flippancy" toward "the grand heroisms of human history."

"The Genteel Tradition"—the label George Santayana applied to Victorian America's reluctance to engage directly with the facts of life—outlived Twain; by most accounts, it perished during World War I. As the creation of both Sam Clemens's talents and ambitions and the values and appetites of his contemporary audience, "Mark Twain" was shaped by that ideology. Think, for example, of how invisible human sexuality is in Twain's work—what would modern humorists do without that topic? However, what most members of his audience heard in Twain's style, with its tang of the frontier and its grip on actual experience, was the voice of freedom. To later writers such as Hemingway, it was also the voice that enabled the modern American writer to take aesthetic possession of the world.

When Twain turned seventy in 1905, the white-tie birthday party that *Harper's Magazine* threw for him was every bit as impressive as the one *The Atlantic Monthly* had thrown for Whittier in 1877. A forty-piece orchestra played accompaniment while 170 guests, including millionaire Andrew Carnegie and African American writer Charles Chesnutt, consumed a seven-course meal and listened to more than a dozen speeches and a congratulatory letter from President Teddy Roosevelt. As a souvenir, each guest was given a foot-high bust of Twain. Like the honorary degree that Oxford University would bestow on Twain two years later, this piece of statuary was a sign that his achievement belonged in the same category as geniuses such as William Shakespeare and Ludwig van Beethoven. However, when at last it was Twain's own turn to speak, his truant disposition took center stage, and most of the formality went out of the event. The topic of his speech was the regimen by which he had managed to live so long. "I have made it a rule," he declared in his beloved deadpan drawl, "never to smoke more than one cigar at a time. I have no other restrictions as regards smoking."

Like his mop of white hair and his bandit's mustache, cigars were a conspicuous prop in the "Mark Twain" image that was as popular as any of his books. Twain did not actually begin wearing the white suit until the year following his seventieth birthday, but when he did, it made headlines too, and delighted his audience. It seemed to put the finishing touch on his character *as* a character; it completed the picture of Twain himself as a symbol of individuality, self-expression, freedom from conformity. It was the visual complement to the pleasure principle he preached at his seventieth birthday party as the moral of his life:

We can't reach old age by another man's road. . . . And I wish to urge upon you this—which I think is wisdom—that if you find you can't make seventy by any but an uncomfortable road, don't you go.

To the generation for whom this image was "Mark Twain," it came as a disconcerting surprise when, two days after his April 21, 1910, death, the *New York Herald* broke the news that Twain had been the author of the book titled *What Is Man?*—a short philosophical dialogue that had been published anonymously in 1906, the same year Twain first emerged in that stunning white suit. According to this little book, "man" is an unthinking, socially programmed machine: "He is moved, directed, COMMANDED, by *exterior* influences—*solely*. He *originates* nothing, himself—not even an opinion, not even a thought." This concept of environmental determinism was familiar to readers in 1906 from the works of the novelists of the generation after Twain's, the literary naturalists such as Émile Zola, Thomas Hardy, and Theodore

Dreiser. And the idea that individuals are conditioned by their culture was already there in Twain's earlier works: implicitly in Huck's assumption that slavery is "natural" and blacks are inferior; explicitly in Hank's asseverations on "training." Hank even says that "training is everything; training is all there is *to* a person." However, Huck and Hank themselves, as memorable, vivid characters, seem to belie such a dehumanizing doctrine.

Mark Twain's Stature as a Writer

Mark Twain himself, who had conquered the world by the force of his personality, originality, and genius, seemed in his own person to provide his contemporaries with an antidote to the intellectual maladies of fin de siècle art and thought. His audience looked at him, with a mix of pride and camaraderie, as glittering proof of the possibilities of making it in America. There is, however, no hint of individual characters amid the humorless abstractions of *What Is Man?* When his audience first learned Twain had written it, their reaction was sentimental: it seemed too bad that the "greatest of American humorists," as a contemporary commentator in *Current Literature* put it, was "a sad-hearted man" ("Mark Twain's" 643). But in the long run it was even better to dismiss the book entirely. When a new edition of *What Is Man?* appeared in 1917, this time with Twain's name on its title page, the reviewer for *The New York Times* simply "refuse[d] to believe" that Twain really meant what it says ("As to Posthumous" 216).

Because they had invested so much in Twain as a source of personal and cultural pleasure, early-twentieth-century readers were completely unprepared to entertain the thesis of one of the first book-length studies of his art and career, *The Ordeal of Mark Twain*, published in 1920 by Van Wyck Brooks. As the title of his book lets readers know from the start, Brooks argues that so far from being someone who mastered his times, Mark Twain "was the supreme victim of an epoch in American history" (324). The great writer that Twain could have been was sacrificed to the role of jester in the court ruled by public opinion. Brooks's reading of Twain was shaped by his own times. He wrote as a member of the so-called lost generation, and his rejection of the philistine culture that idolized Twain was a critical equivalent to the decision made by writers such as Ezra Pound, T. S. Eliot, Gertrude Stein, and Ernest Hemingway to become expatriates in protest against America's cultural inadequacies. However, Brooks rightly cites the signs of despair in so much of what Twain wrote and withheld from publication in his last years as the symptoms of his "ordeal" as an American artist for whom the loving embrace of the available reading public was a suffocating, emasculating stranglehold.

Brooks's iconoclastic book aroused a lot of shocked anger. The most significant response was Bernard DeVoto's *Mark Twain's America* (1932), which reads Twain's career as a triumph that was made possible by the same American culture Brooks saw as destructive. Within Twain's best works, DeVoto states, one finds "the humor of the frontier in its greatest incandescence, realizing its fullest scope and expressing its qualities on the level of genius. In them an American civilization sums up its experience" (240-41). Instead of crippling Twain, the indigenous culture gave him wings. Under different vocabularies, the critical debate about what was gained and what was lost in the complex relationship between Twain and his times continues to this day. Ultimately, individual readers will have to decide that question for themselves.

Interestingly, in their own later works on Twain, Brooks and DeVoto each moved so far toward the other's interpretation of Twain's achievement that they might be said to have changed places. What they were really attacking and defending, with a passion of which they were only partially conscious, was America itself. To his times and since, Mark Twain has seemed to many people to be the representative American— or, as Ken Burns's 2001 Public Television documentary on Twain puts it, with surprising solemnity, not just "an American, but *the* American."

On the other hand, one of Twain's own most cherished fantasies was that of "the mysterious stranger." His last attempt at writing a novel was, in one manuscript version, actually titled that. In this story the "stranger" turns out to be Satan, who finds himself among earthlings in the same unaccountable way that Hank Morgan finds himself among Arthurians. As for himself, Twain saw more than a coincidence in the fact that his birth in 1835 coincided with the passage of Halley's comet across the earth's skies during its seventy-five-year orbit around the sun. He predicted that he would die in 1910, when the comet would again be passing by. He saw himself and the comet as "two indefinable freaks" who "came in together" and so "must go out together." Paradoxically, the more Twain seemed to his American audience to embody their ideal self, their idea of America, the more he felt like a radically estranged outsider. Despite this, however, Twain and his times were as closely linked to each other as the "Siamese" twins he frequently wrote about. He may not be *the* American, but, for better and worse, no writer can tell us more about American culture than he can.

Note

1. Except where otherwise indicated, all quotations from Mark Twain, his publishers, and his reviewers cited in this essay can be found at one or both of the following online sites: Mark Twain Quotations, Newspaper Collections, and Related Resources, http://www.twainquotes.com, administered by Barbara Schmidt; Mark Twain in His Times, http://etext.lib.virginia.edu/railton, administered by Stephen Railton.

Works Cited

Arnold, Matthew. "Civilization in the United States." *The Nineteenth Century* 23 (Apr. 1888).

"As to Posthumous." *New York Times* 3 June 1917.

Brooks, Van Wyck. *The Ordeal of Mark Twain*. 1920. New York: E. P. Dutton, 1970.

DeVoto, Bernard. *Mark Twain's America*. Boston: Little, Brown, 1932.

Dreiser, Theodore. *A Book About Myself*. 1922. Greenwich, CT: Fawcett, 1965.

Freud, Sigmund. *Jokes and Their Relation to the Unconscious*. Trans. James Strachey. New York: W. W. Norton, 1960.

Hemingway, Ernest. *Green Hills of Africa*. New York: Charles Scribner's Sons, 1935.

Kaplan, Justin. *Mr. Clemens and Mark Twain*. New York: Simon & Schuster, 1966.

Mabie, Hamilton W. "Mark Twain the Humorist." *The Outlook* 87 (23 Nov. 1907).

Mark Twain. Dir. Ken Burns. Alexandria: PBS Video/Florentine Films Production, 2001.

"Mark Twain's Pessimistic Philosophy." *Current Literature* 48 (June 1910).

Santayana, George. "The Genteel Tradition in American Philosophy." *The Essential Santayana*. Ed. Santayana Edition. Bloomington: Indiana UP, 2009.

Turner, Frederick Jackson. "The Significance of the Frontier in American History." *Rereading Frederick Jackson Turner*. Ed. John Mack Faragher. New York: Henry Holt, 1994.

Mark Twain's Critical Reception_____

Alan Gribben

Mark Twain's immense talent was recognized relatively early, and almost from the beginning Twain maintained a loyal readership and earned numerous flattering notices. However, during the three most important decades of his writing career—the 1870s through the 1890s—his reputation among the reigning literati of New England was partially clouded by the fact that his books were sold *only* by door-to-door salespeople, not through retail bookstores. Twain got his start with this lucrative method of "subscription" distribution when the American Publishing Company of Hartford, Connecticut, brought out his *The Innocents Abroad* in 1869 and *Roughing It* in 1872. Thereafter, the formerly impoverished newspaper and magazine reporter was understandably reluctant to give up an arrangement that enabled him to build a nineteen-room mansion in the stylish Nook Farm suburb of Hartford in 1874 and outfit it with a fashionable retinue of servants.

The fact that subscription books were seldom advertised in newspapers and magazines ordinarily made it relatively difficult for them to obtain sympathetic reviews—or sometimes any reviews at all. Many elite authors and editors regarded the products of subscription publishing as an inferior class of literature and viewed their persistent sales agents as tawdry nuisances. Fortunately, in Mark Twain's case he gained three countering advantages: the sheer volume of his book sales, which rapidly familiarized the public with his name and writings; the frequent appearances of his stories, sketches, essays, and serialized novels in the leading periodicals of his day; and the unstinting support of the leading literary authority and book reviewer of that day, William Dean Howells. A close personal friend of Twain, Howells was always prompt to praise Twain's books, initially in *The Atlantic Monthly* and, after 1886, in *Harper's Monthly*,

Despite Mark Twain's early and long-lasting success as a writer, five fundamental issues have repeatedly been raised to call into question Twain's standing. In the first place, his early identity as primarily a travel writer confused his contemporaries when he sought to switch over to penning novels (and then went back, intermittently, to releasing travel books). Even today, admirers of Twain's fiction often seem non-plused by his travelogues and view them as regrettable distractions from his "real" work.

The second issue is Twain's increasing tendency to dabble in entre-preneurial business ventures, especially his attempt to own and operate his own publishing firm. His business ventures have complicated and, for many critics, distorted his authorial image. The third handicap, oddly enough, has been Twain's enormous and sustained popularity. Somehow this enduring appeal, which translates into best-selling books, for many critics apparently classifies his stature as suspect and unduly exalted. His fourth difficulty was and remains his primary repu-tation as a humorist. For a sizable number of critics the risible aspects of his writing interfere with the serious social analysis and commen-tary they want to see him dispense. The fact that Twain essentially earned his income by making his readers smile and guffaw has not been a sufficient excuse to certain sober-minded commentators for his comedic episodes.

Finally, there exists the issue of Twain's literary craftsmanship, which has been questioned repeatedly. Can an acknowledged master-piece such as *Adventures of Huckleberry Finn* (1884), which returns in its concluding chapters to its seemingly puerile "boy book" begin-nings, still be considered a masterpiece? *A Connecticut Yankee in King Arthur's Court* (1889) contains many strange artistic decisions; do these mar it to the point of inartistry? What about *The Tragedy of Pudd'nhead Wilson* (1894), in which Twain's racial theories seem to a number of scholars to be hopelessly contradictory? Twain's unfinished "Mysterious Stranger" stories (composed 1897-1908) exist in three overlapping versions; what might one make of these? Or take his auto-biography, written by differing methods at various times and then er-ratically revised in repetitive drafts. What should we think about it?

Let it be said that, for the vast majority of Twain's readers, his strengths assuredly outweigh whatever writerly faults of which he was guilty. Indeed, some of his supposed authorial flaws—if they are indeed flaws—serve to make his books and manuscripts more fascinating for many scholars and critics. At any rate, the depth and range of his literary talents are undeniable. First of all, he left behind a voluminous record of his life and his era. Here was an author who was writing regularly from the time he was a teenager until he lay on his deathbed, and even then he was still asking for pencil and paper, according to one biographical account. Crucially, Mark Twain's contributions to what is now identified as the American colloquial style—a relaxed, conversational tone that set itself against the convoluted, artificial-sounding sentences of American authors who still imitated an earlier British literary mode—are obvious and epochal. Additionally, his capacities for the perfect turn of phrase, uncannily comic timing, and ingratiating, tongue-in-cheek satire won the world's admiration and to this day place him among America's leading writers.

Early Travel Books

Louis J. Budd's book *Mark Twain: The Contemporary Reviews* (1999) makes it possible to follow the outlines of the critical reception of Twain's varied literary output throughout his entire writing career. His first travel book, *The Innocents Abroad*, captured effusive reviews as well as foreseeable carping about a latently subversive tone. The *Hartford Times* (in the city of the book's publisher) called it "fresh, racy and sparkling as a glass of iced champagne, and a good deal better for the health and digestion." In contrast, the *San Francisco Evening Bulletin* fretted that, while most of what Twain wrote "about the Holy Land is true, . . . we could wish that he said it less flippantly, with less levity, and a greater deference to the feelings of those more reverent and strong of faith." The newspaper asked, "Was it right to hold even the most temper-trying" of his fellow travelers "up to public contempt?

. . . Would the author have been pleased if some one of his fellow-passengers had drawn him . . . with all his angularities of character exaggerated—nay, distorted into burlesque, to the public?" Despite these remarks, the same review conceded that, unlike most literary comedians of his day, Twain

> does not rely upon bad spelling and worse puns to make his readers laugh. He is droll, fond of the grotesque and a coiner of absurd conceits; but he possesses that higher quality of humor that is allied to wit. He makes you laugh, but he makes you think as well.

The paper added that *Innocents Abroad* "is full of vigorous vitality—full of brawn and marrow."

The *New York Evening Mail* took pains to condemn the general output of subscription publishing for its "large amount of verbal and pictorial padding," but then went on to acknowledge that "this duodecimo, however, contains a fund of fun. . . . There are many touches of sly and well-aimed satire in the book." Likewise the *Buffalo Commercial Advertiser* complained that the typical "fat octavo joke" book "is sure to pall the taste of an average reader"; by contrast, the editors admitted, Twain's new work "blended facts with fancy, humor with instruction" and thereby "produced a pleasant, piquant and really enjoyable book." When William Dean Howells—who had not yet met Twain—came to write about *The Innocents Abroad,* his defense of the book in *The Atlantic Monthly* was resounding:

> It is always good-natured humor . . . that he lavishes on his reader, and even in its impudence it is charming; we do not remember where it is indulged at the cost of the weak or helpless side, or where it is insolent, with all its sauciness and irreverence.

The published responses to Twain's succeeding books roughly followed a similar pattern: a few critics' feathers were ruffled by the edginess of his tightrope-walking act that tested the boundaries separating the haven of the permissible from the chasms of the impermissible; others objected to Twain's indifference to long-accepted forms and conventions. Meanwhile, most professional readers applauded his inventiveness, daring, and entertainment value.

Twain's second major book, *Roughing It*, a compilation of autobiographical sketches about his stagecoach journey to the Nevada Territory in 1861 and his subsequent experiences in western Nevada, California, and the Sandwich Islands, drew a mixed review in the *Cincinnati Gazette*: "One may not always approve the taste of what is said, yet he can rarely record his dissent without a smile." The reviewer for *The Independent* praised the fact that "his fun is not dependent upon bad spelling or bad grammar. He writes good English, and we can commend the book to all who enjoy the wild Western drollery of which Mark Twain is the ablest living master." The *Boston Evening Transcript* was even more enthusiastic: "The worthies of the 'flush times' of Nevada are so admirably depicted that one is almost induced to call Mark Twain a comic Plutarch."

William Dean Howells, by now Twain's friend, weighed in with several gratifying compliments in *The Atlantic Monthly*:

> The grotesque exaggeration and broad irony with which the life is described are conjecturably the truest colors that could have been used, for all existence there must have looked like an extravagant joke, the humor of which was only deepened by its nether-side of tragedy. . . . It is singularly entertaining, and its humor is always amiable, manly, and generous.

The *Overland Monthly* declared that far from being merely a "book of grotesque humor and rollicking fun," *Roughing It* "abounds in fresh descriptions of natural scenery, some of which, especially in the overland stage-ride, are remarkably graphic and vigorous." Although the *San Francisco Evening Bulletin* lamented that "in a literary point of view the work is hardly up to the standard of *The Innocents Abroad*" and stated that "we miss that eloquence of description adorning a few of his sketches of France," most reviewers agreed with the *New York Tribune* that *Roughing It* offered many "savory pleasantries" and that its many illustrations "are no less comical." (Engraved pictures were a staple of the subscription publishing industry and, indeed, in that day were generally expected to be present in most books featuring literary humor.)

Switching Genres

Among the challenges that Twain presented for book reviewers were his frequent switches of literary genre. In 1876 he departed temporarily from travel narratives and made his first solo venture as a novelist (he had previously tried his hand at extended fiction by collaborating with author Charles Dudley Warner in writing a now largely forgotten volume, *The Gilded Age*, in 1873). Twain's *The Adventures of Tom Sawyer*, the second entry in what would become known as a "boy book" trend in American literature, easily excelled its predecessor, Thomas Bailey Aldrich's *The Story of a Bad Boy* (1869), by intermixing wildly imagined episodes—including a murder in a cemetery, a pirate campout, a treasure hunt, and a search for children lost in a cave—with actual characters and events drawn from Samuel Clemens's river-village boyhood. Book reviewers were generally impressed with the originality and fun of the novel. Howells praised the title character as

> mischievous, but not vicious. . . . In a word, he is a boy, and merely and exactly an ordinary boy on the moral side. . . . There is a scrupulous regard for the boy's point of view in reference to his surroundings and himself, which shows how rapidly Mr. Clemens has grown as an artist.

Across the Atlantic, the *London Standard* promised that "this is a capital boy's book, and will be the more amusing to English boys from the fact that the language, the doings, and all but the human nature differ so widely from those with which they are familiar. . . . Tom Sawyer is a true boy." The *Hartford Evening Post* found that "the characters are drawn with a firm hand and are readily recognized as types o[f] ordinary people having to do with ordinary affairs."

Switching back to travel narratives, Twain returned to European scenes with *A Tramp Abroad* (1880), which the *Saturday Review* complained about being "dull" in places but with parts that are "delightfully bright and clever." Howells admitted that "this book has not the fresh frolicsomeness of the *Innocents Abroad*" but added that "the writer has always the unexpected at his command, in small things as well as great." The reviewer for the *Spectator* was moved to remark that

> there is little in modern literature with which it can be compared outside the previous works of Mark Twain himself. He is the greatest writer living of travels containing an odd mixture of sober truth, droll exaggeration, and occasional buffoonery, all mixed up together in the most incongruous way imaginable.

However, the same reviewer went on to complain of the "great irregularity in the book" and the clumsiness "of manufacturing the jocularity. . . . It bears evidence of having been patched and pieced together from all sorts of odd and old materials." A more glowing notice appeared in London's *Congregationalist*:

> For a thoroughly genial travelling companion, one who knows how to combine instruction with amusement, who notices everything that is worth observing, . . . who is never prosy, but in whose lively chatter there is some good suggestion, commend us to Mark Twain.

New Directions

Delving deeply into English history for materials for a new novel, *The Prince and the Pauper* (1881), Twain gave the world a book so unlike his previous works that *The Atlantic Monthly*'s H. H. Boyesen alerted readers that this was "not by the Twain we have known for a dozen or more years as the boisterous and rollicking humorist." Of one thing Boyesen was certain: "It will be accorded a rank far above any of the author's previous productions." Similar encomiums arrived, congratulating Twain on discarding his trademark traits in favor of New England refinement. Even the southern writer Joel Chandler Harris, reviewing the novel in the *Atlanta Constitution*, declared that "the wild western burlesquer, the builder of elephantine exaggerations and comicalities has disappeared, and in his stead we have the true literary artist."

Edwin Pond Parker began his review of *The Prince and the Pauper* for the *Hartford Courant* by assuring readers that "although the book is sold by subscription only, it has no trace of the cheap, ill-favored aspect common to most subscription-books." At last, Parker announced, "Mark Twain has finally fulfilled the earnest hope of many of his best friends, in writing a book which has other and higher merits than . . . mere humor." *The Century Magazine* had quibbles about an inconsistency of idioms, "a mixture of old and modern," but conceded that "it is certainly effective as a story" although "it appears also to be overweighted with purpose." In the ensuing century the most enthusiastic of these judgments would come to seem erroneous for extolling a less authentic side of Twain's writing abilities.

Despite that encouragement to disavow his own autobiographical experiences, in *Life on the Mississippi* (1883) Twain reverted to type, recounting his colorful piloting days and retracing his old steamboat trips between St. Louis and New Orleans. Lafcadio Hearn called the result "in some respects . . . the most solid book that Mark Twain has written," in the *New Orleans Times-Picayune*, and the *San Francisco Chronicle* termed it "the best book Mark Twain has written since *The Innocents Abroad*." Even today this redolent narrative remains what

Twain aspired it to be, the "standard work" about an immense national waterway.

As one would expect, *Adventures of Huckleberry Finn* provoked numerous and conflicting reviews because it broke new ground in both narrative style and subject matter. English professor and author Brander Matthews, to his credit, saw past the mounting cavils and scolded "old maids of either sex [who] will wholly fail to understand [Huck Finn] or to like him, or to see his significance and his value." Matthews succinctly summarized Twain's achievement: "In *Tom Sawyer* we saw Huckleberry Finn from the outside; in the present volume we see him from the inside." Matthews especially complimented "the sober self-restraint with which Mr. Clemens lets Huck Finn set down, without any comment at all, scenes which would have afforded the ordinary writer matter for endless moral and political and sociological disquisition."

The *New York World*, adopting a contrary view of *Huckleberry Finn*, condemned "this cheap and pernicious stuff" about a "wretchedly low, vulgar, sneaking and lying Southern country boy of forty years ago." The *San Francisco Chronicle*, observing that the Concord Public Library had peremptorily banned Twain's new novel, labeled this action "absurd" and lamented that "there is a large class of people who are impervious to a joke, even when told by as consummate a master of the art of narration as Mark Twain." As though to make this point, the *Boston Daily Advertiser* warmly congratulated the people of Concord for expelling the book and expressed a hope "that the old school of coarse, flippant and irreverent joke makers is going out, to return no more."

When Mark Twain again ventured into English history for novelistic material, cheekily picturing, as the title suggests, *A Connecticut Yankee in King Arthur's Court*, the story inevitably invited furor with its slangy characterizations of the near-sacred knights and ladies of Camelot. Nevertheless, the *Glasgow Herald* discerned that "not parody, but satire is intended." The *London Star*, noting that "there has been the usual amount of perfunctory weeping and wailing about the desecration committed by Mark Twain," nonetheless commended the "SERIOUS

PURPOSE in the book, underlying its rollicking, grotesque, and frankly Philistine humor" and lauded

this queer olla podrida [miscellany] of mediaeval lore and Yankee droller-
ies. It will shock many Tennysonians, who will lift their hands in horror at
the profanation of the grave sanctities of the *Idylls* and the *Morte d'Arthur*.
But there is a certain rude breath of common sense and humanity about *A
Yankee* . . . which is healthy and even stimulating.

Now writing for *Harper's Monthly*, Twain's friend William Dean Howells granted that

he leaves, to be sure, little of the romance of the olden time, but no one is
more alive to the simple, mostly tragic poetry of it. . . . This kind of humor,
the American kind, the kind employed in the service of democracy, of humanity, began with us a long time ago; in fact Franklin may be said to have
torn it with the lightning from the skies.

The Tragedy of Pudd'nhead Wilson drew fewer reviews and seemed
to baffle some of Twain's admirers. The *London Chronicle* opined that
"there is in this volume a good deal of Mark Twain at his best, and not a
little of Mark Twain at his worst. . . . Pathos and bathos, humour and
twaddle, are thrown together in a way that is nothing less than amazing." On the other hand, the *Graphic* in London deemed the novel a
"very uncharacteristically powerful and even deeply affecting story."
The *Athenaeum* faulted aspects of the narrative but extolled "the picture of the negro slave Roxana" with her "gusts of passion or of despair," declaring that "the book well repays reading just for the really
excellent picture of Roxana." *Cosmopolitan Magazine* pronounced
"the people, in all their fatuous prejudice and stolidity," to be so credi-
ble "that the illusion becomes perfect, and we swallow the melodrama
without a qualm—exchange of heirs, haunted house, murder, and all."
A journal called *Public Opinion* reminded its readers that

Mark Twain is an apostle of the unconventional. . . . Being free from reverence for anything merely because it is customary, and being blessed with a fancy which knows no bounds, his readers are sure of meeting improbable situations. . . . Of late years his writings have shown a moral or social aim which, while it is sometimes overwrought and made to bear undue burden, is always of healthy tone.

The *Critic* labeled *Pudd'nhead Wilson* a work

with flashes and touches of genius, and yet the form . . . so crude, so coarse, so erring from the ways of true classicism, so offensive to immemorial canons of taste, that the critic, in spite of his enjoyment and wonder, puts it reluctantly down in the category of unclassifiable literary things—only to take it up and enjoy it again!

Twain's fifth and final travel book, *Following the Equator* (1897; *More Tramps Abroad* in the English edition), garnered general praise. The *London Mail* described it as being

about all sorts of expected and unexpected things, . . . but mainly it is about Mark Twain, and consequently it is keenly enjoyable. In spite of a certain falling off of late, Mark Twain remains the most genuinely spontaneous of living humorists, and the most wittily observant of literary globe trotters.

As with *Pudd'nhead Wilson*, commentators particularly relished the Pudd'nhead Wilson maxims that head each chapter of *Following the Equator*. Indeed, the *Glasgow Herald* predicted that "most of this book will be allowed to perish, but . . . the Pudd'nhead Maxims will certainly be picked out of it and kept with care." The *Athenaeum* summarized a widely shared opinion:

It is too long, and there are passages in it that are too diffuse; but none of his works would stand better for a sample of all his wares—humour, good sense, good nature, genuine good fun, shrewd observation, and bits of description which would be hard to equal in the writings of the most serious travellers.

Life reflected hopelessly:

Order, proportion, sequence and coherence have no conceivable part in his scheme of literary composition. He follows his own sweet will, like a spoiled child who knows he can have his own way if he is only audacious and amusing.

The *Critic* was similarly direct: "Mark Twain has reached the terrible frankness of maturity and fame; he tells tales like Bismarck, regardless whom he hits, so long as the blow is deserved." Chicago's *Dial* magazine extolled the book's

earnestness, moral and humane,—an earnest desire for sincerity and genuineness, but tearing sham to pieces and flinging it to the winds. If Mr. Clemens had not been Mark Twain, he might have been [the iconoclastic Scottish historian and essayist Thomas] Carlyle.

As for form, the *Dial* added, "he is continually stepping from the sublime to the ridiculous, and *vice versa*. As soon as he suspects he is getting eloquent, he at once jumps into outrageous farce."

Mark Twain's Posthumous Reputation

Who were the most influential commentators on Mark Twain's life and writings in the century after his death? In terms of the frequency of citations to their work, transformation of the field of Twain studies, and durability of scholarly reputation, one would have to name four pivotal figures, all of whom became prominent during the 1960s: Walter Blair, Henry Nash Smith, James M. Cox, and Louis J. Budd. Blair's *Mark Twain and Huck Finn* (1960) helped make sense out of *Huckleberry Finn*'s sequences of composition and informed readers about many overlooked details and sources. In *Mark Twain: The Development of a Writer* (1962), Smith delivered a nuanced and groundbreaking study of the evolution of Twain's writing styles that still resonates after half a century. Cox's *Mark Twain: The Fate of Humor* (1966) inspired the postmodern commentators who would follow in later decades, weighing among other things the price that Twain paid for his popularity. Budd examined Twain from political and social perspectives, and he lived to see many tributes paid to his work, especially to *Mark Twain: Social Philosopher* (1962) and *Our Mark Twain: The Making of His Public Personality* (1983).

Various scholars have taken up the work of these pioneers and amplified it. Victor A. Doyno refined Blair's ideas about the genetic growth of *Huckleberry Finn* and added numerous dimensions to our interpretation of Twain's ideas in *Writing "Huck Finn": Mark Twain's Creative Process* (1991) and "Beginning to Write 'Huck Finn': Essays in Genetic Criticism" (2002). Forrest G. Robinson, in particular, extended the types of critical insights that Cox had cultivated in such studies as *In Bad Faith: The Dynamics of Deception in Mark Twain's America* (1986) and *The Author-Cat: Clemens's Life in Fiction* (2007). David E. E. Sloane, like many other scholars, demonstrated Budd's broad influence in *Mark Twain as a Literary Comedian* (1979) and *Adventures of Huckleberry Finn: American Comic Vision* (1988).

In the area of biography, an accelerating parade followed the lead-off work by Albert Bigelow Paine, who alone had the privilege of knowing—and living with and near—his subject. Paine's three-volume *Mark Twain: A Biography* (1912) provided incidents and quotations from Twain's final years that only Paine witnessed and recorded. Justin Kaplan's *Mr. Clemens and Mark Twain* (1966) has survived for decades because of its momentum and conciseness. During the early twenty-first century, a number of competitors to Kaplan's biography began appearing. These have included Everett Emerson's *Mark Twain: A Literary Life* (2000), which focuses closely on Twain's writings; Ron Powers's lyrical *Mark Twain: A Life* (2005); and Jerome Loving's opinionative and challenging *Mark Twain: The Adventures of Samuel L. Clemens* (2010). Several dozen other valuable biographies focus on specific periods or aspects of Twain's life, such as Jeffrey Steinbrink's *Getting to Be Mark Twain* (1991); Philip Ashley Fanning's *Mark Twain and Orion Clemens: Brothers, Partners, Strangers* (2003); Hamlin Hill's *Mark Twain: God's Fool* (1973), a searing exposé of Twain's last ten years; William R. Macnaughton's *Mark Twain's Last Years as a Writer* (1979); Michael Shelden's dazzling and revelatory *Mark Twain: Man in White* (2010), about Twain's last five years; and Karen Lystra's *Dangerous Intimacy: The Untold Story of Mark Twain's Final Years* (2004).

Once dismissed as a lightweight figure in her husband's life, Olivia Langdon Clemens has in recent decades come into her own and is now perceived as displaying an intellect and personality suitably matched to those of her famous husband. This is largely owing to a rehabilitation of her reputation that was initially orchestrated by Laura E. Skandera Trombley's *Mark Twain in the Company of Women* (1994) and Susan K. Harris's *The Courtship of Olivia Langdon and Mark Twain* (1996).

All modern Mark Twain studies have been dependent upon the Mark Twain Papers, a huge collection of primary materials housed in the Bancroft Library at the University of California at Berkeley, and its publishing arm, the Mark Twain Project, which since 1967 has been issuing reliable texts of Twain's unpublished and previously published writings.

Studies of Individual Works

Each of Mark Twain's novels has had a critical history of its own, shaped by its most prominent features and the issues it has raised. *The*

Adventures of Tom Sawyer has yet to receive a book-length treatment that adequately accounts for its strengths and its weaknesses, but excellent articles have been written by Hamlin Hill, Judith Fetterley, and Tom H. Towers, among others. Since the 1970s, there has been a recognition that this first novel about the lives of boys living in a small river town contains darker and more sinister elements than readers perceived during the first century after its publication.

By contrast, the literary scholarship and criticism devoted to Twain's masterpiece, *Adventures of Huckleberry Finn*, is so enormous and complex as to prohibit any brief summary. Laurie Champion's valiant *The Critical Response to Mark Twain's "Huckleberry Finn"* (1991) barely managed to scrape the surface, and a veritable avalanche of subsequent books and articles have descended on the novel since then. (Appraisals of each of these can be found in *American Literary Scholarship*, published by the Duke University Press annually since 1963.) At the clear risk of omitting myriad commendable studies, one can at least single out Jocelyn Chadwick-Joshua's defense of Twain's motives in writing the novel, *The Jim Dilemma: Reading Race in "Huckleberry Finn"* (1998); *One Hundred Years of "Huckleberry Finn": The Boy, His Book, and American Culture*, edited by Robert Sattelmeyer and J. Donald Crowley (1985); *Satire or Evasion? Black Perspectives on "Huckleberry Finn,"* edited by James S. Leonard, Thomas A. Tenney, and Thadious M. Davis (1992); Gary P. Henrickson's "Biographers' Twain, Critics' Twain, Which of the Twain Wrote the 'Evasion'?" in *Southern Literary Journal* (1993); Richard Hill's "Overreaching: Critical Agenda and the Ending of *Adventures of Huckleberry Finn*" in *Texas Studies in Literature and Language* (1991); and a number of essays in *A Companion to Mark Twain*, edited by Peter Messent and Louis J. Budd (2005).

The rampant racism associated with the pro-slavery atmosphere of antebellum Hannibal, Missouri, has been exposed by Shelley Fisher Fishkin's *Lighting Out for the Territory: Reflections on Mark Twain and American Culture* (1996) and Terrell Dempsey's *Searching for*

Jim: Slavery in Sam Clemens's World (2003). Twain's love-hate relationship with England, which was manifested in *A Connecticut Yankee*, received treatment in Howard G. Baetzhold's *Mark Twain and John Bull: The British Connection* (1970). Susan Gillman and Forrest G. Robinson edited a provocative collection of essays about a novel whose onion-peeling messages confound many readers, *Mark Twain's "Pudd'nhead Wilson": Race, Conflict, and Culture* (1990).

All studies of Twain's *The Mysterious Stranger* owe a debt to John S. Tuckey, whose *Mark Twain and Little Satan: The Writing of "The Mysterious Stranger"* (1963) first revealed the inadequacies and chicanery of the posthumous 1916 edition of Twain's fantasy novel. *Centenary Reflections on Mark Twain's "No. 44, The Mysterious Stranger,"* edited by Joseph Csicsila and Chad Rohman (2009), provides a thorough guide to the history of, and assumptions about, Twain's last long work of fiction. Tom Quirk and a half dozen other scholars evaluated Twain's short stories in *Mark Twain: A Study of the Short Fiction* (1997), which was followed by Peter Messent's *The Short Works of Mark Twain: A Critical Study* (2001).

Twain's travel books have received significantly less critical attention than his works of fiction, and only a few scholars have devoted entire monographs to individual books. The travel writings have mostly drawn a scattering of journal articles and chapters discussing their features, such as Lawrence I. Berkove's excellent overview, "Mark Twain: A Man for All Regions," in *A Companion to the Regional Literatures of America*, edited by Charles L. Crow (2003). Nonetheless, a few book titles are worth highlighting. Richard Bridgman broke new ground by taking Twain's travel books seriously in *Traveling in Mark Twain* (1987). Jeffrey Alan Melton's *Mark Twain, Travel Books, and Tourism: The Tide of a Great Popular Movement* (2002) explains Twain's role in popularizing travel and travel writing. Horst H. Kruse took a careful look at a relatively neglected book in *Mark Twain and "Life on the Mississippi"* (1981). Miriam Jones Shillingsburg's *At Home Abroad: Mark Twain in Australasia* (1988) tracked a major portion of Twain's globe-trotting route that he reported in *Following the Equator.*

Reference and Specialized Works

Magnificently complete reference works dedicated to Mark Twain and his writings began multiplying rather miraculously during the 1990s, putting within the easy reach of undergraduates much detailed information that only a few decades earlier Twain specialists had had to scramble to unearth and master. Chief among these was R. Kent Rasmussen's *Mark Twain A to Z: The Essential Reference to His Life and Writings* (1995), later expanded into the two-volume *Critical Companion to Mark Twain: A Literary Reference to His Life and Work* (2007). Also important were James D. Wilson's *A Reader's Guide to the Short Stories of Mark Twain* (1987); E. Hudson Long and J. R. LeMaster's *The New Mark Twain Handbook* (1985); *The Mark Twain Encyclopedia*, edited by LeMaster and James D. Wilson (1993); and David H. Fears's multivolume *Mark Twain Day by Day: An Annotated Chronology of the Life of Samuel L. Clemens* (2008-   ), Gregg Camfield's *The Oxford Companion to Mark Twain* (2003), and the large essays about Mark Twain in many of the *Dictionary of Literary Biography* series volumes. *Mark Twain: The Complete Interviews*, edited by Gary Scharnhorst (2006), rounded up Twain's amusing encounters with newspaper and magazine reporters, which showed him to be ever ready with a memorable remark or an amusing bit of wisdom. *The Quotable Mark Twain: His Essential Aphorisms, Witticisms, and Concise Opinions*, edited by R. Kent Rasmussen (1997) supplies a handy compendium to Twain's best-known quips.

Specialized studies have zeroed in on discrete strands of Mark Twain's thought. Sherwood Cummings's *Mark Twain and Science: Adventures of a Mind* (1988), for example, explored Twain's fascination with scientific discoveries that came to light during his lifetime. Alan Gribben's two-volume *Mark Twain's Library: A Reconstruction*

(1980) assembled the first annotated catalog of his library collection and his reading. Sydney J. Krause examined Twain's literary predilections in *Mark Twain as Critic* (1967). Larzer Ziff drilled toward the very heart of Twain's artistic motivation in an enduring article, "Authorship and Craft: The Example of Mark Twain" in *Southern Review* (1976).

A collection of essays, *The Mythologizing of Mark Twain*, edited by Sara deSaussure Davis and Philip D. Beidler (1984), looked at the phenomenon of Twain's success in consciously shaping his image for posterity. Leland Krauth's *Proper Mark Twain* (1999) estimated the price that Twain was willing to pay for conforming to propriety. Harold K. Bush, Jr., closely appraised Twain's religious beliefs in *Mark Twain and the Spiritual Crisis of His Age* (2007). Joseph L. Coulombe traced the molding effect of Twain's years in Nevada and California in *Mark Twain and the American West* (2003). Gender studies of Twain's writings commenced in the 1990s, deftly noting the frequent instances of cross-dressing and gender confusion throughout his works. Linda A. Morris brought these scholarly inquiries up to date in *Gender Play in Mark Twain: Cross-Dressing and Transgression* (2007).

After Twain's death in 1910, questions about "taste" in his literature gradually dissipated. However, during the last decades of the twentieth century, a troublesome new objection arose over the painfulness to many readers of the casual references to racial epithets and the unemotional, offhanded depictions of African American slavery in his stories and novels, particularly in *Adventures of Huckleberry Finn* and *Pudd'nhead Wilson*. As the narrator of the former book, Huck Finn employs the deeply offensive "N word" more than two hundred times. In this instance Twain was substantially the victim of his times and his artistic credo; adhering to the tenets of the American realism movement, he was committed to accurate renditions of the speech of the Mississippi River valley as he had heard it spoken during the 1840s. Consequently, when setting his fiction in the pre-Civil War South, he found it necessary to employ the term "nigger" and to portray slavery as he had actually seen and heard it practiced. Twain's often-derogatory references to Native Americans in the early and middle parts of his career—though perhaps less forgivable because they were unnecessary for purposes of verisimilitude—were nonetheless common currency at the time he used them, and he inserted them at face value for literary purposes.

Whether now-dated language and unbecoming attitudes will ultimately diminish Twain's twenty-first-century popularity remains to be seen. During the 1980s, a reaction against compulsory assignments of *Huckleberry Finn* in public schoolrooms arose, centered on the book's use of the objectionable word referring to black slaves. Over the ensuing decades, this movement led to the banning of the novel in dozens of middle and high schools. Because texts can never change—unless they are bowdlerized, as Twain's books have often been—Twain's language is likely to lead to further controversy. Several reputable scholars and authors have called for public schools to avoid assigning *Huckleberry Finn* as a textbook and instead require students to read more overtly abolitionist literature, such as Harriet Beecher Stowe's *Uncle Tom's Cabin* (1852). One critic in particular, Jonathan Arac, has made the castigation of this vulnerable aspect of Twain's stature the object of repeated articles and a book, *"Huckleberry Finn" as Idol and Target: The Functions of Criticism in Our Time* (1997). Even a longtime admirer of Twain's works, James S. Leonard, has arrived at the point of conceding that there are "real problems" with teaching the novel in contemporary society. At the beginning of the second decade of the twenty-first century, these concerns still constitute a formidable challenge to the legacy of Mark Twain and the prestige of his literary masterpiece. However, controversy notwithstanding, Mark Twain prevails as one of the eminent figures of nineteenth-century American literature, and most critics continue to include him on every short list of the premier authors produced by the United States.

Works Cited and Consulted

Anderson, Frederick, ed. *Mark Twain: The Critical Heritage*. 1971. New York: Routledge, 1997.

Arac, Jonathan. *"Huckleberry Finn" as Idol and Target: The Functions of Criticism in Our Time*. Madison: U of Wisconsin P, 1997.

Baetzhold, Howard G. *Mark Twain and John Bull: The British Connection*. Bloomington: Indiana UP, 1970.

Berkove, Lawrence I. "Mark Twain: A Man for All Regions." *A Companion to the Regional Literatures of America*. Ed. Charles L. Crow. Malden, MA: Blackwell, 2003.

Blair, Walter. *Mark Twain and Huck Finn*. Berkeley: U of California P, 1960.

Bridgman, Richard. *Traveling in Mark Twain*. Berkeley: U of California P, 1987.

Budd, Louis J. *Mark Twain: Social Philosopher*. Bloomington: Indiana UP, 1962.

_____. *Our Mark Twain: The Making of His Public Personality*. Philadelphia: U of Pennsylvania P, 1983.

_____, ed. *Critical Essays on Mark Twain, 1867-1910*. Boston: G. K. Hall, 1982.

_____, ed. *Critical Essays on Mark Twain, 1910-1980*. Boston: G. K. Hall, 1983.

_____, ed. *Mark Twain: The Contemporary Reviews*. New York: Cambridge UP, 1999.

Bush, Harold K., Jr. *Mark Twain and the Spiritual Crisis of His Age*. Tuscaloosa: U of Alabama P, 2007.

Camfield, Gregg. *The Oxford Companion to Mark Twain*. New York: Oxford UP, 2003.

Chadwick-Joshua, Jocelyn. *The Jim Dilemma: Reading Race in "Huckleberry Finn."* Jackson: UP of Mississippi, 1998.

Champion, Laurie, ed. *The Critical Response to Mark Twain's "Huckleberry Finn."* Westport, CT: Greenwood Press, 1991.

Coulombe, Joseph L. *Mark Twain and the American West*. Columbia: U of Missouri P, 2003.

Cox, James M. *Mark Twain: The Fate of Humor*. Princeton, NJ: Princeton UP, 1966.

Csicsila, Joseph, and Chad Rohman, eds. *Centenary Reflections on Mark Twain's "No. 44, The Mysterious Stranger."* Columbia: U of Missouri P, 2009.

Cummings, Sherwood. *Mark Twain and Science: Adventures of a Mind*. Baton Rouge: Louisiana State UP, 1988.

Davis, Sara deSaussure, and Philip D. Beidler, eds. *The Mythologizing of Mark Twain*. Tuscaloosa: U of Alabama P, 1984.

Dempsey, Terrell. *Searching for Jim: Slavery in Sam Clemens's World*. Columbia: U of Missouri P, 2003.

Doyno, Victor A. "Beginning to Write 'Huck Finn': Essays in Genetic Criticism." *Huck Finn: The Complete Buffalo and Erie County Public Library Manuscript—Teaching and Research Digital Edition*. CD-ROM. 2002.

_____. *Writing "Huck Finn": Mark Twain's Creative Process*. Philadelphia: U of Pennsylvania P, 1991.

Emerson, Everett. *Mark Twain: A Literary Life*. Philadelphia: U of Pennsylvania P, 2000.

Fanning, Philip Ashley. *Mark Twain and Orion Clemens: Brothers, Partners, Strangers*. Tuscaloosa: U of Alabama P, 2003.

Fears, David H. *Mark Twain Day by Day*. Multivolume series. Banks, OR: Horizon Micro, 2008-   .

Fischer, Victor. "Huck Finn Reviewed: The Reception of *Huckleberry Finn* in the United States, 1885-1897." *American Literary Realism* 16 (Spring 1983): 1-57.

Fishkin, Shelley Fisher. *Lighting Out for the Territory: Reflections on Mark Twain and American Culture*. New York: Oxford UP, 1996.

Gillman, Susan, and Forrest G. Robinson, eds. *Mark Twain's "Pudd'nhead Wilson": Race, Conflict, and Culture*. Durham, NC: Duke UP, 1990.

Gribben, Alan. *Mark Twain's Library: A Reconstruction*. 2 vols. Boston: G. K. Hall, 1980.

_____. "A Retrospective: The State of Mark Twain Studies." *A Companion to Mark Twain*. Ed. Peter Messent and Louis J. Budd. Malden, MA: Blackwell, 2005.

_____. "Samuel Langhorne Clemens (Mark Twain)." *Facts On File Bibliography of American Fiction, 1866-1918*. Ed. James Nagel and Gwen L. Nagel. New York: Facts On File, 1993.

Harris, Susan K. *The Courtship of Olivia Langdon and Mark Twain*. New York: Cambridge UP, 1996.

Henrickson, Gary P. "Biographers' Twain, Critics' Twain, Which of the Twain Wrote the 'Evasion'?" *Southern Literary Journal* 26.1 (Fall 1993): 14-29.

Hill, Hamlin. *Mark Twain: God's Fool*. New York: Harper & Row, 1973.

Hill, Richard. "Overreaching: Critical Agenda and the Ending of *Adventures of Huckleberry Finn*." *Texas Studies in Literature and Language* 33.4 (1991): 492-513.

Hill, Richard, and Jim McWilliams, eds. *Mark Twain Among the Scholars: Reconsidering Contemporary Twain Criticism*. Albany, NY: Whitston, 2002.

Horn, Jason Gary. *Mark Twain: A Descriptive Guide to Biographical Sources*. Lanham, MD: Scarecrow Press, 1999.

Kaplan, Justin. *Mr. Clemens and Mark Twain*. New York: Simon & Schuster, 1966.

Krause, Sydney J. *Mark Twain as Critic*. Baltimore: Johns Hopkins UP, 1967.

Krauth, Leland. *Proper Mark Twain*. Athens: U of Georgia P, 1999.

Kruse, Horst H. *Mark Twain and "Life on the Mississippi."* Amherst: U of Massachusetts P, 1981.

LeMaster, J. R., and James D. Wilson, eds. *The Mark Twain Encyclopedia*. New York: Garland, 1993.

Leonard, James S. "Racial Objections to *Huckleberry Finn*." *Early American Literature* 30 (2001): 77-82.

Leonard, James S., Thomas A. Tenney, and Thadious M. Davis, eds. *Satire or Eva-*

---

sion? Black Perspectives on "Huckleberry Finn." Durham, NC: Duke UP, 1992.

Long, E. Hudson, and J. R. LeMaster. *The New Mark Twain Handbook.* New York: Garland, 1985.

Loving, Jerome. *Mark Twain: The Adventures of Samuel L. Clemens.* Berkeley: U of California P, 2010.

Lystra, Karen. *Dangerous Intimacy: The Untold Story of Mark Twain's Final Years.* Berkeley: U of California P, 2004.

Macnaughton, William R. *Mark Twain's Last Years as a Writer.* Columbia: U of Missouri P, 1979.

Melton, Jeffrey Alan. *Mark Twain, Travel Books, and Tourism: The Tide of a Great Popular Movement.* Tuscaloosa: U of Alabama P, 2002.

Messent, Peter. *The Short Works of Mark Twain: A Critical Study.* Philadelphia: U of Pennsylvania P, 2001.

Messent, Peter, and Louis J. Budd, eds. *A Companion to Mark Twain.* Malden, MA: Blackwell, 2005.

Morris, Linda A. *Gender Play in Mark Twain: Cross-Dressing and Transgression.* Columbia: U of Missouri P, 2007.

Paine, Albert Bigelow. *Mark Twain: A Biography—The Personal and Literary Life of Samuel Langhorne Clemens.* 3 vols. New York: Harper & Brothers, 1912.

Powers, Ron. *Mark Twain: A Life.* New York: Free Press, 2005.

Quirk, Tom. *Mark Twain: A Study of the Short Fiction.* New York: Twayne, 1997.

_____, ed. *Mark Twain's "Adventures of Huckleberry Finn": A Documentary Volume.* Detroit: Gale, 2009.

Rasmussen, R. Kent. *Critical Companion to Mark Twain: A Literary Reference to His Life and Work.* 2 vols. New York: Facts On File, 2007.

_____. *Mark Twain A to Z: The Essential Reference to His Life and Writings.* New York: Facts On File, 1995.

_____, ed. *The Quotable Mark Twain: His Essential Aphorisms, Witticisms, and Concise Opinions.* Chicago: Contemporary Books, 1997.

Robinson, Forrest G. *The Author-Cat: Clemens's Life in Fiction.* New York: Fordham UP, 2007.

_____. *In Bad Faith: The Dynamics of Deception in Mark Twain's America.* Cambridge, MA: Harvard UP, 1986.

Sattelmeyer, Robert, and J. Donald Crowley, eds. *One Hundred Years of "Huckleberry Finn": The Boy, His Book, and American Culture.* Columbia: U of Missouri P, 1985.

Shelden, Michael. *Mark Twain: Man in White—The Grand Adventure of His Final Years.* New York: Random House, 2010.

Shillingsburg, Miriam Jones. *At Home Abroad: Mark Twain in Australasia.* Jackson: UP of Mississippi, 1988.

Sloane, David E. E. *"Adventures of Huckleberry Finn": American Comic Vision.* Boston: Twayne, 1988.

_____. *Mark Twain as a Literary Comedian.* Baton Rouge: Louisiana State UP, 1979.

Smith, Henry Nash. *Mark Twain: The Development of a Writer*. Cambridge, MA: Harvard UP, 1962.

Steinbrink, Jeffrey. *Getting to Be Mark Twain*. Berkeley: U of California P, 1991.

Tenney, Thomas A. *Mark Twain: A Reference Guide*. Boston: G. K. Hall, 1977.

Trombley, Laura E. Skandera. *Mark Twain in the Company of Women*. Philadelphia: U of Pennsylvania P, 1994.

Tuckey, John S. *Mark Twain and Little Satan: The Writing of "The Mysterious Stranger."* West Lafayette, IN: Purdue University Studies, 1963.

Twain, Mark. *Mark Twain: The Complete Interviews*. Ed. Gary Scharnhorst. Tuscaloosa: U of Alabama P, 2006.

Wilson, James D. *A Reader's Guide to the Short Stories of Mark Twain*. Boston: G. K. Hall, 1987.

Ziff, Larzer. "Authorship and Craft: The Example of Mark Twain." *Southern Review* 12 (Apr. 1976): 246-60.

"Pluck Enough to Lynch a Man":
Mark Twain and Manhood _____

Hilton Obenzinger

In *Adventures of Huckleberry Finn* (1884), Huck joins a mob howling after Colonel Sherburn and intending to string him up for killing a drunkard whose insults and curses had irritated him one time too many. Sherburn stands on the roof of his porch and disperses the would-be lynch mob with fearless disdain. "The idea of *you* lynching anybody!" he mocks the "loafers" who have been aroused from their torpor in the "one-horse" Mississippi village. "It's amusing. The idea of you thinking you had pluck enough to lynch a *man!*" Sherburn scorns them as cowards who gain what little courage they have parasitically from their leader, whom he sarcastically deems "half-a-man." He goes on:

> "Now the thing for *you* to do is to droop your tails and go home and crawl in a hole. If any real lynching's going to be done it will be done in the dark, Southern fashion; and when they come they'll bring their masks, and fetch a *man* along. Now *leave*—and take your half-a-man with you." (*Huckleberry Finn* ch. 22)

He tosses his gun up across his left arm and cocks it as he says this. The lynch mob decides to beat a hasty retreat. And with this oration, punctuated with the click of the colonel's gun, the spectacle of a "whole man" has been performed from the heights of the roof to Huck and the mob, and to that even greater mob, the mass of readers.

What in Mark Twain's fiction *is* a "whole man"? And is Colonel Sherburn such a whole man? Sherburn, like the novel's feuding Colonel Grangerford, is clearly an educated "gentleman all over," and he appears to be a paragon of southern aristocracy. But Twain's male characters embody American manhood (and boyhood) across all lines of class, race, education, and region. How do we understand the way Twain depicts such diverse personalities as Pap, Jim, Injun Joe, Hank

Morgan, and David (Pudd'nhead) Wilson? How much is masculinity a performance—a certain way of behaving in the eyes of other people, such as in the eyes of a lynch mob or a slave master or an entire society—in Twain's fiction? And how does the "whole man" perform?

Several recognizable nineteenth-century male types appear in Twain's fiction, and it is worth noting their characteristics, even in a schematic fashion. Masculinity, like femininity, is a "cultural invention," as E. Anthony Rotundo puts it in *American Manhood*, and "each culture constructs its own version of what men and women are—and ought to be" (1). Different models of manhood, different sets of attitudes, expectations, and codes, emerged in the course of the nineteenth century. These models, overlaying each other and often operating at the same time, created a potent mix of assumed male norms, settler nationalism, and white supremacy that drove American expansion. During the early part of the century, proper manhood was characterized by postrevolutionary republican virtues—honesty, rejection of luxury, plain speaking—layered over a patriarchal base in which the family and community were central. Parallel to the republican patriarch who bears communal responsibility was the man of the settler-colonial frontier, whether in the West or on the maritime frontier.

The frontier man was independent, taciturn, wise in the ways of the wilderness or the sea, prone to challenging other men through tall tales and initiation hoaxes, and capable of great violence—behavioral norms that Twain knew very well. The aristocratic plantation gentleman presided in the South, paternalistic toward slaves and chivalrous toward women; he was guided by complex codes of honor, particularly the Code Duello—the ancient rules governing when and how to protect honor through ritualized violence, codified by former South Carolina governor John Lyde Wilson in 1838. When this code of honor, insult, and appropriate, regulated violence worked properly, the aristocrat displayed good manners, "even when one gentleman sought the life of another." Adherence to the code "exemplified excellent pedigree."

Nonstructural and noninstitutional outbursts of violence displayed a lack of personal control and were to be avoided at all costs. The code, with its social underpinnings of restrained violence, did not condone unorchestrated mayhem. Southerners hoped to sublimate passion and to keep it "within bounds" after honor had been called into question. The resolution of this moral and ethical dilemma between the natural man of passion and the social man of discipline was to be found in this convoluted form of controlled violence (Steward 8).

In the North, the entrepreneurial man emerged, an individualist who could compete in the growing market economy, self-fashioning his success and identity. The self-made, entrepreneurial man could produce his own world, even through P. T. Barnum-like spectacle and speculative excess. Even more excessive, the confidence man succeeded in fashioning himself through gullibility and fraudulent exchange, while other boundaries between competition and crime were blurred with the emergence of "robber barons." Speculation, expansion, and technological innovation accelerated after the Civil War, while suffragists and the New Woman challenged the accepted boundaries of the female sphere, all of which created new anxieties about male authority. Many middle-class men driven by the stress of competition and fear of failure suffered from neurasthenia, an enervating collapse or breakdown, underscored by a sense that settled, civilized life was inevitably debilitating and emasculating. With the closing of the frontier toward the end of the nineteenth century, Teddy Roosevelt's "strenuous life" was meant to restore masculine vigor; this "passionate" manhood, as Rotundo terms this type, responded to the doubts about male power that swelled toward the end of the century, relieving anxieties through robust physicality and the manly virtues of martial violence, such as the "jolly little war" with Spain in 1898 that became a counterinsurgency operation to conquer the Philippines.

Several models of manhood are easily recognizable in Twain's fiction. However, discussion of masculinity in Twain's fiction has been somewhat limited, perhaps because male characters are so omnipresent that they are *too* visible and, paradoxically, seem almost invisible.

In his essay "Mark Twain and Gender," Peter Stoneley observes that "the notion of manhood is implicitly offered as a naturalized and universalized phenomenon" that can be viewed as "a taken-for-granted *ground*" (68). Critics have discussed Twain's relationships with women at some length, however, and how these relationships reveal his assumptions about men as well.

Shelley Fisher Fishkin argues against the limitations of what she describes as two camps that emerged in the critical literature on Twain's attitudes toward women: "those who felt women were bad for Twain and those who felt Twain was bad for women" (109). Bad for Twain because his wife and other women in his life censored his writing, enforcing the restrictions of feminized propriety, which, Van Wyck Brooks and others contend, severely constrained his creativity; bad for women because his female characters were too few, and those he did create often lacked depth and embodied standard nineteenth-century sentimental notions of the woman's sphere. Stoneley considers Twain's female characters as often being "one-dimensional" and "determined in relation to clumsy and troubling categories: the pure, girlish woman; the fussy, interfering woman; the hungry, dangerous woman" (76). When Twain's female characters do seem to break out of standard feminine roles, they often become mannish, "unsexed" in nineteenth-century terms, such as the vengeful Roxana in *Pudd'nhead Wilson* (1894). Fishkin asserts that readers should move beyond the "two bads" to engage in more complex analyses of gender. Linda A. Morris's *Gender Play in Mark Twain: Cross-Dressing and Transgression* highlights often overlooked gender dynamics, while Susan K. Harris, in "Mark Twain and Gender," "juxtapose[s] Twain's ideas about women to his ideas about men, to 'map,' as it were, his gender assumptions" (163), elaborating how gender concepts of both men and women depend upon each other.

The construction or performance of masculinity in Twain's work is even more problematic because discussions are thoroughly entangled with yet another fiction, that of "Mark Twain" himself. "I know you clear through," Colonel Sherburn addresses the mob. "I was born and raised in the South, and I've lived in the North; so I know the average all around. The average man's a coward." The colonel seems to present an uncanny description of Mark Twain himself, the southerner who also came to know the average man in the North by way of his reconstruction in the West and who stands above the cowardly mob of hypocritical public opinion. While Twain may have drawn upon his own experience and personality to depict Colonel Sherburn—similar to the way he may have tapped into his own technological and political obsessions in *A Connecticut Yankee in King Arthur's Court* (1889) to create Hank Morgan as the avid inventor and creator of the nineteenth century's "new deal" in medieval England—it would be a mistake to conflate "Mark Twain" with any one character in any of his novels.

In addition, "Mark Twain" became the celebrated, public persona through the addition of essays, sketches, travel books, lecture appearances, and newspaper interviews. When readers think of Samuel Clemens, they invariably think of the wise, foolish, witty, courageous, cowardly, disreputable, honorable character Leslie A. Fiedler has described as "a *schlemiel*—or clown—Westerner" (501). The performance of "Mark Twain" became second nature to its author—the persona acting as both an expression and a critique of manhood itself. A full understanding of masculinity and Mark Twain would include the biography of Samuel Clemens, along with analysis of all of the texts and performances that went into creating the persona. Here, I will focus only on the fictional men (and boys as formative men) populating Twain's major novels, particularly *Adventures of Huckleberry Finn*, along with *The Adventures of Tom Sawyer*, *A Connecticut Yankee in King Arthur's Court*, and *Pudd'nhead Wilson*.

In these novels Twain assaults all forms of authority, including the authority of the church, literature, morality, and social conventions. He especially lambastes the presumptions of white supremacy and the prerogatives of male dominance. Many of Twain's men in *Huckleberry Finn* are cruel, corrupt, and bombastic and lack moral compass, even when—like Colonel Sherburn—they seem to display the awareness, competence, and self-assurance assumed of male leaders. Sherburn, for example, excoriates the mob, scornfully declaiming how "average" men undermine the operations of civilization, such as the jury system, through their cowardice. Sherburn is "well born," like Colonel Grangerford, in the mold of a southern plantation gentleman. The portrait of Grangerford is of a very tall, very slim man, a gentleman dressed in a full suit "from head to foot made out of linen so white it hurt your eyes to look at it." Commanding fear and respect, he is a rich man with many slaves, and each member of his family is assigned a personal servant. The Grangerfords are locked in an elaborate, endless feud with the other aristocratic family in the area, the Shepherdsons. The cause of the feud is long forgotten, but the conflict is fueled by the rules of an absurd yet murderous code of honor.

Sherburn's critique of the mob seems compelling, and he does seem to speak from high moral ground—literally, from the roof—except for one problem: He himself is, in fact, a murderer. He has gunned down in cold blood the harmless town drunk, Boggs, for no apparent reason other than the fact that the old fool irritated him. Sherburn really does deserve to be hanged, albeit after being convicted by a jury and sentenced by a judge, and not by a mob. Moreover, not only does his wanton shooting of a harmless drunk demand justice, the murder also violates the southern code of male honor, as the drunken ravings of a man like Boggs are not worthy of the outrage of a southern gentleman like the colonel. Boggs's insulting behavior is not worthy of a duel, much less summary execution. Despite Colonel Sherburn's scathing denunciations of the average man's cowardice, he is no one to admire. In Sherburn, as in Colonel Grangerford, Twain exposes the corrupt southern gentleman as a faulty model of manhood.

Twain also skewers other southern gentlemen, even if they appear respectable. In *Pudd'nhead Wilson*, for example Judge Driscoll is horrified to learn that, after suffering a kick in the behind by Count Luigi, his adopted son, Tom, "had him up in court and beat him" according to the law (ch. 12) instead of challenging him to a duel: "Do you mean to tell me that blood of my race has suffered a blow and crawled to a court of law about it?" In response to this "infamy," the judge disinherits Tom, cursing him as the "base son of a most noble father!" Judge Driscoll, like Grangerford, Sherburn, and the other members of the aristocratic First Families of Virginia, projects a sense of honor and power, wealth and propriety, and adherence to the Code Duello. "Although they helped make and interpret laws, these Missouri mandarins also believed that at times they were above them," observes Dick Steward in *Duels and the Roots of Violence in Missouri*. "Contemptuous of the masses, the men of the bar echoed the voice of democracy, but in reality they had very little respect for the will of the people" (85). The code is so deeply ingrained that the judge privileges it over the rule of law without a second thought, enforcing aristocratic hegemony rather than any demonstration of justice. In a similar fashion, the men of the First Families of Virginia maintain their airs of moral superiority unaffected by the crude reality of their sexual exploitation. They regularly force themselves sexually on their slaves, producing offspring such as Roxana, who is white in all appearances but is marked by a single drop of blood as a slave.

At the beginning of *Pudd'nhead Wilson*, Percy Driscoll, the judge's brother, seeking to punish his slaves for stealing, threatens to sell them down the river to horrid conditions on plantations, a fate "equivalent to condemning them to hell" (ch. 2). However, in an act of mercy, he instead merely sells them locally, and "like a god he had stretched forth his mighty hand and closed the gates of hell against them." With deep satisfaction he notes "that he had done a noble and gracious thing, and he was privately well pleased with his magnanimity," recording the incident in his diary "so that his son might read it in after years and be thereby moved to deeds of gentleness and humanity himself." If the reader is capable of irony (and the townspeople of Dawson's Landing— Roxana included—are decidedly not), the master's charity—like the open secret of the sexual exploitation of the men of the First Families of Virginia, the hypocrisy of Colonel Sherburn's denunciations, or the absurdity of the senseless Grangerford-Shepherdson feud—is exposed as nothing but self-deluded pretense.

After the lynch mob "went tearing off every which way" in the face of Sherburn's defiance, the next paragraph in chapter 22 of *Huckleberry Finn* abruptly begins with Huck's reporting, "I went to the circus." Twain's sudden shifts often take on the quality of dreams, as one extreme scene jumps to the next, often with no apparent connection except for Huck's narrative voice, which produces an evocative, allusive effect. Huck relates how a drunken man at the circus attempts to join the equestrian acrobats and eventually the ringmaster allows him to ride, "if he thought he could stay on the horse." Soon the horse breaks free, and the drunk dangles in apparent danger; but then he stands up, tears off his clothing, and reveals that he is actually part of the circus. Huck completely misunderstands that the apparent drunkard has been putting on an act and that the ringmaster knows very well what he is doing. Huck continues to believe that the individual rider has played a trick on the central authority of the performance. "I felt sheepish enough, to be took in so," he confesses, "but I wouldn't a been in that ring-master's place, not for a thousand dollars."

The circus scene, juxtaposed to the spectacle of Colonel Sherburn and the lynch mob, complements the previous encounter, but this time the scene is explicitly theatrical, a comic performance of mock violence, outrage, and honor, although Huck does not fully understand the game between the circus performers and the audience. In his eyes, the drunken man tricks the competent man of authority—the ringmaster, playing a role similar to that of the dignified interlocutor tripped up by the malapropisms and fractured logic of Tambo and Bones in the blackface minstrel show. Huck identifies with the humiliation of the ringmaster instead of joining in the delight of realizing that it was all a script, a playful exhibition, and the ringmaster was in on the act.

The Boggs-Sherburn and circus scenes are framed by the role-playing of the King and the Duke of *Huckleberry Finn*: earlier, through

Critical Insights

their creations of themselves as royalty and their cracked performances of William Shakespeare; afterward, through their obscene and ridiculous Royal Nonesuch performance—a con job in which the wholly male audience's sense of humiliation would prevent them from revealing that they had been "sold." The two humbugs are frauds playing frauds, burlesque caricatures of aristocrats that are satirical commentaries on southern pretensions of slave owners as born masters and poor whites as beneficiaries of their largess. The King and the Duke's antics frame the scenes of the Boggs murder, Sherburn's confrontation with the lynch mob, and the circus hoax, underscoring how male authority is a form of performance, a bogus masquerade, and how such power is dethroned.

Twain's satire of male competence goes beyond humbugs, circus performers, gentleman murderers, and slave-master aristocrats. For example, Pudd'nhead Wilson is a somewhat sympathetic character, an educated man who suffers long amid the village idiocy of Dawson's Landing. In the courtroom climax of *Pudd'nhead Wilson*, he performs to the public, employing intelligence and arcane knowledge of fingerprints to expose the real murderer of the judge and revealing that Roxana switched the "white" Tom and "black" Chambers during their infancy. However, Wilson, despite his great revelations, still does not come to understand the underlying crime in the narrative. With Roxana, Tom, and Chambers all appearing white, race itself is "a fiction of law and custom" (ch. 2), a social hallucination and not something innate and immutable, like a fingerprint. All he can do is to expose the individual murderer, while remaining oblivious to slavery as a social and moral murderer. He seems competent but, like the rest of the town, incapable of perceiving the bitterly ironic hallucination of race on which the slave system is based. The "tragedy" of the novel is partly Roxana's vain effort to outwit the system and its consequences in ruined lives and murder. However, in great part, the tragedy lies in the fact that Pudd'nhead Wilson—who is hailed and elected mayor after his triumph—does not have the clarity of vision to understand the absurdity of racism. He really is a pudd'nhead.

Hank Morgan, the "boss" in *A Connecticut Yankee in King Arthur's Court*, presents a portrait of the entrepreneurial, self-made man. He is competent and enlightened, the incarnation of the innovative Yankee, "a practical Connecticut man" who disdains slavery of any sort. When he awakens in Arthurian England, he decides to transform the backward medieval society into a "rationally constructed world" (ch. 13) filled with modern technology and democratic institutions. As part of his revolution, he creates what he calls a "man-factory," a West Point-like school in which he takes in young men untainted by superstition and servile mentality to educate them "up to revolution-grade" (ch. 13) in order "to banish oppression from this land and restore to all its people their stolen rights and manhood without disobliging anybody" (ch. 14). He has confidence in technology and commerce, and he is optimistic in the capacity of his "man-factory" to transform people, despite his repeated qualms about human nature.

Hank realizes that "a superior man like me ought to be shrewd enough to take advantage" (ch. 5) of the ignorance of the backward English, and he vows to "boss the whole country inside of three months" (ch. 2). He does become the Boss, and he displays increasing disdain for the "white Indians" (ch. 2) whom he has decided to save through his benevolent dictatorship. However, his plan turns to horror. "The more power Hank acquires," Lawrence I. Berkove observes, "the more he thinks of himself as inherently superior and the more his democratic professions are contradicted by his admitted ambitions. He looks down on—most undemocratically—the people he encounters, and he never treats any of them as his equals" (98). In his arrogance, Hank combines the characteristics of a conquistador and a shrewd industrialist to become "a giant among pigmies, a man among children" (ch. 8).

When Hank comes across St. Stylite, a hermit who repeatedly bows on his pillar in prayer, Hank decides it's "a pity to have all this power going to waste" (ch. 22). He rigs elastic cords to the hermit to run a sewing machine to manufacture shirts. Twain often creates comic burlesques by taking otherwise serious or exalted activities and describing them in profane or commercial terms, and the method works well in this scene. However, the St. Stylite sewing machine also displays the industrialist's ability to dehumanize. A similar dehumanization occurs in the explosive marvels Hank learned while working in the Colt munitions factory in Connecticut before his transport to the past; the violence throughout the novel, such as Hank's feat of blowing up the fountain to outdo Merlin, seems harmless at first, like mock cartoon violence (although Hank's ridiculous chant in German about mass murder seems to be an eerie adumbration [ch. 23]), but by the end of the novel, the satire turns dark. The grim Sand-Belt massacre is no longer humorous, and the failure of Hank's enterprise stands out in bold relief. It is a failure not only of industrial society but also of Hank's moral sense. Only through domesticity and the confusion of dreams and reality does he recover any sense of self, abandoning his ambitions of domination. The man-factory has been exposed as mechanical and inhuman; it is just as immoral to create a man in a factory as it is to turn a man into a factory.

Tom Sawyer grows to manhood in his overcharged "factory" of fantasies. Through adventures and mischief he will grow up to become a man of the ruling elite, although perhaps not a Colonel Sherburn or a Hank Morgan, and his antics anticipate yet another type of manhood. At the end of *The Adventures of Tom Sawyer*, "Judge Thatcher hoped to see Tom a great lawyer or a great soldier someday" (ch. 35), and the reader gets a sense that Tom would become a leader of the republic, or at least of St. Petersburg. However, the Tom Sawyer in *Huckleberry Finn* is not identical to the playful boy in *Tom Sawyer*. In Huck's book, Tom's mischief is far more toxic, and he cares far less for the consequences of his actions—even to the point of risking his own life and the lives of his friends. He treats Jim callously like a plaything—an object for his own gratification—even though Tom knows Jim has been legally freed, in order to engineer the script of his "evasion." When Aunt Sally wants to know why Tom schemed to set Jim free, "seeing he was already free," Tom replies with exasperation: "Well, that *is* a question,

I must say; and *just* like women! Why, I wanted the *adventure* of it; and I'd a waded neck-deep in blood to . . ." (*Huckleberry Finn* ch. 42). Aunt Polly enters and interrupts his explanation, but he has already said enough to convey that he defines his male identity through the performance of his savage fantasies. Nonviolent rationality is a feminine attribute; violent fantasy turning to bloody reality marks him as a man.[1]

The novels *Tom Sawyer* and *Huckleberry Finn* appeared as part of the post-Civil War "bad boy" book craze launched by Thomas Bailey Aldrich's *The Story of a Bad Boy* in 1869. Through the late nineteenth and early twentieth centuries, numerous bad-boy books would recount the mischievous childhoods of their now-respectable middle-class authors, mostly as memoirs but also as fiction. The misdeeds of these bad boys range from the pranks of Aldrich's young Tom Bailey to the sadistic practical jokes that George Peck's bad boy inflicts on his father in episode after episode in *Peck's Bad Boy and His Pa* (1883). The rage in bad-boy books paralleled the increasing anxieties of out-of-control boys in a quickly expanding industrial and urban society. Romantic notions of childhood as a unique period in life took hold at the same time that the repressive apparatus of truant officers and reform schools established itself.

According to the prominent contemporary psychologist G. Stanley Hall, "Normal children often pass through stages of passionate cruelty, laziness, lying, and thievery" (qtd. in Mailloux 112), and the child, especially a boy, "is in the primitive age." According to Hall's theory, "The instinct of the savage survives in him" (qtd. in Bederman 78), and as the savage boy grows, he moves through evolutionary stages that lead, eventually, to the civilized man. If parents were to tolerate some of the wild behavior of boys and curb the more dangerous ones, they would encourage boys to grow up to be mature men; boyhood's savagery would offset the danger of neurasthenia or nervous exhaustion facing civilized, overrefined adult men. So Tom Sawyer, as a middle-class boy who is being groomed to join the ruling elite, is expected to be mischievous. His cruel and dangerous practical joke at Jim's expense in *Huckleberry Finn* can thus be seen as a typical exercise in learning and enforcing gender roles.

For the perceptive reader, Tom's fantasy life raises other concerns: May the boy be father to the man? May Tom grow up still thoughtlessly toying with the lives of others? Years later, Twain addressed these possibilities, spelling out what Tom's passionate masculinity would mean in a full-grown man:

> Mr. [Teddy] Roosevelt is the Tom Sawyer of the political world of the twentieth century; always showing off; always hunting a chance to show off; in his frenzied imagination the Great Republic is a vast Barnum circus with him for a clown and the whole world for an audience; he would go to Halifax for half a chance to show off, and he would to hell for a whole one. (qtd. in Gibson 26)

The bombastic, imperialist president could be the grown-up Tom Sawyer, but Tom Sawyer (in both novels), as well as Hank Morgan and David Wilson, also have appealing characteristics. They are flawed, their models of manhood (or boyhood) may be targets of satire, and they may even be tragic failures, in a sense, but they behave according to socially sanctioned norms: Hank Morgan as a Yankee entrepreneur, David Wilson as an educated freethinking rationalist, Tom Sawyer as an exuberant fantasist and adventurer.

There are other men throughout Twain's novels who step outside normative roles, often as villains. For example, *Huckleberry Finn*'s King and Duke actually do run a vast Barnum-like circus as part of their huckster schemes. These two humbugs, hardly harmless, are willing to bilk naive people of their money and, even more cruelly, to sell Jim back into slavery, motivated entirely by their own gain. They present the worst aspects of entrepreneurial manhood, despite their absurd acts as fallen aristocrats.

Pap Finn embodies the excluded, poor white of the "one-horse" villages of the river. However, he is a monster, a vicious child abuser denouncing how the law could stand between him and "a man's own son, which he has had all the trouble and all the anxiety and all the expense of raising," but actually bemoaning his inability to grab Huck's money. Pap's only sense of worth comes from asserting his meager white supremacy, expressed in his drunken "Call this a govment" rant about the educated "mulatter" who was able to vote.

Injun Joe is a murderer without the protection of class and race afforded to a Colonel Sherburn. Joe is driven by his rage at his ambiguous position as a half-breed Indian in a society primarily defined along the black-white color line, explaining his drive for revenge against Widow Douglas for the actions of her late husband: "He had me *horsewhipped!*—horsewhipped in front of the jail, like a nigger!" (*Tom Sawyer* ch. 29). Despite his outcast status as a half-breed, he is, at least, not a slave, and he feels deeply injured to be treated as one. To the Welshman hearing of Joe's plans to torture Widow Douglas, his violence is due to his innate Indianness, but Joe's marginal social position offers a way other than blood to understand his rage. Twain's compassionate response to his horrible death underscores Joe's humanity, in spite of his criminal violence. Still, despite the injury Joe suffers, he, too, is a murderer, and no example of manhood. Interestingly, these villains—with the exception of Tom Driscoll in *Pudd'nhead Wilson*, who is a weak, selfish scion of the slave-master aristocracy, even if he is actually "black" and has been raised under false pretenses—all exist on the margins of society, and their excesses revolve around their desire for money.

Also on the margins are some of the most moving male characters who come closest to being "whole" men depicted by Twain. For example, as a slave, Jim is subservient and childlike in his ignorance and superstition, and it would seem he has no basis to be an example of manhood. However, he reveals his true character through the course of his travels with Huck, although in order to survive as a slave he is constantly forced to hide behind his mask of servile acquiescence, particularly in going along with Tom's bizarre "evasion." In his minstrel-like logomachies or dialogues with Huck, such as their debate over "King Sollerman," Jim reveals his ability to outwit Huck through logic, despite his ignorance. He also reveals his feelings as a father through his desire to buy his wife and children out of bondage, or even steal them, the way he gets "low and homesick" when he remembers his wife and children, and the powerful, anguished account of how he learned that his daughter was deaf (*Huckleberry Finn* ch. 23). *Tom Sawyer* and *Huckleberry Finn* depict worlds of absent or abusive fathers, and in that regard Jim stands out as an exception, in relation to his daughter and as father figure for Huck. Huck observes, with naive irony, "I do believe he cared just as much for his people as white folks does for their'n. It don't seem natural, but I reckon it's so" (ch. 23), and in many respects Huck becomes "his people." In *The Jim Dilemma: Reading Race in "Huckleberry Finn,"* Jocelyn Chadwick-Joshua demonstrates persuasively how the novel satirizes racism within the constraints and expectations of its time. Chadwick-Joshua regards Jim as having "the marks of a hero," and she enumerates "the constellation of his virtues":

> his sense of honor, ethics, loyalty, indomitable faith in the nuclear family (a faith that extends into guardianship of Huck Finn), masterful ability to manipulate language, sturdy sense of duty, grasp of the deep meaning of friendship, clear perception of himself as a man, unintimidating wisdom, desire to be self-reliant, and conscious awareness of taking risks. (xii)

Jim also takes control of the situation when he warns Huck away from looking at the face of the dead body in the house floating down the river—"it's too gashly" (ch. 9). Only in the last chapter of the novel do we learn why Jim has kept Huck in the dark, when he explains that Pap "ain't a comin' back no mo'" because "dat wuz him." Jim used Huck for his escape, purposely hiding the truth so that Huck would continue to stay on the raft to protect him. He deceived Huck about the death of his father, but only to save himself, and ironically Jim becomes more of a father to Huck as a result.

Of course, the biggest liar in *Huckleberry Finn* is Huck himself, although he too lies to save himself, not to construct elaborate fantasies at the expense of others as Tom does. Through his lies, the outcast boy demonstrates powerfully what a man he will become. Morality for Huck is contingent, always depending on circumstances and personal relationships. He seeks to save Jim, even though all of what he knows to be morality tells him that he is stealing someone else's property; but he decides to go to Hell, nevertheless (ch. 31).

Earlier in the novel, Huck is tempted to betray Jim but refuses, explaining to himself:

> Well, then, says I, what's the use you learning to do right, when it's troublesome to do right and ain't no trouble to do wrong, and the wages is just the same? I was stuck. I couldn't answer that. So I reckoned I wouldn't bother no more about it, but after this always do whichever come handiest at the time. (ch. 16)

What comes handiest to Huck is to follow the influence of friendship and sympathy—even if such an impulse leads to spiritual damnation, to Hell. "I begun to think how dreadful it was, even for murderers, to be in such a fix," Huck says, contemplating what to do about the thieves he left behind on the sinking riverboat. He reaches a type of moral conclusion: "I says to myself, there ain't no telling but I might come to be a murderer myself, yet, and then how would *I* like it?" (ch. 13). Even in this instance, with thieves who are not friends, like Jim, Huck works out a rough Golden Rule.

In his marginalized status, with his improvised morality, and through the constant performance of lies, Huck displays the decency, courage, and honesty Twain expects from a man. However, like Pudd'nhead Wilson and other characters in Twain's Mississippi novels, Huck cannot see beyond the definitions of the slave system. He never understands his decision to free Jim as an attack on the system—he would be horrified to be called an abolitionist—but only as an attempt to help a friend. He always considers himself to be doing wrong, and he is shocked when Tom, an upstanding boy, decides to help him free Jim.

Years later, Twain would excoriate the "lies of silent assertion," particularly "the silent assertion [about slavery] that there wasn't anything going on in which humane and intelligent people were interested" ("My First Lie" 440). Huck, by placing his friendship above the law and conventional morality, has acted against the lies of the slave system, but only by instinct. In some ways, this is similar to the way Judge Driscoll placed more value on the Code Duello than on the legal system. However, there is a difference: as Twain describes in an 1895 notebook entry alluding to *Huckleberry Finn*:

> I should exploit the proposition that in a crucial moral emergency a sound heart is a safer guide than an ill-trained conscience. I sh'd support this doctrine with a chapter from a book of mine where a sound heart and a deformed conscience come into collision and conscience suffers defeat. (qtd. in Blair 143)

In this instance, deformed conscience, like the laws that enforce slavery, is worthy of defeat.

Huck and Jim demonstrate some of the strongest positive attributes of a man, in Twain's eyes: friendship and loyalty. The relationship between the boy and the slave takes on many characteristics, including surrogate father and son, equal brothers (at least on the raft), hero and sidekick (although the roles switch back and forth), even though these dynamics are no longer possible off the raft, and Jim plans on returning to what passes as civilization in St. Petersburg and redeeming his real family. Jim and Huck share admiration for Tom Sawyer, but as Tom's subordinates and not as his equals. Tom is the measure of right behavior. "Do you reckon Tom Sawyer would ever go by this thing?" Huck exclaims to Jim about boarding the wrecked steamboat they pass on the river.

Not for pie, he wouldn't. He'd call it an adventure—that's what he'd call it; and he'd land on that wreck if it was his last act. And wouldn't he throw style into it?—wouldn't he spread himself, nor nothing? Why, you'd think it was Christopher C'lumbus discovering Kingdom Come. I wish Tom Sawyer *was* here. (ch. 12)

At the end of Tom's farcical "evasion," with Huck declaring "old Jim, you're a free man *again*," Jim praises the mastermind of the adventure:

En a mighty good job it wuz, too, Huck. It 'uz planned beautiful, en it 'uz *done* beautiful; en dey ain't *nobody* kin git up a plan dat's mo' mixed-up en splendid den what dat one wuz. (ch. 40)

However, at the end, when Tom explains the torchlight procession and brass band that he would engineer to greet Jim after "he managed to set a nigger free that was already free before," he reveals that Jim remains a plaything for his grand fantasies. In the book's last chapter, Tom invites Huck to join him "for howling adventures amongst the Injuns, over in the Territory," but Huck declines, deciding "to light out for the Territory ahead of the rest," rejecting the fussy female attention of Aunt Sally—but also rejecting Tom's adventures for the real-life one of survival.

At the end of *Tom Sawyer*, Tom elaborates his game of forming a gang of robbers but sets the boundaries of the proper bad boy: "But, Huck, we can't let you into the gang if you ain't respectable, you know" (ch. 35). By the end of *Huckleberry Finn*, Huck knows all too well—and rejects all forms of respectability, fleeing friendship with Tom as well as Aunt Sally's attempts to "sivilize" him. *Huckleberry Finn* depicts male friendship movingly, but it also presents a satire of the uneven class and race dynamics that corrode male bonds.

So, what did Twain consider a "whole" man? Considering the characters in these novels—even the more sympathetic ones, such as the first Tom Sawyer, Huck, Jim, Hank Morgan, and Pudd'nhead Wilson—they all seem flawed, all not quite whole. Twain was depicting men realistically through humor and satire, and no doubt Colonel Sherburn's call for a whole man was just a bombastic claim. In these novels, especially *Huckleberry Finn*, we can feel the contradictions between idealized manhood and crude reality among the ricocheting ironies.

There are moments of exemplary manhood in all these novels, such as the display of moral courage by King Arthur in *Connecticut Yankee*. But perhaps the clearest, most consistent, even exalted depiction of male character can be found in the person of a girl. *Personal Recollections of Joan of Arc* (1896) is generally regarded as one of Twain's least successful novels—although it also happened to be his favorite—and it is certainly beyond the scope of the major works considered in this essay. One reason Twain may have favored this novel might have been because of the depiction of Joan of Arc as heroic yet humble, courageous in battle yet abhorring violence, loving life yet ready to face death, and other characteristics identifiable as nineteenth-century expressions of male virtues.

When Joan begins to have her visions and is given her mission to save France, she displays a "new light in the eye," and she carries herself with a "new bearing" that was "born of the authority and leadership which had this day been vested in her by the decree of God." Her eyes and the way she carries herself assert "authority as plainly as speech could have done it, yet without ostentation or bravado. This calm consciousness of command, and calm unconscious outward expression of it, remained with her thenceforth until her mission was accomplished" (*Joan of Arc* bk. 1, ch. 7). What is important is her mission, not her social standing or false honor, and certainly not fantasies (even though she was accused of inventing her visions), even if she carries out her military campaign reluctantly: "My disposition being toward peace and quietness, and love for all things that have life; and being made like this, how could I bear to think of wars and blood, and the pain that goes with them, and the sorrow and mourning that follow after?" (bk. 2, ch. 33). But she does carry out the duty of her mission, loyal unto death, despite the need to shed blood. Despite the satirical dismantling of male presumption in Twain's major novels, the young Joan expresses Twain's persistent sentimental notions of loyalty, bravery, honesty, necessity, and quiet humility that underlay his sense of idealized manhood. Ironically, all of this is expressed by a girl.

Notes

Thanks to my undergraduate researchers Brynn Forte and Jenna Tonn, and to Shelley Fisher Fishkin for her critical response.
1. For a full analysis of Tom's role, see my essay "Going to Tom's Hell in *Huckleberry Finn*."

Works Cited

Bederman, Gail. *Madness and Civilization: A Cultural History of Gender and Race in the United States, 1880-1917*. Chicago: U of Chicago P, 1995.

Berkove, Lawrence I. "*Connecticut Yankee*: Twain's Other Masterpiece." *Making Mark Twain Work in the Classroom*. Ed. James S. Leonard. Durham, NC: Duke UP, 1999.

Blair, Walter. *Mark Twain and Huck Finn*. Berkeley: U of California P, 1960.

Chadwick-Joshua, Jocelyn. *The Jim Dilemma: Reading Race in "Huckleberry Finn."* Jackson: UP of Mississippi, 1998.

Fiedler, Leslie A. Afterword. *The Innocents Abroad, or, The New Pilgrim's Progress* by Mark Twain. New York: Signet Classics Penguin, 1966.

Fishkin, Shelley Fisher. "Mark Twain and Women." *Feminist Engagements: Forays into American Literature and Culture*. New York: Palgrave Macmillan, 2009.

Gibson, William M. *Theodore Roosevelt Among the Humorists: W. D. Howells, Mark Twain, and Mr. Dooley*. Knoxville: U of Tennessee P, 1980.

Harris, Susan K. "Mark Twain and Gender." *A Historical Guide to Mark Twain*. Ed. Shelley Fisher Fishkin. New York: Oxford UP, 2002.

Mailloux, Stephen. *Rhetorical Power*. Ithaca, NY: Cornell UP, 1989.

Morris, Linda A. *Gender Play in Mark Twain: Cross-Dressing and Transgression*. Columbia: U of Missouri P, 2007.

Obenzinger, Hilton. "Going to Tom's Hell in *Huckleberry Finn*." *A Companion to Mark Twain*. Ed. Peter Messent and Louis J. Budd. Malden, MA: Blackwell, 2005. 401-15.

Critical Insights

Rotundo, E. Anthony. *American Manhood: Transformations in Masculinity from the Revolution to the Modern Era*. New York: Basic Books, 1993.

Steward, Dick. *Duels and the Roots of Violence in Missouri*. Columbia: U of Missouri P, 2000.

Stoneley, Peter. "Mark Twain and Gender." *A Companion to Mark Twain*. Ed. Peter Messent and Louis J. Budd. Malden, MA: Blackwell, 2005. 66-77.

Twain, Mark. "My First Lie and How I Got Out of It." *Tales, Speeches, Essays, and Sketches*. Ed. Tom Quirk. New York: Penguin, 1994.

Kindred Rivals:
Mark Twain and Ambrose Bierce_____
Lawrence I. Berkove

Of all the authors who were contemporaries of Mark Twain, none had as much in common with him as Ambrose Bierce. When Twain's relationship with Bierce went well, it sometimes rose to the level of lukewarm. Usually, however, the two men kept their distance from each other, a respectful, polite distance at best, but occasionally a frigid and biting distance. Most scholars who know both authors think there was some antipathy between them. This perhaps overstates the case, but it is noteworthy that Twain and Bierce were not more friendly. Despite having genuine differences, they shared many striking similarities in their lives, in positions they held on a large variety of topics, and in some of their literary techniques. Twain is unarguably the superior author and richly deserves his reputation, but Bierce, a more remarkable author than is generally recognized, remains undervalued.

Comparisons of the two writers turn up so many parallels that either they arrived at amazing resemblances of mind, values, and works independently or there are grounds for the possibility that each may have been more aware of the other's work than he admitted, and that they may have engaged in a rivalry that involved reciprocal borrowing. If that proves to be the case, it would constitute additional evidence that Twain was not as original as he is generally believed to be.[1] However, such a conclusion would not diminish Twain's genius, as no author develops in a vacuum. Moreover, in most cases, Twain improved upon the originals from which he is known to have borrowed. Such a conclusion should encourage further inquiry into the influences on him of other authors.

Comparisons begin with Twain's and Bierce's biographies. Both men were born into low-income families in tiny rural communities— Twain in Florida, Missouri, in 1835; Bierce in Ohio's Horse Cave settlement in 1842. Both of their families soon moved to larger and more established towns—Twain's family relocated to Hannibal, Missouri, where he spent most of his boyhood. His youth in that Mississippi River town was his first formative experience and has come to be popularly known as the "Matter of Hannibal." He would later use Hannibal as the backdrop for much of his fiction, most notably *The Adventures of Tom Sawyer* (1876), *Adventures of Huckleberry Finn* (1884), *The Tragedy of Pudd'nhead Wilson* (1894), "The Man That Corrupted Hadleyburg" (1899), and the posthumously published *No. 44, The Mysterious Stranger.* Bierce's family, with nine children, moved first to a farm near Circleville, Ohio, later to Warsaw, Indiana, and finally to Elkhart, Indiana. The recognizable presence of these early homes is abundant in Twain's fiction but sparse in Bierce's fiction. A reason for this may be found in a stanza Carey McWilliams quotes from an autobiographical poem Bierce wrote and published in the November 3, 1883, issue of the *Wasp*:

> With what anguish of mind I remember my childhood,
>> Recalled in the light of a knowledge since gained;
> The malarious farm, the wet, fungus grown wildwood,
>> The chills then contracted that since have remained.
> The scum-covered duck pond, the pigstye close by it,
>> The ditch where the sour-smelling house drainage fell,
> The damp, shaded dwelling, the foul barnyard nigh it
>> *(Biography* 26)

Bierce's bleak recollection of his boyhood homes is possibly also in the unflattering descriptions of some of the rural communities he depicts in his short stories. Bierce was a stickler for unvarnished truth throughout his entire career, and his literalism and concomitant refusal to paint over the disagreeable facts of commonplace existence may be one reason he never matched Twain in popularity. However, the real difference between Twain's and Bierce's attitudes toward their boyhood homes might not be as great as first appears, especially when it is realized that Twain typically began his fictions with romantic illusions that when stripped away reveal ugly aspects of initially attractive fictional characters and communities, such as St. Petersburg, Pikesville, and Dawson's Landing. Scholar Victor A. Doyno has suggested that Huck Finn's preference for food in "a barrel of odds and ends" in which "things get mixed up, and the juice kind of swaps around" (*Huckleberry Finn* ch. 1, p. 2) was Twain's indirect hint that Huck, shunned by the respectable families of seemingly benign St. Petersburg to fend for himself, foraged for food in a swill barrel before it was poured into a hog trough.[2]

The Civil War

Seven years older than Bierce, Twain had some time to pursue his career interests before the Civil War in 1861 interrupted both of their lives. As is well known, Twain spent some of his prewar years in the printing trade at home and in various cities of the eastern United States. Later, he realized one of his boyhood dreams and became a steamboat pilot on the Mississippi River between St. Louis and New Orleans. This second formative experience in his life, now popularly known as the "Matter of the River," became another source for much of his literature. Bierce, on the other hand, did not have much time for personal development. With the help of a benevolent uncle, he left his immediate family around the age of seventeen and enrolled in the respected Kentucky Military Institute, where he spent at least a year and learned military fundamentals and developed some advanced skills in topographical engineering and mathematics. In 1860, he returned to Indiana and worked at several jobs until President Abraham Lincoln issued a call for military volunteers on April 15, 1861. Four days later, Bierce enlisted for a three-month period. A bare month later, his unit was sent to western Virginia and saw action at Philippi, one of the first land battles of the Civil War.

The Civil War caused a major difference in Twain's and Bierce's lives, but one that grew less important over the years. On July 18, 1861, Twain left St. Louis for Nevada Territory, to be a secretary to his brother Orion, who had been appointed secretary of the new territorial government. In reality, Twain fled the Civil War. In *Roughing It* (1872), Twain states that he expected to be in Nevada for three months—the length of time generally believed by people in both the North and South that hostilities would last before an accommodation was reached. Instead, Twain stayed in Nevada nearly three years, through May 1864. From there he went to California, where he remained until December 1866, except for a four-month visit to Hawaii between March and July 1866.

After his first few months in the West, Twain entered journalism—a profession from which he was never thereafter completely separated. His five and one-half years in the Far West constituted his third major formative experience, during which he accumulated what can be called the "Matter of the West." Twain became a professional writer during that time and also acquired a reputation as a humorous speaker that followed him when he arrived in New York in January 1867 and helped establish him in the East.

For Bierce, the Civil War was *the* formative experience of his life. He served in the Union Army almost continuously from 1861 until 1865, except for a three-month furlough in 1864 to recover from a head wound. For a soldier, no engagement in which he fights is "minor," but among the major battles that Bierce endured were Shiloh (which was a seminal experience in the formation of his philosophy and came for him to epitomize warfare), Chickamauga, Missionary Ridge, Stones River, and Kennesaw Mountain. Through most of his military career, he was a lieutenant and a topographical engineer whose job was to reconnoiter prospective battlegrounds and prepare maps of the terrain. As his wounds testify, his was not a safe rear-echelon position. By the time he received a medical discharge in January 1865, he had seen more action than most Civil War veterans and, probably, more than most future literary figures.

Bierce was discharged from the army with the rank of lieutenant. Later, as a civilian, he received an honorary brevet commission as major, which skipped him over the intermediary rank of captain, and he was thenceforth occasionally addressed as "Major Bierce." Although Bierce undoubtedly deserved the tardy promotion and took pride in the title, none of his stories glorifies war. On the contrary, he was sharply skeptical of anything approaching a romantic view of war. He acquired a reputation as a military authority and harshly criticized military incompetence, especially among officers, some of them famous, who foolishly or willfully risked or wasted the lives of their soldiers.

After the war, Bierce worked for the federal government's Reconstruction program in the South, serving in Selma, Alabama, as agency aide to the special agent for the Treasury Department (*Sole Survivor* 69). The corruption he observed from that post eroded what little idealism he had left, so when his admired former leader, General W. B. Hazen, offered him a place on an army mapping expedition to California, he accepted. When he arrived in California in 1866 and discovered that the commission in the regular army he expected was not offered him, he resigned from the army, took a position as a night watchman at the San Francisco Sub-Treasury, and began writing for the *San Francisco News-Letter and California Advertiser.* This launched him into a new career, and for the rest of his life he supported himself as a journalist and achieved national prominence, especially for "Prattle," his weekly feature column of commentary.

Face-to-Face Meetings

While Bierce and Twain were both still early in their writing careers, they met each other in California, probably during the mid-1860s. Carey McWilliams believes that by that time Bierce already admired Twain and was studying his writings "to sharpen lethiferous wit against bovine humor" (*Biography* 83) and that their first meeting was humorous and friendly (87-88). If so, the friendship soon took a rocky path. By February 19, 1870, Bierce in his *News-Letter* column remarked on Twain's recent marriage to Olivia Langdon with a charge that Twain had calculatedly chosen "some one with a fortune to love— some one with a bank account to caress" (qtd. in McWilliams, *Biography* 88). Roy Morris, Jr., records a subsequent accusation from Bierce that Twain's wife's wealth had made it unnecessary for him to lecture anymore and that he could now indulge his "native laziness." Still later, when Twain's father-in-law died, Bierce ironically approved in print the marriage because Livy's inheriting a quarter of a million dollars had removed any doubt concerning the "propriety of the transaction" (125). Even making allowances for the rough humor of the West of that era, Bierce's comments were nasty, and if they reached Twain's ears, they would have caused resentment. There is no reason to believe that Twain learned of them,[3] but they indicate either hostility or jealousy at some level in Bierce.

Twain and Bierce met again in 1872 in London, England, where Bierce—who by then had also married an affluent woman—was now living and making his living writing for hire, especially for the British humor magazine *Fun*. McWilliams says of this period that "Bierce and Twain met often and became quite good friends" (*Biography* 88). This is perhaps a bit too strong. Although the two men occasionally socialized with each other, even in their early years they seemed to regard each other as rivals. For example, while they were both in London, they were invited to a dinner at a club at which Bierce was engaged to speak. He chose to tell in a humorous way about his first meeting with Twain. However, while Bierce was speaking, Twain managed to look bored in such a way as to upstage and undercut him. Bierce saw this and faltered in his delivery. Bierce was proud, and, according to Morris, he was white-faced with humiliation when he sat down; he never again spoke in public (142-43). It is true that Twain and Bierce occasionally complimented each other to third parties (Grenander, "'Five Blushes'" 170), but the record of Bierce's subsequent brief and scattered comments about Twain in publications tends to be on the sarcastic side.[4] The few references to Twain in his private letters are either innocuous or mildly friendly, and in one of his late letters, he affects disingenuously to have barely known Twain and to have met with him only several times (*Much Misunderstood* 151).

After Twain returned to the United States in 1874, he wrote a damning letter about Bierce to his British publisher, Chatto & Windus, in which he described Bierce's 1873 book *Nuggets and Dust* as "the vilest book that exists in print—or very nearly so" and claimed that "for every laugh that is in his book, there are five blushes, ten shudders and a vomit. The laugh is too expensive."[5] Although both M. E. Grenander and one of the editorial notes to volume 6 of *Mark Twain's Letters* (102) see this letter aimed narrowly at *Nuggets and Dust*, the possibility remains that Twain sensed a rival in Bierce and, as he did with such potential competitors as the "Phunny Phellows" humorists, emphatically denied any tie to his works.

It is unlikely that Bierce knew of Twain's letter, but what he could not have missed fourteen years later was the marked underrepresentation of his work in *Mark Twain's Library of Humor* (1888). Published by Twain's own firm, Charles L. Webster & Co., this anthology understandably gave prominence to Twain, including some of his best short fiction and extracts from books. But it included only seven brief fables of relatively trivial significance written by Bierce.

Writing Careers

Twain's genius as a writer had appeared almost from the beginning of his career in Nevada, but Bierce also hit the ground running. Although it took him almost a quarter of a century after the Civil War to begin writing the extraordinary tales that now establish him as the most important author to have come out of that war, long before those tales Bierce was already recognized as one of the leading and most versatile authors of the West. His work had appeared in the *Overland Monthly*,

Argonaut, and *Wasp*—leading literary journals on the West Coast. Approximately one-third of his total fictional output had been written by 1886.[6] Much of it is humor at least as good as other authors' works in *Mark Twain's Library of Humor,* and some of it consists of pieces close in quality to the Twain items that were included. Bierce's "Why I Am Not Editing 'The Stinger'" (1874) and "Mr. Masthead, Journalist" (1879) parallel Twain's own "How I Edited an Agricultural Paper Once" (1870). Bierce's "Jupiter Doke, Brigadier-General" (1885) is choice and unlike anything Twain wrote until the lesser-quality "Luck" (1891).

While Twain lent his pen name to *Mark Twain's Library of Humor,* most of the selecting was actually done by William Dean Howells and Charles H. Clark,[7] but Bierce did not know that. If no rivalry existed between them before the book came out, Bierce would now have reason to feel slighted. If a rivalry had already existed, it would have been further fueled.

Shock, Humor, Wit, and Satire

Twain maintained ties with his former associates in Nevada and California and undoubtedly was kept informed of literary news there, in which Bierce featured prominently. Meanwhile, from his own occasionally sour or snide comments on Twain, it is certain that Bierce kept apprised of Twain's growing reputation. More than that, McWilliams reports, Bierce admonished the poet George Sterling to reread *Huckleberry Finn (Biography* 88). However, did either man appreciate what the other was doing? No hard evidence exists to answer that question definitively, but the similarities in what they wrote are too many to be dismissed as mere coincidences. On the surface, it is evident that they covered the same ground, often in much the same way, and they sometimes wrote similar pieces inspired by the same sources. Some of the most apparent similarities are outlined below.

Gory Details to Induce Shock

Bierce has long been notorious for his use of gory details to shock readers. He used them as early as 1873 in *Fun*, and he continued to use them throughout most of his writing career. However, as Gladys Bellamy points out, in such early works as "The Great Prize Fight" (1863) and "A Bloody Massacre near Carson" (1863), Twain anticipated Bierce's lifelong development of this technique (100-101). In Bierce's fiction, shock is seldom if ever used as an end in itself; almost always it is used as a means to induce readers to face up to and reflect on unpleasant realities. Twain also, as early as "Cannibalism in the Cars" (1868), displayed a similar use and then went on to devise ways of concealing and delaying shock until after readers penetrated his stories' surfaces and reached their content level.

Humor and Wit

Both Twain and Bierce have been praised for being humorists and wits, both produced notable examples of both genres, and both gave thought to distinctions between humor and wit. Their ideas on these distinctions changed subtly over the years and deepened. In 1885, Twain observed:

> Wit & humor—if any difference, it is in *duration*—lightning and electric light. Same material, apparently; but one is vivid, brief & can do damage— tother fools along & enjoys elaboration. (*Notebooks* 162)

He later elaborated on the differences among humor, wit, and comedy in his well-known essay "How to Tell a Story" (1895). However, in the "Pudd'nhead Wilson's New Calendar" epigram that heads chapter 10 of *Following the Equator* (1897), he wrote: "Everything human is pathetic. The secret source of Humor itself is not joy but sorrow. There is no humor in heaven."

As previously mentioned, M. E. Grenander thought of Bierce as a wit and Twain as a humorist. This reflects Bierce's own view of himself. In a "Prattle" discussion of the subject, he wrote:

> Humor is tolerant, tender; its ridicule caresses; wit stabs, begs pardon— and turns the weapon in the wound. Humor is a sweet wine, wit a dry; we know which is preferred by the connoisseur.

He then added, "They may be mixed, forming an acceptable blend" (*Examiner* March 23, 1903). An earlier example of his idea of wit occurs in a "Prattle" response to a letter writer: "L. C.—If the paragraph 'made you laugh' it was not 'witty.' Wit is not laughable. N.B.—I'm assuming that you understand what you read" (*Examiner* February 5, 1893). It is hardly profitable to pursue hairsplitting distinctions among wit, humor, comedy, irony, sarcasm, satire, and sardonicism, inasmuch as they overlap. Both authors exhibit all of these literary techniques, but Twain expressed a preference for humor and Bierce for wit, and both authors in the final analysis transcend pigeonholing by any or all of these distinctions.

Another form of wit was Twain's and Bierce's use of often cynical aphorisms. R. Kent Rasmussen notes that Twain always had a gift for the "superbly turned phrase" (xiv), but it was Bierce who as early as 1874 began writing satirical definitions. In 1875, he composed a piece titled "The Demon's Dictionary," and in March 1881 he began a feature series in the *Wasp* titled "The Devil's Dictionary" that attracted much notice. He later expanded this dictionary, which he eventually published as a book. The genre of the aphorism, however, sometimes forces meaning to be subordinated to wit, and Bierce apparently found that mere quotableness could misrepresent his thinking. From 1885 through 1909, he published less sensational but deeper epigrams, first in the *Wasp* and after 1887 in his syndicated columns in Hearst periodicals. The cynical maxims of Twain's "Pudd'nhead Wilson's Calendar" in *Pudd'nhead Wilson* and "Pudd'nhead Wilson's New Calendar" in *Following the Equator* thus had precedent in the already famous definitions and epigrams that Bierce had popularized.

Cynical Satires of Moralistic Fables and Folktales

Twain's best-known pieces in this category are "The Story of the Bad Little Boy Who Didn't Come to Grief" (1865) and "The Story of the Good Little Boy Who Did Not Prosper" (1870). Later developments of his along this line include "Some Learned Fables for Good Old Boys and Girls" (1875) and "Little Bessie" (1908-1909). These tales are transparently ironic and, through the employment of the Sunday-school narrative style used to entertain and instruct children, undercut conventional religious morality. In 1873, in some of his contributions to *Fun*, Bierce began mocking conventional morality for its romantic shallowness in such parodic sketches as "The Magician's Little Joke," "The Grateful Bear," and "Converting a Prodigal," which last bears comparison to Twain's "Story of the Bad Little Boy." Under the guise of obvious humor, both Twain and Bierce thus evinced a cynically bleak view of human nature.[8]

Possible Imitations

Some evidence suggests each man might have had an earlier work of the other in mind when he wrote a later piece of his own. This is not to claim that Twain and Bierce plagiarized each other, but that though their styles certainly differed and their plots may have varied, they still used similar situations and central ideas. For example, Bierce's "Perry Chumley's Eclipse" (1874), though amusing, weakly resembles Twain's sparkling "A Full and Reliable Account of the Extraordinary Meteoric Shower of Last Saturday Night" (1864). However, as the latter's publication antedated Bierce's arrival in California, similarities in the two stories may have been only coincidental. A nearer resemblance can be found in both men's interests in the idea of erecting a monument to the Bible's Adam. Howard G. Baetzhold reports that the genesis for Twain's satirical "A Monument to Adam," which was published in *Harper's Weekly* in 1905, was an interest he first had in 1879 that subsequently found expression in an 1883 talk "On Adam" (522). Meanwhile, Bierce published his own satirical piece titled "A Monument to Adam" (which mentions Twain) in the *Californian* of 1880; it was reprinted in 1890 in the *Wasp*. Even if both men independently developed an interest in the topic at the same time, Bierce's earlier publication of his piece makes it eligible to be considered a precursor to Twain's work. Similarly, Bierce's tale "The Famous Gilson Request" (1878) anticipates by more than twenty years Twain's "The Man That Corrupted Hadleyburg" (1899). Both stories, Robert L. Gale observes, are satirical and expose human avarice and civic self-righteousness (93-94).

Even more directly, both authors wrote sketches not only on the same topic but also with almost identical titles. Twain's 1865 piece "Just 'One More Unfortunate'" describes a girl in jail who pretends to be simple, innocent, and unassuming but is actually just the opposite. There is no subtlety in Twain's style; he frankly denounces the girl as "competent to take charge of a University of Vice." In 1871, Bierce published a brief sketch in the *San Francisco News-Letter* titled "One More Unfortunate" that at first seems to be pathetically describing a young woman bent on suicide, but it turns out that the girl has a romantic crush on a policeman and is trying to entrap him into becoming involved with her. The sketch is skillful, understated, and in the manner of classical Cynicism analyzes conduct for an underlying agenda. Bierce concludes the sketch without obvious moralizing, the last line only describing ironically that on the woman's "clean, delicate face" was "an expression that can only be described as frozen profanity."

In 1868, Bierce published in the *News-Letter* a series of four satires purporting to be observations by a traveler from a hitherto unknown Asian country on American culture as he observed it in San Francisco ("Letters from a Hdkhoite"). Naive and idealistic, the traveler attempts to understand what he sees by reference to what he knows from his own country. A contrast results, generally to the disadvantage of San Francisco. The influence of Oliver Goldsmith's *Letters from a Citizen of the World* (1762) and Jonathan Swift's *Gulliver's Travels* (1726) is easily seen in these accounts. In 1870-1871, Twain wrote a similar short series, "Goldsmith's Friend Abroad Again," for the *Galaxy*. Openly indebted to Goldsmith's *Letters*, Twain's series was an exposé of California's corrupt system of justice from the point of view of a naive and innocent Chinese traveler. In 1875, he wrote "The Curious Republic of Gondour" for *The Atlantic Monthly*. That sketch is a Swiftian account of a visit to an imaginary land with better laws than our own. Between 1888 (when Edward Bellamy's *Looking Backward* was published) and 1907, Bierce again returned to Gulliverian social satires with eleven short pieces that were later amalgamated into a single work: "The Land Below the Blow." Although Swift and Goldsmith were the ultimate inspirations for these works of Bierce and Twain, Bierce was first into print with "Letters from a Hdkhoite" and might thereby have been a more immediate model than Goldsmith for Twain. On the other hand, Twain's success with "Gondour" might have moved Bierce to return to his Gulliverian satires.

Both authors also wrote pieces in the subgenre of "future history." In these works, generally both satirical and pessimistic, narrators from some point in the future look back on what are for Twain's and Bierce's readers the present and try to make sense of the scattered and almost obliterated remnants of the once-glorious American civilization and detect the causes of its demise.

Hoaxes

Both Bierce and Twain learned the technique of the hoax from the masters of Nevada's Sagebrush School. Twain, of course, lived and worked in Nevada from 1861 to 1864, and he kept up friendships with some of his Nevada associates through the rest of his life. Elsewhere, it has been advanced at length that much of Twain's most important fiction, most especially his novels, have subtle hoaxes deep in their cores that when recognized reveal powerful and surprising themes that unify the individual works and relate all of them to each other.[9] Bierce also had direct contact with Sagebrush authors both from his position as editor of the *Argonaut*, which published contributions of some of them, such as Dan De Quille and Joe Goodman, sometimes in the same issues with his own contributions, and especially from his occasional visits to Nevada's Comstock Lode and his close personal friendship with Sam Davis, one of the most accomplished Sagebrush authors.[10]

In one of his essays, Carey McWilliams perceptively observes that it is impossible to discuss Bierce apart from the tradition of the hoax ("Introduction" iii-vi). Although this statement certainly applies to Bierce's penchant for literary pranks, such as his parts in the Poe hoax and the early book *The Dance of Death* (1877), it also extends to some of his best-known stories, such as "The Death of Halpin Frayser" (1891), the Parenticide Club tales (1886-1893), "Moxon's Master" (1899), and most particularly and brilliantly his masterpiece, "An Occurrence at Owl Creek Bridge" (1890).[11] Apart from their use in common of the technique of the hoax, Twain and Bierce evince themes that, though not identical, are close in their artistic subtlety and pessimistic content.

Religious Parallels

Both Twain and Bierce were raised in frontier Calvinism. The influence of this on Twain was seminal and far too involved to be summarized adequately here other than to say that a deep and bitter criticism of God is explicit and notoriously abundant in the writings of Twain's last two decades. Also, that although Twain remained a believer, his opposition to God in the form of heretical Calvinism is central to many if not most of his works of fiction.[12] Bierce was only slightly influenced by his Calvinist background, but he, too, expressed a lifelong antipathy to religion, especially Christianity. Bierce remained interested in and informed about theology during his entire life but replaced formal adherence to a religious creed with an engagement with philosophy. He was particularly attracted to classical Stoicism and Cynicism, both of which emphasized moral conduct. Classical Stoicism emphasized Reason as the guide to behavior; classical Cynicism advocated following Truth but tested all claims to it for underlying agendas. Bierce explicitly acknowledged the importance to him of both philosophies in his weekly newspaper columns in the *San Francisco Examiner*, and their presence can be seen operating in the stands those columns take. His stories, however, put those philosophies on trial and derive no small measure of their power from demonstrating the ultimate failure of philosophy to cope with life.

Like Twain, whose examples of similar skepticism of, or outright hostility to, Christianity and its professional promoters are well known and easily available, Bierce never tired of exposing clergymen and avid devotees of all religions for hypocrisies, ignorant or mean-spirited positions, and illegal activities. So many instances of this occur in his journalism that only a few selections will have to represent the range. In a cynical response, for example, to a reader's letter, he wrote, "'Heaven and Hell, as taught to us,' are neither places nor conditions; they are parts of an apparatus for picking pockets" (*Examiner* December 2, 1894). On July 3, 1887, he published a poem in which he satirized the egotistic cupidity and the deep distrust of God underlying the prayers for rain of Illinois farmers: "Send *us* the showers, Lord, and parch the plains./ Of Indiana./. . . ./We've sold our wheat already— high: that crop's/ Beyond Thy Power." This sentiment closely parallels Twain's attack on Special Providences in "The Second Advent" (1881).

In 1891, when Rabbi Jacob Voorsanger of San Francisco complained that Bierce had been unfairly critical of him, Bierce replied in the *Examiner*, "I have ever taken an unholy delight in making mischief in all the houses of the Lord." All other denominations have had their turn, he wrote, "will he [Rabbi Voorsanger] decline his inning at the spit?" Bierce then proceeded to a larger point, a characteristic theme of his:

It is not for . . . any priest of any religion, to complain of injustice. Through all the centuries of history the trail of every priesthood has been a trail of blood—the blood of those who dared to believe otherwise than they. Whenever and wherever they have had the power they have conducted their controversies with fire and sword: they have combated [*sic*] heretical doctrine by removing the heads that entertained it. (September 6, 1891)

This position is so close to Twain's that it would be virtually impossible to be certain of its authorship were it not verifiable that Bierce wrote it.

Unlike Twain, however, Bierce's "crusade" against Christianity did not include Christ. Twain retained an ambivalent default Trinitarian belief in Christ and respected the human Christ as a dispenser of mercy and salvation while despising the divine Christ for introducing Hell (*Letters from Earth* 46). In contrast, Bierce always praised Christ but regarded him not as divine but as a "lightning moral calculator." Bierce stated that, for himself, the ultimate test of right was what

"under the circumstances, would Christ have done?"—the Christ of the New Testament, not the Christ of the commentators, theologians, priests, and parsons. The test is perhaps not infallible, but it is excellently simple and gives as good practical results as any. (*Examiner* June 28, 1891)

Coming from different perspectives, therefore, both Bierce and Twain arrived at a similar practical conclusion. They also fully agreed on the position that Bierce articulated when he wrote that "in the matter of width the gulf between Christianity and Christ is no floor-crack" (December 25, 1898). For both men, the institution of Christianity was a diminution, a warping, even a perversion of the best of that for which Christ stood.

Despite their hostility toward institutionalized religion and God, both Twain and Bierce gave evidence of being uncomfortable with their intellectual conclusions and showed signs during their careers of a concern with supernaturalism and God. As early as *Roughing It*

(1872), but also in *Huckleberry Finn* (1884) and *A Connecticut Yankee* (1889), there is muted evidence of Twain's belief in a malevolent deity. Especially in his last period, a number of Twain's works—some left unpublished or incomplete—reflect a mind obsessed with manifestations of a deity and the appearance of angels, spirits, and mysterious strangers. The most extensive and searching of these works is the posthumously published *No. 44, The Mysterious Stranger* (written 1902-1908). Its protagonist, a youth in medieval Austria named August Feldner, is taught by a supernatural being named Forty-Four to regard the universe as literally unreal, essentially a thought projection. Forty-Four's last instruction to August can be read as an inducement to use his mind to create his own world. This "inducement," however, intimidates August with its overwhelmingly daunting challenge for a mortal and imperfect human to act like God. As much, therefore, as Twain was disposed to consider God as intending no good to the majority of humanity, and life between the cradle and the grave as a sort of hell, in the final analysis he recognized that if God were evil, fallible humans would make even worse deities.[13]

Although Bierce professed to be an unbeliever, several of his pieces suggest his dismay at the idea of existence without meaning. Probably the best known of these pieces is "An Inhabitant of Carcosa" (1886), a nightmarish tale of obliteration and spiritual desolation. McWilliams speculates that it might have had its genesis in Bierce's Civil War experiences in Coosa County, Alabama (*Biography* 67). In a revealing and remarkable *Examiner* column Bierce wrote on July 24, 1887, about some of his recurring dreams, he included the following stanza that expressed the "dreadful truth" of the "extravagant fancy" of another, similar nightmare:

> Man is long ages dead in every zone,
> The angels all are gone to graves unknown;
> The devils, too, are cold enough at last,
> And God lies dead before the great white throne!

Bierce later inserted this stanza in "Finis Aeternitatis," a longer poem that ends as a satire on a contemporary millionaire; however, the satire appears to be unsatisfactorily tacked on to what started out to be a serious religious reflection on a hauntingly empty universe.[14] Admittedly, such ventures are rare in the majority of Bierce's works, but toward the end of his life, in his last published fiction, such as "The Moonlit Road" (1907), "A Resumed Identity" (1908), "The Stranger" (1909), and, most particularly, "Beyond the Wall" (1908), Bierce tentatively but seriously explores the possibility of postmortem existence, a spiritual dimension in which souls might complete missions and even unite with each other in fulfilling love.

Although both Twain and Bierce were critical of institutionalized religion and God, both at times conceived of a God who created grandeur and inspired awe. In 1886, Bierce wrote the following poem, titled "Creation," for his column in the *Wasp*:

> God dreamed—the suns sprang flaming into place,
> And sailing worlds with many a venturous race!
> He woke—His smile alone illumined space.

In 1909, Twain wrote the manuscript of *Letters from the Earth*, which would not be published until 1962. On its first page appears the following passage:

> He [God] lifted His hand, and from it burst a fountain-spray of fire, a million stupendous suns, which clove the blackness and soared, away and away and away, diminishing in magnitude and intensity as they pierced the far frontiers of Space, until at last they were but as diamond nail-heads sparkling under the domed vast roof of the universe.

The contrast of the former considerations of a malevolent or meaningless world with these glorifications of an imagined deity are inconsistencies within the works of both authors, but these inconsistencies themselves constitute another similarity. The age in which both men lived was damaging to faith. Some found peace of mind in one extreme or the other: unquestioning faith or radical unbelief. Ultimately, it was common particularities of both Bierce and Twain that although their stands on religion were angry, they derived no pleasure from them, and while both men were characterized by skepticism, both also allowed expression to the impulse of their will to believe.

Social Criticism and Antipathy to War and Imperialism

Twain and Bierce were among the most outspoken social critics of their time. From his early journalistic experiences in Nevada and California to the end of his life, Twain attacked in prose and fiction a broad spectrum of injustices: the corruption of justice, racism, unethical business practices, sham, pretense, misdemeanors of the high and mighty, the materialism of the Gilded Age, and betrayal of public trust. As for Bierce, it is impossible to read more than three or four of his weekly columns without encountering the fearless, almost reckless scourging of rogues, scoundrels, and fools that earned him the sobriquet of "the man with the burning pen." He became a predecessor of the muckraker movement when in 1896 his investigative journalism led the successful assault on Collis P. Huntington's railroad refunding bill scam. In short, both men were profoundly involved in the day-to-day affairs of their time and place and attacked many of the same targets.

Twain's hatred of war manifested as early as "The Private History of a Campaign That Failed" (1885) and in the chapters on the Battle of the Sand-Belt in *A Connecticut Yankee*. It thereafter appeared with increasing frequency and explicitness in such works as "The Chronicle of Young Satan" (1900), "The War Prayer" (1905), and "Glances at History (Suppressed)" (1906?). At first supportive of the Spanish-American War of 1898, Twain became disillusioned by America's decision to retain some of its wartime conquests, and he immediately became involved in the cause of anti-imperialism, which overlapped with his scorn of shallow appeals to unthinking patriotism and his basic antipathy to war. He did not know war at first hand, but as "The War Prayer" demonstrates, he did not need personal experience to intuit its horrors. Similarly, his humanitarianism overrode his sectarian patriotism, and he could empathize with Spaniards, Filipinos, Chinese, and aboriginal Australians and Tasmanians, as well as African Americans, when they were victimized by the brutal arrogance of his own nation, race, or culture. At heart, he was oppressed by the legacy of Cain, the ancient flaw of human nature that perversely inclines humans to murder one another. He blamed God for having created it and humans for possessing and acting on it.

Of Bierce it can be said that he came to hate war during his service in the Civil War. Vincent Starrett realized this in his perceptive observation that the stories of Bierce and Stephen Crane are "enduring peace tracts" (60). None of Bierce's tales glorifies war. The Civil War shocked him. It was not just the spectacle of armies fighting a modern war with horrifying new technology that troubled him, but the gory particulars of individual situations that he could not forget: units being decimated in minutes by virtually solid onslaughts of shredding lead and iron; soldiers being mangled and disemboweled and left on the battlefield, sometimes still alive, for animals to eat or for fire to burn; the agonies and screams of the wounded; incompetents ordering men into hopeless charges and fatal traps; bravery wasted and mediocrity rewarded. Whatever religious belief Bierce might have brought with him to the war, he lost it in combat. "Heroism," "glory," "triumph"—these became hollow words for him. "Divine purpose" and "justice" became abstract terms whose meanings conflicted with the details of fields of corpses and numberless personal tragedies.

These memories stayed with Bierce and tormented him through the rest of his life. It took him almost a quarter of a century after the war to begin to exorcise them by writing stories. By focusing on the perceptions and mental processes of their protagonists, his war tales raise realism to a new level and expose in their protagonists' minds the pain, suffering, and, frequently, the self-deceptions of war. Still, Bierce did not go to the extreme of automatic opposition to all war; he understood that there are times when war may be justified. In his columns on the Spanish-American War, Bierce initially supported American military action, but as soon as he realized that the war was not one of national necessity, he became critical of it in his columns—one of the extremely few Americans to do so publicly during the war. As he saw the ineptness of the way the military was conducting the war, his commentaries became ironic. Once the war turned imperialistic, Bierce directed his irony toward the McKinley administration, and he thereafter flayed the nation's reaction to the Philippine insurrection and its intention to rule the territories and populations it had "liberated."[15] Bierce did not approve of imperialism but accepted that Nature drove it as part of its impartial law of "survival of the fittest" and expected that just as America annexed territory now because it could, in the future it would be effaced in its turn and replaced by some other power that would conquer its way to eminence.[16] Considering therefore that Twain's initial response to war was to flee it and Bierce's was to enlist, each man ultimately drew much closer to the other's position.

Conclusions

This study of the relationship of Twain and Bierce neither pretends to be exhaustive nor denies that there might be more than one cause for particular similarities. However, is it likely that there is no common denominator for *all* or most of them? It would seem willfully obtuse to dismiss all of Twain's and Bierce's similarities as coincidences; there are too many—the above list is not complete—and they are too close to have been merely accidental. The purpose of this study has been to consider two contemporary authors who are rarely mentioned in the same context and who are ranked very differently as literary figures, and to recognize that there exists a case for connecting them.

In life, Twain and Bierce seemed to have little regard for each other, but what passed before as indifference or hostility may now be understood as rivalry. It would have been difficult for Bierce to be detached from Twain's growing fame; indeed, the record of his *Examiner* acerbities suggests that he read more of Twain's work than he later chose to admit. Resentment or envy could well have been at work. Twain, on his part, was notoriously indisposed to acknowledge literary indebtednesses, and neither his denials nor his silences can be trusted to give us an accurate account of his sources. He was widely disliked on the Comstock for his hoaxes and sharp satires but also for his unacknowledged borrowings, and it is now recognized that his famous derogations of such authors as Bret Harte, Edgar Allan Poe, and even Sir Walter Scott did not prevent him from acquiring ideas and information from them. Insofar as Twain kept abreast of literary developments in America and especially the writers of the Far West, it is hard to imagine that he remained in the dark about what Bierce, one of the foremost and most talked-about literary figures of California, was doing. It is more improbable that both authors remained ignorant of or uninterested in each other's writings than that both at some level felt the other to be a competitor, semisurreptitiously took note of what that other was doing, and sympathetically resonated to it in subsequent writings of his own.

Time has a way of clarifying things and putting them into better perspective. We have learned more about both authors and how to read them more productively. As a result, Twain has outgrown the once-popular stereotype of him as only a genial humorist and a warmhearted spinner of delightful stories about an idyllic rural America. But of all the important authors of the nineteenth century, Bierce even now remains one of the most underestimated, although some scholarship reflects a broad-based competence in Bierce's work instead of just a narrow focus on one or two stories. However, now that S. T. Joshi and David E. Schultz have recently edited and made available almost all of Bierce's fiction and many of his other writings,[17] it is to be hoped that Bierce will attract more attention of the highly professional kind that has been lavished on Twain. Twain remains an unaccountable literary genius, a giant for the ages, but Bierce, too, is outstanding in his own right and, at least in his masterpiece "An Occurrence at Owl Creek Bridge," reaches the level of Twain. This is no small accomplishment. Both authors, properly understood, are moralists at heart and literary artists of surprising range and depth. Whatever the personal reasons for their uncongeniality, we can now get past that and see that in their minds and writings there was much that made them kindred.

Notes

1. Over the years, scholars have traced unacknowledged but detectable "borrowings" or adaptations by Twain of particular passages from some other author's work into a work of his own. Within only my own experience, in three items listed in the bibliography I have documented conclusive evidence that specific passages in *Roughing It, Life on the Mississippi,* and *Huckleberry Finn* derive directly from material first published by Twain's former Nevada roommate Dan De Quille. Gladys Bellamy kindly excuses the borrowings from frontier humor as unconscious (46), and Walter Blair less kindly but still gently explains them as "unconscious plagiarism" (127). However, these borrowings are more than a few, and they form a pattern. Twain once explicitly denied the "crime" of plagiarism (Bellamy 45), although his unacknowledged borrowings were noticed in his own time, and he could not have remained totally unaware of the open resentment they caused. Scholarly recognitions of these "borrowings" have been so scattered and infrequent as to be neglected, and their cumulative importance remains unassessed.

2. Doyno made this suggestion in a talk I attended. See also Tom Towers's article "'Never Thought We Might Want to Come Back'" for a negative view of St. Petersburg in *Tom Sawyer.* In chapter 3 of *Heretical Fictions,* Joseph Csicsila and I corroborate Tower about St. Petersburg and extend his interpretation to other towns that Twain seems at first to idealize. Towers goes on to place Twain among the leaders of the "revolt against the small town" movement in American literature.

3. Negative comments in newspapers about Twain from his former western associates were not uncommon. Although he had some strongly loyal friends, he was not very popular in either Nevada or California. Even his friends Joe Goodman (Berkove, *Insider Stories* 557) and Arthur McEwen (33) admit this, and when Twain's future father-in-law wrote to some of Twain's former associates for character references, many of the replies were unsatisfactory.

4. I wish to thank S. T. Joshi and David Schultz for giving me access to their extensive file of Bierce's journalism and letting me see for myself the records of Bierce's comments about Twain.

5. See Grenander's essay "'Five Blushes, Ten Shudders, and a Vomit'" (170-71)

and volume 6 of *Mark Twain's Letters* (101-2), especially note 1, which speculates that Twain wrote only a narrowly focused opinion that in effect headed off an invitation to write a "puff" of Bierce's book *Nuggets and Dust* (1873), which Chatto & Windus had also published. Grenander offers a more deeply argued defense of the book as wit instead of humor and suggests several reasons Twain denigrated it as a work of humor, including resentment of the book's disparagement of American humorists (of whom Twain, of course, was one) and resentment toward the publishers for not respecting his pen name (175-77).

6. Volume 1 of the three-volume edition of *The Short Fiction of Ambrose Bierce* contains all the tales and sketches that Bierce is known to have published through 1886.

7. See Gohdes's foreword in *Mark Twain's Library of Humor* (vii-ix).

8. The sketches that Bierce wrote in England, long almost inaccessible but mentioned here, are included in volume 1 of *The Short Fiction of Ambrose Bierce*.

9. *Heretical Fictions* offers extended analyses of five of Twain's novels that identify distinctive themes that are carried through those works by their use of the hoax.

10. In a published 1915 memoir of Bierce, Davis wrote of their forty-year friendship. In addition, Davis's own short story, "The Reporter's Revenge," qualifies as a possible source for Bierce's "Owl Creek." For more information on these items and Bierce's connections with Sagebrush authors, see Berkove, *A Prescription for Adversity.*

11. See *A Prescription for Adversity* for discussions of all these and similar tales, and especially chapter 6, which is entirely devoted to "Owl Creek."

12. This is the main thesis of *Heretical Fictions.*

13. See chapter 6 of *Heretical Fictions* for a fuller discussion of this story.

14. This column, with the poem, is reprinted in *A Sole Survivor* (307-11). "Finis Aeternitatis" appears in "Black Beetles in Amber" in *The Collected Works of Ambrose Bierce* (5: 65-67).

15. Bierce's newspaper columns covering the Spanish-American War, the Philippine insurrection, and other international hostilities from 1898 to 1901 have been collected in *Skepticism and Dissent.*

16. For Bierce's views on the natural causes of "expansionism" see his *Skepticism and Dissent* (85-87, 126-27, 182-85) and Berkove, *A Prescription for Adversity* (40-47).

17. See the list of works cited, under Bierce, for a partial listing.

Works Cited and Consulted

Baetzhold, Howard G. "A Monument to Adam." *Mark Twain Encyclopedia*. Ed. J. R. LeMaster and James D. Wilson. New York: Garland, 1993. 522-23.

Bellamy, Gladys. *Mark Twain as a Literary Artist*. Norman: U of Oklahoma P, 1950.

Berkove, Lawrence I. "Dan De Quille and 'Old Times on the Mississippi.'" *Mark Twain Journal* 24.2 (Fall 1986): 28-35.

_____. "Dan De Quille and *Roughing It*: Borrowings and Influence." *Nevada Historical Society Quarterly* 37.1 (Spring 1994): 52-57.

_____. "New Information on Dan De Quille and 'Old Times on the Mississippi.'" *Mark Twain Journal* 26.2 (Fall 1988): 15-20.

_____. *A Prescription for Adversity: The Moral Art of Ambrose Bierce.* Columbus: Ohio State UP, 2002.

_____, ed. *Insider Stories of the Comstock Lode and Nevada's Mining Frontier, 1859-1909.* 2 vols. Lewiston, NY: Edwin Mellen Press, 2007.

Berkove, Lawrence I., and Joseph Csicsila. *Heretical Fictions: Religion in the Literature of Mark Twain.* Iowa City: U of Iowa P, 2010.

Bierce, Ambrose. *The Collected Works of Ambrose Bierce.* 10 vols. New York: Neale, 1909-1912.

_____. *The Fall of the Republic, and Other Political Satires.* Ed. S. T. Joshi and David E. Schultz. Knoxville: U of Tennessee P, 2000.

_____. *A Much Misunderstood Man: Selected Letters of Ambrose Bierce.* Ed. S. T. Joshi and David E. Schultz. Columbus: Ohio State UP, 2003.

_____. *The Short Fiction of Ambrose Bierce: A Comprehensive Edition.* 3 vols. Ed. S. T. Joshi, Lawrence I. Berkove, and David E. Schultz. Knoxville: U of Tennessee P, 2006.

_____. *Skepticism and Dissent: Selected Journalism, 1898-1901.* Ed. Lawrence I. Berkove. Ann Arbor, MI: UMI Research Press, 1980.

_____. *A Sole Survivor: Bits of Autobiography.* Ed. S. T. Joshi and David E. Schultz. Knoxville: U of Tennessee P, 1998.

Blair, Walter. *Mark Twain and Huck Finn.* Berkeley: U of California P, 1962.

Branch, Edgar Marquess. *The Literary Apprenticeship of Mark Twain.* Urbana: U of Illinois P, 1950.

Fears, David H. *Mark Twain Day by Day.* Vols. 1-2. Banks, OR: Horizon Micro, 2008-2009.

Gale, Robert L. *An Ambrose Bierce Companion.* Westport, CT: Greenwood Press, 2001.

Gohdes, Clarence. "Foreword." *Mark Twain's Library of Humor.* 1888. New York: Bonanza, 1969.

Grenander, M. E. *Ambrose Bierce.* New York: Twayne, 1971.

_____. "'Five Blushes, Ten Shudders, and a Vomit': Mark Twain on Ambrose Bierce's *Nuggets and Dust*." *American Literary Realism* 17 (1984): 169-79.

McEwen, Arthur. "Heroic Days on the Comstock." 1893. *The Life and Times of the "Virginia City Territorial Enterprise."* Ed. Oscar Lewis. Ashland, OR: Lewis Osborne, 1971. 29-36.

McWilliams, Carey. *Ambrose Bierce: A Biography.* 1929. Hamden, CT: Archon Books, 1967.

_____. "Introduction." *Bierce and the Poe Hoax*, by Carroll D. Hall. San Francisco: Book Club of California, 1934.

Morris, Roy, Jr. *Ambrose Bierce: Alone in Bad Company.* New York: Oxford UP, 1995.

Rasmussen, R. Kent, ed. *The Quotable Mark Twain: His Essential Aphorisms, Witticisms, and Concise Opinions*. Chicago: Contemporary Books, 1997.

Sketches of the Sixties by Bret Harte and Mark Twain; Being forgotten material collected for the first time from "The Californian," 1864-1867. San Francisco: John Howell, 1927.

Starrett, Vincent. *Buried Caesars*. Chicago: Covici-McGee, 1923.

Towers, Tom. "'Never Thought We Might Want to Come Back.'" *Modern Fiction Studies* 21 (Winter 1975-76): 509-20.

Twain, Mark. *Adventures of Huckleberry Finn*. 1884. Ed. Victor Fischer and Lin Salamo. Berkeley: U of California P, 2002.

_____. *Best Short Stories of Mark Twain*. Ed. Lawrence I. Berkove. New York: Modern Library, 2004.

_____. *Collected Tales, Sketches, Speeches, and Essays, 1852-1910*. 2 vols. Ed. Louis J. Budd. New York: Library of America, 1992.

_____. *The Complete Essays of Mark Twain*. Ed. Charles Neider. Garden City, NY: Doubleday, 1963.

_____. *Early Tales and Sketches*. 2 vols. Ed. Edgar Marquess Branch and Robert H. Hirst. Berkeley: U of California P, 1979-1981.

_____. *Fables of Man*. Ed. John S. Tuckey. Berkeley: U of California P, 1972.

_____. *Letters from the Earth*. Ed. Bernard DeVoto. New York: Harper & Row, 1962.

_____. *Mark Twain's Letters*, vol. 6, *1874-1875*. Ed. Michael B. Frank and Harriet Elinor Smith. Berkeley: U of California P, 2002.

_____. *Mark Twain's Library of Humor*. 1888. New York: Bonanza, 1969.

_____. *Mark Twain's Mysterious Stranger Manuscripts*. Ed. William M. Gibson. Berkeley: University of California Press, 1969.

_____. *Notebooks and Journals*, vol. 3. Ed. Robert Pack Browning, Michael B. Frank, and Lin Salamo. Berkeley: U of California P, 1979.

_____. *A Pen Warmed-Up in Hell: Mark Twain in Protest*. Ed. Frederick Anderson. New York: Harper & Row, 1972.

CRITICAL
READINGS

Mark Twain as a Travel Writer_____

Larzer Ziff

As hateful as he insisted that he found the genre, Twain was to return to the travel book again and again after the 1880 publication of *A Tramp Abroad*. Most obviously he did so because unlike fiction, the rewards of which were never certain, his travel writing could, conservatively, be expected to produce a profit and, optimistically, to generate large earnings. Risk was all but eliminated by the fact that a travel book was made up in great part of letters that had been contracted and remunerated in advance by newspapers and magazines. Revenues from book sales, therefore, were in addition to income already realized from the work, albeit it was necessary to revise and supplement the journalistic letters before they found book form: they needed, as Twain said, "to have some of the wind and water squeezed out of them."[1] Those contracted letters, however, also obligated Twain to produce on schedule week after week for months at a stretch and he was a lazy man, or at least a man who forever called himself lazy because he did his best work at unanticipated hours and in unexpected seasons rather than within any regimen. He loathed the travel-letter arrangement as an affront to his constitution even as he abominated the sheer physical exertion and petty mental calculations connected with leaving one place only to set up in another which would soon be left. Characteristically he appears at his happiest—and his narratives are often at their best—not when he is at a site but when he has nothing to do but lie back in stagecoach or steamship and drawl on as he awaits an arrival he more than half-wishes will never come.

It is, nevertheless, a mistake to understand Twain's repeated return to the travel narrative as primarily linked to his financial circumstances. There is a deeper, more literary, connection. Twain was a master at revealing character through dialogue and capturing in the printed marks on the page the pitch and stress of the spoken American tongue—to read his work is to hear it. He could deploy the vocabularies and rhythms of a range of dialects, and tell a comic story past its climax but to the wistful, softly expressed afterthought that undermined that climax and brought the story tumbling down under its own weight; which is to say not only were his content and manner comic but so was his form. Twain, however, was not an accomplished maker of extended plots. He is at his best in his short pieces or in the incidents within his novels, while the plots of the novels as a whole rely upon coincidence and mistaken identities and often evoke the tedium of a good joke that goes on too long. Even *Huckleberry Finn*, his masterpiece, is weakened by the incongruity of the final episodes. . . .

In his last years, lying abed and dictating what he called his "Autobiography," Twain refused to proceed chronologically but insisted on jumping from the memory of a given event to the memory of another that his unreined mind associated with it even though the remembered events occurred decades apart and sometimes were further disconnected by one having been a personal experience and the other an item he had read in the newspaper. He justified this erratic—yet always traceable—course by claiming he had invented "a form and method whereby the past and the present are constantly brought face to face, resulting in contrasts which newly fire up the interest all along like contact of flint with steel" (*Autobiography*, 2:245). This seems a somewhat overstated justification for garrulous rambling, but, then, Twain at his best always rambled and to recognize this is to identify a fundamental connection between his mental and his physical wanderings.[2] A journey's serial progress from place to place stimulated his mind's parallel excursion along a path of linked memories. Far from being antipathetic to his literary practice as he often proclaimed it to be, travel writing was a perfect vehicle for Twain's imagination.[3]

* * *

Twenty-six years of age, Sam Clemens in 1861 headed for the Nevada Territory in flight from the Civil War and in pursuit of he knew not quite what. After the war had disrupted traffic on the Mississippi and put a halt to his budding career as a steamboat pilot on that river, he spent several weeks with a band of fellow Missouri townsmen who had formed themselves into a troop of Confederate irregulars. But not much time was needed to show him his essential inability to participate in the rituals of military discipline with a straight face—it seemed to be such playacting. When, moreover, the playacting turned grim with a shooting that led Clemens to fear that he may actually have participated in a killing, he was ready to make a rapid exit from the stage. His brother Orion was leaving for the West to take up the post of secretary to the governor of the Territory of Nevada and Sam set out with him. There he would do what just about every other man, young, old, and in-between was doing, try his hand at mining.

The flush times of Nevada silver and California gold were to find their most enduring image in the picture of them Clemens eventually drew after he became the author Mark Twain. But for some four years following his arrival in the Washoe in 1861 he worked and loafed with miners, exploding the charges that laid bare the vitals of the Nevada mountains, and skimming the skin off the California earth to sift through the beds of her hillside streams. More than once he thought sudden wealth was his, but the mineral fortune at his fingers' ends always managed to wriggle into the palm of another. Together with miners, vagabonds, speculators, horse traders, and courtroom hangers-on he played crude and often violent practical jokes upon newly arrived greenhorns, but from these Westerners he also learned the subtle art of the vernacular comic story—to tell it with a straight-faced seriousness that grew longer and graver in direct ratio to the outrageous improbability of what was being said.

Some seven years after he left the West, Twain told the story of his mining ventures in *Roughing It* (1872). When all of his attempts at working mines and trading in mine stocks had brought him up against the blank wall of failure, he said, a partner stirred him to make one last try at working their claim. Accordingly, armed with a long-handled shovel he descended into an eight-foot shaft in order to clear it of loose rocks and dirt: "You must brace the shovel forward with the side of your knees till it is full, and then, with a skilful toss, throw it backward over your left shoulder. I made the toss and landed the mess just on the edge of the shaft and it all came back on my head and down the back of my neck. I never said a word, but climbed out and walked home. I inwardly resolved that I would starve before I would make a target of myself and shoot rubbish at it with a long-handled shovel. I sat down and gave myself up to solid misery—so to speak."[4] "So to speak" qualifies the desperation considerably because it is at this point in his account that the failed miner reveals that he had earlier amused himself with writing letters to the Virginia City (Nevada) Daily *Territorial Enterprise*, which had printed them. Now returning to his cabin from his defeat at the end of a shovel he found a letter inviting him to become city editor of the *Enterprise* at a salary of twenty-five dollars a week. Although Sam Clemens did not then realize it, he had finally hit pay dirt. From that time forward he was to write for a living and refine the ore within himself into Mark Twain.

From Nevada Twain eventually drifted into California and continuing newspaper work which in March 1866 eventuated in his stepping aboard the *Ajax* to sail to the Hawaiian (Sandwich) Islands in order to furnish letters to the *Sacramento Union*. He spent four months and a day there, wrote twenty-five letters to the *Union* about the islands, and after his return to San Francisco, on the basis of the local fame his letters had earned he announced a public lecture on his experiences. He thus launched the platform career he was to continue to pursue throughout his working life, locked in the cycle of travel leading to writing leading to lecturing, which, of course, involved further travel that led to further writing, and so forth.

The Hawaiian letters were revised six years later to form the final chapters of *Roughing It* although they are rather disconnected from the pictures of the West that make up the greater part of the book. By that time Twain, an established author living in the East, had a national audience that consisted of *all* members of the average reading family—women and men, girls and boys—an uncommon phenomenon for an American author. His books were sold by subscription rather than in bookstores, the publisher's agent calling door-to-door with sample pages brimming with illustrations, and, equally important, sample bindings from cloth to hand-tooled Morocco, with which to entice a householder who in most cases purchased but one or two books a year into putting his name on the subscription list. The buyer, as Justin Kaplan writes "was typically rural, a farmer or small tradesman with little education, for whom bulk was an index of value" (p. 62); hence Twain's filling out a book about the continental West with the Hawaiian letters. Subscription books ran over 600 pages. George Ade, who grew up with such books, called them "front-room literature." They were not to be read from cover to cover any more than the front room itself was to be occupied on weekdays. . . .

Mark Twain's travel narratives combined into one audience readers customarily divided by different interests. It included not only women, the conventional readers of novels, and boys and young men, the conventional readers of sensational journal tales, but men who usually read nothing at all save the newspaper, the ledger, and the Bible. No American author of his time attracted so many male readers, and this massive quantitative addition to the limited reading public enjoyed by other authors early established and long maintained his celebrity. As the *St. Louis Republican* said of Twain's Sandwich Island lecture, delivered there in March 1867, "He succeeded in doing what we have seen Emerson and other literary men fail in attempting—he interested and amused a large and promiscuous audience."[5]

The distinctive approach that attracted male readers was developed in the days of Twain's Western journalism when he had no readership other than the kind of men with whom he had worked, drunk, and played in Virginia City, Angel's Camp, and San Francisco. The nature of such an audience may readily be inferred from a reading of the original travel letters from Hawaii. Although literate, its members are distrustful of the literary and welcome an outlook that validates their suspicion that diction is polished in direct proportion to its detachment from the actual—truth needs only plain talk. They are curious about the way other men in other places go about making a living and keen to improve the opportunities this may suggest to them, but they are proud to be Americans and savagely defensive in the face of older and more cultured societies. Willing to learn and even sympathize with the viewpoint of nonwhites they nevertheless equate being American with being white and however sympathetic they may be to others are not so to the point of relinquishing their feeling of superiority to them. Over the course of his career Twain came to disagree with many of the convictions held by such readers, but he never lost his sense of who they were and how their attention was to be held, even when he intended to laugh them out of their views and shame them into his.

Earlier, however, the author of the Hawaiian letters was very much one of the boys—booted, tobacco-chewing, westerners who are confident they are the true representatives of the national character. And, indeed, as with the addition of new states the nation became more western in the second half of the nineteenth century, so the national tone also became more western. Even easterners acknowledged there was something more American about a region that had never been under what Hawthorne called "the damned shadow of Europe." Learning his craft by addressing westerners, Mark Twain was, in effect, learning how to address a nation; William Dean Howells was to call him the "Lincoln of our literature."

The letters from Hawaii are a mix of keen observations that seek to inform and gross distortions that seek to amuse. In them Twain experiments with ways in which he can provide his readers with accurate physical descriptions of the islands, speculate on their potential value to the United States, and explain the nature of their government and society, yet keep those readers' attention with laughter. One solution was to provide himself with an invented companion who could stand in for the uneducated, rough-and-ready reader, rooted in the particulars of physical life and distrustful of idealization. This companion, Mr. Brown, can be relied upon to bring any excursion into the literary ether back to earth with a thump. He will respond to Twain's praise of the superior warmth of the Hawaiian climate and the superior cleanliness of the houses and streets of Honolulu when compared with San Francisco by complaining about the heat and detailing the awesome array of insects that annoy during the day and make sleep impossible at night. Both commentators invite laughter: the narrator Twain who has allowed himself to soar too far from the plane of actuality in his enthusiastic descriptions, and his pedestrian companion Brown who cannot grasp the larger implications of what he sees because of the flea bite on his hand. Twain is thus able to fulfill the travel narrative's obligation to provide description and information while also carrying on a comic critique of the travel form.

Brown is an amusing prop and he or his equivalents were to reappear in later travel narratives. But the more challenging task was to develop a single authorial voice that could be both funny yet listened to on serious matters, convey a sense of an ambience larger than the sum of particulars yet avoid the bookishness of what Bayard Taylor would call "earnest impressions." Even as Twain employed Brown he was moving to replace him by incorporating his outlook into a first-person account that could also see beyond the details. Most commonly he combined the two—the literary observer and the horse-sense commentator—by following up descriptions that might appear to be echoes of nineteenth-century parlor literature with a comment that undercut without quite disabling them. In *Innocents Abroad*, for example, he writes, "Toward nightfall, the next evening, we steamed into the great artificial harbor of the noble city of Marseilles, and saw the dying sunlight gild its clustering spires and ramparts, and flood its leagues of environing verdure with a mellow radiance that touched with an added charm the white villas that flecked the landscape far and near." Immediately after which he adds, the brackets are his. "[Copyright secured according to law.]"[6] If Twain thus satirizes conventional travel literature, he is having his cake as well as eating it: he does not mock the literary until he has shown that he can be literary if he so chooses. The laugh comes only after he has displayed what he can do. When he really wishes to marshall an all-out assault on descriptive twaddle he most frequently does so by carrying a passage to absurdity: "The table d'hote was served by waitresses dressed in the quaint and comely costume of the Swiss peasants. This consists of a simple gros de paine, trimmed with ashes of roses, with overskirt of sacre bleu ventre sans gris, cut bias on the off side, with facings of petit polonaise and narrow insertions of pate de fois gras backstitched to the mise en scene in the form of a jeu d'esprit" (*Tramp Abroad*, p. 340).

As early as the Hawaiian letters Twain evinced a stunning ability to use similes drawn from the banal, even vulgar, experience of his readers with which to picture with exactness the exotic. His taste was not always impeccable: "The red sun looked across the placid ocean through the tall, clean stems of the coconut trees," he told his California readers, "like a blooming whiskey bloat through the bars of a city prison."[7] An arrestingly precise picture, but one so coarse in tone it destroys what it achieves. More often than not, however, even while still addressing a California audience Twain was emerging from such slips in taste while retaining his striking eye for the simile that was both unexpected yet just right. The top of a coconut palm looks like "a feather duster struck by lightning" (p. 229); that's dead accurate. . . .

In one of the letters to the *Alta California*, Twain wrote on March 2, 1867 that "Prominent Brooklynites are getting up a great European pleasure excursion for the coming summer, which promises a vast amount of enjoyment for a very reasonable outlay" (p. 111). Originating among members of Henry Ward Beecher's Pilgrim Church, the leisurely excursion to the Holy Land by way of Europe would be made in a ship exclusively devoted to that purpose—no venture in group tourism on so extended a scale had ever before been undertaken. With the fare fixed at $1,250 in American currency and passengers advised to carry $500 in gold for further expenses, the *Quaker City* was to be equipped with a library, musical instruments, and a printing press for the production of a daily newspaper. The Reverend Henry Ward Beecher and General William Tecumseh Sherman were advertised to be among the 110 passengers the steamer would be accommodating on a voyage schedule to last from June to November although the possibility of its being extended if the passengers so desired was held open. "Isn't it an attractive scheme?" Twain wrote. "Five months of utter freedom from care and anxiety of every kind, and in company with a set of people who will go only to enjoy themselves, and will never mention a word about business during the voyage" (p. 113). His letter was both a report to the readers of the *Alta California* and a petition to its management to underwrite the cost of his participation.

The company who went "only to enjoy themselves" proved, on the whole, to be a dreary, hymn-singing lot of "venerable fossils." They duplicated on a large scale the characteristics of a devout believer Twain had observed on board the ship that had carried him from San Francisco to the Isthmus. During a storm when the sea flowed into the forward cabin and washed the carpet bags aft this pattern of devotion had clasped a stanchion with one arm and held it firmly as he prayed, while with the other arm he grabbed each carpet bag as it floated past, making sure it was not his before he reached out for another. "Any man of judgment cannot but think well of his modesty," Twain wrote, "in only relying on Providence to save the ship but looking out for his carpet sack himself" (*Travels with Mr Brown*, p. 17).

In the event, neither the Reverend Beecher nor General Sherman could make it—indeed even a well-advertised actress found she had other commitments. But if the celebrities could not make the voyage Mark Twain could and the voyage gained him a celebrity to rival Beecher and Sherman. He wrote fifty-eight letters about the tour to the *Alta California* as well as six for the New York *Tribune*, and one each for two other newspapers, but reprinted none verbatim when he assembled them into *The Innocents Abroad*. Published in July 1869, it "has been the most popular book of foreign travel ever written by an American."[8]

When he reported on Hawaii and his journey from California to New York, Twain described places about which a relatively scant literature existed. But he was keenly aware of the vast amount of writing that existed on France, Italy, and the Holy Land, and that his readers were, on the whole, familiar with it. "I make small pretence," he wrote at the outset, "of showing any one how he *ought* to look at objects of interest" (*Innocents*, p. v); that's what other books do. Rather he will suggest to the reader how he would see Europe if he looked with his own eyes rather than those of previous travelers.

This outlook led him to two bold, not to say outrageous, commitments: he would ignore sites that bored him, regardless of how famous they might be; and he would pit his opinions against the standing truths, however uncouth this might reveal him to be. Although he meant to be scornful of the Moors he observed in North Africa when he wrote that they "like other savages, learn by what they see; not what they hear or read" (p. 86); that was very much the kind of "savagery" to which he himself adhered in both his finest moments of comic deflation of the pompous and his worst moments of adolescent mockery of the cultivated.

The Innocents Abroad is a book about touring, not traveling, and that is its strength. The tour was laid out in advance and Twain embarked on it because everything had been prepared for him. He didn't know the language of any country he visited and his foreign acquaintanceship was limited to guides, hoteliers, waiters, and shopkeepers. At no point did he pretend otherwise or wish to alter this condition—to imagine he was a traveler rather than a mere tourist—because he brilliantly perceived that the originality of his work compared with other books of travel would reside in his paying closer attention to the tourist experience and to tourists themselves than to the places visited. *Innocents Abroad* is a book about the comic adventures of a group of tourists far more than it is about the places they visit. They are, indeed, innocents abroad, clueless as to where to go and how to react except as steered by guides and prompted by travel books and they are marvelously fit subjects for the comic art.

Although by dint of being their observer Twain separates himself from his fellows he does not absolve himself from being a tourist. In an echo of Bayard Taylor's refusal to wear the customary protections donned by tourists against the desert sun he remarks that "No Arab wears a brim to his fez, or uses an umbrella, or any thing to shade his eyes or his face," but unlike Taylor he spurns these not because he wishes to be like an Arab but because he sees what the others look like and doesn't want to look like them: "They travel single file; they all wear the endless white rag of Constantinople wrapped round their hats, and dangling down their backs; they all hold white umbrellas, lined with green, over their heads" (p. 466), and so costumed they ride bouncing along, knees up, elbows out, umbrellas popping up and down. "It will be bad enough to get sun-struck, without looking ridiculous into the bargain." (p. 467).

Unlike Taylor, too, is his opinion of foreigners. On Fayal in the Azores, "The community is eminently Portuguese—that is to say, it is slow, poor, shiftless, sleepy, and lazy" (p. 55). Italians are a happy, cheerful, contented, superstitious, poverty-stricken, indolent, and worthless lot. The "priestcraft" to which they submit "suits these people precisely; let them enjoy it, along with the rest of the animals" (p. 209). Arabs are filthy, squalid, simple, superstitious, disease-tortured creatures and are by nature a thankless and impassive race who possess all the distempers that are born of indolence and iniquity.

Such unqualified ridicule of other peoples is slightly leavened by the absoluteness with which it is affirmed, as if in being so sweeping Twain relies upon the reader's sense that these generalizations are completely subjective, offered as examples of his comic irascibility rather than as objective truths. Yet even granting this somewhat doubtful contention, the heaped-up diction of derision goes beyond comic intent or even scorn to convey an almost violent abhorrence of other peoples because they are not clean, not sensible, not industrious, not modern—not, in a word, American. His fellow tourists "entered the country [of the Bible] with their verdict already prepared, and they could no more write dispassionately and impartially about it than they could about their own wives and children" (p. 511). In opposition to such passionate partiality, however, Twain's authorial position was not one of dispassionate objectivity. Rather, he offered a different but equally passionate partiality. The comic corollary of seeing with one's own eyes demanded that conventional observations be contradicted, and so at times he not so much saw with his own eyes as with the eyes of others and then inverted the view.

At its best Twain's commitment to taking a position opposed to that of the most prominent travel books on the Holy Land results in sharp-eyed observations such as those on the Sea of Galilee, the oft-described "beauty" of which he exposes as a fiction, first by comparing it with the true beauty of Lake Tahoe, which is fresh in his memory, and then by quoting and analyzing the descriptions of the Sea of Galilee in revered texts (such as *The Crescent and the Cross* and *Tent Life in the Holy Land*) to show that those books actually unsay what they claim to say: "Nearly every book concerning Galilee and its lake describes the scenery as beautiful. No—not always straightforward as that. Sometimes the *impression* intentionally conveyed is that it is beautiful, at the same time that the author is careful not to *say* that it is in plain Saxon. But a careful analysis of these descriptions will show that the materials of which they are formed are not beautiful and can not be wrought into combinations that are beautiful" (pp. 510-11). Such close reading plays a significant part in all of Twain's writing because he believes, in effect, that deceptions, even authorial self-deceptions, will be betrayed by the very language in which they are presented. Ultimately his view of language is nominalistic; he does not believe in any reality that is larger than the sum of the observed details. At its worst such nominalism prevents the possibility of seeing a truth that may transcend the particulars of a scene. A group of Arabs lounging about a well, for example, reminds him of the biblical illustrations he had "worshipped" as a child except that in the pictures there was no dirt, desolation, ugly features, sore eyes, or raw-backed donkeys; no "disagreeable jabbering in unknown tongues; no stench of camels; no suggestion that a couple of tons of powder placed under the party and touched off would heighten the effect and give to the scene a genuine interest and a charm which it would always be pleasant to recall, even though a man lived a thousand years" (p. 544). When the crescendo of dislikes finally erupts into a fantasy of destruction we understand this is only comic exaggeration; what is actually being exploded are not real Arabs but the meretricious generalizations about life in the Holy Land (and by implication in the Bible) that run completely counter to observed details. And yet we may still remain disturbed. Must a keen eye for details necessarily blow to bits the possibility of seeing beyond them to a larger verity? The question applies to more than literary technique; it applies to how people whose everyday life differs radically in its details from those of the observer are to be understood by that observer.

"Travel and experience mar the grandest pictures and rob us of the most cherished traditions of our boyhood" (p. 597), Twain writes. What, then, do they supply? Why do tourists tour? Twain answers: "We wish to learn all the curious, outlandish ways of all the different countries, so that we can 'show off' and astonish people when we get home. We wish to excite the envy of our untraveled friends with our strange foreign fashions which we can't shake off. All our passengers are paying strict attention to this thing, with the end in view I have mentioned" (p. 233).

This adolescent desire to be envied, prominently on display in *Tom Sawyer*, for example, was a constant motivating factor in Twain's life. He went upon the river, he said, because of the distinction it would bring him in the eyes of the boys back home. " I first wanted to be a cabin-boy, so that I could come out with a white apron on and shake a table-cloth over the side, where all my old comrades could see me; later I thought I would rather be the deck-hand who stood on the end of the stage-plank with a coil of rope in his hand because he was particularly conspicuous,"[9] and finally, of course, he decided upon the most enviable position of all, steamboat pilot.

Similarly, when the war closed river traffic and he headed for the West, he did so, he said, because he envied his brother the glory he would acquire back home because of his travels, and he deliberately expressed this envy in terms of the comically naive wonder of an adolescent, even though he was at the time of going West twenty-six, and at the time of writing about it thirty-two: "Pretty soon he would be hundreds and hundreds of miles away on the great plains and deserts, and among the mountains of the Far West, and would see buffaloes and Indians, and prairie dogs, and antelopes, and have all kinds of adventures, and may be get hanged or scalped, and have ever such a fine time, and write home and tell us all about it, and be a hero" (*Roughing It*, p. 19). Reason enough, then, to accompany his brother and gain his share of the envy of those back home.[10]

This, however, is but half of the matter. In the sentences that follow his description of himself and his fellow tourists as traveling in order to be able to "astonish people when we get home," Twain writes: "The gentle reader will never, never know what a consummate ass he can become, until he goes abroad. I speak now, of course, in the supposition that the gentle reader has not been abroad, and therefore is not already a consummate ass" (p. 233), and therein resides the power of Twain's travel writing and the persisting appeal of *Innocents Abroad*. He is, as the other great nineteenth-century common man of American literature, Walt Whitman, said of himself, both in and out of the game. He can exploit the comic potential of his fellow tourists because he recognizes his share in their aspirations. His frequent reversion to an adolescent outlook is a constant reminder of his participation in the national naivete—the unsophistication of the plush-parlor, church-going, unliterary, provincial, flag-waving, American middle class—even while he satirizes it.

In the face of Old World civilization Twain's characteristic response is to bring to the monuments of European art an unabashedly materialistic yardstick and an aggressively patriotic political outlook. There is, doubtless, a good deal that is defensive about this. Unable to appreciate the aesthetics of masterpieces he is expected to admire he changes the frame of reference from art to politics and considers them in terms that permit him to reject them. So in Paris, "miles" of paintings by the old masters lead him to say: "Some of them were beautiful, but at the same time they carried such evidences about them of the cringing spirit of those great men that we found small pleasure in examining them. Their nauseous adulation of princely patrons was more prominent to me and chained my attention more surely than the charms of color and expression which are claimed to be in the pictures" (p. 137). If this is vulgar in the sense of lacking in refinement, it is vulgar also in the sense of being representative of ordinary people. Twain, too, had patrons, and patrons he could identify almost as precisely as could a painter employed by a nobleman, because his books were sold by subscription. He did not "cringe" to his patrons but he certainly spoke to them in terms of values he shared with them, and these were a respect for material attainment as a measure of worth and the belief that American democracy was the best political system in the world.

"Medicis are good enough for Florence," Twain writes. "Let her plant Medicis and build grand monuments over them to testify how gratefully she was wont to lick the hand that scourged her" (p. 245). His friends abuse him, he says, because he fails to see the beauty in the productions of the old masters. He cannot help but see it now and then, he admits, "but I keep on protesting against the groveling spirit that could persuade those masters to prostitute their noble talents to the adulation of such monsters as the French, Venetian and Florentine Princes of two and three hundred years ago" (p. 260). Whatever the shortcoming of his aesthetic sensibility his reaction carries the doughty strain of republicanism that may be viewed, for example, in John Adams's remark to Jefferson that "Every one of the fine Arts from the earliest times have been enlisted in the service of Superstition and Despotism."[11] Yet it also points to the feeling of inadequacy that arose within him when he confronted the civilizations of the Old World. Although he was able to cite his democratic instincts in defense of his uneasiness in the presence of the fine arts, he was unable to bring the same impulses to bear upon his reaction to the degradation he saw in the streets. Rather than regarding filth and poverty as the effect of the same political conditions that had reserved to a few the capacity to patronize art, he recoiled in disgust as if the condition of the poor was a natural consequence of their racial identity. In effect, Twain aestheticized the life of the common people whose lands he visited, finding it repellently ugly, even as he politicized the monuments of art, finding them socially oppressive. Underlying his shifting criteria was a desire to provide a rationale for his sorely challenged sense of American superiority.

The mechanical arts are the American arts, Twain asserts. Just as the popes have patronized and preserved art so "our new, practical Republic is the encourager and upholder of mechanics. In their Vatican is stored up all that is curious and beautiful in art; in our Patent Office is hoarded all that is curious or useful in mechanics" (p. 305). The imbalance of the comparison is glaring and the implication that fine arts and mechanical arts cannot coexist is faulty, but in this rambling giant of a book in which themes disappear to reemerge again, Twain can also be compelling when comparing European culture with American. He says of his inability to write about Rome: "What is there in Rome for me to see that others have not seen before me? What is there for me to touch that others have not touched? What is there for me to feel, to learn, to know, that shall thrill me before it pass to others? Nothing whatsoever" (p. 267). The series of questions is almost wistful, coming as it does from a writer who has most to say when a site has acquired a history of commentaries which he can proceed to demolish as he gets at the details before him. Twain's restraint appears to proceed from genuine awe. The overwhelming presence of Rome cannot be laughed away. With nothing left for him as a writer to discover, he turns the tables and in the pages following talks of what a resident of the Campagna would discover in America: people without a mother church; no foreign soldiers to protect the government; common literacy; glass windows; wooden houses; fire companies; insurance companies; newspapers;

printing presses; Jews treated just like human beings; people who can complain about the government and take hold of it themselves; people who know more than their grandfathers and employ modern mechanical methods. In its way this is, after all, a description of Rome.

The *Quaker City* called at the Azores, Gibraltar, Marseilles, Genoa, Leghorn, Civita Vecchia, Naples, Athens, Constantinople, Sebasatapol, Odessa, Yalta, and Smyrna, remaining at some ports long enough for the tourists to make extended excursions to inland cities or take overland routes and meet it at a further port of call. "Such was our daily life on board the ship—" Twain wrote after returning home, "solemnity, decorum, dinner, dominoes, devotion, slander. It was not lively enough for a pleasure trip; but if we had only had a corpse it would have made a noble funeral excursion" (p. 645). Yet traveling without the constant care of changes of vehicle, lodgings, and diet, without the problem of baggage transport and the nuisance of dealing with servants and officials suited him extremely well.

When the *Quaker City* stopped at Odessa for recoaling Twain was relieved to learn from his guidebooks that there were no sights to see in the city "and so we had one good, untrammeled holy day on our hands" (p. 388). Nothing so sets the tourist off from the traveler as does such an attitude which, until Twain converted it into comic art, was precisely what travel literature strove to avoid. "The voices raised against 'mere tourism,'" James Buzzard has written, "were often those raised also against the spread of technology and machinery" (p. 32); so that, for example, travel by rail was decried as antitravel. John Ruskin said that it was like being sent as a package. Mark Twain, however, reveled in the luxury of steamships and the speed of fast trains and constantly measured foreign life against the material standard achieved in America. Insofar as travel is seen as necessitating work for its results he emerges in *Innocents Abroad* as the consummate antitraveler even as his account of such antitravel endures as the most popular travel book ever written by an American.

* * *

Elisha Bliss, proprietor of the American Publishing Company, which had published *Innocents Abroad*, urged Twain to supply an account of his Western experiences to follow upon the great success of that book. Twain started on it in 1870, the year after *Innocents* was published, and *Roughing It* appeared in 1872. Like its predecessor it too was sold by subscription and it too contained more than 600 heavily illustrated pages. It did not, however, sell nearly so well. Considered as a physical object "the finished book showed too many seams, betraying its origin as a cut-and-paste operation with inconsistent text and careless drawings"[12] that placed it visually in the company of comic monthlies, editorial cartoons, and dime novels.

Yet with this said, *Roughing It* is clearly superior to *Innocents Abroad* as a literary work, and since Twain's day has been far more frequently reprinted. Its picture of the American West in the boom times that followed the gold rush and the unearthing of the Comstock Lode continues to be the classic portrait of that era and its comic episodes—the purchase of the genuine Mexican plug, the great landslide case, Buck Fanshaw's funeral, or the cat who didn't like quartz mining, to name a few—are fresh at each rereading because, unlike jokes that climax in a punch line, the joy they provide is embedded in the telling. *Innocents Abroad* was written unit by unit as the travels described were taking place, but *Roughing It* is a retrospective work. Although it too is largely episodic and often follows the path of associations rather than the track of travel, it has a theme that underlies the separate incidents and provides a unity lacking in *Innocents Abroad*. *Roughing It* is a narrative of travels that changed the traveler from an innocent into a veteran, in Western terms, from a greenhorn into an old settler—one great difference from the East being that in the West becoming an old settler is a matter of acquiring a set of habit-changing experiences rather than accumulating years of residence. And it is a narrative of the scenes and adventures that changed the bumptious young fool who piled into the stagecoach at St. Joseph and journeyed across the continent to Fort Laramie, South Pass, Salt Lake City, Carson City, and the California gold fields into a master storyteller. Significantly, although less apparently, it is also a view of the American West that for all the youthful naivete of its protagonist is informed by the maturity of an author who has traveled abroad and brings that knowledge to his sense of what is uniquely American.

Some seventy hours out of St. Joe and rolling along in a stagecoach, Twain saw his first coyote (which he consistently spelled "cayote") and described him thus: "The cayote is a long, slim, sick and sorry-looking skeleton, with a gray wolf-skin stretched over it, a tolerably bushy tail that forever sags down with a despairing expression of forsakenness and misery, a furtive and evil eye, and a long, sharp face, with slightly lifted lip and exposed teeth. He has a general slinking expression all over" (*Roughing It*, pp. 48-49). In fuller illustration of the coyote's manner, he describes what happens when a swift-footed dog, especially one that has a good opinion of himself, sets out to chase the coyote. The pursued coyote begins at a trot with a fraudful smile that encourages the dog who speeds up and, panting fiercely, approaches to within twenty feet of the coyote only to find that however great his exertion he cannot close that distance even though the mangy coyote still is going at a soft trot and, indeed, seems even to be slackening speed so as not to run away from him. Maddened the dog gives a last desperate burst, when in an instant there is a rushing sound and "behold that dog is solitary and alone in the midst of a vast solitude!" (p. 51). The dog recognizes too late that he has been fooled by the coyote's seeming shiftlessness into believing in his own superiority. He is taught differently through humiliation.

Many a reader of Twain has recognized in that anecdote a parable of Twain's Western experience. The trim and natty townsman looks at the shabby settler and is confident of his superiority. The shabby settler encourages him in this belief, indeed seems in effect to admit his inferiority. Yet somehow the dandy can never quite overtake the rustic in whatever dealing they have although not until the rustic decides the deception has gone on long enough and in an instant speeds away does it dawn upon him that instead of outsmarting the country yokel he has been taken in by him. In a series of early incidents in *Roughing It*, Twain is like the town dog—purchasing an uncontrollable nag under the impression that "genuine Mexican plug" is the name of a choice breed, giving himself up for dead in a blizzard when he is but fifteen steps from a station house as even his horse knows—ignorant of the ways of the West and confident in his eastern ways. But through a series of humiliations he learns to put on a face that no longer mirrors his mind, and like the coyote he takes on the coloration of his environment. The comic narrator who emerges does not betray any consciousness that the tale he tells is funny—the town dog would be chuckling in advance, approach his punch line with guffaws, and even repeat it a few times—but seems dead serious about his story and apparently puzzled by the laughter it evokes.

When after crossing Scott's Bluff Pass Twain first saw alkali water lying in the road, he recalls, it excited him because he could add it to the list of things which he had seen and many other people had not: it was "a thing to be mentioned with eclat in letters to the ignorant at home." But Twain the writer of this account is no longer the young fool who first saw alkali water, no longer, that is, a tourist, and he goes on to reflect that his brother and he were "the same sort of simpletons as those who climb unnecessarily the perilous peaks of Mont Blanc and the Matterhorn, and derive no pleasure from it except the reflection that it isn't a common experience" (pp. 72-73). Looking back on his Western experience through the lens of his more recent pilgrimage to Europe and the lands of the Bible, he saw that the value of travel resided in the shedding of false ideas of the world and the acquisition of self-knowledge rather than in the collection of sights to be displayed back home as tokens of one's superiority. Through travel Twain learned to unlearn sham beliefs, and *Innocents Abroad* is full of the fun of such unlearning. What might be called the greenhorn chapters of

Roughing It play further variations on the theme, but in the latter work one sees this negative process accompanied by the positive emergence of the man who was always there.

"Every now and then, in these days, the boys used to tell me I ought to get one Jim Blaine to tell me the stirring story of his grandfather's old ram—but they always added that I must not mention the matter unless Jim was drunk at the time—just comfortably and sociably drunk" (p. 383); so begins the fifty-third chapter of *Roughing It*. What follows is a small masterpiece that is not just Mark Twain in his prime but American humor at its best. Blaine gets drunk in the right degree one night, the boys summon Twain, they all crowd into the miner's small, candle-lit cabin, seat themselves on empty powder kegs, and Jim Blaine commences the story of the old ram: "There never was a more bullier old ram than what he was. Grandfather fetched him from Illinois—got him from a man by the name of Yates—Bill Yates—maybe you might have heard of him; his father was a deacon—Baptist—and he was a rustler, too; a man had to get up ruther early to get the start of old Thankful Yates; it was him put the Greens up to jining teams with my grandfather when he moved west" (p. 384). That first is the last mention of the celebrated ram. Mention of the Greens leads to Sarah Wilkerson whom Seth Green married which brings up Sile Hawkins who wanted to court her and so one name continues to lead to another, each attached to an incident or detail that vividly renders the person that bears the name: old Miss Wagner had to borrow a glass eye to receive company in but more often than not the glass eye dropped out without her noticing it, "being blind on that side you see;" Uncle Lem, standing under a scaffold, had his back broken in two places when a bricklayer with a hod full of bricks fell on him. That was no accident; divine providence had appointed him to be under the scaffold in order to break the bricklayer's fall. His dog was with him but was not appointed because he would have seen the man falling and stood from under: "A dog can't be depended on to carry out a special providence." And so Blaine's tale proceeds in a crescendo of violent yet harmless incidents, much in the manner of the maiming explosions that cheerfully occur in animated cartoons. Extraordinary as they are, the incidents are nevertheless grounded in the culture of rural, midwestern America. Although Blaine never gets back to the ram, his string of associations coheres into an indelible picture of a people and their ways: election day shenanigans, quiltings, Dorcas Society meetings, westward migrations, church affiliations. Moreover as one name reminds Blaine of another and he connects them through courtships, marriages, and deaths, despite the violence contained in almost every incident his discourse comes to resemble nothing so much as the talk at a family gathering, say at Thanksgiving, that is overheard by a curious child. As the elders catch up on family and neighborhood news, mention of one person leading to gossip about another, through their talk they in effect build the community into which the eavesdropping child is socialized.

Blaine's story is an ingeniously packed example of the larger coherence that can arise from an artful pursuit of associations. In his books, to be sure, Twain never followed his associative rambling in a direct line away from the starting point without once looking back. For example, a description of sagebrush as useful as a fuel but useless as a vegetable leads him to say that only mules and jackasses eat it, because, he muses, they and camels "have appetites that anything will relieve temporarily but nothing satisfy." When he was traveling in Syria, for example, a camel ate his overcoat and the contents of its pockets— percussion caps, cough candy, and fig paste—but choked to death on the manuscript letters he was writing for the home papers. Finally though, unlike Jim Blaine he does circle back: "I was about to say, when diverted from my subject, that occasionally one finds sagebrushes five or six feet high, and with a spread of branch and foliage in proportion" (p. 36). What the reader remembers, however is the camel not the sagebrush. The story of the old ram is both a conscious expansion into irresistible absurdity of an important structural element in all of Twain's travel writing and a breathtaking demonstration of the patterns of coherence that emerge when the mind is let loose to ramble. "Since I digress constantly," Twain finally tells himself, "perhaps it is as well to eschew apologies altogether and thus prevent their growing irksome" (p. 352). He's right.

The Indians in *Roughing It* are targets of Twain's not-so-funny irascibility as most foreign peoples were in *Innocents Abroad*, principally because he is intent on debunking the noble savages of Fenimore Cooper, Emerson Bennett, and the melodramas of the popular stage. Romance quickly falls away once an actual Indian is encountered, he says, and what one sees is treacherous, filthy, and repulsive. Where a literature exists Twain continues to seek originality in contradicting it, which is not, as has been observed of similar passages of *Innocents Abroad*, seeing with one's own eyes so much as it is seeing with the eyes of others but reversing the image they see.

Twain, however, looks more closely at the Chinese in the West than he does at the Indians. What had been written about them was, in the main, negative; Bayard Taylor's absolute terror at the idea of Chinese immigration into the country is an example. But Twain's positive view comes not so much from an automatic reversal of such literature as it does from personal observation of the Chinese community and a scorn for the kind of humanity represented by those who persecute the Chinese. In his comments on the subject he sounds a note that will grow stronger in each succeeding decade of his life as he increasingly attacks the ignorance and hypocrisy on which the complacencies of American social, political, and religious life are based, using his observations of other people to drive this message home. "All Chinamen can read, write and cipher with easy facility—pity but all our petted *voters* could" (p. 392), he writes with special reference to laws that discriminate against the Chinese. He characterizes the Chinese as industrious and quick to learn, sympathetically discusses their desire to be interred in China and the burial societies that exist for this purpose, and concludes:

They are a kindly disposed, well-meaning race, and are respected and well treated by the upper classes all over the Pacific coast. No Californian *gentleman or lady* ever abuses or oppresses a Chinaman under any circumstances, an explanation that seems to be much needed in the East. Only the scum of the population do it—they and their children; they, and naturally and consistently, the policemen and politicians, likewise, for they're the dust-licking pimps and slaves of the scum, there as elsewhere in America. (p. 397)

Henceforth he was to use exotic cultures to expose the hollow core of American self-satisfaction rather than to find those cultures wanting by American standards.

In *Roughing It* we are told of John Smith, a Nevada hay rancher, who becoming suddenly rich through his interest in a mine was able to travel in Europe. "When he came back he was never tired of telling about the fine hogs he had seen in England, and the gorgeous sheep he had seen in Spain, and the fine cattle he had noticed in the vicinity of Rome" (p. 321). John Smith advised everybody to travel because one could never imagine what surprising things there were in the world unless one did so. His story is offered as amusement, but there is a subtext. The hay rancher's failure to have had Westminster Abbey, the Escorial, or the Coliseum register upon his imagination while his mind remained, as it were, in the barnyard, may cause a laugh, but the burden of his tale is that he used his travel to reassess the value of what he knew best back home. On the larger scale of manners and morals this was how Mark Twain would come to approach his travel.

Excerpted from "Mark Twain" in *Return Passages: Great American Travel Writing, 1780-1910* (2000), pp. 171-180, 183-185, 187-200. Copyright © 2000 by the Yale University Press. Reprinted with permission of the Yale University Press.

Critical Insights

Notes

1. *Mark Twain's Autobiography* (New York: Harper & Brothers, 1924), 2 vols., 1:245.

2. In his excellent study, *Traveling in Mark Twain* (Berkeley: University of California Press, 1987), Richard Bridgman suggests that the mind's associative wandering is analogous to travel. Speaking of his study, Bridgman writes, "As the looseness of the travel account provided a particularly receptive vehicle for such materials, this essay is obliged to think as much about psychological patterns as geographical ones" (p. 4).

3. This extends to some of his fiction also, most notably *Huckleberry Finn*, which arranges its incidents along the line of a journey down the Mississippi and contains descriptions of the different kinds of communities and types of characters encountered along the way—a travelogue through Mississippi River society, circa 1845.

4. Mark Twain, *Roughing It* (New York: Oxford University Press, 1996), p. 294.

5. *Mark Twain's Travels with Mr. Brown*, ed. Franklin Walker & G. Ezra Dane (New York: Alfred A. Knopf, 1940), p. 136.

6. Mark Twain, *The Innocents Abroad* (New York: Oxford University Press, 1996), p. 93.

7. *Mark Twain's Letters from Hawaii*, ed. A. Grove Day (New York: Appleton-Century, 1966), p. 215.

8. *Traveling with the Innocents Abroad*, ed. Daniel Morely McKeithan (Norman: University of Oklahoma Press, 1958), p. xi.

9. Mark Twain, *Life on the Mississippi* (New York: Oxford University Press, 1966), p. 66.

10. In *The Beaten Track, European Tourism, Literature, and the Ways of Culture, 1800-1918* (Oxford: Clarendon Press, 1993), James Buzzard has argued that travelers such as Twain describes himself to be, and tourists such as he observes, travel in order to convert the " 'culture' encountered through travel into exchangeable items, tokens of cultural accomplishment that are legal tender in the sign-market of personal acculturation at home. . . . Symbols of Europe become commodities that tourists exchange by displaying them to an audience, which responds (or is imagined to respond) by recognizing the tourist as a person of culture" (p. 225). This is persuasive; Twain abroad with innocents admits as much when he talks of showing off back home. Moreover, as a writer of travel letters he does not even await the return home but "shows off" from the start.

11. *The Adams-Jefferson Letters*, ed. Lester J. Cappon (Chapel Hill: University of North Carolina Press, 1959), 2:502.

12. Beverly R. David & Ray Sapirstein, "Reading the Illustrations in *Roughing It*," p. 28, appended to the Oxford Edition, op. cit.

The Adventures of Tom Sawyer:
A Nightmare Vision of American Boyhood_____

Cynthia Griffin Wolff

Twain's second book of boyhood has more or less cornered one segment of the American Dream. Read with admiration (read during the
long years when *Moby-Dick* was relegated to obscurity), it captured
both our lofty goals and our tragic weaknesses; and if it is not "the"
American epic, it has epic dimensions. By comparison, its predecessor
seems unworthy of serious attention (a "comic idyll of boyhood," says
Leo Marx dismissively, on his way to a lengthy analysis of *The Adventures of Huckleberry Finn*)—no more than idealized reminiscences,
pulp fantasies of an "Everyboy." Yet Huck himself is more particular
about his antecedents: "You don't know about me," he says at the beginning of his story, "without you have read a book by the name of 'The Adventures of Tom Sawyer,' but that ain't no matter. That book was made
by Mr. Mark Twain, and he told the truth, mainly." In the first instance,
this is where he has "been before"—the world of this other fiction—and
one explanation for the questing need that fills Huck's own tale must be
found here, in the fabricated town of St. Petersburg on the Mississippi.

We are certainly correct to see Huck as heroic—an American Odys-
seus (or Hamlet); but if, for the sake of contrast, we diminish the complexity of Tom Sawyer's world—relegating it to the simplistic category
of "All-American Boyhood"—we will find ourselves led seriously
astray.

It is no easy thing for an adult American reader to get at the "real"
world of this novel. Our culture has provided us with too many colorful, fleshed-out reproductions of it: a bicentennial stamp depicting
Tom and the whitewashed fence; commemorative plates and pictures;
and countless stage and film productions—each one full of life and
merriment, each exuding the security of childhood-as-it-ought-to-be in
small-town America. And every one of these sentimental evocations is
false to the original.

In fact, Tom's world would be difficult to capture faithfully on film—impossible, perhaps, on stage: it is a phantom town inhabited largely by ghostly presences. Consider, for example, the buildings that actually appear in the novel; consider *all* of them. To begin with, there are private dwellings: Aunt Polly's house, Jeff Thatcher's house (where Becky visits), the Douglas mansion, the Welshman's farm, and the "haunted" house where Tom and Huck so nearly lose their lives. Then there are institutional buildings designed specifically to bedevil an active boy: the church and the schoolhouse. However, all of these— houses, church, school—are places from which an average, energetic male youth is expected to flee: "his" world, the world to be explored and conquered, lies beyond—in lush Edenic woods, a river, and (presumably) a healthy, industrious town of tolerable size. And here the shadow world begins. There is a river; there are woods. But of the town, only menacing fragments await. Two taverns (one housing criminals), a courthouse, a jail, and a deserted slaughterhouse. Nothing more.

Let us be more specific. No stores are mentioned in the novel. No blacksmiths. No livery stable. No bank. Mark Twain, who renders the steamboat's arrival so vibrantly in *Life on the Mississippi*, put no busy wharf in the world of this fiction—no commercial steamboat traffic at all. Every bit of the bustling business that an impressionable reader might impute to Tom Sawyer's world is, in fact, notably absent from the novel; the only downtown buildings that actually do appear in the St. Petersburg of Twain's creation are those few grisly emblems of crime and punishment. Two taverns, a courthouse, a jail, and a deserted slaughterhouse.

Placed against this somber background is a complex society of children, so tightly knit and so emotionally engaging that it tends to dominate the reader's attention. Ben Rogers and Billy Fisher and Joe Harper and Amy Lawrence and Jeff Thatcher: such names in this novel attach to people with specific histories and relationships, friendships and enmities, all of the subtle qualities that make them seem distinctive and "real." The slow accretion of this children's world renders Tom's and Huck's activities with a kind of palpable, three-dimensional plausibility.

> "Say—what is dead cats good for, Huck?"
>
> "Good for? Cure warts with."
>
> "No! Is that so? I know something that's better."
>
> "I bet you don't. What is it?"
>
> "Why spunk-water."
>
> "Spunk-water! I wouldn't give a dern for spunk-water."
>
> "You wouldn't, wouldn't you? D'you ever try it?"
>
> "No, I hain't. But Bob Tanner did."
>
> "Who told you so?"
>
> "Why he told Jeff Thatcher, and Jeff told Johnny Baker, and Johnny told Jim Hollis, and Jim told Ben Rogers and Ben told a nigger, and the nigger told me. There now!"

The very vividness of these children, then, makes all the more remarkable the peculiar air of vagueness, of faceless generality, that permeates Twain's evocations of most adult gatherings.

Consider these paragraphs describing Muff Potter's capture:

> Close upon the hour of noon the whole village was suddenly electrified with the ghastly news. No need of the as yet undreamed-of telegraph; the tale flew from man to man, from group to group, from house to house, with little less than telegraphic speed. . . . Horsemen had departed down all the roads in every direction and the Sheriff "was confident" that he would be captured before night.
>
> All the town was drifting toward the graveyard. Tom's heartbreak vanished and he joined the procession. . . . Arrived at the dreadful place, he wormed his small body through the crowd and saw the dismal spectacle. . . . He turned, and his eyes met Huckleberry's. Then both looked elsewhere at once, and wondered if anybody had noticed anything in their mutual glance. But everybody was talking. . . .

"Poor fellow!" . . . "Muff Potter'll hang for this if they catch him!" This was the drift of the remark; and the minister said, "It was a judgment; His hand is here."

Now Tom shivered from head to heel; for his eye fell upon the stolid face of Injun Joe. At this moment the crowd began to sway and struggle, and voices shouted, "It's him! it's him! he's coming himself!"

"Who? Who?" from twenty voices.

"Muff Potter!" . . .

People in the branches of the trees over Tom's head said he wasn't trying to get away—he only looked doubtful and perplexed.

"Infernal impudence!" said a bystander.

Here we have a convocation of most of the townsfolk. Yet not one is given a name (only the "outsiders"—Muff Potter and Injun Joe). Instead, there is a torrent of collective nouns: whole village, man to man, group to group, horsemen, all the town, the crowd, anybody, everybody, the crowd, voices, people, a bystander. Even the dignitaries remain nameless; they are merely "the Sheriff" and "the minister." When it is compared with the density of the scenes depicting children, this collection of citizens becomes vaporous: as "people" within the novel, they can scarcely be said to exist. No more than anonymous shadows—appropriate, indeed, to the illusory town of which they are citizens. Small wonder, then, that films and pictures falsify. Of necessity they give substance to entities—buildings and businesses and hurrying, excited people—that either do not exist at all within this fictional world or are, at best, only partially realized.

Since this is a boy's story, it is only fair to ask what a boy in such a world might make of himself. Given the character of the town Twain has created, given the social possibilities of St. Petersburg as we know it through this novel, what will Tom Sawyer become when he is a man? The question cannot be answered.

Initially Twain had intended the novel to be a kind of *bildungsroman*: as Justin Kaplan reports, it was to have had four parts—"'1,

Boyhood & youth; 2 y & early manh; 3 the Battle of Life in many lands; 4 (age 37 to [40?]).'" Yet the finished novel shows no sign of this early intention. In fact, Twain writes his "conclusion" with a kind of defensive bravado: "So endeth this chronicle. It being strictly a history of a *boy*, it must stop here; the story could not go much further without becoming the history of a *man*." At least one reason for the author's decision may be found in the very nature of the world he was moved to create. There are no available men in it—no men whom Tom can fancy himself imitating—no newspaper office with a garrulous editor, no general store owner to purvey gossip and candy, no lawyer lounging in an office buzzing with flies and heavy with the odor of musty books. Of course there *is* Judge Thatcher, "a fine, portly, middle-aged gentleman with iron-gray hair." But Judge Thatcher presides in the county seat, twelve miles away; he enters the novel only very briefly in chapter IV (to witness Tom's triumph-turned-humiliation in Bible class) and thereafter disappears entirely until chapter XXXII, when he is summoned to rejoice in the safe return of the children from the cave. Many adults who have not read *Tom Sawyer* since the days of their youth are apt to recall Judge Thatcher as a rather more vivid personage than he truly is in the novel. Perhaps we are recollecting cinematic images, or perhaps our own imaginations supply his presence because we feel compelled to remedy the novel's deficiencies and "normalize" the town. But the stubborn fact remains. The town is not normal, certainly not congenial to a boy's coming of age.

It is, of course, a matriarchy (and in this respect, contrasts markedly with the various patriarchal systems that Huck encounters in his journey down the river), a world that holds small boys in bondage. The town that we are shown in this book is saturated with gentility, that is, with women's notions. A man may dispense Bible tickets or conduct the ceremony on Sundays; but the church service, the Sunday School exercises, the daily ritual of family prayers—these are all clearly defined as fundamental components of something that Aunt Polly (and other women like her) have defined as "duty" or "morality." Similarly,

          Critical Insights

the mayor himself may judge the elocution contest; but this masculine salute to "culture" merely reinforces already established female allegiances to the melancholy and banally "eloquent" in literature. The very opening word of the novel establishes the situation. "'Tom!'" The boy's name called by his impatient aunt. "'Tom!'" The demanding tone permeates the novel, no other voice so penetrating or intrusive. What is a male child to do against this diminutive drill master? Surrender is out of the question: the dismal results of capitulation greet him in mournful, not quite masculine figures. Mr. Walters, the superintendent of the Sunday School, "a slim creature of thirty-five, with a sandy goatee and short sandy hair; he wore a stiff standing-collar . . . a fence that compelled a straight lookout ahead, and a turning of the whole body when a side view was required." And, more contemptible, "the Model Boy, Willie Mufferson [who took] as heedful care of his mother as if she were cut glass. He always brought his mother to church, and was the pride of all the matrons. The boys all hated him, he was so good."

Rebellion, however, is no easy thing to manage. Tom cannot bring himself to dislike Aunt Polly. Occasionally, he admits to loving her; and when he genuinely saddens her (as during his disappearance to the island), he discovers that "his heart [is] full of pity for her." Pity and its cousin guilt: these are Aunt Polly's most formidable weapons (no less so for being used without guile). "'She never licks anybody,'" Tom complains as he sets about beginning to whitewash the fence. "'She talks awful, but talk don't hurt—anyways it don't if she don't cry.'" Tom might be able to contend with open anger, but he receives only reproaches that insinuate themselves into that budding thing called "conscience." Discovered after a stealthy trip abroad at night, "Tom almost brightened in the hope that he was going to be flogged; but it was not so. His aunt wept over him and asked him how he could go and break her old heart so; and finally told him to go on, and ruin himself and bring her gray hairs with sorrow to the grave, for it was no use for her to try any more. This was worse than a thousand whippings, and Tom's heart was sorer now than his body. He cried, he pleaded for forgiveness, promised to reform over and over again." In Tom's world, female children are no easier to deal with than their adult models. Becky Thatcher rules him by alternating tears with lofty reproaches; and although Tom's angry feelings toward her are a good deal more available to him than any genuinely hostile feelings he might have toward the generation of mothers, he nonetheless continues to wish for a more direct and "manly" emotional code. "He was in a fine rage. . . . He moped into the schoolyard wishing she were a boy, and imagining how he would trounce her if she were."

With no acceptable model of "free" adult masculinity available, Tom does his best to cope with the prevailing feminine system without being irretrievably contaminated by it. His principal recourse is an entire repertoire of games and pranks and superstitions, the unifying motif of which is a struggle for control. Control over his relationship with Aunt Polly is a major area of warfare. Thus the first scene in the book is but one type of behavior that is repeated in ritual form throughout the book. Tom, caught with his hands in the jam jar—about to be switched. "'My! Look behind you, aunt!' The old lady whirled round, and snatched her skirts out of danger. The lad fled, on the instant, scrambled up the high board fence, and disappeared over it. His Aunt Polly stood surprised a moment, and then broke into a gentle laugh. 'Hang the boy, can't I never learn anything? Ain't he played me tricks enough like that for me to be looking out for him by this time?'" Crawling out his bedroom window at night is another type of such behavior, not important because it permits this or that specific act, but significant as a general assertion of the right to govern his own comings and goings. Bartering is still another type of this behavior. Trading for blue Bible coupons or tricking his playmates into painting the fence—these are superb inventions to win the prizes of a genteel society without ever genuinely submitting to it.

The logical continuation of such stratagems would be actual defiance: the rebellion of authentic adolescence to be followed by a manhood in which Tom and his peers might define the rules by which society is to be governed. But manhood never comes to Tom; anger and defiance remain disguised in the games of childhood.

Twain offers these pranks to us as if they were no more than humorous anecdotes; Aunt Polly is always more disposed to smile at them than to take them seriously. However, an acquiescence to the merely comic in this fiction will blind us to its darker side. A boy who seeks to control himself and his world so thoroughly is a boy deeply and constantly aware of danger—justifiably so, it would seem, for an ominous air of violence hangs over the entire tale. It erupts even into the apparently safe domestic sphere.

When the children depart from their schoolmaster in chapter XXI to begin the lazy summer recess, they leave him disgraced—his gilded, bald pate blazing as the ultimate spectacle in the school's pageant. "The boys were avenged. Vacation had come." Mr. Dobbin (even his name invites laughter) is hilariously humiliated, and he is apt to linger in our memories primarily as the butt of a good joke. Yet for most of the children most of the time, he is a source of genuine terror.

The one "respectable" man whom Tom sees regularly, Mr. Dobbin, is a sadist. Having reached maturity with the unsatisfied ambition to be a doctor, he spends his free time perusing a book of "anatomy" (that is, a book with pictures of naked people in it). His principal active pleasure is lashing the children, and the preparations for the approaching commencement exercises merely provide an excuse to be "severer and more exacting than ever. . . . His rod and his ferule were seldom idle now—at least among the smaller pupils. . . . Mr. Dobbin's lashings were very vigorous ones, too; for although he carried, under his wig, a perfectly bald and shiny head, he had only reached middle age and there was no sign of feebleness in his muscle. As the great day approached, all the tyranny that was in him came to the surface; he seemed to take a vindictive pleasure in punishing the least shortcomings." If the village itself (with taverns, courthouse, jail, and deserted slaughterhouse) is composed of the elements of crime and punishment, then Mr. Dobbin might be construed as one of the executioners—-

disarmed at only the final moment by the boys' "revenge" and exiting to catcalls and laughter. The joke is a fine exercise in imaginative power, but it does not fully succeed in countering the potency of the masculine "muscle" that is used with such consistent vindictiveness and violence.

Violence is everywhere in Tom's world. Escape to the island does not answer: random, pitiless destruction can find a frightened boy just as lightning, by chance, can blast a great sycamore to fall on the children's camp and signify that catastrophe is never far away.

Clearly, Tom is a major figure in the play of violence, yet his part is not clear. Is he victim or perpetrator? Is the violence outside of him, or is it a cosmic reflection of something that is fundamental to his own nature?

His games, for example, have a most idiosyncratic quality; the rebellion and rage that never fully surface in his dealings with Aunt Polly and the other figures of authority in this matriarchal world find splendid ventilation in fantasy. Richly invigorated by his imagination, Tom can blend the elements of violence and control exactly to suit his fancy. Acquiescent to society's tenets in real life, in daydreams Tom is always a rebel.

> The idea of being a clown recurred to him now, only to fill him with disgust. For frivolity and jokes and spotted tights were an offense, when they intruded themselves upon a spirit that was exalted into the vague and august realm of the romantic. No, he would be a soldier. . . . No—better still, he would join the Indians, and hunt buffaloes and go on the warpath in the mountain ranges and the trackless great plains of the Far West, and away in the future come back a great chief, bristling with feathers, hideous with paint, and prance into Sunday school, some drowsy summer morning, with a blood-curdling war-whoop, and sear the eyeballs of all his companions with unappeasable envy.

Safe in his own fictional world, Tom participates in carefully constructed rituals of devastation. He and his cohorts may be outlaws of any kind; however, whatever roles they choose, there are always careful sets of regulations to be followed. In games, control reigns supreme: "'Guy of Guisborne wants no man's pass. Who art thou that—that—' 'Dares to hold such language,' said Tom prompting—for they talked 'by the book,' from memory."

The real import of these rules—this rigid regimentation of boyish fantasy—becomes clear several times in the novel as the children play. "Huck said: 'What does pirates have to do?' Tom said: 'Oh, they have just a bully time—take ships and burn them, and get the money and bury it in awful places in their island. . . .' 'And they carry the women to the island,' said Joe; 'they don't kill the women.' 'No,' assented Tom, 'they don't kill the women—they're too noble.'" And at the conclusion:

> "Tom Sawyer's Gang—it sounds splendid, don't it Huck?"
>
> "Well, it just does, Tom. And who'll we rob?"
>
> "Oh, most anybody. Waylay people—that's mostly the way."
>
> "And kill them?"
>
> "No, not always. Hide them in the cave till they raise a ransom."
>
> "What's a ransom?"
>
> "Money. You make them raise all they can. . . . That's the general way. Only you don't kill the women. You shut up the women, but you don't kill them. . . . It's so in all the books."

Pirates and robbers and Indians. Such are the figures of Tom's creation; and so long as they remain merely imaginary, governed by the "code" of play, they are clearly harmless. "You don't kill women. . . . It's so in all the books."

Given the precarious balancing of control and violence in Tom's fantasies, we can easily comprehend his terrified fascination with Injun Joe's incursions into the "safety" of St. Petersburg. Accidentally witness to Injun Joe's murderous attack, Tom's first response is characteristic: he writes an oath in blood, pledging secrecy. "Huck Finn and Tom Sawyer swears they will keep mum about this and they wish they may Drop down dead in Their tracks if they ever tell and Rot." It is an essentially "literary" maneuver, and Tom's superstitious faith in its efficacy is of a piece with the "rules" he has conned from books about outlaws. However, Injun Joe cannot easily be relegated to the realm of such villains. It is as if one element in Tom's fantasy world has torn loose and broken away from him, roaming restlessly—a ruthless predator—genuinely and mortally dangerous.

He has murdered a man, but perversely, he does not flee. Instead, he loiters about the town in disguise, waiting for the moment to arrive when he can take "revenge." Humiliated once by the Widow Douglas's husband (no longer available to the Indian's rage), Joe plans to work his will upon the surviving mate. "'Oh, don't kill her! Don't do that!'" his nameless companion implores.

> "Kill? Who said anything about killing? I would kill *him* if he was here; but not her. When you want to get revenge on a woman you don't kill her—bosh! you go for her looks. You slit her nostrils—you notch her ears like a sow! . . . I'll tie her to the bed. If she bleeds to death, is that my fault? I'll not cry, if she does."

It is almost a parody of Tom's concocted "rules" for outlaws; even Injun Joe flinches from killing a woman. Sadistic torture (of a clearly sexual nature) is sufficient.

His grievance is twofold: against the absence of the man who would be his natural antagonist; and then against the woman who has inherited the man's property and authority. Seen in this light, his condition is not unlike the hero's. Tom, denied the example of mature men whom he might emulate, left with no model to define an adult nature of his own. Tom, adrift in a matriarchal world—paying the continuous "punishment" of guilt for the "crime" of his resentment at genteel restraints, conceiving carefully measured fantasies within which to voice (and mute) his feelings. Injun Joe is Tom's shadow self, a potential for retrogression and destructiveness that cannot be permitted abroad.

Yet genuine vanquishment is no easy task. No other adult male plays so dominant a role in the novel as Injun Joe. Indeed, no other male's name save Huck's and Tom's is uttered so often. The only contender for adult masculine prominence is that other angry man, Mr. Dobbin. But the schoolmaster's vicious instincts are, in the end, susceptible to control through humor: he can be humiliated and disarmed by means of a practical joke. After all is said and done, he is an "acceptable" male, that is, a domesticated creature. The Indian, an outcast and a savage, is unpredictable; he may turn fury upon the villagers or act as ultimate executioner for Tom. When Tom's tentative literary gestures prove insufficient, desperate remedies are necessary. Twain invokes the ultimate adventure. Death.

Death has several meanings for Tom. On the one hand, it is the final loss of self—a relinquishment of control that is both attractive and frightening. Confronted with reverses, Tom sometimes longs for the blissful passivity of death, deterred primarily by the sneaking fear that "guilt" might be "punishable" even in the unknown land to which he would travel. "It seemed to him that life was but a trouble, at best, and he more than half envied Jimmy Hodges, so lately released; it must be very peaceful, he thought, to lie and slumber and dream forever and ever, with the wind whispering through the tree and caressing the grass and the flowers over the grave, and nothing to bother and grieve about, ever any more. If he only had a clean Sunday-school record he could be willing to go, and be done with it all."

On the other hand, properly managed, "death" might be the ultimate assertion of control, the means a boy might use in this puzzling female world to win a satisfactory "self" after all. "Ah," Tom's fantasy runs, "if he could only die *temporarily!*"

The triumph of "temporary death" and the fulfillment of that universal fantasy—to attend one's own funeral and hear the tearful eulogies and then to parade boldly down the aisle (patently and impudently alive)—is the central event in the novel. The escapade is not without its trials: a terrible lonesomeness during the self-imposed banishment and a general sense of emptiness whenever Tom falls to "gazing longingly across the wide river to where the village lay drowsing in the sun." Yet the victory is more than worth the pain. Temporarily, at least, Tom's fondest ambitions for himself have come true. "What a hero Tom was become, now! He did not go skipping and prancing, but moved with a dignified swagger as became a pirate who felt that the public eye was on him." He has definitely become "somebody" for a while—and he has achieved the identity entirely upon his own terms.

Yet this central miracle of resurrection is merely a rehearsal. Its results are not permanent, and Tom must once again submit to death and rebirth in order to dispatch the specter of Injun Joe forever.

The escapade begins lightheartedly enough: a party and a picnic up river into the countryside. Yet this moderated excursion into wilderness turns nightmare in the depths of the cave. "It was said that one might wander days and nights together through its intricate tangle of rifts and chasms, and never find the end of the cave. . . . No man 'knew' the cave. That was an impossible thing." Existing out of time, the cave is a remnant of man's prehistory—a dark and savage place, both fascinating and deadly. Once lost in the cave, Tom and Becky must face their elemental needs—hunger, thirst, and the horror, now quite real, of extinction. For Tom alone, an additional confrontation awaits: he stumbles upon Injun Joe, who has taken refuge in this uttermost region. The temptation to despair is very great; however, "hunger and wretchedness rise superior to fears in the long run. . . . [Tom] felt willing to risk Injun Joe and all other terrors." Thus he begins his long struggle out. Holding a length of a string lest he be separated from Becky, he tries one dark pathway, then another, then "a third to the fullest stretch of the kite-line, and was about to turn back when he glimpsed a far-off speck that looked like daylight; dropped the line and groped toward it, pushed his head and shoulders through a small hole and saw the broad Mississippi rolling by!" Born again upon his beloved river, Tom has earned his reward.

Afterwards, as Tom recounts his adventures to an admiring audience, he becomes a "hero" once again—now the hero of his own adventure story. Even more, he has become rich from finding buried treasure; Judge Thatcher conceives a great opinion of his future and says that he hopes "to see Tom a great lawyer or a great soldier some day." Endowed with an excess of acceptable identities which have been conferred upon him as the result of his exploits (no clearer, certainly, about the particulars of the adult male roles identified by them, but nonetheless christened, as it were, into the "rightful" inheritance of them), Tom seems to have surmounted the deficiencies of his world.

Yet it is a hollow victory after all. Just as Tom must take on faith the pronouncement of his future as a "great lawyer" or a "great soldier" (having no first-hand information about these occupations), so we must accept the validity of his "triumph." The necessary condition for Tom's final peace of mind (and for his acquisition of the fortune) is the elimination of Injun Joe. And this event occurs quite accidentally. Taking the children's peril as a warning, the villagers have shut the big door to the cave and triple-bolted it, trapping Injun Joe inside. When the full consequences of the act are discovered, it is too late; the outcast has died. "Injun Joe lay stretched upon the ground, dead, with his face close to the crack of the door. . . . Tom was touched, for he knew by his own experience how this wretch had suffered. . . . Nevertheless he felt an abounding sense of relief and security, now."

Tom's final identification with the savage, valid as it certainly is, gives the lie to the conclusion of this tale. What do they share? Something irrational and atavistic, something ineradicable in human nature. Anger, perhaps; violence, perhaps. Some unnamed, timeless element.

The poor unfortunate had starved to death. In one place near at hand, a stalagmite had been slowly growing up from the ground for ages, builded by the water-drip from a stalactite overhead. The captive had broken off the stalagmite, and upon the stump had placed a stone, wherein he had scooped a shallow hollow to catch the precious drop that fell once in every three minutes with the dreary regularity of a clock-tick—a dessert-spoonful once in four-and-twenty hours. That drop was falling when the Pyramids were new; when Troy fell; when the foundations of Rome were laid; when Christ was crucified; when the Conqueror created the British empire; when Columbus sailed; when the massacre at Lexington was "news." It is falling now; it will still be falling when all these things shall have sunk down the afternoon of history and the twilight of tradition and been swallowed up in the thick night of oblivion. . . . It is many and many a year since the hapless half-breed scooped out the stone to catch the priceless drops, but to this day the tourist stares longest at that pathetic stone and that slow-dropping water when he comes to see the wonders of McDougal's Cave. Injun Joe's cup stands first in the list of the cavern's marvels; even "Aladin's Palace" cannot rival it.

Whatever Injun Joe represents in this fiction—whatever his complex relationship may be to Tom—he cannot be dealt with by summary banishment. Shut up by fiat; locked away. It is an ending with no resolution at all.

Taken seriously as a psychological recommendation, the ultimate disposition of the problem of Injun Joe offers no solution but that of denial. Lock away the small boy's anger; lock away his anti-social impulses; shut up his resentments at this totally feminine world; stifle rebellion; ignore adult male hostility: they are all too dangerous to traffic with.

Thus Tom's final "self" as we see it in this novel is a tragic capitulation: he has accommodated himself to the oddities of his environment and given over resistance. A resolution to the story is established not by changing the bizarre quality of the fictional world (not even by confronting it), but by contorting the small hero into compliance. He becomes that worst of all possible things—a "Model Boy"—the voice of conformity in a genteel society. Huck complains. "'The widder eats by a bell. . . . Everybody's so awful reg'lar a body can't stand it.'" And Tom responds. "'Well, everybody does that way, Huck. . . . If you'll try this thing just awhile longer you'll come to like it. . . . Huck, we can't let you into the gang if you ain't respectable you know.'"

He has even lost his sense of humor.

The fault is Twain's, of course. Tom has earned the right to "be somebody"; but his creator's vision has faltered. Twain averts his attention from the struggle that should be central and shrinks from uncivilized inclinations. In the end, his hero must settle for security in a world that will always be run by its women.

However, Huck continues doubtful. And in his own book, he pursues the quest for fathers. Fully to understand his needs, we must know—exactly—where he has been before. Here, in *The Adventures of Tom Sawyer*.

From *The Massachusetts Review* 21, no. 4 (1980): 93-105. Copyright © 1980 by *The Massachusetts Review*. Reprinted by permission from *The Massachusetts Review*.

The Realism of *Huckleberry Finn*_____

Tom Quirk

"Hast seen the White Whale?" gritted Ahab in reply.

"No; only heard of him; but don't believe in him at all," said the other good-humoredly. "Come aboard!"

"Thou are too damned jolly. Sail on. Hast lost any men?"

"Not enough to speak of—two islanders, that's all;—but come aboard."

—*Moby-Dick*, chapter 115, "The *Pequod* Meets the *Bachelor*"

"It warn't the grounding—that didn't keep us back but a little. We blowed out a cylinder-head."

"Good gracious! anybody hurt?"

"No'm. Killed a nigger."

"Well, it's lucky; because sometimes people do get hurt."

—*Adventures of Huckleberry Finn*, chapter 32

I

The second of these passages, too familiar to require much commentary, is frequently instanced as a dramatic rendering of much that is noteworthy about *Huckleberry Finn*: the centrality to the novel's purpose of questions of racial prejudice; the transparent irony disclosed in Aunt Sally's anxious question and her genuine relief that no "people" were injured; the canniness of Huck himself, who, though perplexed by this sudden relative who calls him "Tom," knows enough about human nature to invent yet another fictional experience and to adopt yet another persona on the instant, but who is totally unaware of the satire, irony, or humor of his own remark. Huck knows his audience *inside* the novel; time and again he sizes up his situation in an antagonistic adult world and plays to the several desires, fears, and biases of those who confront or question him. However (despite his amiable introduction to us in the opening paragraph, his final summary complaint about the "trouble" he has had telling his story, and his closing adieu, "YOURS TRULY, HUCK FINN"), Huck is often indifferent to or ignorant of his effects upon an audience *outside* the book, which is to say us as readers.

If realism depends upon a certain consensual understanding of the world, an understanding, that is, of what Henry James said we cannot, one way or another, "not know," then the realism of *Huckleberry Finn* stands in peculiar relation to other realist works. As Michael Davitt Bell has shown, Twain's attachment to the announced principles of literary realism is tenuous at best,[1] and what is true for Twain is even more true for his young narrator. For Huck not only does not knowingly participate in this consensus understanding, but he also is supremely unqualified to render it in his narrative. Time and again, Huck proves that he can readily adapt to the moves of the game, but no one has taught him the logic of it. The origins of feuds, the behavior of pirates and robbers, the decor of the Grangerford house, the prerogatives of royalty, all these remain obscure and mysterious to him, but he quickly sizes up the situation and plays his part as best he can.

The first passage comes from as famous a book. Yet so far as I know this exchange and its coincidentally parallel expression in *Huckleberry Finn* have gone virtually unnoticed. There may be several explanations for this. Among them, and one perhaps worth exploring, involves the difference between the romanticism of *Moby-Dick* and the realism of *Huckleberry Finn*. That difference may be as simple as the distinction between motive and action, the difference, that is, between quest and escape—between the pursuit (all defiant of necessity and contingency, fixed upon some insane object and driven by some overruling passion) and the "scrape" (the unanticipated event somehow managed, eluded, or negotiated). Ahab bends the will of his crew to his purpose and dispenses with genial observances and courtesies; Huck caters to whim and courts favor, always with an eye to the nearest exit. The unmarried captain of the *Bachelor*, as with most of Melville's bachelors, is an emblem of moral complacency and lavish good humor, in command of a full cargo and homeward bound. Aunt Sally is a type, an equal mixture of Christian goodwill, blind bigotry, and doting affection, glad to receive the boy whom she takes to be her nephew. *Moby-Dick* is characterized by its symbolic trappings, its metaphysical inquiries, its lyrical spontaneity, its Shakespearean "quick probings at the very axis of reality," as Melville said in "Hawthorne and His Mosses."

But *Huckleberry Finn* works by other means: It subverts the same high drama that promotes its episodes (Boggs's drunken swagger, for example, results in his murder, but the dramatic emphasis is upon the town's perverse fascination with his dying; a distempered gang calls for the lynching of Colonel Sherburn, but what they receive is an upbraiding lecture on mob cowardice). It indulges on the happiest terms in reflective moments through the benign auspices of folklore, superstition, and enviable credulity. Ishmael's crow's-nest reverie is blasted by the anxious recognition that he hovers over "Descartesian vortices," but Huck and Jim argue the origins of stars—the moon must have laid them after all—and no one gets hurt. *Huckleberry Finn* displays much less of the Melvillean interest in an "Anacharsis Clootz deputation" of humanity than in the solidarity of two, a "community of misfortune" as Twain would later describe the partnership of Huck and Jim. In the above cited passages, Melville's is a throwaway line, Twain's an epitome of vernacular realism.

Huckleberry Finn, like *Moby-Dick*, is a storyteller's story. In both books the teller and the tale vie for our attention. Ishmael, the yarn-spinner, is intent on chasing to their dens the significances of his experiences, though it is seldom the case that we as readers feel that these adventures are existentially *his* at all. Huck, too, is a receptacle of impressions, but they are filtered through a distinctively adolescent consciousness—quick to perceive, slow to comprehend.

But there are two "authors" of *Huckleberry Finn*, Mark Twain and Huck Finn, and there are also two distinct fictive worlds established by them. Twain presents us with a world that must be judged, Huck with a world that must be inhabited. If both authors are realists, however, their realism is of different orders of experience. Huckleberry Finn's story is primarily a record of feeling, not cognition, and as Twain once remarked, "emotions are among the toughest things in the world to manufacture out of whole cloth; it is easier to manufacture seven facts than one emotion."[2] The "quality of felt life" that Henry James claimed is central to the realist aesthetic is fulfilled in Huck's story; the deadly satirical thrusts of a man slightly outraged by life are largely the result of Twain's management of that same narrative.

The difference between Mark Twain's realism and Huck Finn's may be seen at a glance in comparable passages from *Life on the Mississippi* and *Huckleberry Finn*:

I had myself called with the four o'clock watch, mornings, for one cannot see too many summer sunrises on the Mississippi. They are enchanting. First, there is the eloquence of silence; for a deep hush broods everywhere. Next, there is the haunting sense of loneliness, isolation, remoteness from the worry and bustle of the world. The dawn creeps in stealthily; the solid walls of black forest soften to gray, and vast stretches of the river open up and reveal themselves; the water is glass-smooth, gives off spectral little wreaths of white mist, there is not the faintest breath of wind, nor stir of leaf; the tranquility is profound and infinitely satisfying. Then a bird pipes up, another follows, and soon the pipings develop into a jubilant riot of music. . . . When the light has become a little stronger, you have one of the fairest and softest pictures imaginable. You have the intense green of the massed and crowded foliage near by; you see it paling shade by shade in front of you; . . . And all this stretch of river is a mirror, and you have the shadowy reflections of the leafage and the curving shores and the receding capes pictured in it. Well, that is all beautiful; soft and rich and beautiful; and when the sun gets well up, and distributes a pink flush here and a powder of gold yonder and a purple haze where it will yield the best effect, you grant that you have seen something that is worth remembering.[3]

In chapter 19, Huck and Jim watch "the daylight come":

Not a sound, anywheres—perfectly still—just like the whole world was asleep, only sometimes the bull-frogs a-cluttering, maybe. The first thing to see, looking away over the water; was a kind of dull line—that was the woods on t'other side—you couldn't make nothing else out; then a pale place in the sky; then more paleness, spreading around; then the river softened up, away off, and warn't black any more, but gray; you could see little dark spots drifting along, ever so far away—trading scows, and such things; and long black streaks—rafts; sometimes you could hear a sweep streaking; or jumbled up voices, it was so still, and sounds come so far; and by and by you could see a streak on the water which you know by the look of the streak that there's a snag there in a swift current which breaks on it and makes that streak look that way; and you see the mist curl up off of the water, and the east reddens up, and the river, and you make out a log cabin in the edge of the woods, away on the bank on t'other side of the river, being a wood-yard, likely, and piled by them cheats so you can throw a dog through it anywheres; then the nice breeze springs up, and comes fanning you from over there, so cool and fresh, and sweet to smell, on account of the woods and the flowers; but sometimes not that way, because they've left dead fish laying around, gars, and such, and they do get pretty rank; and next you've got the full day, and everything smiling in the sun, and the song-birds just going it! (156-57)

Disclosed here are the obvious differences to be expected between a genteel and a vernacular narrator, or more properly between an adult and a child. Twain's passage is deliberate—shaped by rhetorical motive, organized logically in homogenous time and space, varied in diction, consistent in tone, and obedient to the terms of its announced purpose. Descriptive detail corroborates the preordained sentiment; the hushed silence, the creeping mists, the massed color and softening light contribute to, even validate, the "enchantment" of the scene.

Huck's description moves by statement and correction—there is "not a sound," he says, "but only sometimes"; the air is "sweet to smell" but "sometimes" there is a dead gar laying around. There is in

Huck's passage the unembarrassed monotony of phrasing—the word *streak* is used three times in the same clause. And Huck dispenses with explanatory remark. Twain's river is a mirror in which are to be found the reflections of wood and shore; but when Huck says "and the east reddens up, and the river" there is no authorial indication that the river reflects the red of the sky, for his world need not answer to the laws of optics. The phenomenon is local to his perception; it would not occur to him that the scene is an "effect." Huck's river at dawn is shifting impressions first and only incidentally a world of objects—the "little dark spots," we are told by way of an appositive, are trading scows; the "dull line," the woods; the "long black streaks," rafts. His world is populated by things, but they don't authorize his experience. And he does not belabor the mental corrections necessary to make such a world.

Twain's description is a "composition," a self-conscious act of language so constructed that we may grant that the scene is "worth remembering." Whether or not his depiction is memorably phrased, it stands as admiration of a natural event whose picturesque existence is independent of his rendering. Huck's scene is merely recalled, and one feels that without his consciousness to sustain it, the world itself might dissolve. For all that, however, Huck's landscape is the more tolerant; it admits the coexistence of the duplicity of cheats and stench of rotting fish with the music of birds. Huck is ever alert to treachery and snare, yet without condemning, he delivers an undiminished natural scene and exults in a privileged moment. Twain, by contrast, aims at a universal sentiment that is tonic relief from the "worry and bustle of the world."

Twain's presence pervades *Huckleberry Finn*, but with few exceptions, he is loyal to the terms of the book and favors Huck's unmediated world of feeling over his own often angry conviction.[4] That is, however strong Twain's own sentiments, he typically recognized that his first artistic responsibility was to a rendering of the authenticity of Huck's adolescent sensibility. The realism of *Huckleberry Finn* is disclosed alternately by the thread of Huck's consciousness, not yet come to full awareness of how fully implicated in events it is, and by the palpable events that seem randomly strung upon it, which is to say by the narrative itself. These are inevitably interwoven, and often tangled, but it is well to take up the teller and the tale separately.

II

One of the things to be observed about the realism of *Huckleberry Finn* is that Huck's voice functions much like Whitman's multivalent "I" in "Song of Myself"—he is the narrator of his chronicle and the author of his book; he is the chief witness of events and, emotionally at least, the principal victim of them; he is ruled and to a degree protected by the laws of the republic and the customs of place, but only accidentally a citizen of and never a voice in the dominant culture that so mystifies him.

Both as "author" and as narrator, Huck typically forgoes representational depiction. He himself has seen the Aunt Sallys of the world before, and he is far less interested in disclosing her character than in dealing with the situation. Huck's own considerable experience in the world (the result of having fended for himself most times, not of playing the detached observer of life), as remarkable as it is regrettable in a fourteen-year-old child, outfits him for his adventures. In this sense, the realism of the quoted passage above, and dozens of others like it, is presupposed in the telling itself.[5] Unlike Ahab, Huck takes the world on its terms, not his own, and experience has taught him how to best navigate its treacheries and to delight in its beauties.

Huck's wary canniness is frequently the source in *Huckleberry Finn* of the sort of narrative detachment so often associated with realist writing; it is also the source of a special pathos. When Huck sees the king and the duke tarred and feathered, men who "didn't look like nothing in the world that was human," he is incapable of hardening himself to their plight. Huck finally concludes, "Human beings *can* be awful cruel to one another" (290). This familiar scene is moving not because it effectively dramatizes Twain's attitudes toward the damned human race, nor for that matter because it serves as moral pronouncement (these two con men are scalawags through and through and deserve the sort of treatment they at long last receive). Nor, I believe, does it signal Huck's moral development, or as Leo Marx would have it, "a mature blending of his instinctive suspicion of human motives with his capacity for pity."[6] Instead, it is the unlooked for and disquieting revelation, somewhat surprising in a boy as familiar with the world as Huck is, that gives the moment force.

For Huck has witnessed earlier far greater and more disturbing cruelty than this: the murderous treatment of Jim Turner on the *Walter Scott*; the killing of Buck Grangerford, which still troubles his sleep; Boggs's gasping out his last breath under the weight of a family Bible; not to mention the thievery and calculated deceptions of the king and the duke themselves. What he hasn't before recognized, indeed does not fully recognize even as he speaks his sad conclusion, is the universal human condition of cruelty. Nor has he yet developed the righteous, which is to say the "civilized," indignation that would serve as defense against his own spontaneous impulses.

Huck and Tom have no opportunity to help these con men, and they go on home. But Huck is feeling "kind of ornery and humble," not so brash as before, even though he knows he hasn't done anything to cause the event he has just witnessed. Only two chapters earlier, in his famous decision to tear up the letter to Miss Watson and to "go to hell" and to help Jim, Huck's sympathies had prevailed against his training. Twain once observed in reference to a similar internal struggle in chapter 16, that this is a chapter "where a sound heart and a deformed conscience come into collision and conscience suffers defeat." His analogous moral decision in chapter 31 is a temporary triumph, however; as Harold H. Kolb, Jr., has remarked, "Huck never defeats his deformed conscience—it is we [as readers] who do that—he simply ignores it in relation to Jim."[7] When he sees the punished king and duke, however, Huck finds that a conscience, deformed or otherwise, has little to do with whether you do right or wrong or nothing at all. And precisely at that moment conscience moves in on him: "If I had a yaller dog that didn't know no more than a person's conscience, I would pison him. It takes up more room than all the rest of a person's insides, and yet ain't no good, nohow" (290).

Perhaps Huck is never so vulnerable as at this moment. His unwanted recognition, followed hard and fast by voracious conscience, has its inverted equivalent in *Moby-Dick* when Ahab realizes his quest is self-destructive but that he must press on nevertheless, and he drops his tear into the sea. For in Huck's response to the frenzied throng of townspeople exacting their revenge on these rapscallions and the image of the pair who do not look human, he concludes upon the human condition. Ahab is driven by interior impulses that extinguish all "natural" longings and lovings; but Huck, just as relentlessly, and simply by virtue of being alive and growing up, is being drawn into this inhuman, human world.

Robinson Jeffers, in "Shine, Perishing Republic," would have his children keep their distance from the "thickening center" of corruption:

> And boys, be in nothing so moderate as in love of man, a
> clever servant, insufferable master.
> There is the trap that catches noblest spirits, that caught
> they say—God, when he walked the earth.

This is a belated wisdom, reduced to fatherly advice, that, boys being boys, will likely go all unheeded. But Twain (or Huck rather) dramatizes his troubled understanding at the moment of its birth; his conclusion is the unstudied remark, not yet a conviction, no longer a perception. For Huck, corruption has no center but spreads out evenly before him, just as he has left it behind in the wake of his flight; it presents no scrape to be mastered or outlived but the general human condition. And Huck is not yet wise; his insight yields instantly to vague, unaccountable feelings of guilt. And this, too, is a dimension of the realism of the book, for he is a boy more ruled by feeling than sober reflection. *Huckleberry Finn* has sometimes been described as a picaresque novel without the picaro. This may be a meaningful statement if our understanding of the genre is qualified by the variations of it Cervantes accomplished in *Don Quixote*, a novel Twain read several times, Tom Sawyer at least once, and Huck not at all. Still, Huck is not quite an idealist, not yet a rogue. His mischievousness is typical of a boy his age, and it is combined with a special, sometimes ridiculous tenderness.

Huck is often capable of pseudomoralizing, citing his Pap as authority for lifting a chicken or borrowing a melon. This is also true when, in chapter 22, he dodges the watchman and dives under the circus tent: "I had my twenty-dollar gold piece and some other money, but I reckoned I better save it. . . . I ain't opposed to spending money on circuses, when there ain't no other way, but there ain't no use in *wasting* it on them" (191). Once inside, though the audience is hilarious, Huck is "all of a tremble" to see the danger of the drunken horseback rider. When, at length, he recognizes that he has been taken in by this performer, he is so admiring of him and the bully circus itself that he claims if he ever runs across it again, "it can have all of *my* custom, every time" (194).

In this relatively slight episode are compactly blended the multiple functions of Huck as author, character, narrator, and comic device. As author, he tries to make the circus scene vivid to us, but he is not equal to the task. His rendering of the performance is notable for its descriptive flatness. The passages are sprinkled with a few vernacular metaphors, but unlike his disturbing description of his Pap in chapter 5, Huck's language here is indefinite and vague. The men are dressed in their "drawers and undershirts," he says, and the ladies have lovely complexions and are "perfectly beautiful." What is vivid, however, is his faltering speech, his slightly breathless excitement. As narrator, he gropes for adjectives and falls into abstractions and platitudes. Huck is mastered by the spectacle, which is simultaneously his experience and his subject matter. But as boy, he is true to childlike enthusiasm and typically replaces descriptive detail with hyperbolic affidavits of his rapt attention: it was "the splendidest sight that ever was"; the women looked like "real sure-enough queens"; it was a "powerful fine sight"; "I never see anything so lovely"; "they done the most astonishing things" (191-92). At length, he becomes the straight man to his own joke. So pleased is he with the sight that he promises the circus can have his business any time, evidently unaware of the humor of the remark, that his "custom" has in no way damaged his purse.

Huck is worldly wise but never jaded, as this episode dramatizes, but the significance of his pranks are defined less by youthful motive than by the terms of the adventure. The charm of what Neil Schmitz calls his "Huckspeech" (speech "written as spoken, talked into prose")[8] can be, and is, radically redefined by narrative context. There is prankishness involved, for example, when Huck plays his joke on Jim after they have been separated in the fog, but he receives a tongue-lashing that so cuts him that he "humbles himself to a nigger." Huck's manufacture of his own murder in order to escape the potentially lethal abuse of his Pap is grotesque to be sure, but it is highly dramatic too, and Huck regrets that Tom is not handy to throw in "the fancy touches" (41). He laments Tom's absence as well in an episode that is a mixture of romantic escapade and existential urgency when, in chapter 12, he and Jim undertake to save Jim Turner from certain death. The same may be said for his efforts to preserve the Wilks girls' fortune from the hands of the king and the duke.

As humorist Huck is humorless, as hero he is only accidentally heroic, and as narrator he seems never quite to know where to place the accent. He is constitutionally incapable of distilling from his supposed experience either the ultimate conditions or the deeper significance of his adventures. Huck never doubts the existence of the "bad place" and the "good place"; in fact, he believes them to be all that Miss Watson has told him. However, while he can imagine the fires of hell and the monotony of playing harps and singing forever, he scarcely comprehends eternity and has little interest in it. His famous declaration "All right, then, I'll *go* to hell" (271) is not accompanied with an exclamation point. The statement is matter-of-fact and to be taken literally, for Huck is a literal-minded boy. He is temperamentally suited to the bad place (wickedness is in his line, he says), and he will give up trying to achieve the other place. But his decision is also the resignation of self-acceptance, a declaration, that is, of the acceptance of the world's judgment upon him, not the resolution to abide by some higher moral authority, as is sometimes claimed. It is just this quality that gives the scene its special pathos. Huck is not built right, and the fact that he is social and moral refuse is hardly arguable.

Huck is caught between stern rebuke ("Don't scrunch up like that, Huckleberry"; "Don't gap and stretch like that") and enforced social acceptance ("Pray every day, Huckleberry"; "Chew your food, Huckleberry"). But he remains the same boy the town allowed to sleep in a hogshead, stay away from school, and make do for himself. Caught on the horns of this dilemma, there is nevertheless a strong undercurrent of self-affirmation; Huck is filled with self-recrimination and self-condemnation, but never self-loathing: When Jim is bitten by the rattlesnake, he curses himself as a "fool" for not remembering that the mate was apt to join the dead one he had placed in Jim's blanket; he is sorry for the outcome and his stupidity but not the impulse. Huck devoutly tries to admire Emmeline's poetic "tributes" and drawings because he accepts the Grangerford family faith that she was a saint; he even steals up into her room and browses through her scrapbook when he begins to "sour" on her. He often regrets that Tom Sawyer is not around to throw some style into his plans, but Huck never fully accepts the world's corrections or refusals of him. And this same realistic disclosure of a young boy's self-consciousness, in the hands of Mark Twain, becomes a satirical vehicle as well.

Twain often employs a satirical strategy in Huck that he seems to have observed in himself and to have dramatized in *A Tramp Abroad*. The narrator of that book does not condemn violent alien customs (most particularly the revolting German student duels) but instead curses himself for failing to comprehend the wisdom of received tradition. The same is true of countless occasions in *Huckleberry Finn* where Twain's intent, as opposed to Huck's, is to expose sham, pretense, and outright silliness: Huck is perplexed that the widow makes him "grumble over the victuals" even though there is nothing wrong with them; he takes it on faith that Emmeline Grangerford's pictures are "nice," but they always give him the "fan-tods"; he goes to church with the Grangerfords and hears a sermon about brotherly love and "preforeordestination," and everyone agrees it was a good sermon, and it must be so because, for Huck, it proved to be "one of the roughest Sundays" he had ever run across.

Tom Sawyer variously describes Huck as a lunkhead, an idiot, or a saphead for failing to comprehend the observances required of pirates, robbers, or royalty. Huck never disputes Tom's basic superiority or his own cultural and moral ignorance; after all, Tom is "full of principle" (307). In fact, Huck is flabbergasted that Tom is willing and eager to help him free Jim, and he regrets his own betrayal of his friend for not insisting that he not sink so low:

> Here was a boy that was respectable, and well brung up; and had a character to lose; and folks at home that had characters; and he was bright and not leatherheaded; and knowing, and not ignorant; and not mean, but kind; and yet here he was, without any more pride, or rightness, or feeling, than to stoop to this business, and make himself a shame, and his family a shame, before everybody. I *couldn't* understand it, no way at all. (292-93)

As a realistic portrayal of one boy's concern for another, the statement is touching; as satire, it is deadly—all the more so when we learn that Miss Watson has already freed Jim in her will and that Tom knows it.

Twain once astutely remarked that, unlike *Tom Sawyer, Huckleberry Finn* is not a book for boys but for those who used to be boys. It is not altogether clear Twain recognized this distinction at the time of writing the novel, so strong was his identification with his created character, but the instinctive decision to have an unwashed fourteen-year-old out-cast tell a story ultimately meant for readers whose own innocence was behind them proved to be an enabling one. As a character or narrative consciousness, Huck is pure possibility—his future casually spreads out before him, luxuriant in meandering adventures and antics, free-dom and easiness. But he is doomed as well—for every adult reader knows (though because we are adults we are often reluctant to admit it) that his delightful caginess and high jinks depend less on moral pur-pose than on youthful energy; his escapes and accommodations are destined to become evasions and compromises in the end.[9] Huck does not know this, he hasn't even considered the issue; but we his grown-up readers do, and every vile specimen of humanity surveyed in this rich cross section of America confirms it. Huckleberry Finn set out to tell a story and did the best he could. By degrees, it became apparent to Mark Twain that the boy was writing a novel.

III

Perhaps *novel* is too narrow a word. In his "Notice," and apparently after some deliberation, Twain chose to describe his book as a "narra-tive." In any event, the tale Huck tells is all slapdash and Oh, by the way, as mixed up in its way as the king's recitation of Hamlet's solilo-quy; the book Twain wrote is another matter.

Huckleberry Finn is a highly episodic book, and the arrangement of episodes observes no incontestable narrative logic. The feud chapters precede rather than follow the Boggs shooting not for self-evident ar-tistic reasons but because we are to suppose that is the order in which Huck lived them. The episodic density of the book thins considerably as the narrative progresses, the last half being dominated by the lost heirs episode and the evasion chapters. But this is not because these events are more important than earlier ones but because in the several-year gestation of the book Twain himself had acquired the capacity to make more of less. That capacity, it is true, sometimes degenerates into artifice and burlesque, as in the strategy to acquire one of Aunt Sally's spoons, but it likewise betrays an author's professionally calculated attitude toward his material. Moreover, Twain had commercial as well as artistic motives impelling him to finish his book; undoubtedly, in the final burst of composition in 1883, he approached his narrative, in part, as a commodity that was too long in production. Besides, he had his own newly formed publishing company ready to print and promote it.

The *reason* some episodes follow others might be more confidently pursued by examining how the novel grew and took shape during the seven years of its intermittent composing. That is a story too complicated to tell here.[10] It is enough to say, perhaps, that Huck Finn, as character and voice, was a metaphor for Twain's mind: through his identification with the boy he might indulge nostalgically in vagrant thoughts and happy recollections, and particularly in the early stages of composition he might satisfy his own desire to escape the cares of a world that was too much with him. And when he was in more aggressive moods, through the satirical latitude Huck's perspective on events permitted him, Twain could deal scathingly with his several hatreds and annoyances—racial bigotry, mob violence, self-righteousness, aristocratic pretense, venality and duplicity, along with several lesser evils. His complaints about these and other matters found their way into Huck's narrative.

W. D. Howells once affectionately complained that he wished Mark Twain might rule his fancy better, and for his part, Twain contributed to the public image of him as a jackleg novelist. However, not since the work of such critics as Gladys Bellamy, Sydney Krause, William Gibson, Walter Blair, Victor Doyno, or Henry Nash Smith, to name only a few, has anyone been able to celebrate Twain's maverick genius at the expense of his literary art. Still, we cannot dismiss out of hand Mark Twain's claim that he merely served as the "amanuensis" to his creative imagination, and in fact on the first page of the manuscript of the novel he gave his book the working title "Huckleberry Finn/Reported by Mark Twain." By the end of the first paragraph, however, even that modest claim seems too much.

From the manuscript we know that Twain had at first begun his tale with "You will not know about me . . ." before he fully accepted Huck's ungrammatical authenticity and, with it, all the multiplying implications of the decision. "You don't know about me," Huck begins, "without you have read a book by the name of 'The Adventures of Tom Sawyer.'" Clearly, Mark Twain cannot serve even as the reporter of Huck's narrative, and, besides, he is not to be trusted, for we have it on Huck's authority that he told some "stretchers" in recounting Tom's story. Within the first three sentences, Huck has politely dispensed with "Mr. Mark Twain" and introduced himself as an orphan in more ways than one.

Except perhaps for the opening lines of "Song of Myself," there may be no more audacious beginning to an extended work of the imagination. Mysteriously, we are forced, or rather agree, to assume what Huck assumes, not because we are in the seductive presence of someone afoot with his vision, but because Huck amuses us. He makes us laugh and, later, cry; we want to be with him and to hear him speak. Just as mysteriously, we assume, or rather never ask, how such a book written by a boy could come to be, nor do we require of it even the most fundamental elements of fictional probability.

Even without Kemble's illustration of Huck writing a letter to Mary Jane Wilks in chapter 28, we can easily imagine him in the act of writing itself—squinting one eye, holding his tongue between his teeth, tightly clenching his pencil as he begins to record his adventures. It is somewhat more difficult, however, to imagine when or why Huck tells his story. We know that he has finished it before he lights out for the Territory and that he has presumably spent about as much time writing as it took for Tom's bullet wound to heal. But the only apparent motive he has in the writing is to correct the forgivably exaggerated account of Tom and him that Mark Twain had published as "The Adventures of Tom Sawyer." (It would be out of character for Huck to assume that anyone might actually be interested in his thoughts or exploits.) More perplexing is the fact that Tom Sawyer was published in 1876, but the novel takes place in the 1830s or 1840s, and it never occurs to Huck that he ought to explain this curious discrepancy. It is equally unimaginable that Huck should have lit out for New York instead of the Indian Territory to seek a publisher for the completed manuscript. The very conditions of the fiction that is his book are perhaps the biggest stretcher of all.

It is not for nothing that Twain added the elaborate introductory apparatus to his novel—the heliotype image of him as a frontispiece, sternly presiding over his book; his parenthetical identification of Huck as "Tom Sawyer's Comrade"; his setting of the scene and the time of the novel; his "Notice" and his "Explanatory." These were no doubt, in part, attempts to reassert his own authorial presence in the narrative to follow, but Twain has also rather generously and succinctly made up for some of Huck's literary failings. Huck, after all, never tells us the when or where of this narrative, but Twain does—the Mississippi Valley, forty to fifty years ago. Perhaps Huck did not know, after all, that his story ought to display some interest in motive, plot, or moral, and Twain in his "Notice" somewhat protectively and very authoritatively warns us away from even noting their absence in the narrative. At the same time, in his "Explanatory," Twain calls attention to one of the book's chief virtues, the careful attention to and realistic rendering of dialect. We can imagine Huck straining to parse out a sentence, but we hardly expect him to have taken the same pains Twain did in fashioning the speech of his characters.

Huck's story as novel is impossibility followed by implausibility and linked together by unlikelihood. To give a merely incidental example, when in chapter 17 Huck wakes up after his first night at the Grangerford house, he has forgotten that he is now George Jackson. That much is realistic; the reader, too, is apt to get lost in the dizzying array of Huck's aliases. But Huck tricks Buck into giving the name away:

"Can you spell, Buck?"

"Yes," he says.

"I bet you can't spell my name," says I.

"I bet you what you dare I can," says he.

"All right," says I, "go ahead."

"G-o-r-g-e J-a-x-o-n—there now," he says. (136)

Then Huck privately writes the name down because "somebody might want *me* to spell it, next." One need not be a metafictionist to see the difficulty here. Huck, as narrator, has spelled George Jackson correctly from the beginning, along with any number of other, more difficult names—Harney Shepherdson, Emmeline Grangerford, Lafe Buckner, Silas Phelps, "Henry the Eight," Colonel Sherburn (how Huck was able to sound out *Colonel* is a permanent puzzle). Are we to suppose that in the few months since this exchange with Buck occurred that Huck has undergone some orthographically redemptive experience? My point here is not to indulge in fastidious fault-finding but rather to note that in the course of reading these sorts of questions simply don't come up. The enchantment, the atmosphere of mind, conveyed by Huck's narrative presence is too pleasing, too hypnotic, to permit skepticism. There is considerable magic in the realism of *Huckleberry Finn*.

However improvised and shapeless the boy's narrative is, it nonetheless miraculously coheres almost in spite of itself. More often than not, the plot thickens only to dissolve into another overlapping adventure. We expect Colonel Sherburn to get lynched; but he does not. What really happened to Buck Grangerford; Huck won't tell us. We become interested in the romance of Miss Sophia and Harney Shepherdson, but all we know of their star-crossed love affair is that they got across the river safely. We pity Boggs's sixteen-year-old daughter and ask for revenge; but what we get in her potential hero, Buck Harkness, is a coward and someone looking "tolerable cheap" at that. We hope that the king and duke get their just deserts, but then are made to feel sorry for them when they do. We wish to see the Wilks girls reunited with their money and their nearest kin, but in the climactic scene of this episode the crowd rushes forward to the coffin and Huck takes the opportunity amid the confusion to get away from there, and we, his readers, however much a part of us might want to linger, are willingly drawn after him. The Wilks girls' adventure is abruptly over, and Huck's has acquired new life.

And the two principal plot devices, it turns out, are false leads, Hitchcockean MacGuffins: Huck is fleeing from Pap, but Pap, we learn at last, was the dead man in the floating house thirty-four chapters and several hundred miles ago. Jim is escaping from the dreadful edict of Miss Watson to sell him down the river, but, again, we eventually discover that he had been freed two months earlier in her will. Time and again, the action that enlists our interest is discarded, diverted, or thwarted. In "Chapter the Last" Twain, through several disclosures made by several characters, goes about tying up the loose ends of the story as quickly and efficiently as a calf-roper with the rope clenched between his teeth: Jim owns himself, and his early prophecy that he will be a rich man is fulfilled; Pap is dead, and thus Huck has free use of his six thousand dollars to finance a trip west; Tom is recovered from his bullet wound, and we now know why he had consented to free Jim.

If there is no plot to speak of, there remain nevertheless discernible mythic, structural, and satirical patterns throughout the novel—patterns of flight and absorption, prophecy and fulfillment, retreat and return, death and rebirth, initiation and emergence, repetition and variation. And there are multiple themes and issues as well—of the comic and devastating effects of Christian piety and absurd sentimentality, of obnoxious aristocratic privilege and backwater vulgarity, of marginalization and co-optation, of intuitive sympathy and utilitarian conduct, of inflexible racist bigotry and the dignifying enlargements of open friendship. Then there is the clear advance over and inestimable contribution to the tradition of American humor that is accomplished in the example of the book itself. These patterns, themes, and achievements are certainly "there" within the novel to the extent that criticism and interpretation can make them so, but they would be invisible to Huck and likely hazy to Twain himself. All of them may be comprehended, perhaps, in the insightful remark of Henry Nash Smith: Twain's "technical accomplishment was of course inseparable from the process of discovering new meanings in his material. His development as a writer was a dialectic interplay in which the reach of his imagination imposed a constant strain on his technical resources, and innovations of method in turn opened up new vistas before his imagination."[11]

The four groups of working notes for the novel Twain jotted down between 1879 and 1883 nevertheless reveal that Twain's imaginative reach was at times blind groping. Among other things, Twain considered including in his narrative a Negro sermon, the legend of a Missouri earthquake, a house-raising, a village fire, a hazing, elocution lessons, an encounter with alligators, a quilting bee, a candy-pulling, a temperance lecture, a duel, a lynching, an accidental killing with an "unloaded" gun, an auction, a dog messenger, and (most improbably of all) an elephant given to Huck and Tom so that they might ride around the country and "make no end of trouble."[12] Twain was always tempted by burlesque, of course, and the fact that he resisted the several temptations suggested by this list of creative brainstorms testifies to more than a bit of artistic restraint. However, many have felt he so yielded to his fondness for burlesque in the final evasion episode that he irreparably damaged Huck's integrity and credibility, subjected Jim to a series of unnecessary degradations, subverted the terms of Huck and Jim's friendship he had so patiently developed, and ultimately betrayed his reader's confidence.

That is an issue individual readers will decide, but the working notes indicate at least the range of possibilities Huck's adventures suggested to the author, a range so vast as to become arbitrary. The only requirements of his then developing narrative, it seems, were that Huck should have been the witness to the events, or to a recitation of them by another, and that Huck narrate them. This is merely to say that Twain banked on the realism of a literary manner over and above the realism of subject matter. Any and all of the events recorded in his working notes conceivably could have happened along the Mississippi, of course, but they indicate no definite narrative direction. And many episodes he did dramatize are no less adventitious than those he contemplated. After all, he did choose to include witch pies and rope ladders, hidden treasure and secret tattoos, sideshows and soliloquies, feuds and romances, ghost stories and fistfights. And as palpable as the river is in the book, it is absolutely incredible that a runaway slave should be trying to get to Canada on its current.

If Twain did not in every instance manage to rule his fancy, he does seem to have tried to coordinate the several products of it. The most obvious example of this sort of artistic management is in the telling juxtaposition of the Boggs shooting with the drunken bareback rider at the circus. In the first episode, the actual physical suffering of Boggs and the emotional grief of his daughter are mixed with the sham of pious sentiment and the predictably perverse fascination of the townspeople, who shove each other aside to get a good look at a dying man. At the circus, Huck's worrying over the supposed drunk is sincere, but the man's peril is merely show business. There are other paired episodes or details as well: the actual deafness of Jim's daughter and the deaf-and-dumb hoax of the duke; the real rattlesnake on Jackson's Island that bites Jim and the garter snakes with buttons tied to their tails in the shed at the Phelps farm; Huck's captivity in his Pap's cabin and the gruesomely imagined evidence of his invented murder, and Jim's captivity in the shed on the Phelps farm and the ridiculous traces of Tom's romantic prescriptions that convince the townsfolk that Jim is a raving lunatic; Huck's efficient attempts to save Jim Turner aboard the *Walter Scott* and Tom's embroidered and leisurely efforts to rescue Jim in the evasion episode. Each of these correspondences, and others as well, mark with deadly satirical effect the difference between realistic urgency and contrived hoax. They also mark how artfully Twain blended the two.

Many of the characters and episodes in *Huckleberry Finn* can be explained as inspired narrative twists that keep the plot moving along, broaden the range of Huck and Jim's adventures, and permit the author to indulge in such imaginative improvisation as might occur to him. The most important of these are the introduction of the king and duke in chapter 19 and the reemergence of Tom Sawyer in chapter 33. When Twain allowed the king and duke to commandeer the raft, he violated the sanctity of the craft and the river itself. But it was also an enabling move, for now his characters could travel in daylight and the author could survey in freer fashion the manners and language of life along the river. The maneuver also helped explain away the difficulty of moving an escaped slave into the Deep South, since Huck and Jim now have considerably less say in events. The fantastic reintroduction of Tom Sawyer, who suddenly becomes the superintendent of affairs and relaxes the deadly serious consequences of Huck's decision in chapter 31 to help Jim, turned Huck's experiences and commitment into disappointingly fanciful pranks. But at least it provided a strategy, however improbable, for concluding a book that might have drifted along forever.

Huckleberry Finn was published in England in 1884; coincidentally, Henry James published his famous essay "The Art of Fiction" the same year. Twain's novel passes most of the tests for the art of the novel that James proposes there—that it be interesting, that it represent life and give the very "atmosphere of mind" in contact with experience, that it "catch the color, the relief, the expression, the surface, the substance of the human spectacle." It also happens to fulfill the requirements of some critics and the expectations of many readers that James holds up for skeptical scrutiny—that it have a "happy ending," that it be full of incident and movement, that it have an obvious moral purpose. Coincidentally, too, James compares in the same essay two novels he had at the time been reading—Robert Louis Stevenson's *Treasure Island* and Edmond de Goncourt's *Chérie*. The first, he notes, "treats of murders, mysteries, islands of dreadful renown, hairbreadth escapes, miraculous coincidences, and buried doubloons"; the second seeks to trace "the development of the moral consciousness of a child." James approves of Stevenson's novel because it achieves what it attempts, whereas De Goncourt's, in his estimation, does not. James probably did not imagine, even as he struck the comparison, that any writer, much less an American writer, might effectively fuse both attempts in a single project, but he certainly would have approved the attempt.

Not that Twain would have given a fig for James's approval. In such matters, W. D. Howells was Twain's admired comrade, as Hawthorne was Melville's. Even so, after Twain had finished his novel and was making revisions, he wrote Howells with a certain petulant self-confidence that he, at least, was happy with the result: "And *I* shall *like* it, whether anybody else does or not." Melville's summary remark to Hawthorne upon the achievement of *Moby-Dick*, to risk one final comparison, is similarly defiant: "I have written a wicked book, and feel spotless as a lamb." The wickedness of *Huckleberry Finn* is not the wickedness of *Moby-Dick*, of course, but it is the sort one might expect of Huck Finn, and maybe Mark Twain. For Huck had been brought up to it, and the rendering of it was right in Twain's line.

From *Coming to Grips with "Huckleberry Finn": Essays on a Book, a Boy, and a Man* (1993), pp. 83-105. Copyright © 1993 by the Curators of the University of Missouri. Reprinted with permission of the University of Missouri Press.

Notes

1. "Mark Twain, 'Realism,' and Huckleberry Finn," in *New Essays on "Huckleberry Finn,"* ed. Louis J. Budd (Cambridge: Cambridge University Press, 1985), 35-59.
2. *Life on the Mississippi* (New York: Viking Penguin, 1986), 228-29.
3. Ibid.
4. Twain does speak his own mind from time to time—most obviously when he has Colonel Sherburn scold the mob in chapter 22, and perhaps most interestingly when he chooses to speak through Jim about the benefits of industry and progress in parts of chapter 14.

5. Shaped as he is by experience, however, Huck remains innocent in an important way. Unlike Colonel Sherburn, say, who has traveled in the North and lived in the South and is therefore able to proclaim on the cowardice of the "average" man (190), Huck's perspective has not frozen into an attitude. Not only is the narrative point of view of this novel presexual, as has so often been observed, but it is also prepolitical, even preideological. Huck, in his efforts to help Jim, may worry that he may become a "low-down Abolitionist," but the quality of that anxiety is rather more like a thousand childhood myths—e.g., the worry children have that, having made an ugly face, it will "stick."

6. "Mr. Eliot, Mr. Trilling, and Huckleberry Finn," *The American Scholar* 22 (Autumn 1953): 423-40.

7. Twain, quoted in Walter Blair, *Mark Twain and Huck Finn* (Berkeley and Los Angeles: University of California Press, 1960), 143; Kolb, "Mark Twain, Huck Finn, and Jacob Blivens: Gilt-Edged, Tree-Calf Morality in the *Adventures of Huckleberry Finn*," *The Virginia Quarterly Review* 55 (Autumn 1979): 658.

8. *Of Huck and Alice: Humorous Writing in American Literature* (Minneapolis: University of Minnesota Press, 1983), 96.

9. Twain knew this, too; in a cranky moment, he predicted that Huck would grow up to be just as low-down and mean as his Pap.

10. Walter Blair and, more recently, Victor A. Doyno have provided us with full and perceptive book-length studies of the evolution of the novel. See Blair, *Mark Twain and Huck Finn*, and Doyno, *Writing Huck Finn: Mark Twain's Creative Process* (Philadelphia: University of Pennsylvania Press, 1991).

11. *Mark Twain: The Development of a Writer* (Cambridge: Harvard University Press, 1962), 113.

12. The working notes for *Huckleberry Finn* are reproduced in the California-Iowa edition of the novel, 711-61.

"Huckleberry Fun" _____

Everett Carter

The first thing to say about *Huckleberry Finn* is that it is a funny and pleasurable book. A true professional, Mark Twain wanted his writing to earn its and his way, and he knew that the best way to find readers was to mine the vein of humor whose first product was the pure gold of "The Jumping Frog of Calaveras County." He subscribed easily, comfortably, instinctively to the oldest traditions of his craft—that it should delight and instruct, and in that order. First, to give delight, to give pleasure, and *Huckleberry Finn* constantly gives the deepest, the primary kind of pleasure—that of the child in all of us. He also wanted to instruct, and the instruction in *Huckleberry Finn* is the important undertone. The overtone is the delight, the triumph of pleasure over pain, of hope over fear, of life over death; the undertone is the flow of satiric criticism. First the pleasure, then the instruction.

The novel's delight is immediate: "You don't know about me, without you have read a book by the name of 'The Adventures of Tom Sawyer,' but that ain't no matter. That book was made by Mr. Mark Twain, and he told the truth, mainly." That "mainly" sets the tone; the story will be playful, will imitate life but at the distance of pretense, will be like life, but at a safe remove. The book will have the perspective of youthful deflation of the adult world; it will establish the identity of the true author, who will control both the overtone of comedy and the undertone of satire.

The next sentences in chapter 1 contemplate the important pleasure of the happy ending. Huck reminds us of the triumph of the first installment of his small saga—the winning of $6,000, "all gold," that was his part of the reward for the downfall of Injun Joe. With this emphasis, the reader is pointed in the direction of true comedy; the $6,000, "all gold," will be there at the conclusion to symbolize, in hard cash, the happy ending.

The language of the opening sentences furthers the comic tone. Part of our delight in it is our admiration of its wit—our appreciation of the expert manipulation of language to imitate the speech of a partially educated boy of a specific region. Another joy is the more selfish pleasure of superiority; we laugh at those who know the rules less well than we, and who inhabit an area where an "inferior" dialect is spoken. A further invitation to smile is in the manipulation of the sentence's rhythm: the "mainly," coming after the pause of the comma, and after the speaker has apparently finished his thought. We hear, and see, the comic lecturer as he pauses, looks innocently about him, and adds the deflating "mainly."

The next sentences establish the important element of hedonistically happy childhood, the return to infantile messiness. "[I]t was rough living in the house all the time, considering how dismal regular and decent the widow was in all her ways; and so when I couldn't stand it no longer, I lit out. I got into my old rags, and my sugar-hogshead again, and was free and satisfied." The comic tone of this passage is signaled by the words "regular and decent," reminding readers of *Tom Sawyer* that it was the Widow Douglas who had "snaked" Huck out of the "wet" and had given him the first of many homes he would long for. Huck's rebellion is the cheerful, lighthearted protest of the child against the acknowledged moral superiority of the parent. The Widow's attitudes are the moral touchstones of the book; her position is emphasized by the immediate introduction of the ugly Miss Watson, who will be the truly repressive figure, the one from whose tyranny both Huck and Jim will escape. Huck's wallowing in the mud is comic when it occurs in the context of the good and beneficent parent who will be there to clean him up; it becomes serious rebellion in the context of an evil "parent," Miss Watson, and the soon-to-be-introduced real parent, the awful Pap Finn. Huck accepts the moral authority of Widow Douglas, avowing himself a believer in the Widow's "Providence," a beneficent one in which "a poor chap would stand considerable show," and a heretic in Miss Watson's repressive religion under which "there warn't no help for [a poor chap] any more."

After introducing himself, after alluding to the author of his story, after telling of the Widow and Miss Watson, Huck describes his meetings with Tom and with "Miss Watson's big nigger, named Jim." Both characters are shown first in their roles in the pure comedy. Jim will play the buffoon, yielding the easiest and most primitive stimulus to laughter—our feeling of superiority to someone beneath us. Tom will be shown as he constantly converts reality into make-believe. (Both will also perform important roles in the didactic elements of the novel, Tom as an exemplar of sentimental absurdity, Jim as the medium of the novel's satiric attack on the Southern attitudes toward race.)

With the coming of winter, Huck is dismayed by signs of the reappearance of his vicious father. He immediately transfers titular ownership of his fortune to Judge Thatcher, who has been caring for it, giving Huck the reasonable 5 percent interest it has been earning. By the transfer, Huck places the money out of his predatory father's reach. Judge Thatcher, along with Widow Douglas, is a good "parent," and with her he provides a stable moral center, located in a "decent and regular" society, a center that is necessary to establish the comic aspect of the satiric undertone. Pap Finn will be the contrast to this society, a contrast that will enable the reader to see the moral thrust of the satire. For the time being, however, I will concentrate on the pure humor of this first part of the plot, the delight in Huck's ability to triumph over obstacles and reach a "happy ending."

Kidnapped by his terrible father, Huck finds his life in danger. He resourcefully saws out a portion of a bottom log of his cabin prison and escapes in a canoe that has conveniently floated into his care. He meets Jim, who has escaped from his oppressor, Miss Watson, and together they live a short island idyll of childlike primitivism. Together they investigate a ruined house that has floated down the Mississippi, a "house of death"; in one corner lies a dead man. This brief episode focuses the comic tone. From the house of death they emerge joyfully with the small things of life, "an old tin lantern, and a butcher knife without any handle, and a bran-new Barlow knife worth two bits in any store. . . ." The list goes on, and ends with a wooden leg: "the straps was broke off of it, but, barring that, it was a good enough leg, though it was too long for me and not long enough for Jim." The conversion of possible pain and crippling to the joy of bacchanalian absurdity ends with Huck telling us, "We got home all safe."

Huck finds out that Jim has a price on his head. The two pile onto a raft and start their voyage down the Mississippi River. Never mind that freedom lay more certainly to the north; the tip of Illinois, a free state, lies south of St. Petersburg, and anyway the current flows south, and Mark Twain goes with the flow, even after the runaways miss the Illinois landfall in a fog. Before they do, they meet another life-threatening adventure and emerge from it unscathed. This time another derelict structure is involved, a wrecked steamboat named the *Walter Scott* (the symbolism will play a part in the satiric undertone, but in terms of the pure comedy the episode is another example of comic triumph). Trapped aboard the wreck with a gang of murderous thieves, Huck and Jim steal their boat, leaving the gang to drown. (Huck will try to save them by one of his wonderfully shrewd ruses, but the murderous gang will get their just deserts.)

At this point, Huck plays the same kind of thoughtless joke on Jim that he and Tom played in the first pages of the novel, showing the same childlike heedlessness. Huck's remorse, when Jim shows his pain, is the important first step in developing the major element of the novel's satiric purpose. (For the moment I will simply mark it and return to the comic overtone.) A steamboat smashes the fugitives' raft, and Huck alone starts on an important new adventure in the "House Beautiful" of the Grangerfords. The episode is largely satirical, with both the gentle satire on sentimental art, and the bitter satire on the Southern code of false honor. But it also provides another in the series of the novel's "happy endings." Escaping from the horror of the senseless, murderous family feud, Harney Shepherdson and Sophia Grangerford, with Huck's help, elope: "they'd got across the river and was safe." Jim, too, has escaped death, and Huck rejoins him on the raft and in the river.

When two Mississippi confidence men, the self-styled Duke of Bridgewater and Dauphin of France, take over the raft (Huck, typically, has helped them escape from some of their angry victims), these "lowdown humbugs and frauds" are the occasion for a variety of satires on nobility (these examples of royalty, says Jim, "do smell so") and on human gullibility (the poster for their public performance reads "Ladies and Children Not Admitted"; "If that don't fetch them," says the Duke, "I don't know Arkansaw"). The Duke and the Dauphin also provide us with the pure comedy of wit as they deliciously garble Shakespearean passages: "To be, or not to be; that is the bare bodkin/ That makes calamity of so long life. . . . But soft you, the fair Ophelia:/ Ope not thy ponderous and marble jaws. . . ." The rascals take their parts as well in the series of fortunate escapes and happy endings that continue to give readers the joy of deflected pain and averted danger. The most important of these episodes is the attempted swindling of Mary Jane Wilks and her sisters, a scheme that Huck characteristically thwarts with courage and craft. His success invokes the classical satisfaction of witnessing the dupers duped. The con men lose not only their stolen fortune, but all their earlier ill-gotten gains as well when Huck arranges for the restitution of the orphans' inheritance. Further gratification is provided by the eventual fate of the two swindlers. The reader does not, for the most part, share in Huck's sweetness of character that permits him to sympathize with the two frauds as they are tarred and feathered. Instead, we feel the comic satisfaction of witnessing poetic justice.

The last of the con men's villainies has been the selling of Jim for a share in the announced reward for his capture. The buyer, Silas Phelps, coincidentally, is Tom Sawyer's uncle, a happy coincidence since it creates the possibility of the eventual revelation of Jim's having already been freed. The last chapters, descending into the burlesque that often attracted Mark Twain's wayward genius, are devoted to the important objects of his satiric ridicule—the warping of Southern mentality by the falsehoods of meretricious literature, and the immorality of the Southern attitudes toward race. However, they are also the climax of the reassuring succession of affirmative endings. After Tom Sawyer has succeeded in getting himself shot (in the leg, of course—a curable wound), his rescue is effected by Jim, of whom the doctor says he had never seen "a better nuss or faithfuller, and yet he was risking his freedom to do it. . . ." The final scene comprises the classic comic finale: the revelation of an extraneous, gratuitous Providence, a "god from the machine," that turns the chaos into order and instantly transforms potential tragedy into comedy. Jim is in chains, and Huck is poor because "pap's been back before now, and got it all away from Judge Thatcher. . . ." No, says Tom, Jim is already "as free as any cretur that walks this earth! . . . Miss Watson died two months ago, and . . . set him free in her will." As for Old Man Finn, Jim reveals that it was his corpse that was huddled in "the house of death"; Huck's fortune is "all there yet—six thousand dollars and more. . . ."

It has taken ten chapters of satiric overkill to reach this happy conclusion. Convinced that false romanticism had been the cause of the moral downfall of the American South, Mark Twain put Huck and Jim through an ordeal by Tom's mad devotion to sentimental literature. In its first pages, the novel sounds the note of the first great comic novels in the Western tradition. Like Don Quixote, Tom substitutes the falsity of romance for the truth of reality. A Sunday school picnic is transformed into "a whole parcel of Spanish merchants and rich A-rabs." An old tin lamp becomes the means of summoning "a lot of genies." Unreconstructed by his early errors of fantasy, he drops into the Phelps plantation with the same warped vision: reality distorted by books of heroes: "Baron Trenck," "Casanova," "Benvenuto Cheleeny," "Henry IV." True comic satire, holding up vice and error to ridicule, must have a norm against which to measure the error, and Huck provides such a norm with his hardheaded empiricism. He looks at reality with his own eyes (like Mark Twain, he is after all "from Missouri"): "there warn't no Spaniards and A-rabs, and there warn't no camels nor no elephants. It warn't anything but a Sunday-school picnic. . . ." Then Mark Twain made sure to have him add the typically Twainian anticlimactic absurdity: "and only a primer class at that." Considering Tom's claim for the magical properties of an oil lamp, Huck does not reject it out of hand. Like the good empiricist he is, he "reckoned" he would "see if there was anything in it." He got a lamp, performed the experiment, rubbed away; nothing happened, and so he "judged that all that stuff was only just one of Tom Sawyer's lies." Faced at the end with the problem of freeing Jim from his captivity in one of the Phelps's slave cabins, Huck proposes his commonsensical solution: lift the bed leg up and remove the chain, take the key from the outside wall, and open the door. When Tom objects, proposing his ridiculous alternatives, Huck's response is: "I see in a minute it was worth fifteen of mine, for style, and would make Jim just as free a man as mine would, and maybe get us all killed besides."

The continuing satire directed against false romanticism is overshadowed by the deeper satire directed against the inhumanity of slavery and the ugliness of racial prejudice. The device of irony becomes the principal weapon of the satirist, using the small ironies that are effective devices of comic satire, not the large irony that is the hallmark of the tragic mode. Small ironies—reversals of meaning—are used to show us the disease of wrong human action when measured against a norm of health agreed upon by author and reader. A moral accord, the satiric covenant, is always present between author and reader, giving both the pleasure of the hope of reform, the comic possibility of a return to health. Large irony, universal irony, is fatal and unalterable, implying the malevolence of a seemingly rational but really absurd universe. The ironies of *Huckleberry Finn* are of the first kind, the comic ironies that imply the possibility of a return of a diseased society to health. Ironically, it is Pap Finn, the most evil of the Southern spokesmen for white prejudice, who inadvertently but surely establishes the norm of social health against which we measure his, and the unreconstructed South's, aberrations as he rails against the "govment" of the free Northern states. Pap, who "had been drunk over in town, and laid in the gutter all night," goes to "ripping again. . . . Whenever his liquor begun to work, he most always went for the govment. . . ." "Oh, yes," he whines, "this is a wonderful govment, wonderful. Why, looky here. There was a free nigger there, from Ohio. . . . And what do you think? they said he was a p'fessor in a college. . . . And that ain't the wust. They said he could vote. . . . Thinks I, what is the country a-coming to? . . . They call that a govment that can't sell a free nigger till he's been in the State six months. . . ." Pap Finn, very early in the novel, ironically establishes the moral norm against which Southern social inadequacies are to be measured, and from this point on the reader is secure in his alliance with the author when he creates his small, stable ironies. Whatever Pap Finn is for, the reader is conditioned to be against; whatever he is against, the reader is for. The social structure of the Northern free states becomes the standard of health from which Southern society deviates and to which, hopefully, it can be helped to return by the small ironies of comic satire. These ironies are bound up with the realistic vision that sees the boy as necessarily a product of the mores and attitudes of his society, and the characterization of Huck Finn will adhere to this reality. He will, in the course of his adventures, learn that Jim is not a thing, but a human being, and one of the best he has known. And yet, being a creature of his society, he cannot translate this knowledge from the individual to the class: blacks in the abstract will remain things for him, and his "conscience" will always chide him for violating society's injunction against stealing another (white) person's "things."

Twain has made sure to make this point by placing Huck's first crisis of "conscience" immediately after his discovery of Jim's warm humanity. Huck has played another joke on him, this time letting Jim believe he was dead. Jim's sorrow and his dignified rebuke ("trash is what people is dat puts dirt on de head er dey fren's en makes 'em ashamed") plunges Huck into an agony of remorse in which Jim, who has been up to then a commodity, becomes a warm, dignified, loyal human being. But just a page later, when Jim says he is "all over trembly and feverish to be so close to freedom," Huck's reaction shows that his discovery of Jim's humanity has not been translated into a general truth about slaves and slavery. Huck feels "trembly" too; Jim, he tells himself, is almost free "and who was to blame for it? Why, *me*. I couldn't get that out of my conscience. . . . Conscience says to me, 'What had poor Miss Watson done to you, that you could see her nigger go off right under your eyes and never say one single word?' . . ." Jim goes on to say that "the first thing he would do when he got to a free State he would go to saving up money and never spend a single cent, and when he got enough he would buy his wife . . . and then they would both work to buy the two children, and if their master wouldn't sell them, they'd get an Ab'litionist to go and steal them."

Secure in the knowledge of his reader's assured complicity in the irony, Twain describes Huck's reaction: "It most froze me to hear such talk. . . . Here was this nigger which [note the "which"] I had as good as helped to run away, coming right out flat-footed and saying he would steal his children—children that belonged to a man I didn't even know; a man that hadn't ever done me no harm." He writes a letter to Miss Watson, betraying Jim, feels "good and all washed clean of sin," and then remembers Jim's love and loyalty. His "sound heart" triumphs over his false social "conscience." He tears the letter up. "All right, then, I'll *go* to hell." The complicity between author and reader is seamless: the ironies of Huck's inverted morality, his conviction that he is bad when he has done good, compels the reader to detest the society that has so warped the boy's sense of good and evil, and to cheer the "sound heart" that instinctively allies itself with the humanistic society that Pap Finn has earlier, unwittingly, established as the norm of moral health.

An appreciation of the overtone of pure humor and the undertone of satire should not ignore the depths of sadness and pathos that are there in the novel, as they are in most great comic inventions: the loneliness of Huck, the awful killings between the feuding Southern families, the pathetic drunkard murdered mercilessly by a Southern "aristocrat"; above all, the horror of a system that reduces people to commodities and trains its children to be unthinking accomplices in the crime. Anybody killed in the steamship explosion? asks Aunt Sally. "No'm. Killed a nigger." "Well, it's lucky; because sometimes people do get hurt." The numbing horror of this exchange between good-natured Aunt Sally and good-hearted Huck almost cancels out the fun and pleasure we feel in reading *Huckleberry Finn* and has convinced many modern readers and critics that the work is a tragedy. But this evidence of the power of social prejudice is a statement about a particular society, one that Mark Twain hoped could be reformed, and not a tragic statement about an inevitable human condition. We have learned about a norm of healthy social behavior through the ironic drunken rant of Old Man Finn. We know that Aunt Sally's moral blindness is not inevitable. Pap Finn's ravings have shown us that there are societies where humans can be treated as humans; the possibilities of social health are there in the depiction of the racial callousness of otherwise dear, sweet, humane Sally and otherwise warm, loyal, and loving Huck Finn, making this most painful of the satiric thrusts a part of an ultimately comic vision. The dominant mood of *Adventures of Huckleberry Finn* is an affirmation in which the undertones of healing satire merge with the overtone of pure humor to make it America's comic masterpiece.

From *Making Mark Twain Work in the Classroom*, edited by James S. Leonard (1999), pp. 131-139. Copyright © 1999 by Duke University Press. All rights reserved. Reprinted with permission of Duke University Press.

Huck, Jim, and American Racial Discourse _____

David L. Smith

> They [blacks] are at least as brave, and more adventuresome [compared to whites]. But this may perhaps proceed from a want of fore-thought, which prevents their seeing a danger till it be present. . . . They are more ardent after their female: but love seems with them to be more an eager desire, than a tender delicate mixture of sentiment and sensation. Their griefs are transient. Those numberless afflictions, which render it doubtful whether heaven has given life to us in mercy or in wrath, are less felt, and sooner forgotten with them. In general, their existence appears to participate more of sensation than reflection. To this must be ascribed their disposition to sleep when abstracted from their diversions, and unemployed in labor.
>
> —Thomas Jefferson, *Notes on the State of Virginia* (187-88)

Almost any Euro-American intellectual of the nineteenth century could have written the preceding words. The notion of Negro inferiority was so deeply pervasive among those heirs of "The Enlightenment" that the categories and even the vocabulary of Negro inferiority were formalized into a tedious, unmodulated litany. This uniformity increased rather than diminished during the course of the century. As Leon Litwack and others have shown, even the Abolitionists, who actively opposed slavery, frequently regarded blacks as inherently inferior. This helps to explain the widespread popularity of colonization schemes among Abolitionists and other liberals.[1] As for Jefferson, it is not surprising that he held such ideas, but it is impressive that he formulated so clearly at the end of the eighteenth century what would become the dominant view of the Negro in the nineteenth century. In many ways, this Father of American Democracy—and quite possibly of five mulatto children—was a man of his time and ahead of his time.[2]

In July of 1876, exactly one century after the American Declaration of Independence, Mark Twain began writing *Adventures of Huckleberry Finn*: a novel which illustrates trenchantly the social limitations which American "civilization" imposes on individual freedom. The book takes special note of ways in which racism impinges upon the lives of Afro-Americans, even when they are legally "free." It is therefore ironic that *Huckleberry Finn* has often been attacked and even censored as a racist work. I would argue, on the contrary, that except for Melville's work, *Huckleberry Finn* is without peers among major Euro-American novels for its explicitly anti-racist stance.[3] Those who brand the book "racist" generally do so without having considered the specific form of racial discourse to which the novel responds. Furthermore, *Huckleberry Finn* offers much more than the typical liberal defenses of "human dignity" and protests against cruelty. Though it contains some such elements, it is more fundamentally a critique of those socially constituted fictions—most notably romanticism, religion, and the concept of "the Negro"—which serve to justify and to disguise selfish, cruel, and exploitative behavior.

When I speak of "racial discourse," I mean more than simply attitudes about "race" or conventions of talking about "race." Most importantly, I mean that "race" itself is a discursive formation, which delimits social relations on the basis of alleged physical differences.[4] "Race" is a strategy for relegating a segment of the population to a permanent inferior status. It functions by insisting that each "race" has specific, definitive, inherent behavioral tendencies and capacities, which distinguish it from other "races." Though scientifically specious, "race" has been powerfully effective as an ideology and as a form of social definition, which serves the interests of Euro-American hegemony. In America, race has been deployed against numerous groups, including Native Americans, Jews, Asians, and even—for brief periods—an assortment of European immigrants.

For obvious reasons, however, the primary emphasis historically has been on defining "the Negro" as a deviant from Euro-American norms. "Race" in America means white supremacy and black inferiority[5]; and "the Negro," a socially constituted fiction, is a generalized, one-dimensional surrogate for the historical reality of Afro-

American people. It is this reified fiction which Twain attacks in *Huckleberry Finn*.

Twain adopts a strategy of subversion in his attack on race. That is, he focuses on a number of commonplaces associated with "the Negro," and then he systematically dramatizes their inadequacy. He uses the term "nigger," and he shows Jim engaging in superstitious behavior. Yet he portrays Jim as a compassionate, shrewd, thoughtful, self-sacrificing and even wise man. Indeed, his portrayal of Jim contradicts every claim presented in Jefferson's description of "the Negro." Jim is cautious, he gives excellent advice, he suffers persistent anguish over separation from his wife and child, and he even sacrifices his own sleep in order that Huck may rest. Jim, in short, exhibits all the qualities that "the Negro" supposedly lacks. Twain's conclusions do more than merely subvert the justifications of slavery, which was already long since abolished. Twain began this book during the final disintegration of Reconstruction, and his satire on antebellum Southern bigotry is also an implicit response to the Negrophobic climate of the post-Reconstruction era (Berkove; Gollin; Egan, esp. 66-102). It is troubling, therefore, that so many readers have completely misunderstood Twain's subtle attack on racism.

Twain's use of the word "nigger" has provoked some readers to reject the novel. (See Hentoff.) As one of the most offensive words in our vocabulary, "nigger" remains heavily shrouded in taboo. A careful assessment of this term within the context of American racial discourse, however, will allow us to understand the particular way in which the author uses it. If we attend closely to Twain's use of the word, we may find in it not just a trigger to outrage, but more importantly, a means of understanding the precise nature of American racism and Mark Twain's attack on it.

Most obviously, Twain uses "nigger" throughout the book as a synonym for "slave." There is ample evidence from other sources that this corresponds to one usage common during the Antebellum period. We first encounter it in reference to "Miss Watson's big nigger, named

Jim" (Ch. 2). This usage, like the term "nigger stealer," clearly designates the "nigger" as a piece of property: a commodity, a slave. This passage also provides the only apparent textual justification for the common critical practice of labelling Jim, "Nigger Jim," as if "nigger" were a part of his proper name. This loathsome habit goes back at least as far as Albert Bigelow Paine's biography of Twain (1912). In any case, "nigger" in this sense connotes an inferior, even subhuman, creature, who is properly owned by and subservient to Euro-Americans.

Both Huck and Jim use the word in this sense. For example, when Huck fabricates his tale about the riverboat accident, the following exchange occurs between him and Aunt Sally:

> 'Good gracious! anybody hurt?'
> 'No'm. Killed a nigger.'
> 'Well, it's lucky, because sometimes people do get hurt.' (Ch. 32)

Huck has never met Aunt Sally prior to this scene, and in spinning a lie which this stranger will find unobjectionable, he correctly assumes that the common notion of Negro subhumanity will be appropriate. Huck's off-hand remark is intended to exploit Aunt Sally's attitudes, not to express Huck's own. A nigger, Aunt Sally confirms, is not a person. Yet this exchange is hilarious, precisely because we know that Huck is playing upon her glib and conventional bigotry. We know that Huck's relationship to Jim has already invalidated for him such obtuse racial notions. The conception of the "nigger" is a socially constituted and sanctioned fiction, and it is just as false and as absurd as Huck's explicit fabrication, which Aunt Sally also swallows whole.

In fact, the exchange between Huck and Aunt Sally reveals a great deal about how racial discourse operates. Its function is to promulgate a conception of "the Negro" as a subhuman and expendable creature, who is by definition feeble-minded, immoral, lazy, and superstitious. One crucial purpose of this social fiction is to justify the abuse and exploitation of Afro-American people by substituting the essentialist fiction of

"Negro-ism" for the actual character of individual Afro-Americans. Hence, in racial discourse every Afro-American becomes just another instance of "the Negro"—just another "nigger." Twain recognizes this invidious tendency of race-thinking, however, and he takes every opportunity to expose the mismatch between racial abstractions and real human beings.

For example, when Pap drunkenly inveighs against the free mulatto from Ohio, he is outraged by what appears to him as a crime against natural laws (Ch. 6). In the first place, a "free nigger" is, for Pap, a contradiction in terms. Indeed, the man's clothes, his demeanor, his education, his profession, and even his silver-headed cane bespeak a social status normally achieved by only a small elite of white men. He is, in other words, a "nigger" who refuses to behave like a "nigger." Pap's ludicrous protestations discredit both himself and other believers in "the Negro," as many critics have noted. But it has not been sufficiently stressed that Pap's racial views correspond very closely to those of most of his white Southern contemporaries, in substance if not in manner of expression. Such views were held not only by poor whites but by all "right-thinking" Southerners, regardless of their social class. Indeed, not even the traumas of the Civil War would cure Southerners of this folly. Furthermore, Pap's indignation at the Negro's right to vote is precisely analogous to the Southern backlash against the enfranchisement of Afro-Americans during Reconstruction. Finally, Pap's comments are rather mild compared to the anti-Negro diatribes which were beginning to emerge among politicians even as Twain was writing *Huckleberry Finn*. He began writing this novel during the final days of Reconstruction, and it seems more than reasonable to assume that the shameful white supremacist bluster of that epoch—exemplified by Pap's tirade—informed Twain's critique of racism in *Huckleberry Finn*. (See Pettit, *Mark Twain and the South*, 35-50.)

Pap's final description of this Ohio gentleman as "a prowling, thieving, infernal, white-shirted free-nigger" (Ch. 6) almost totally contradicts his previous description of the man as a proud, elegant, dignified figure. Yet this contradiction is perfectly consistent with Pap's need to reassert "the Negro" in lieu of social reality. Despite the vulgarity of Pap's personal character, his thinking about race is highly conventional and, therefore, respectable. But most of us cannot respect Pap's views, and when we reject them, we reject the standard racial discourse of both 1840 and 1880.

A reader who objects to the word "nigger" might still insist that Twain could have avoided using it. But it is difficult to imagine how Twain could have debunked a discourse without using the specific terms of that discourse. Even when Twain was writing his book, "nigger" was universally recognized as an insulting, demeaning word. According to Stuart Berg Flexner, "Negro" was generally pronounced as "nigger" until about 1825, at which time Abolitionists began objecting to that term (57). They preferred "colored person" or "person of color." Hence, W. E. B. Du Bois reports that some black Abolitionists of the early 1830s declared themselves united "as men, . . . not as slaves; as 'people of color,' not as 'Negroes'" (245). Writing a generation later in *Army Life in a Black Regiment* (1869), Thomas Wentworth Higginson deplored the common use of "nigger" among freedmen, which he regarded as evidence of low self-esteem (28). The objections to "nigger," then, are not a consequence of the modern sensibility but had been common for a half century before *Huckleberry Finn* was published. The specific function of this term in the book, however, is neither to offend nor merely to provide linguistic authenticity. Much more importantly, it establishes a context against which Jim's specific virtues may emerge as explicit refutations of racist presuppositions.

Of course, the concept of the "nigger" entails far more than just the deployment of certain vocabulary. Most of the attacks on the book focus on its alleged perpetuation of racial stereotypes. Twain does indeed use racial stereotypes here. That practice could be excused as characteristic of the genre of humor within which Twain works. Frontier humor relies upon the use of stock types, and consequently, racial stereotypes are just one of many types present in *Huckleberry Finn*. Yet while valid, such an appeal to generic convention would be unsatisfactory, because it would deny Twain the credit which he deserves for the sophistication of his perceptions (see Ellison, Hansen, Lynn).

As a serious critic of American society, Twain recognized that racial discourse depends upon the deployment of a system of stereotypes which constitute "the Negro" as fundamentally different from and inferior to Euro-Americans. As with his handling of "nigger," Twain's strategy with racial stereotypes is to elaborate them in order to undermine them. To be sure, those critics are correct who have argued that Twain uses this narrative to reveal Jim's humanity. Jim, however, is just one individual. Much more importantly, Twain uses the narrative to expose the cruelty and hollowness of that racial discourse which exists only to obscure the humanity of all Afro-American people.

One aspect of *Huckleberry Finn* which has elicited copious critical commentary is Twain's use of superstition (see especially Hoffman, "Jim's Magic"). In nineteenth century racial discourse, "the Negro" was always defined as inherently superstitious.[6] Many critics, therefore, have cited Jim's superstitious behavior as an instance of negative stereotyping. One cannot deny that in this respect Jim closely resembles the entire tradition of comic darkies (see Woodard and MacCann), but to observe this similarity is a negligible feat. The issue is, does Twain merely reiterate clichés, or does he use these conventional patterns to make an unconventional point? A close examination will show that in virtually every instance, Twain uses Jim's superstition to make points which undermine rather than revalidate the dominant racial discourse.

The first incident of this superstitious behavior occurs in Chapter 2, as a result of one of Tom Sawyer's pranks. When Jim falls asleep under a tree, Tom hangs his hat on a branch. Subsequently, Jim concocts an elaborate tale about having been hexed and ridden by witches. The tale grows more grandiose with subsequent retellings, and eventually Jim becomes a local celebrity, sporting a five-cent piece on a string around his neck as a talisman. "Niggers would come miles to hear Jim tell about it, and he was more looked up to than any nigger in that country," the narrator reports. Jim's celebrity finally reaches the point that "Jim was most ruined, for a servant, because he got so stuck up on account of having seen the devil and been rode by witches." This is, no doubt, amusing. Yet whether Jim believes his own tale or not—and the "superstitious Negro" thesis requires us to assume that he does—the fact remains that Jim clearly benefits from becoming more a celebrity and less a "servant." It is his owner, not Jim, who suffers when Jim's uncompensated labor diminishes.[7]

This incident has often been interpreted as an example of risible Negro gullibility and ignorance, as exemplified by blackface minstrelsy. Such a reading has more than a little validity, but can only partially account for the implications of this scene. If not for the final sentence, such an account might seem wholly satisfactory, but the information that Jim becomes, through his own storytelling, unsuited for life as a slave, introduces unexpected complications. Is it likely that Jim has been deceived by his own creative prevarications—especially given what we learn about his character subsequently? Or has he cleverly exploited the conventions of "Negro superstition" in order to turn a silly boy's prank to his own advantage?

Regardless of whether we credit Jim with forethought in this matter, it is undeniable that he turns Tom's attempt to humiliate him into a major personal triumph. In other words, Tom gives him an inch, and he takes an ell. It is also obvious that he does so by exercising remarkable skills as a rhetorician. By constructing a fictitious narrative of his own experience, Jim elevates himself above his prescribed station in life. By becoming, in effect, an author, Jim writes himself a new destiny. Jim's triumph may appear to be dependent upon the gullibility of other "superstitious" Negroes, but since we have no direct encounter with them, we cannot know whether they are unwitting victims of Jim's ruse or not. A willing audience need not be a totally credulous one. In any case, it is intelligence, not stupidity, which facilitates Jim's triumph. Tom may have had his chuckle, but the last laugh, clearly, belongs to Jim.

In addressing Jim's character, we should keep in mind that fore-thought, creativity and shrewdness are qualities which racial discourse—see Thomas Jefferson—denies to "the Negro." In that sense, Jim's darky performance here subverts the fundamental definition of the darky. For "the Negro" is defined to be an object, not a subject. Yet does an object construct its own narrative? Viewed in this way, the fact of superstition, which traditionally connotes ignorance and unsophistication, becomes far less important than the ends to which superstition is put. This inference exposes, once again, the inadequacy of a positivist epistemology, which holds, for example, that "a rose is a rose is a rose." No one will deny the self-evidence of a tautology; but a rose derives whatever meaning it has from the context within which it is placed (including the context of traditional symbolism.) It is the contextualizing activity, not *das Ding-an-sich*, which generates meaning. Again and again, Twain attacks racial essentialism by directing our attention, instead, to the particularity of individual action. We find that Jim is not "the Negro." Jim is Jim, and we, like Huck, come to understand what Jim is by attending to what he does in specific situations.

In another instance of explicitly superstitious behavior, Jim uses a hairball to tell Huck's fortune. One may regard this scene as a comical example of Negro ignorance and credulity, acting in concert with the ignorance and credulity of a fourteen-year-old white boy. That reading would allow one an unambiguous laugh at Jim's expense. If one examines the scene carefully, however, the inadequacy of such a reductive reading becomes apparent. Even if Jim does believe in the supernatural powers of this hairball, the fact remains that most of the transaction depends upon Jim's quick wits. For example, the soothsaying aside, much of the exchange between Huck and Jim is an exercise in wily and understated economic bartering. In essence, Jim wants to be paid for his services, while Huck wants free advice. Jim insists that the hairball will not speak without being paid. Huck, who has a dollar, will only admit to having a counterfeit quarter. Jim responds by pretending to be in collusion with Huck. He explains how to doctor the "quarter" so that "anybody in town would take it in a minute, let alone a hair-ball" (Ch. 4). But obviously it is not the hair-ball who will benefit from acquiring and spending this counterfeit coin (cf. Weaver and Williams).

In this transaction, Jim serves his own interests while appearing to serve Huck's interests. He takes a slug which is worthless to Huck, and through the alchemy of his own cleverness, he contrives to make it worth twenty-five cents to himself. That, in antebellum America, is not a bad price for telling a fortune. But more importantly, Twain shows Jim self-consciously subverting the prescribed definition of "the Negro," even as he performs within the limitations of that role. He remains the conventional "Negro" by giving the white boy what he wants, at no real cost, and by consistently appearing to be passive and subservient to the desires of Huck and the hair-ball. But in fact, he serves his own interests all along. Such resourcefulness is hardly consistent with the familiar, one-dimensional concept of "the superstitious Negro."

And while Jim's reading is formulaic, it is hardly simple-minded. He sees the world as a kind of Manichean universe, in which forces of light and darkness—white and black—vie for dominance. Pap, he says, is uncertain what to do, torn between his white and black angels. Jim's advice, "to res' easy en let de ole man take his own way" (Ch. 4), turns out to be good advice, because Huck greatly enjoys life in the cabin, despite Pap's fits of drunken excess. This mixture of pleasure and pain is precisely what Jim predicts. Admittedly, Jim's conceptual framework is not original. Nonetheless, his reading carries considerable force, because it corresponds so neatly to the dominant thematic patterns in this book, and more broadly, to the sort of dualistic thinking which informs much of Twain's work. (To take an obvious example, consider the role reversals and character contrasts in *Pudd'nhead Wilson* or *The Prince and the Pauper.*) And most immediately, Jim's comments here reflect tellingly upon his situation as a black slave in racist America. The slave's fate is always torn between his master's will and his own.

In this reading and other incidents, Jim emerges as an astute and sensitive observer of human behavior, both in his comments regarding Pap and in his subtle remarks to Huck. Jim clearly possesses a subtlety and intelligence which "the Negro" allegedly lacks. Twain makes this point more clearly in the debate scene in Chapter 15. True enough, most of this debate is, as several critics have noted, conventional minstrel show banter. Nevertheless, Jim demonstrates impressive reasoning abilities, despite his factual ignorance. For example, in their argument over "Poly-voo-franzy," Huck makes a category error by implying that the difference between languages is analogous to the difference between human language and cat language. While Jim's response—that man should talk like a man—betrays his ignorance of cultural diversity, his argument is perceptive and structurally sound. The humor in Huck's conclusion, "you can't learn a nigger how to argue," arises precisely from our recognition that Jim's argument is better than Huck's.

Throughout the novel, Twain presents Jim in ways which render ludicrous the conventional wisdom about "Negro character." As an intelligent, sensitive, wily and considerate individual, Jim demonstrates that one's race provides no useful index of one's character. While that point may seem obvious to many contemporary readers, it is a point rarely made by nineteenth-century Euro-American novelists. Indeed, except for Melville, J. W. DeForest, Albion Tourgee, and George Washington Cable, white novelists virtually always portrayed Afro-American characters as exemplifications of "Negroness." In this regard, the twentieth century has been little better. By presenting us a series of glimpses which penetrate the "Negro" exterior and reveal the person beneath it, Twain debunks American racial discourse. For racial discourse maintains that the "Negro" exterior is all that a "Negro" really has.

This insight in itself is a notable accomplishment. Twain, however, did not view racism as an isolated phenomenon, and it was his effort to place racism within the context of other cultural traditions which produced the most problematic aspect of his novel. For it is in the final chapters—the Tom Sawyer section—which most critics consider the weakest part of the book, that Twain links his criticisms of slavery and Southern romanticism, condemning the cruelties which both of these traditions entail. (See Altenbernd.) Critics have objected to these chapters on various grounds. Some of the most common are that Jim becomes reduced to a comic darky (e.g., Marx, Schmitz), that Tom's antics undermine the seriousness of the novel, and that these burlesque narrative developments destroy the structural integrity of the novel. Most critics see this conclusion as an evasion of the difficult issues which the novel has raised. There is no space here for a discussion of the structural issues, but it seems to me that as a critique of American racial discourse, these concluding chapters offer a harsh, coherent, and uncompromising indictment.

Tom Sawyer's absurd scheme to "rescue" Jim offends, because the section begins with Huck's justly celebrated crisis of conscience, which culminates in his resolve to free Jim, even if doing so condemns him to hell. The passage which leads to Huck's decision, as familiar as it is, merits reexamination:

> I'd see him standing my watch on top of his'n, stead of calling me, so I could go on sleeping; and see him how glad he was when I come back out of the fog; and when I come to him again in the swamp, up there where the feud was; and such like times; and would always call me honey, and pet me, and do everything he could think of for me, and how good he always was; and at last I struck the time I saved him by telling the men we had small-pox aboard, and he was so grateful, and said I was the best friend old Jim ever had in the world, and the *only* one he's got now; and then I happened to look around, and see that paper. . . . I studied a minute, sort of holding my breath, and then says to myself: 'All right, then, I'll *go* to hell'—and tore it up. (Ch. 31)

The issue here is not just whether or not Huck should return a contraband[8]—an escaped slave—to its proper owner. More fundamentally, Huck must decide whether to accept the conventional wisdom, which defines "Negroes" as subhuman commodities, or the evidence of his own experience, which has shown Jim to be a good and kind man and a true friend.

Huck makes the obvious decision, but his doing so represents more than simply a liberal choice of conscience over social convention. Twain explicitly makes Huck's choice a sharp attack on the Southern church. Huck scolds himself: "Here was the Sunday school, you could a gone to it and if you'd done it they'd a learnt you, there, that people that acts as I'd been acting about that nigger goes to everlasting fire" (Ch. 31). Yet despite Huck's anxiety, his choice is obviously correct. Furthermore, by the time that Twain wrote these words, more than twenty years of national strife, including Civil War and Reconstruction, had established Huck's conclusion regarding slavery as a dominant national consensus. Not even reactionary Southerners advocated a reinstitution of slavery. Since the Southern church had taught that slavery was God's will, Huck's decision flatly repudiates the church's teachings regarding slavery. And implicitly, it also repudiates the church as an institution by suggesting that the church functions to undermine, not to encourage, a reliance on one's conscience. To define "Negroes" as subhuman removes them from moral consideration and therefore justifies the callous exploitation of them. This view of religion is consistent with the cynical iconoclasm which Twain expressed in *Letters from the Earth* and others of his "dark" works.[9]

In this context, Tom Sawyer appears to us as a superficially charming but fundamentally distasteful interloper. His actions are governed not by conscience but rather by romantic conventions and literary "authorities." Indeed, while Tom may appear to be a kind of renegade, he is in essence thoroughly conventional in his values and proclivities. Despite all his boyish pranks, Tom represents a kind of solid respectability— a younger version of the Southern gentleman, as exemplified by the Grangerfords and the Shepherdsons (see Hoffman, *Form and Fable*, 327-28). Hence, when Tom proposes to help Huck steal Jim, Huck laments that "Tom Sawyer fell, considerable, in my estimation. Only I couldn't believe it. Tom Sawyer a *nigger stealer!*" (Ch. 33). Such liberating activity is proper for Huck, who is not respectable, but not for Tom, who is. As with the previous example, however, this one implies a deep criticism of the status quo. Huck's act of conscience, which most of us would now endorse, is possible only for an outsider. This hardly speaks well for the moral integrity of Southern (or American) "civilization."

To examine Tom's role in the novel, let us begin at the end. Upon learning of the failed escape attempt and Jim's recapture, Tom cries out, self-righteously: "turn him loose! He ain't no slave; he's as free as any creature that walks this earth" (Ch. 42). Tom has known all along that his cruel and ludicrous scheme to rescue the captured "prisoner" was being enacted upon a free man; and indeed, only his silence regarding Jim's status allowed the scheme to proceed with Jim's cooperation. Certainly, neither Huck nor Jim would otherwise have indulged Tom's foolishness. Tom's gratuitous cruelty here in the pursuit of his own amusement corresponds to his less vicious prank against Jim in Chapter 2. And just as before, Twain converts Tom's callous mischief into a personal triumph for Jim.

Not only has Jim suffered patiently, which would in truth represent a doubtful virtue. (Jim is not Uncle Tom.) Jim demonstrates his moral superiority by surrendering himself in order to assist the doctor in treating his wounded tormentor. This is hardly the behavior which one would expect from a commodity, and it is *precisely* Jim's status—man or chattel—which has been fundamentally at issue throughout the novel. It may be true that Tom's lengthy juvenile antics subvert the tone of the novel, but they also provide the necessary backdrop for Jim's noble act. Up to this point, we have been able to admire Jim's good sense and to respond sentimentally to his good character. This, however, is the first time that we see him making a significant (and wholly admirable) moral decision. His act sets him apart from everyone else in the novel except Huck. And modestly (if not disingenuously), he claims to be behaving just as Tom Sawyer would. Always conscious of his role as a "Negro," Jim knows better than to claim personal credit for his good deed. Yet the contrast between Jim's behavior and Tom's is unmistakable. Huck declares that Jim is "white inside" (Ch. 40). He apparently intends this as a compliment, but Tom is fortunate that Jim does not behave like most of the whites in the novel.

Twain also contrasts Jim's self-sacrificing compassion with the cruel and mean-spirited behavior of his captors, emphasizing that white skin does not justify claims of superior virtue. They abuse Jim, verbally and physically, and some want to lynch him as an example to other slaves. The moderates among them, however, resist, pointing out that they could be made to pay for the destruction of private property. As Huck observes: "the people that's always the most anxious for to hang a nigger that hain't done just right, is always the very ones that ain't the most anxious to pay for him when they've got their satisfaction out of him" (Ch. 42). As if these enforcers of white supremacy did not appear contemptible enough already, Twain then has the doctor describe Jim as the best and most faithful nurse he has ever seen, despite Jim's "resking his freedom" and his obvious fatigue. These vigilantes do admit that Jim deserves to be rewarded, but their idea of a reward is to cease punching and cursing him. They are not even generous enough to remove Jim's heavy shackles.

Ultimately, *Huckleberry Finn* renders a harsh judgment on American society. Freedom from slavery, the novel implies, is not freedom from gratuitous cruelty; and racism, like romanticism, is finally just an elaborate justification which the adult counterparts of Tom Sawyer use to facilitate their exploitation and abuse of other human beings. Tom feels guilty, with good reason, for having exploited Jim, but his final gesture of paying Jim off is less an insult to Jim than it is Twain's commentary on Tom himself. Just as slaveholders believe that economic relations (ownership) can justify their privilege of mistreating other human beings, Tom apparently believes that an economic exchange can suffice as atonement for his misdeeds. Perhaps he finds a forty-dollar token more affordable than an apology. But then, just as Tom could only "set a free nigger free," considering, as Huck says, "his bringing-up" (Ch. 42), he similarly could hardly be expected to apologize for his pranks. Huck, by contrast, is equally rich, but he *has* apologized to Jim earlier in the novel. And this is the point of Huck's final remark, rejecting the prospect of civilization. To become civilized is not just to become like Aunt Sally. More immediately, it is to become like Tom Sawyer.

Jim is, indeed, "as free as any creature that walks this earth." In other words, he is a man, like all men, at the mercy of other men's arbitrary cruelties. In a sense, given Twain's view of freedom, to allow Jim to escape to the North or to have Tom announce Jim's manumission earlier would be an evasion of the novel's ethical insights. While one may escape from legal bondage, there is no escape from the cruelties of this "civilization." There is no promised land, where one may enjoy absolute personal freedom. An individual's freedom is always constrained by one's social relations to other people. Being legally free does not spare Jim from gratuitous humiliation and physical suffering in the final chapters, precisely because Jim is still regarded as a "nigger." Even if he were as accomplished as the mulatto from Ohio, he would not be exempt from mistreatment. Furthermore, since Tom represents the hegemonic values of his society, Jim's "freedom" amounts to little more than an obligation to live by his wits and to make the best of a bad situation.

Slavery and racism, then, are social evils which take their places alongside various others which the novel documents, such as the insane romanticism that inspires the Grangerfords and Shepherdsons blithely to murder each other, generation after generation. Twain rejects entirely the mystification of race and demonstrates that Jim is in most ways a better man than the men who regard him as their inferior. But he also shows how little correlation there may be between the treatment one deserves and the treatment one receives.

If this conclusion sounds uncontroversial from the perspective of

1984, we would do well to remember that it contradicts entirely the over-whelming and optimistic consensus of 1884. And no other nineteenth-century novel so effectively locates racial discourse within the context of a general critique of American institutions and traditions. Indeed, the novel suggests that real individual freedom, in this land of the free, cannot be found. "American civilization" enslaves and exploits rather than liberates. It is hardly an appealing message.

Given the subtlety of Mark Twain's approach, it is not surprising that most of his contemporaries misunderstood or simply ignored the novel's demystification of race. Despite their patriotic rhetoric, they, like Pap, were unprepared to take seriously the implications of "free-dom, justice, and equality." They, after all, espoused an ideology and an explicit language of race which was virtually identical to Thomas Jefferson's. Yet racial discourse flatly contradicts and ultimately renders hypocritical the egalitarian claims of liberal democracy. The heart of Twain's message to us is that an honest person must reject one or the other. But hypocrisy, not honesty, is our norm. For too many of us continue to assert both racial distinction and liberal values, simulta-neously. If we, a century later, continue to be confused about *Adventures of Huckleberry Finn*, perhaps it is because we remain more deeply committed to both racial discourse and a self-deluding opti-mism than we care to admit.[10]

Notes

1. The literature on the Abolition movement and on antebellum debates regarding the Negro is, of course, voluminous. George Fredrickson's excellent *The Black Image in the White Mind* is perhaps the best general work of its kind. Fredrickson's *The Inner Civil War* is also valuable, especially pp. 53-64. Leon Litwack closely examines the ambivalence of Abolitionists regarding racial intermingling (214-46). Benjamin Quarles presents the most detailed examination of black Abolitionists, though Vincent

Harding offers a more vivid (and overtly polemical) account of their relationships to white Abolitionists (101-194).

2. The debate over Jefferson's relationship to Sally Hemings has raged for two centuries. The most thorough scholarly accounts are by Fawn Brodie, who suggests that Jefferson did have a prolonged involvement with Hemings, and by Virginius Dabney, who endeavors to exonerate Jefferson of such charges. Barbara Chase-Riboud presents a fictionalized version of this relationship in *Sally Hemings*. The first Afro-American novel, *Clotel; Or the President's Daughter* (1853) by William Wells Brown, was also based on this alleged affair.

3. For dates of composition, see Blair. For a discussion of Melville's treatment of race, Carolyn Karchner's *Shadow Over the Promised Land* is especially valuable. Articles on *Benito Cereno* by Joyce Adler and Jean Yellin are also noteworthy. Rayford Logan and Lawrence J. Friedman provide detailed accounts of the racist climate in Post-Reconstruction America, emphasizing the literary manifestations of such attitudes. Friedman's discussion of George Washington Cable (99-118), the outspoken Southern liberal, is very informative. For a general historical overview of the period, C. Vann Woodward's work remains unsurpassed. John W. Cell offers a provocative reconsideration of Woodward's arguments, and Joel Williamson's new book documents the excessively violent tendencies of Southern racism at the end of the century.

4. My use of "racial discourse" has some affinities to Foucault's conception of "discourse." This is not, however, a strictly Foucauldian reading. While Foucault's definition of discursive practices provides one of the most sophisticated tools presently available for cultural analysis, his conception of power seems to me problematic. I prefer an account of power which allows for a consideration of interest and hegemony. Theorists such as Marshall Berman (34-35) and Catherine MacKinnon (526) have indicated similar reservations. Frank Lentricchia, however, has made a provocative attempt to modify Foucauldian analysis, drawing upon Gramsci's analysis of hegemony. See Foucault, *The Archaeology of Knowledge, Power/Knowledge* (esp. 92-108), and *The History of Sexuality*, (esp. 92-102).

5. This is not to discount the sufferings of other groups. But historically, the philosophical basis of Western racial discourse—which existed even before the European "discovery" of America—has been the equation of "good" and "evil" with light and darkness (or, white and black). (See Derrida; Jordan, 1-40; and West, 47-65.) Economically, the slave trade, chattel slavery, agricultural peonage, and color-coded wage differentials have made the exploitation of African-Americans the most profitable form of racism. Finally, Afro-Americans have long been the largest American "minority" group. Consequently, the primacy of "the Negro" in American racial discourse is, to use Althusser's term (87-126), "Over-determined." The acknowledgment of primary status, however, is hardly a claim of privilege.

6. Even the allegedly scientific works on the Negro focused on superstition as a definitive trait. See, for example, W. D. Weatherford and Jerome Dowd. No one has commented more scathingly on Negro superstition than William H. Thomas, who was, by American definitions, a Negro himself.

7. Hoffman in *Form and Fable* (331) reveals an implicit understanding of Jim's creativity, but he does not pursue the point in detail.

8. This term became a part of the official military vocabulary during the Civil War, referring to a slave who had gone "AWOL."

9. A number of works comment on Twain's religious views and the relation between his critiques of religion and of racism. See Ensor; Pettit, "Mark Twain and the Negro"; and Gollin.

10. I would like to thank my colleagues, David Langston and Michael Bell, for the helpful suggestions which they offered to me regarding the essay.

Works Cited

Adler, Joyce. "Melville's *Benito Cereno*: Slavery and Violence in the Americas." *Science and Society*, 38 (1974), 19-48.

Altenbernd, Lynn. "Huck Finn, Emancipator." *Criticism*, 1 (1959), 298-307.

Althusser, Louis. *For Marx*. London: Verso Editions, 1979.

Berkove, Lawrence I. "The Free Man of Color in *The Grandissimes* and Works by Harris and Mark Twain." *The Southern Quarterly*, 18.4 (1981), 60-73.

Berman, Marshall. *All That Is Solid Melts into Air*. New York: Simon & Schuster, 1982.

Blair, Walter. "When Was *Huckleberry Finn* Written?" *American Literature*, 30 (March 1958), 1-25.

Brodie, Fawn. *Thomas Jefferson, an Intimate History*. New York: Norton, 1974.

Brown, William Wells. *Clotel: Or the President's Daughter*. New York: Arno Press, 1969.

Cell, John W. *The Highest Stage of White Supremacy*. New York: Cambridge University Press, 1982.

Chase-Riboud, Barbara. *Sally Hemings*. New York: The Viking Press, 1979.

Clemens, Samuel. *Adventures of Huckleberry Finn*. Eds. Scully Bradley, Richmond Croom Beatty, E. Hudson Long, and Thomas Cooley. 2nd ed. New York: Norton, 1977.

Dabney, Virginius. *The Jefferson Scandals*. New York: Dodd, Mead, 1981.

Derrida, Jacques. "White Mythology." *New Literary History*, 6 (1974), 5-74.

Dowd, Jerome. *Negro Races*. New York: Macmillan, 1907.

Du Bois, William E. B. *The Souls of Black Folk. Three Negro Classics*. Ed. John Hope Franklin. New York: Avon, 1965.

Egan, Michael. *Mark Twain's Huckleberry Finn: Race, Class and Society*. Atlantic Highlands, NJ: Humanities Press, 1977.

Ellison, Ralph. "Change the Joke and Slip the Yoke." *Shadow and Act*. New York: Vintage, 1964, 45-59.

Ensor, Allison. *Mark Twain and the Bible*. Lexington: The University of Kentucky Press, 1969.

Flexner, Stuart Berg. *I Hear America Talking*. New York: Van Nostrand Reinhold, 1976.

Foucault, Michel. *The History of Sexuality*. Vol. 1. New York: Vintage, 1980.

_____. *Power/Knowledge.* Ed. Colin Gordon. New York: Pantheon, 1980.

Fredrickson, George M. *The Black Image in the White Mind.* New York: Harper Torchbooks, 1971.

_____. *The Inner Civil War.* New York: Harper Torchbooks, 1971.

Friedman, Lawrence J. *The White Savage: Racial Fantasies in the Postbellum South.* Englewood Cliffs, NJ: Prentice-Hall, 1970.

Gollin, Richard and Rita. "*Huckleberry Finn* and the Time of the Evasion." *Modern Language Studies*, 9 (Spring 1979), 5-15.

Gramsci, Antonio. *Selections from the Prison Notebooks.* New York: International Publishers, 1971.

Hansen, Chadwick. "The Character of Jim and the Ending of *Huckleberry Finn.*" *Massachusetts Review*, 5 (Autumn 1963), 45-66.

Harding, Vincent. *There Is a River.* New York: Harcourt Brace Jovanovich, 1981.

Hentoff, Nat. "Huck Finn Better Get Out of Town by Sundown." Column. *The Village Voice*, 27 (May 4, 1982).

_____. "Is Any Book Worth the Humiliation of Our Kids?" Column. *The Village Voice*, 27 (May 11, 1982).

_____. "Huck Finn and the Shortchanging of Black Kids." Column. *The Village Voice*, 27 (May 18, 1982).

_____. "These Are Little Battles Fought in Remote Places." Column. *The Village Voice*, 27 (May 25, 1982).

Higginson, Thomas Wentworth. *Army Life in a Black Regiment.* Boston: Beacon Press, 1962.

Hoffman, Daniel. *Form and Fable in American Fiction.* New York: Oxford University Press, 1961.

_____. "Jim's Magic: Black or White?" *American Literature*, 32 (March 1960), 47-54.

Jefferson, Thomas. *Notes on the State of Virginia. The Portable Thomas Jefferson.* Ed. Merrill D. Peterson. New York: Viking, 1975.

Jordan, Winthrop. *White Over Black.* New York: Norton, 1968.

Karchner, Carolyn. *Shadow Over the Promised Land.* Baton Rouge: Louisiana State University Press, 1980.

Lentricchia, Frank. "Reading Foucault (Punishment, Labor, Resistance)." *Raritan* 1.4: 5-32.

_____. "Reading Foucault (Punishment, Labor, Resistance)." Part 11. *Raritan* 2: 41-70.

Litwack, Leon F. *North of Slavery.* Chicago: The University of Chicago Press, 1961.

Logan, Rayford. *The Negro in American Life and Thought: The Nadir, 1877-1901.* New York: The Dial Press, 1954.

Lynn, Kenneth S. *Mark Twain and Southwestern Humor.* Boston: Little, Brown, 1959.

MacKinnon, Catherine A. "Feminism, Marxism, Method, and the State: An Agenda for Theory." *Signs*, 7:3 (1982), 515-44.

Marx, Leo. "Mr. Eliot, Mr. Trilling and *Huckleberry Finn.*" *The American Scholar*, 22 (Autumn 1953), 423-40.

Paine, Albert Bigelow. *Mark Twain: A Biography*. New York: Harper, 1912.

Pettit, Arthur G. "Mark Twain and the Negro, 1867-1869." *Journal of Negro History*, 56 (April 1971), 88-96.

_____. *Mark Twain and the South*. Lexington: The University of Kentucky Press, 1974.

Quarles, Benjamin. *Black Abolitionists*. New York: Oxford University Press, 1969.

Schmitz, Neil. "Twain, *Huckleberry Finn*, and the Reconstruction." *American Studies*, 12 (Spring 1971), 59-67.

Thomas, William Hannibal. *The American Negro*. New York: The Negro Universities Press, 1969. Reprint of 1901 ed.

Weatherford, W. D. *Negro Life in the South*. New York: Young Men's Christian Association Press, 1910.

Weaver, Thomas and Williams, Merline. "Mark Twain's Jim: Identity as an Index to Cultural Attitudes." *American Literary Realism*, 13 (Spring 1980), 19-30.

West, Cornel. *Prophesy Deliverance*. Philadelphia: Westminster Press, 1982.

Williamson, Joel. *The Crucible of Race*. New York: Oxford University Press, 1984.

Woodard, Fredrick and MacCann, Donnarae. "*Huckleberry Finn* and the Traditions of Blackface Minstrelsy." *Interracial Books for Children Bulletin*, 15:1-2 (1984), 4-13.

Woodward, C. Vann. *Origins of the New South*. Baton Rouge: Louisiana State University Press, 1971.

_____. *The Strange Career of Jim Crow*. Third Edition. New York: Oxford University Press, 1974.

Yellin, Jean Fagan. "Black Masks: Melville's 'Benito Cereno.'" *American Quarterly* 22 (Fall 1970), 678-89.

Connecticut Yankee:
Twain's Other Masterpiece

Lawrence I. Berkove

Teaching *Connecticut Yankee* can be an exceptionally rewarding experience because the book is far better than is generally realized. Written at the height of Twain's powers, *Connecticut Yankee* approaches the skill, complexity, and tragic force of *Huckleberry Finn*, and it is definitely one of Twain's greatest works. Students react positively to it, for it illuminates the thought and art of Mark Twain in unique and surprising ways. Despite its ultimate pessimism, students appreciate it for its honesty in articulating moral and philosophical issues that they are confronting. Because teaching *Connecticut Yankee* is closely tied to interpretation, in this essay I will explain my interpretation of the novel simultaneously with my method of teaching it.

As with many great novels, there are some obstacles to a satisfactory reading of *Connecticut Yankee*, but they are on the surface and can be resolved at a deeper level. Teachers who prepare for them will be richly repaid by an unusual amount of student participation and a variety of insights and aesthetic enjoyment. They will be able to turn to good advantage what are thought to be difficulties but are better regarded as opportunities: the change in the novel from a humorous to a tragic tone, the fact that Twain's art and ideas are not yet thoroughly understood, the novel's seeming lack of structural and thematic unity, and the unexpected impact on it of Calvinistic thought.

The first problem—the shift in tone from humorous to tragic—is easily understood. It stems from the fact that virtually no one reads Mark Twain without some preconceptions, stemming from his popular reputation as a humorist, of what to expect. Readers who anticipate a book full of laughs will not be disappointed in the earlier chapters, but the later chapters will puzzle and upset them. The first lesson to be taught a class by way of preparation, therefore, is that although Mark Twain was a humorist, he was not *only* a humorist, nor was his humor, typically, an end in itself. Some background is necessary to understand what follows from this premise.

Mark Twain was a hoaxer. Perhaps no other writer in literature had so profound an appreciation and mastery of the hoax. It is Twain's primary literary technique and runs through his entire oeuvre, from "The Dandy Frightening the Squatter" (1852) to the late "What Is Man?" (1906) and the posthumously published *The Mysterious Stranger* (1916). *Connecticut Yankee* is intricately laced with hoaxes.

A hoax is a deception. In its familiar forms of tall tales and practical jokes, it is often humorous, especially when the butt of the humor is someone whose pompousness or overconfidence strikes an audience as ripe for a comeuppance. In its extended and specialized sense as a fraud or swindle, however, or to those who are the butts of cruel practical jokes, hoaxes may be quite painful or even tragic. Pascal Covici has noted that "the humor of Mark Twain often turns out to be no laughing matter."[1] Readers expect the target of the hoax to be one or more of the characters in a work of fiction; it always comes as a shock when they learn that *they* are the author's real target. In Twain's most important works, and certainly in *Connecticut Yankee*, clues to underlying main themes are often presented disarmingly, in humorous contexts or in seemingly offhand statements, and they are easily overlooked. Thus, readers often discover with shock at a book's ending that they have missed the point of what is happening in the same way that characters in the work have. Twain does not do this gratuitously, but as a way, first, to make the reader experience the force of the hoax and, then, to reflect on its nature. Thus, it is a mistake to dismiss as bad writing what may seem to be narrative problems or unsatisfactory conclusions; chances are that they are part of a subtly laid hoax.

The deepest pattern for Twain's hoaxes is to be found in his religion, which he interpreted heretically. Students may be surprised or upset to learn that Twain did not believe that God was benevolent, but anyone who reads *The Mysterious Stranger* fragments, or *What Is Man?* or *Letters from the Earth*, works composed after *Connecticut Yankee*, cannot reach any other conclusion, and evidence has long been established that Twain viewed God as a trickster and a tyrant. The origin of Twain's views is in the Calvinistic doctrines he learned as a youth, especially those which taught that God had predestined existence, had made human nature corrupt, and had assigned most human beings to hell. By creating Adam and Eve as fatally limited, Twain reasoned, God set them up from the first to make the wrong choice in the Garden of Eden. Subsequent generations of humans, now burdened with original sin, do even less well in the postlapsarian world of temptations and tribulations. Doubly damned by both predestination and a nature so corruptly sinful that even lives totally spent in apparently virtuous thought and action will not redeem them, humans cannot do otherwise than to merit hell. The fact that they have consciences only makes it worse, because they then castigate themselves for failing to do better, even when it is impossible for them to do so. As Twain viewed life and the "damned human race," therefore, humans were programmed to fail from the beginning of creation by a Catch-22 system. They are thus the butt of God's rather grim practical joke or hoax. Twain saw this predestined pattern repeated in nature, history, society, and individual human beings. He objected to its injustice and deception and devoted much of his literature to describing existence as he saw it in the forlorn hope that he could expose its cruelty. But until the 1890s, when his reputation was established, he dared not express these views outright since that would have alienated the readers of his time. One of Twain's greatest abilities was that of writing at two simultaneous levels: one a plot entertaining enough to be enjoyed, the other a serious but submerged counterplot that, if detected, would reveal to his readers that an instructive hoax had been played on them so that they might fully appreciate what it meant to be taken in. *Connecticut Yankee* perfectly exemplifies this approach.

This takes us to the second problem: that Twain has depths not yet adequately understood. He is a magnificent writer, much better even than some of his advocates realize. The same care that we are accustomed to take with every word and phrase in a Henry James novel may be profitably applied to *Connecticut Yankee*; Twain is no less accomplished an artist. Many scholars see in Twain flashes of brilliance, but not the consummate artistry that characterizes great literature. As a result, a good deal of scholarship engages in a sort of special pleading. Impressive ideas and flashes of literary skill are recognized in both *Huckleberry Finn* and *Connecticut Yankee*; but although we are asked to credit Twain with literary greatness, his novels are widely believed not to hold together. Expecting *Connecticut Yankee* to be funny, many commentators, recognizing that there is no way to find humor in the conclusion, have reasoned that Twain changed his mind mid-course, and that the novel consequently breaks in two. But if we do not expect the novel to be humorous, then it succeeds—powerfully—as a serious hoax.

Another objection to the novel's artistry is the appearance of elements of apparent autobiography. As resemblances between Twain and the protagonist Hank Morgan emerge, some critics feel this detracts from the integrity of the book as a work of fiction. This is a peculiar objection, for it is not at all uncommon for authors to create characters with resemblances to themselves, and for those characters not always to be admirable. Authors write best from what they know, and they ought to know themselves best. As long as Mark Twain is thought to be only a diamond in the rough, someone who can start a novel but not finish it, and who almost but not quite transcends the lack of formal education or some stabilizing feature of his personality or economic condition, there will be ingenious explanations of why *Connecticut Yankee* appears to fall short of formal excellence. Again, this approach is fatally flawed by an incomplete understanding of Twain's genius and neglects the fact that some of the world's outstanding writers succeeded despite the lack of a formal education or perfect personalities. Although Ben Jonson claimed that Shakespeare had "smalle Latin and lesse Greek," he still recognized Shakespeare's greatness. We know next to nothing of Homer and relatively little about Cervantes, yet today no one doubts their surpassing literary achievements. We are in the position of knowing a great deal about Mark Twain, but it would be a case of not seeing the forest for the trees to be so convinced for biographical reasons that Twain was artistically limited as to deny actual evidence of the success of *Connecticut Yankee*.

A third problem is the question of the novel's unity—that is, the harmonic relevance of all parts to its final effect. Most experienced novel readers prefer novels in which there are no loose ends and everything seems to flow together synergistically. We must admit that *Connecticut Yankee*'s unity is not immediately obvious. The first half appears to be funny; the conclusion is grim. There are seemingly digressive chapters in it, such as those in which Hank Morgan appears to serve, transparently, as a mouthpiece for Twain's personal biases. There are also important passages that a careful reader might find difficult if not impossible to accept. Nevertheless, each case where an objection might be raised is actually, paradoxically, evidence of the novel's unity. I will explain.

The best way I have found to proceed with *Connecticut Yankee* is to require that the class finish a first reading of the novel before a discussion of it takes place because it is necessary to move back and forth in the text. Having already informed my students of the previously stated objections to the novel's structural and thematic unity, and my belief that these objections can all be overcome and the novel seen as a work of extraordinary and surprising power and brilliance, I have piqued their curiosity and presented them with a challenge. This approach in itself is a refreshing change from the conventional way of dealing with classics of literature; now both the author and the teacher are out on a limb and something new may be discovered. Since I have required the novel to be read before discussion of it begins, they will already have comprehended the force of the objections to its unity and be interested in how I can prove the contrary.

I begin the proofs by asking my students to allow, for the time being, two basic assumptions. The first is that Hank Morgan is a fictional character, under Twain's control at all times, even (and maybe especially) when he seems to most resemble Twain. The second is that *Connecticut Yankee* should be judged as a unified novel; if its parts can be seen to be unified, then the novel is successful; if not, not. Students have usually been willing to grant these requests because they are seen to be reasonable and potentially beneficial. My students consistently have been eager to be engaged in fresh discovery. Once the assumptions are granted, we can proceed with solving the problems raised above.

The first of them is the question of how the novel is organized. It is constructed as a fiction in two senses of the word: that we are reading something that is not fact, and that even the fictional information we receive is not dependable. The plot is conveyed within several narrative frames. The outermost one, in the "A Word of Explanation" and "Final P.S. by M.T." chapters, is told to us by a narrator who refers to himself as "I" and signs himself "M.T." This narrator must be fictitious, although "M.T." would seem to signify Mark Twain; if not, we have to believe that Twain actually had the experience of meeting Morgan and reading his manuscript. The narrative was supposedly preserved by Clarence, who also contributes the penultimate chapter, "A Postscript by Clarence." Unless we wish to believe that the events literally happened, then Clarence's part in the narrative is also fictitious. Inside these frames is Hank's account, supposedly written retrospectively as a record of his experiences in sixth-century England.

Apart from noting the obvious, that Hank must also be fictitious, we have to deal with his reliability as a narrator. This is a critical element of the novel, and the failure of readers to recognize him as unreliable has commonly misled them. Hank is not unreliable in that he deliberately lies to us or withholds information. On the contrary, he gains our confidence by his openness, his good nature and good sense, and his benevolent intentions toward his new situation. In addition, we can identify with him because he is like one of us: an average American, and not someone, from a class above or below us with a lifestyle or values that we do not share. He also reminds us (frequently) that he is democratic, and we see that his enemies are the enemies of the common man: tyranny, ignorance, and superstition. Nevertheless, Mark Twain once described him as a "nincompoop," and the fact of the matter is that however much Hank professes to understand the events and personalities he encounters, he does not understand them enough, nor does he even understand himself. He almost never questions his own judgment, his true motives, or his actions, despite a growing inconsistency between what he professes and what he is and does. As a consequence, he is as much the victim of his own unreliability as we are.

He believes himself to be the "boss," in control even when his schemes begin to go awry or backfire and when surprises happen to him. Inasmuch as it is difficult to see Hank as unreliable from the outset, it is best to defer discussion of Hank's reliability until the class is well into the discussion of the novel and is scrutinizing the text more carefully. As the novel is reviewed, abundant evidence will be found to demonstrate that Hank's character has remained fixed throughout the novel, and that just as we have been hoaxed into trusting him, he has been hoaxed into believing himself in control of events.

A more subtle organizing element in the novel is its pervasive and critical use of dreams.[2] As early as the "A Word of Explanation" chapter, the narrator tells us how his adventure began with his reading of Thomas Malory's "enchanting" book, *Morte d'Arthur,* "a dream of the olden time." As he reads, he himself "dream[s] again." While in this mood, the stranger he met earlier comes to his room, begins his narrative, then becomes sleepy and gives "M.T." a palimpsest to read while he retires to his own room. Even in the second line of chapter 1, Hank describes the summer landscape: "as lovely as a dream and as lonesome as Sunday"—apparently contradictory impressions. A young girl appears with a hoop of red poppies in her hair—the allusion to opium supplying another suggestion of dream state—and walks "indolently along, with a mind at rest, its peace reflected in her innocent face." Mental indolence and innocence again appear to be contradictory.

Once Hank has been brought to Camelot, he "moved along as one in a dream." Every day he awakens expecting his dream to have vanished, but it persists. He continues to half believe that he is still dreaming until Clarence informs him that he is to be burned at the stake the next day. He compromises the difference between dream and reality when he realizes the imminent danger of the situation: "I knew by past experience of the life-like intensity of dreams, that to be burned to death, even in a dream, would be very far from being a jest, and was a thing to be avoided, by any means, fair or foul, that I could contrive" (chapter 5).

This is a good point at which to pause and discuss with the class if we can really know dream from reality, and whether there is ultimately any great difference between them when it is possible to die for real in a dream just as it is in "reality." The novel continues to make many references to dreams, including waking daydreams, such as King Arthur's dream of conquering Gaul (chapter 31) and Hank's dream of creating a republic (chapter 42). Again, the point to be emphasized is that much more of our lives may be spent in "dreams" than just those obvious times when we are sleeping, and that the line between dream and reality is not as sharp and provable as it appears to be. Inasmuch as Hank's dying words at the novel's end raise further questions about what is dream and what reality, the topic is one that has to have been deliberately built into the text. If students are asked to track all references to dreams in the novel, they will find distinct and compelling patterns that will lead to lively discussions.

Another, more subtle principle of organization inheres in the fact that the novel begins at the end. Everything has already happened to Hank Morgan in the sixth century when Clarence takes over. Everything has already happened to Clarence when a "reborn" Hank takes over again in his proper age, the nineteenth century. Almost everything has happened to the reborn Hank when the narrator, "M.T." takes over, and everything *has* happened by the time M.T. finishes with a P.S. The reader is therefore induced to get emotionally involved in what is essentially a history of past events that are beyond change. The point at issue here is Twain's main theme: *that everything has already happened and that the hope of change is a vain dream.* If this idea sounds hellish, it is no accident. Twain's frequent references to the "damned human race" literally reflected his conviction that life was part of hell and that any other belief was illusion. This is both a powerful and a deeply disturbing notion, and therefore I do not state it at the beginning of a study of *Connecticut Yankee* but let the idea take shape gradually, as the class comes to see that it, and only it, can account for the novel's events and effects.

After the discussion of how Twain's deeply held but heretical beliefs about religion appear to be at odds with his reputation as a humorist, I explain that it is not my purpose to deny that Twain is a master humorist; that would be patently insupportable. I resolve the apparent contradiction by pointing out, as Covici maintains and as I have noted, that Twain's humor "often turns out to be no laughing matter." Humor is often disarming, and I therefore urge students to look carefully for serious issues beneath the humor. Twain's humorous effects are often a sugar-coating over some bitter or pessimistic idea, or they are a strategy to set up the reader for a hoax. Additionally, once the seriousness of the counterplot is realized, humor serves, by its incongruity, to intensify the novel's tragic effect.

My discussion of the text begins with a demonstration of its formal unity. My first points relate to the frame structure; its presence at least suggests that Twain made an effort to impart shape to the novel. Next, I move on to show that everything in the novel, from the first chapter on, points inevitably to the final Battle of the Sand-Belt. This is a critical part of my argument. It is necessary to demonstrate it, if only to counter the claim that the novel "breaks" between a humorous beginning and a grim end. Indeed, everything I say about the novel furthers this point, because I use it to advance my interpretation that the novel is a work of tragedy rather than of comedy, and that its main theme is the denial of the possibility of human freedom. Some of the evidence that supports my position follows.

We know from biography that the first part of *Connecticut Yankee* which Twain worked out was the section dealing with the Battle of the Sand-Belt.[3] It is not surprising, therefore, that the first chapter of the novel, "A Word of Explanation," contains some quiet allusions to the violent end. When "M.T." is told by the stranger that he saw the bullet hole made in the armor of Sir Sagramor le Desirous, his reaction is "electric surprise." These words are the first foreshadowings of the uses of guns and electricity at the Battle of the Sand-Belt. Later in the chapter, the foreshadowing continues ironically as Hank recounts how he learned his real trade in the "great Arms Factory"—the Colt Company—of Hartford; he learned to make "guns, revolvers, cannons, boilers, engines, all sorts of labor-saving machinery." It may be a bit unusual and more than a little grim to describe guns, revolvers, and cannons as "labor-saving machinery," but that is how Hank's guns and revolvers function in the Battle of the Sand-Belt.

Hank later in the book muses on the determining force of heredity and training and how humans early get into molds they cannot break out of. But in the first chapter we see the mold into which Hank has been cast: a maker of armaments and other "labor-saving machinery." He remains unaware of how this fact determines what he will do in sixth-century England, but once these considerations are mentioned to students, they quickly see how this beginning shapes his actions. A disturbing pattern emerges in the novel of his association with explosives and killing, and each incident contributes incrementally to the momentum leading to the final battle.

The first use of explosives occurs in chapter 7, when Hank destroys Merlin's Tower; the second is in chapter 23, where Hank restores a fountain with dynamite. The next reference to it occurs obliquely, in chapter 25, where Hank listens with great pleasure to a cadet from his military academy lay out "the science of war" and "wallow in details of battle and siege, of supply, transportation, mining and countermining . . . infantry, cavalry, artillery, and all about siege guns, field guns, gatling guns, rifled guns, smooth bores, musket practice, revolver practice . . . ." This passage is reminiscent of the scene in Book II of *Gulliver's Travels* where Gulliver enthusiastically tells the King of Brobdingnag of the wonders of gunpowder and is surprised when the King responds with horror at the "inhuman" invention. It is relevant to note here that the first modern educational institution Hank founds in Arthur's kingdom is a kind of West Point, and the cadet is a proud product of Hank's "civilization."

Another incident occurs in chapter 27, when Hank dispatches a couple of hostile knights with a dynamite bomb. "Yes, it was a neat thing, very neat and pretty to see. It resembled a steamboat explosion on the Mississippi; and during the next fifteen minutes we stood under a steady drizzle of microscopic fragments of knights and hardware and horse-flesh."[4] By this time, even those students who are sympathetic to Hank can see that he is deadly and that his humorous way of describing events conceals a personality insensitive to the horror of his actions.

Hank introduces revolvers in chapter 39, "The Yankee's Fight with the Knights." As Hank shoots knight after knight out of the saddle, the rest of the knights break and run. At this, Hank declares "The march of civilization was begun." Hank is not ironic, but Twain is.

When the knights again assemble to attack him after the Interdict, we discover in chapter 42 that Hank's "civilization" consists not only of factories but also of bombs hidden in each factory that can be detonated from a central location. With this discovery, the ominous association of Hank with deadly "labor-saving machinery," quietly begun in "A Word of Explanation," has ripened to the point where most students can see that the mass destruction of the Battle of the Sand-Belt is the logical conclusion of an unmistakable pattern that Hank himself does not recognize. The modern civilization that Hank wishes to bestow upon the sixth century is in reality deadlier by orders of magnitude than the crudely violent one of King Arthur's age. The point is made subtly in chapter 10, "The Beginning of Civilization," when Hank unconsciously associates nineteenth-century civilization with hell as he compliments himself with having surreptitiously introduced modernity into the sixth century. He crows about how nineteenth-century civilization is "booming" under the nose of the sixth century and how it is "fenced" away from general view. It is now an "unassailable" fact, like "any serene volcano, standing innocent with its smokeless summit in tile blue sky and giving no sign of the rising hell in its bowels." He thinks of himself standing with his "finger on the button . . . ready to turn it on and flood the midnight world with light." All of the quoted words and passages clearly foreshadow the Battle of the Sand-Belt with Hank's unassailable strong point, the booming of the guns, the electric fences, the spotlights, and the flood. The association of this civilization with hell is explicit. Does Hank see it? No. Does Twain? With this unusually dense linkage of clues, can there be any doubt?

Another way in which everything leads to the Battle of the Sand-Belt is developed by the way that Hank attempts to further democracy. Hank talks a lot about democracy, but his words are contradicted by his actions. That Hank considers himself a "Yankee of the Yankees" associates him in most readers' eyes with democracy. Even his title of "Boss" seems mild and homey compared to titles like "king," "emperor," and "Caesar." But it quickly becomes apparent that he has tremendous power and is not hesitant to use it, and that he is feared like a mysterious stranger from another world—which he in fact is.[5] The more Hank reflects on despotism, the more attractive it becomes to him. Each time he seems to reject being a despot, he actually moves closer to that role. Furthermore, it is no accident that of all surnames Twain could have given to Hank, he chose one that links him with Morgan le Fay.[6] At first, the two will seem antithetically different, but when Hank is compared at the end with Morgan le Fay, similarities will appear. And at what point in the novel do we learn Hank's last name? Chapter 39! Why is it so delayed, if not to both establish and obscure the comparison?

The more power Hank acquires, the more he thinks of himself as inherently superior and the more his democratic professions are contradicted by his admitted ambitions. He looks down on—most undemocratically—the people he encounters, and he never treats any of them as his equals. On the contrary, he repeatedly confesses his resentment at not being a noble, and has hardly a good word to say about kings. Only Arthur repeatedly demonstrates kingly qualities that wring admiration from Hank, despite himself.

Hank claims to scoff at magicians like Merlin, but then brags about the magic he himself does. Ask your students to define magic. Most will say that it consists of tricks that are not understood. Hank's tricks are technological effects that no one in the sixth century could understand, but every reader of the novel does. Clearly, therefore, to us he is no magician. But, despite Hank's scorn of Merlin, Merlin *is* a real magician. In chapter 3, Hank ridicules Merlin's tiresomely windy repetition of how he directed Arthur to acquire the sword Excalibur from a mysterious hand in a lake. Hank calls it a lie, but if we give credence to the story of Arthur, Merlin's account is accurate, and Arthur, who is also in the hall, does not contradict Merlin. Merlin also casts a spell at the end of the novel that puts Hank into a thirteen-century sleep. Merlin has powers beyond understanding.

Hank also aspires to be a prophet, and in chapter 8 he ventures to prophesy future history. This passage is particularly interesting for several reasons. One is that Hank's "prophetic" powers are really a unique kind of hindsight. A second is that Hank (apparently inadvertently) compares himself in this passage to "adventurers," "wantons," and "drabs"—hardly a compliment. A third is that Hank here demonstrates a knowledge of history. In other words, he knows what "will" happen because from his vantage point as a nineteenth-century person, it already has. This is a highly significant point that we will return to shortly. A fourth, and final, significance of the passage is Hank's apparent unawareness of the fact that prophets do not make things happen, but merely predict what has been destined. Only God can predestine and make things happen.

Hank increasingly wishes to be "adored" and "revered." Heretofore, Hank compared himself with other humans, but this new aspiration implies divine status. This may be an unconscious goal from Hank's perspective, but that Hank is in competition with God is a facet of the novel which Twain must have deliberately constructed. As early as chapter 7, Hank resolves to emulate Robinson Crusoe in that he would have to "invent, contrive, create, reorganize things." The first verb is innocent, but "contrive" has a negative connotation, and "create" is reminiscent of Genesis 1:1. "Reorganize things" also sounds innocent until one reflects that for Hank to undertake to reorganize the sixth century into the nineteenth century means he will have to overwrite the history that has already occurred and been recorded and remake the world according to his pattern. In effect, Hank is about to challenge God on His creation. Later in the same chapter, Hank resents Merlin for spreading a report that Hank does not create miracles because he cannot. Of course, Merlin is correct, but Hank spends the rest of the chapter giving the illusion that he can make miracles happen.

In chapter 8, Hank compliments himself for having "done my entire public a kindness in sparing the sun." We know that Hank did not literally spare the sun but merely used his knowledge of past eclipses to predict that one which already had occurred was about to happen. This is a critical point, which I will soon develop further, but right now the issue is that Hank seems to have convinced himself that he is capable of creating miracles.

Chapter 26, "The First Newspaper," further develops Hank's tendency to think of himself as divine in its allusions to the birth of Christ as told in the gospels of Matthew and Luke. The original meaning of gospel is "good word" or "good news," and it is this sense that Twain uses when Hank says that "[o]ne greater than kings had arrived—the newsboy. But I was the only person in all that throng who knew the meaning of this mighty birth, and what this imperial magician had come into the world to do." The central passage is worth quoting. Hank shows the newspaper to some monks, who cross themselves and describe it as "a miracle, a wonder! Dark work of enchantment." When he finishes reading from it in a "low voice," he gives it to the monks to handle.

So they took it, handling it as cautiously and devoutly as if it had been some holy thing come from some supernatural region. . . . These grouped bent heads, these charmed faces, these speaking eyes—how beautiful to me! For was not this my darling, and was not all this mute wonder and interest and homage a most eloquent tribute and unforced compliment to it? I knew, then, how a mother feels when women, whether strangers or friends, take her new baby, and close themselves about it with one eager impulse, and bend their heads over it in a tranced adoration that makes all the rest of the universe vanish out of their consciousness and be as if it were not, for the time. I knew how she feels, and that there is no other satisfied ambition, whether of king, conqueror or poet, that ever reaches half way to that serene far summit or yields half so divine a contentment.

During all the rest of my séance . . . I sat motionless, steeped in satisfaction, drunk with enjoyment. Yes, this was heaven; I was tasting it once, if I might never taste it more.

The religious imagery in this passage is unmistakable, and so is its similarity to the account of Christ's birth in the manager. Notice, moreover, that Hank's perspective is that of a parent—and one who is in heaven. And what is this newspaper, the Camelot *Weekly Hosannah* (a Hebrew word meaning "please save us," used to praise God), about? This first issue that Hank reads from so dramatically is about the "miracle" of Hank's restoration of a well. In other words, Hank creates his own gospel to praise himself.[7]

Hank's power continues to grow. But when he seems close to the point where he can realize his "dream" of advancing England abruptly into the nineteenth century, the Interdict strikes. From one point of view, the Interdict is not only sudden, it is entirely unsuspected and seems like a flaw in the novel. But from God's point of view, Hank is aspiring to rival Him. It is therefore logical that God's church be the instrument that brings Hank down. The Roman Catholic Church is treated with some criticism by Hank, and because he is afraid of its power, he tries to neutralize it by encouraging the development of a host of Protestant denominations. But, at the end, it is the only institution that is still strong enough to oppose Hank, and if it is authoritarian, it is still better than Hank's authoritarianism, which, as we see in the Battle of the Sand-Belt, is a more hideous and deadly despotism than the "despotism of heaven." As much as Mark Twain himself hated the grip that the church had on men's minds and hearts, he recognized in this novel that its power might be all that stood between man and a worse and more fallible master—man himself.

Despite Hank's frequently repeated affirmations that he understands human nature, he does not. Nor does he reflect on what he has become. Instead, he brags a great deal about his power: "I was no shadow of a king; I was the substance; the king himself was the shadow" (chapter 8). He is condescending to the villagers of Abblasoure in chapters 31 to 34 and decides to confer on them the benefit of his supposedly superior understanding of the theory of political economy. When they realize, however, that he has tricked them into confessing some illegal acts, they fear for their lives, for he has the power of life and death over them. He admits only that he has "overdone" his trick a little, but it is obvious that he has fundamentally overestimated himself and underestimated them. When he is sold into slavery (or, it can be said, *back into* slavery, for he began in the sixth century as a slave), he has been given a lesson in political economy far more sophisticated than the one he thought to teach: in a *completely* free market, where titles and political "rights" are not recognized, a man is ultimately worth only what some buyer is willing to pay for him in the expectation of some capacity for utility. This is an elementary lesson in natural, practical economics. The villagers already understand it, but Hank does not.[8]

Hank claims at several points in the novel that he has destroyed the institution of knighthood, but, as we know, it outlasts him. To put it down each time, he has to use more and more force, which he does even when it should be clear to him—as it is clear to everyone else—that England is with the knights and not with him. This confrontation, of course, raises the question in a new way of how democratic Hank actually is. Can Hank be democratic in any meaningful sense of the term if he looks down on all of his constituents and is a frightening Boss to them, if he is never elected to any term of office, if he insists on opposing the majority of the population, and if he even will kill whoever opposes him—no matter how many—in order to create his "dream of a republic"? The novel remarkably anticipated the predicament in which the United States found itself in Vietnam, where, in the name of democracy, it waged war against the majority of the population. Twain's Hank, especially insofar as he may be thought of as a representative American—"a Yankee of the Yankees"—therefore raises interesting questions for a class: What is democracy? Is Hank democratic? If not, how did he get to be what he is? Is he really benefiting England? Is he better or worse than the leaders that the English already have? Can a democracy be wrong? If the majority is not always right, how is right determined? And so on.

Many ironies in the novel also can be linked to this theme. Take, for example, Hank's invention of "Man-Factories," in which he intends to transform groveling peasants into men suitable for democracy. But ask your students if men can be mass-produced in a factory. Then ask how successful Hank was at doing so. What became of all his "men" when the Interdict struck? At the end, he is left only with boys. Or take Hank's plan to start a patent office. That sounds fair, but with his thirteen-century start on the rest of England, who is going to benefit from that office? Does Hank, in fact, invent anything himself? Does he not simply remember how to build what he knew in his own century? If a rough parallel can be established between, on the one hand, a nineteenth-century Hank and sixth-century England, and, on the other, developed countries and undeveloped countries in our time, what can be inferred about Mark Twain's views of democracy and of progress?

These themes and others will be found readily enough by students who are encouraged to think of Hank's character as consistent and to look for other evidence of unity. The hardest part of teaching the novel, however, consists of the case for its denial of the possibility of freedom. The evidence for this denial is more subtle than the previous patterns, but it is abundant.

We go back to the beginning of the book for this theme and ask some hard questions. Virtually every student today is familiar with movies or literature about time travel, and with the possibility of changing the future if someone could get to the past and cause some things to be different. Now it is time to ask if it is not more likely that it is impossible to change the past. Given a perfect and omnipotent God, His plan for the world would also be perfect (i.e., complete, incapable of improvement, and immutable). Therefore, even if an individual from one age were by some miracle permitted to visit another age, that miracle would also be part of God's plan and the time traveler would not be free to alter the course of the other age's history, which God had predestined at Creation. Insofar as students are at all familiar with their religions or with the Bible, it is productive to point out that both the Old Testament and the New Testament describe a God who is omnipotent and omniscient, who defines the future, causes things to happen, and will not be frustrated.

It is not necessary for students to be religious believers to interpret this novel, but they must be open-minded enough to appreciate that Twain had some relevant views on God and on freedom vs. predestination and that those views show up in ways that cause things to turn out as they do. It may be enough to ask: if there is a God who is omnipotent and omniscient, then, logically, how can we be free? One way I define freedom is: the ability to surprise God. If this definition is used, it should be apparent that either God cannot be surprised, or He is not omniscient and omnipotent. For most religions, predestination is easily understandable, but freedom is the great mystery. For Twain—at least as I understand him—there was no mystery. He believed that freedom could not and did not exist; it was an illusion.[9]

The evidence for predestination in *Connecticut Yankee* is substantial. The most dramatic evidence is Hank's ability to predict eclipses.

Of course, he does not really predict them; he knows about them because they have already occurred, but new ones are predictable. This is important because the very ability to predict them implies a fixed and immutable order in which any eclipse is, from a cosmic perspective, already an accomplished fact. Hank never reflects on this fact, nor does he grasp a corollary: that because no change is possible in an immutable system, neither he nor anyone else is free. *Connecticut Yankee* also implies that time replays itself in endless, simultaneous recycling. That Ecclesiastes may intend this continuous cycle when it says that "there is no new thing under the sun" may be an unconventional and also disturbing view of biblical revelation. Nevertheless, have your students look at the first chapter of Ecclesiastes and ask them to consider how much of the novel is explained by it. You may wish to assign themes based on individual verses.

Hank not only knows about eclipses, but he also knows a good deal of history: personalities, events, and dates. He knows these things because they have already happened and are fixed. Changing the time of an eclipse is a revision of God's plan that is beyond him, but so also is history unchangeable. It was not *meant* for him to have any lasting effect on the sixth century, and that is the way it works out. In other words, all the plans he lays and everything he does are only evanescent. They are not going to last; everything is an illusion. He is taken in by it, and so is every reader who thinks or hopes that Hank is going to be successful, all the while suppressing the real-world knowledge that nothing "modern" happened in the sixth century and that the nineteenth century did not occur until the nineteenth century.

Hank is optimistic and energetic, but everything that he thinks he accomplishes just sets him up for a harder fall at the end. He thinks a lot but never reflects, and so he misses some clues, including a major one that almost all readers also miss. It occurs in chapter 2 just after Clarence tells Hank that it is 19 June 528, and Hank wonders how this can be verified. If there is any troublesome passage in the novel, this is it: "But all of a sudden I stumbled on the very thing, just by luck. I knew that the only total eclipse of the sun in the first half of the sixth century occurred on the 21st day of June, A.D. 528, O.S., and began at 3 minutes after 12 noon." The chance that anyone would just casually happen to know this detail is almost nil. Students always snicker when we start to discuss it because it is something they are sure is forced on Twain's part. If a coincidence, it is mind-boggling. Hank calls it "luck," but what is luck? Ask the class to define the word. Where does it come from? If there is an omnipotent and omniscient deity, where can luck fit in? All through the novel there are similar, though not so dramatic, examples of luck, or coincidence, or chance, or Providence. Again, define "chance" and "coincidence." If we grant an omnipotent and omniscient deity, there can be no luck, no coincidence, no chance. Nothing happens by accident in a predestined world, i.e., one ruled by Providence.

It never occurs to Hank (not to mention most readers) that he was *meant* to know this strange bit of information, just as he was meant to know history, and just as he was meant to know the trades he learned in the Colt factory at Hartford, so that the Battle of the Sand-Belt would occur, and yet all his efforts would turn out to be vanity. This is the message that Twain would communicate through the efforts and failure of the Yankee Hank Morgan: that only what is meant to happen, happens.

Chance, accident, luck, coincidence—euphemistic cloaks for Providence, itself a euphemistic term for God's control—are what truly drive the events in this novel. In chapter 2, Hank says that "being a practical Connecticut man, I now shoved this whole problem out of my mind till its appointed day and hour should come." *Appointed?* Hank speaks more truly than he realizes. All events in the story fall into their appointed times and places.

Take, for instance, the tournament in chapter 9. Sir Gareth and Sir Dinadan are about to joust with each other when, "by malice of *fate*," Sir Dinadan sits by Hank and tells him the one joke that Hank hates most. When he finishes, Sir Dinadan laughs at his own joke "like a *demon*" and goes off to the contest. When Hank opens his eyes he sees Gareth strike Dinadan very hard "and I *unconsciously* out with the prayer, 'I hope to gracious he's killed.' But by *ill-luck*" Gareth crashes into Sir Sagramor, who catches Hank's remark and thinks it meant for him. I have italicized the three words here that are thematically linked to each other. An ominous fate or ill-luck rules this event, and Hank participates, even though unconsciously. So what? Where does it lead? It leads directly to a challenge to Hank from Sir Sagramor four or five years in the future. That in turn leads directly to chapter 39, "The Yankee's Fight with the Knights." In that fight, Hank makes a lasso and its "snaky spirals" yank Sagramor out of his saddle. Other challengers arise, and Hank "snakes" five more to the ground. Sir Lancelot comes forward and the "fateful coils" do their work again. Hank has earlier described this contest as a "duel of the gods," and now that he appears to have won, he basks in the applause, "drunk with glory," and thinks, "The victory is perfect—no other will venture against me—knight-errantry is dead." Hank is full of hubris, and his comeuppance is about to happen. He has been overconfident, as usual, and Sagramor challenges him again after Merlin steals the lasso. Hank meets Sagramor with a secret weapon, never before used, a revolver, and kills him. Other knights charge Hank, and he shoots them out of their saddles. When the rest break and flee, Hank thinks to himself, "Knight-errantry was a doomed institution. The march of civilization was begun."

We have already discussed the irony of this passage. Hank is hubristically overconfident again; knight-errantry is not doomed, and "civilization" is not what Hank thinks it to be. He sees none of this, but the reader can—and the reader also can understand that everything has led up to this point, and this point leads to the Interdict, and the Interdict leads to the Battle of the Sand-Belt. This novel is not disjointed at all, but, on the contrary, tightly organized. The real control in Hank's life is invisible, but the reader can detect Providence's shadowy presence obliquely through Hank's references to such clues as "dreams," "chance," "luck," "accident," "fate," "demon," and "snakes." These words reappear in chapter 42, when Arthur and Mordred's armies face each other to parley for peace. Neither side trusts the other. A ghost warns Arthur in a dream, but the battle is precipitated by "accident": a snake bites a knight's heel, the knight forgets the order not to lift his sword and takes it out to slash at the snake, and the battle takes place— as recorded in the story of Arthur, and as was therefore immutably fated.

Two main points remain to be discussed. The first is the Battle of the Sand-Belt itself. Hank is abandoned by all of his civilization except for Clarence and fifty-two boys. Why boys? Because, being young, they were the only ones he succeeded in indoctrinating. Now, why fifty-two? There are fifty-two weeks in a year, so perhaps this is an allusion to the passing of time. (Another reference to time might be in the name of Hank's wife, Alisande—i.e., all is sand.) There are also fifty-two cards in a deck. This allusion therefore may be to chance, luck, fate— or to deception, if the deck is considered stacked.

Hank and his supporters are located in a cave surrounded by thirteen electric fences set in sand. Why thirteen? There are thirteen cards in a suit. Sand reinforces the pattern of time, and cards the design of fate. But an additional, more powerful answer might be supplied by considering the circular fences as an allusion to Dante's hell. Draw thirteen concentric circles, each one representing the circling electric fences. Inside the inmost circle draw another circle. That represent's Hank's cave. Call the space inside that circle the nineteenth century. Then the next spaces moving outward are the eighteenth, seventeenth, sixteenth centuries, etc., until you come to the space inside the outermost circle. That will be the sixth century. If my surmise is correct, what Twain is implying is that all of existence is within hell, and progress is a damned delusion, for, as in the *Inferno*, the closer one gets to the center, the deeper and more awful is the damnation.

The innocent little girl Hank first sees in Camelot, therefore, with her mind at rest, is damned, born into a cruel age and destined for a hard life. But her damnation is ameliorated by her inactive—dreaming—

mind. The married couple Hank takes out of Morgan le Fay's hellish dungeon have achieved some peace of mind by escaping their lot through dreams. If Hank were successful in awakening them, and they saw what toll the years in the dungeon had taken on each other, how damnably cruel it would be! In Twain's circles, the more the mind is exercised, the more it conceives of hell; the more conscious it is of its situation, the more hell it suffers. Hence, Hank's final dreaming wish to be reunited with his wife, Sandy, is more than an expression of natural affection; it is also a pathetic request to return to a simpler existence in one of the outer circles where the dreams are not so "real" and "hideous."

One of Dan Beard's original illustrations of chapter 18 depicts a barred slit window with an inscription over it: "All hope abandon ye who enter here." The quotation from Dante is not in the novel's text, but Twain had read Dante and he approved the illustration. There is, however, an important difference between Dante's hell and Twain's in *Connecticut Yankee*. Dante's hell is separate from the rest of the world and is complete; *Connecticut Yankee*'s hell merges with the world and is as endless as time.

The last point to be considered is how Hank reached the sixth century. He tells us he got into a crowbar fight with a man called Hercules and was laid out "with a crusher alongside the head that made everything crack," and he then woke up in sixth-century England. Ask your students what would normally happen to someone hit a crusher to the head with a crowbar wielded by a Hercules. Realistically, he would be killed. We must at least, therefore, entertain the possibility that Hank died in that fight and that he is able to move between time periods because he is not a creature of one life, but that he has a sort of life-in-death existence, doomed—or damned—to wander forever with haunting memories of other lives. This is suggested to us by Hank's brief, tragic, but unpursued glimpse of his essential individuality in chapter 18 as a "microscopic atom . . . in this plodding sad pilgrimage, this pathetic drift between the eternities. . . ." This is a chilling as well as powerful insight into the depth of Twain's double despair at the "damned human race" and the cruelty of its existential delusion.

The purpose of this interpretation, of course, is not to convince anyone of its literal truth—I do not recommend using literature as a medium of divine inspiration, and do not myself believe in the novel's paradigm of hell any more than I do in Dante's—but it is meant to help readers understand Twain and to appreciate him as a great artist. *Connecticut Yankee*, like *Huckleberry Finn* before it, is a denial of the possibility of human freedom.[10] This is a remarkable book to come out of the American nineteenth century, which we think of as so dedicated to the affirmation of freedom, but the truth is that Twain, like many of his fellow nineteenth-century authors, e.g., Melville, Dickinson, Crane, and Bierce, among others, had serious doubts about the nature and extent of human freedom. What ultimately keeps Twain from being a depressing author as well as a tragic one is, paradoxically, his American hatred of slavery, cruelty, and injustice, even if the tyrant is a malevolent deity. Twain may even be described as a literary Prometheus who, regardless of great personal cost, devoted himself to bringing the light of truth to man. Both in Twain's literature and in his heart was a deep and sincere yearning to be free. That may be why Hank at times resembles Mark Twain, because as an actor in the drama of life, Twain, like Hank, sought freedom; but as an author-observer he did not believe man was worthy of freedom or that freedom was even possible.

As the underlying structure of *Connecticut Yankee*'s themes is uncovered and students discover its astonishing unity and artistic sophistication, they will take away a fresh respect for Twain and for literature. They will not begrudge its not having been consistently humorous when they recognize that it has caused them to be more thoughtful about human destiny and that it has made a difference in their lives.

Notes

1. Pascal Covici, Jr., "Humor," *Mark Twain Encyclopedia* (New York: Garland, 1993), 380. Covici's section on "Hoax" in the encyclopedia is also worth reading but a fuller discussion of both these topics is in his *Mark Twain's Humor: The Image of a World* (Dallas: Southern Methodist University Press, 1960).

2. I discuss the centrality of the dream motif to the novel in "The Reality of the Dream: Structural and Thematic Unity in *A Connecticut Yankee*," *Mark Twain Journal* 22 (Spring 1984): 8-14. Information from that article is abstracted in this essay, but the full explication contains many additional details that should be helpful in the classroom.

3. See Howard G. Baetzhold's entry on *Connecticut Yankee* in the *Mark Twain Encyclopedia*, 174-78. He recapitulates an earlier essay (listed in the entry's bibliography) on the course of the novel's composition and notes that as early as 1886 Twain had revealed to an audience his plan to have Hank, from behind electrified barbed wire fences, machine-gun Arthur's enemies. Baetzhold takes cognizance of the facts that Twain's views about the novel began shifting soon afterward and that Hank ultimately fought the chivalry of England instead of Arthur's enemies. Baetzhold, understandably, places interpretive emphasis on Twain's remarks about the novel that he was writing, whereas I place greater emphasis on the text itself and on the Calvinistic beliefs that constituted Twain's deepest convictions and that were meshed with his creative impulses.

4. Considering that Mississippi River steamboat explosions were normally regarded as horrible disasters, that Twain's brother was mortally injured in one, and that Twain never forgot the anguish of watching his brother and others die, Hank's description of the explosion as "very neat and pretty to see" must have been loaded by Twain to be bitterly ironic.

5. The motif of a sinister, mysterious stranger first appears in Twain's works in "The Celebrated Jumping Frog of Calaveras County" (1865), and it recurs over the rest of his career. Usually, however, the mysterious stranger is seen from the standpoint of characters with whom readers can identify; he is an outsider, an "other." In causing time, the world, and everything that is in it to be viewed in *Connecticut Yankee* from the perspective of a mysterious stranger, Twain powerfully inverts the motif and subtly implies that no matter how potent a mysterious stranger may seem to humans, even he is controlled by an omnipotence beyond him.

6. The name "Morgan" also has relevant negative associations with the famous pirate, Henry Morgan, and the powerful financier, John Pierpont Morgan.

7. A more complete interpretation of the relevance of chapter 26 to the rest of the novel can be found in my article, "The Gospel According to Hank Morgan's Newspaper," *Essays in Arts and Sciences* 20 (October 1991): 32-42.

8. Hank's pratings about market value reflect theoretical discussions in nineteenth-century America about the value of labor. Twain, on the other hand, had been personally familiar before the Civil War with the institution of slavery, and afterward he knew firsthand that "wage slave" could be more than a figure of speech. Theory, therefore, becomes in the novel another sort of dream that blinds one to hellish reality. For an ex-

tended discussion of the significance of political economy to the novel, see my article, "*A Connecticut Yankee*: A Serious Hoax," *Essays in Arts and Sciences* 19 (May 1990): 28-44.

9. Twain's religious background can be readily learned by reading the section on Calvinism in any reputable encyclopedia or handbook of Christian theology. I have dealt more specifically with the degree to which Twain adhered to the Calvinistic teachings of his youth and how he applied them to his major writings, in "Mark Twain's Mind and the Illusion of Freedom," *Journal of Humanities* [Kobe, Japan], special issue (March 1992): 1-24. Because it is presently difficult to get access to this publication, I will send an offprint to anyone who sends me a request and a self-addressed envelope with adequate postage.

10. My interpretation of *Huckleberry Finn* is developed in "The 'Poor Players' of *Huckleberry Finn*," *Papers of the Michigan Academy of Sciences, Arts, and Letters* 53 (1968): 291-310.

Mark Twain as a Science-Fiction Writer_____

David Ketterer

I

Can a giant in the Brobdingnagian realm of world literature also be a
giant in the Lilliputian world of science fiction? There is surely no a pri-
ori reason why not. A case might be made for such writers as Poe,
Verne, Wells, Huxley, Orwell, and, of course, Swift, whose masterpiece I have alluded to above. Whatever further names might be suggested, it is very unlikely that that of Mark Twain would figure among
them. A major writer, certainly, but what possible connection has the
author of Tom Sawyer and *Huckleberry Finn* with science fiction?
None at all, it would appear, from consulting what is to date the best
history of the genre: Mark Twain (being a trademark rather than a
pseudonym, the full form should always be used) does not merit a single reference in Brian Aldiss's *Billion Year Spree*.[1] On the other hand,
in the course of a ten-page appraisal, Darko Suvin affirms that, had certain "fragmentary sketches . . . been completed and published, [Mark
Twain] would have beyond a doubt stood instead of Wells as the major
turning point in the tradition leading to modern SF, and instead of
Stapledon as the inventor of fictional historiography."[2]

There would seem, then, to be a complete spectrum of possibilities.
At one extreme Mark Twain is not a science-fiction writer at all; at the
other he is comparable to Wells and Stapledon. It seems necessary at
the outset to confront the question of definition: what is science fiction? The term "scientification" was coined by Hugo Gernsback in
1926 and, by way of explanation, applied retrospectively to the work of
Verne, Wells, and, less convincingly, Poe.[3] Some years ago, C. S.
Lewis pointed out that science fiction is not a "homogeneous genre." Is
it therefore, as Robert M. Philmus implies, a "heterogeneous genre," or
is a heterogenous genre a contradiction in terms?[4] There is no question
that an element of heterogeneity characterizes the material collected in
this volume. A genre, it must be recognized, can never be a watertight

compartment—many combinations are permissible. Any generic labeling must depend upon matters of emphasis.

Distinctions in emphasis are established on the basis of the relationship (signaled by the author as a reading convention) between the fictional world and the world of consensus reality. To add the label "science fiction" to the title of a novel directs the reader to take the events, beings, places, or states described as belonging on a literal level to the predominantly material aspects of the vast area that we designate as the unknown. (The supernatural unknown is the domain of visionary literature.) By contrast, the label "fantasy" tells the reader that the universe of the novel is self-contained, realistic on its own terms but discontinuous (except by way of allegorical translation usually in psychological or moral terms) with the known world. This is a world not of the unknown so much as of the unreal. It might appear to follow from this that any attempt to combine the magical or fairy-tale elements of fantasy with the scientific or logical elements of science fiction is misguided and can lead only to incoherence. This is not always the case. The intrusion of the fantastic into what appears to be a science-fiction or a naturalistic text often simply alters the function of the fantasy material. Instead of being encouraged to think about psychology and morality, the reader must consider matters of epistemology: How do we know what we think we know about the nature of reality, and how do we know that what we think we know is accurate? It is the function of epistemology to relate any debate about the real and the unreal to the relationship between the known and the unknown.

Mark Twain is deeply concerned with epistemological questions. Consequently, although elements of science fiction and fantasy mingle freely in much of the work included in this collection, an overall sense of science fiction marks each selection. I have excluded a number of marginal cases that strike me as more fantasy than science fiction, as well as numerous pieces, including the Mysterious Stranger Manuscripts, that involve such biblical characters as Adam, Eve, and Satan, in the spirit of humorous domestication or moral and epistemological inquiry. Everything that I have included, in one way or another, participates in, bears on, or moves toward the development of science fiction.

Mark Twain's importance in the history of science fiction rests partly on the fact that he was the first American writer to exploit fully the possibilities for humor in science fiction.[5] He worked a narrow but rich vein that finds its current apotheosis in the work of Kurt Vonnegut, Jr. As a science-fiction writer and humorist, Mark Twain drew on the traditions of the literary hoax and the tall tale, both constituents of American frontier humor. The importance of the hoax form to Mark Twain's art has been ably demonstrated by Pascal Covici. What is less well appreciated is the relationship between the literary hoax and science fiction.[6] In fact, Mark Twain's career as a science-fiction writer began with what he claimed was an accidental hoax, a piece entitled "Petrified Man" published in the *Territorial Enterprise* on 5 October 1862.

This hoax initiates a significant motif in Mark Twain's work—what might be called a mania for preserved corpses. There is a clear development from the playful "Petrified Man" to the heat-mummified corpses of "The Great Dark" (drafted in August and September 1898) which provides a ready index to the general nature of Mark Twain's changing attitudes. Among the material specifically related to "The Great Dark," we find frozen corpses in the 1884 story outline that I have entitled "The Generation Iceberg" (see appendix C) and in "The Enchanted Sea Wilderness" (written in 1896). A complete listing of this line of succession should also take account of the more or less preserved corpse of St. Charles Borromeo and the petrified monk in chapters 18 and 28 respectively of *The Innocents Abroad* (1869); the concluding reference in chapter 55 of *Life on the Mississippi* (1883) to a cave containing the corpse of a girl that her father had preserved in an alcohol-filled copper cylinder; the dried dead people in *Tom Sawyer Abroad* (1894); the angry man petrified by Little Satan in the first of the Mysterious Stranger Manuscripts (written 1897-98); and the concluding analogy in "My Debut as a Literary Person" (1899) with the mother and child mummified during the volcanic demise of Pompeii. (This last instance links the petrification theme with Mark Twain's notion of his art—and petrifying humor—as a means of preservation.) Overall, these preserved corpses serve successively as objects of humor, curiosity, sorrow, and horror.

Apparently, the twenty-six-year-old Sam Clemens (the "Mark Twain" persona was not born until four months later) intended "Petrified Man" to satirize a mania for cases of natural petrifaction. The piece was received as factual, however, and reproduced in newspapers across the country, readers having failed to notice that the human statue in the story is thumbing its nose. Clemens includes an incidental "scientific" reference to the role that a deposit of limestone sediment, caused by dripping water, played in anchoring the petrified man to the spot. There is a virtually exact parallel to this at the conclusion of Vonnegut's *Cat's Cradle*. The religious leader Bokonon states that, if he was younger, he would avail himself of the freezing properties of a substance called "Ice Nine" in order to solidify himself in an identical attitude of disrespect: "I would take from the ground some of the blue-white poison that makes statues of men; and I would make a statue of myself, lying on my back, grinning horribly, and thumbing my nose at You Know Who." Is this insult an act of homage on Vonnegut's part to a writer he recognizes, with anxiety, Harold Bloom might add, as his strong precursor?[7]

Cat's Cradle is an end-of-the-world story. The prevalence of this theme in science fiction, whether presented literally or as a metaphor for major change, is the most obvious indicator of the genre's apocalyptic character. Mark Twain's science fiction includes only one literal account of the world's end, "Earthquake Almanac" (1865), which concludes with the world being shaken to pieces by a gigantic earthquake. The almanac form, which operates in the murky area where fortune-telling, futurology, and science fiction overlap, also provides a historical link between science fiction and the literary hoax. Although Mark Twain is not intending a serious hoax here, Jonathan Swift successfully perpetrated an almanac hoax with his *Predictions for the Ensuing Year by John Bickerstaff* (1708). Indeed, not only does Swift prefigure Mark Twain's career as a literary hoaxer but in time Mark Twain's vision became increasingly Swiftian. If Mark Twain is Vonnegut's precursor, Swift deserves credit as a precursor of Mark Twain's science fiction.

II

It is a truism in Mark Twain criticism that his work displays a development from the relatively light-hearted to the pessimistically philosophical. This "switch" is reflected in his science fiction. The more frivolous material includes "Petrified Man," "Earthquake Almanac," "A Curious Pleasure Excursion," "The Curious Republic of Gondour," "A Murder, A Mystery, and a Marriage," and "Captain Stormfield's Visit to Heaven." Darko Suvin seems to have followed H. Bruce Franklin in citing *Those Extraordinary Twins* (1894) as an instance of Mark Twain's science fiction.[8] If this opinion is correct, the piece might properly belong with my list of Mark Twain's less serious science fiction. There is no doubt that this story, concerned as it is with humourously exploiting the problems of Italian Siamese twins who share a single body, raises uniquely speculative psychological questions. But Siamese twins do exist and, in fact, Mark Twain had the Tocci twins in mind.[9] Consequently, I would argue that *Those Extraordinary Twins* is not science fiction.

Mark Twain shared with Poe an interest in the possibility of crossing the Atlantic by balloon. Although balloon travel itself was real enough—Mark Twain ascended in one in Paris in 1879—it was the thought of traveling such a great distance that places, say, Poe's "The Balloon Hoax" in the general area of science fiction.[10] In 1868, Mark Twain began a story about a Frenchman's balloon journey from Paris to Illinois, but abandoned the project with the American publication of Jules Verne's *Five Weeks in a Balloon* (1869). (I have included this unfinished draft as appendix A, to which I have supplied the title "The

Mysterious Balloonist" because of the presence of one of Mark Twain's mysterious strangers.) Mark Twain returned to the idea of trans-Atlantic balloon travel in a story written in 1876 entitled "A Murder, a Mystery, and a Marriage." Years later, in *Tom Sawyer Abroad* (1894), Tom, Huck, and Jim are accidentally borne aloft while examining a balloon invented by a mad professor. After a number of landings, adventures, and narrow escapes, they find themselves in Cairo.

"A Murder, a Mystery, and a Marriage" was not published until years after Mark Twain's death. In 1945 Lew D. Feldman and Allan Hyman bought the manuscript and arranged to have sixteen copies printed by Manuscript House. When the slim volume appeared, the trustees of the Mark Twain estate successfully prosecuted the publishers for violation of copyright.[11] As a result, the story remains essentially unknown, and presumably will remain so until it appears in a volume of the University of California edition of the Mark Twain Papers. Although I was unable to obtain permission to publish the tale, a detailed synopsis appears in appendix B. It is about a Frenchman named Jean Mercier who, having tipped his employer Jules Verne out of a balloon, drifts from France to America where he becomes involved in the small-minded affairs of the people of Deer Lick, Missouri.

It would be misleading to classify "A Murder, a Mystery, and a Marriage" as science fiction, although the piece does illustrate what may be understood as an ironic, or at least uncomfortable, relationship between the tall tale and science fiction. ("Petrified Man" does much the same thing for the relationship between the literary hoax and science fiction.) Verne's science-fiction novels, it is claimed, are actually tall tales. But the marvelous balloon voyage in Mark Twain's story is presumably true, that is to say, a genuine science-fiction element. Mark Twain is making extrapolated use of one of those marvels of communication ("railways, steamboats, telegraphs and newspapers") which the insular villagers exclude from their awareness as equivalent to "the concerns of the moon."[12] For them it is part of a science-fiction world.

Their limited horizons find an analogue in the money-grubbing, mean-spiritedness of the Gray brothers. Like the French devil in Poe's "The Devil in the Belfry" (1839), the French outsider in Mark Twain's story (which belongs to the enclosed-world tradition exemplified by Johnson's *Rasselas* [1759], Poe's story, and Wells's "The Country of the Blind" [1904]) serves to awaken the villagers to the extraordinary nature of the reality beyond their narrowly circumscribed environment. He is the bearer of a broader and truer reality that will destroy their village world—the realm of the imagination (which perhaps the lovers to some degree symbolize) will eclipse the dull, factual world. The murder of David Gray by the French balloonist may be understood as symbolically analogous to the destruction of a limited reality. The "apocalyptic" structure that may thus be symbolically teased out of this story corresponds to what I have argued elsewhere is the structure of science fiction.[13] Furthermore, read in this admittedly oblique way, the story's rather incongruous events do make a logical kind of sense.

But, even at this early stage of his career, Mark Twain's faith in the possibility of expansive bright worlds was fainthearted. As one might expect of the author of "Petrified Man," he fears being duped by a tall tale, as no doubt do the villagers. Yet, at the same time, he wants to put himself beyond the boundaries of Deer Lick because it is the inhabitants of such places who are most susceptible to being taken in by tall tales (for example, they accept Jean Mercier's fictional identity and the amateurishly fabricated evidence incriminating the man wrongly arrested for David Gray's murder). Consequently, Jules Verne, one of the early masters of science fiction, is treated in a peculiarly ambiguous fashion. On the one hand, he is exposed and seemingly attacked as a charlatan; on the other hand, Mark Twain's story vindicates Verne's speculations about balloon travel. True, Mark Twain damns Verne to hell, but the revelation which it is projected Verne will publish as "Eighteen Months in a Furnace" might well correspond to the Satanic gospel espoused by Mark Twain in his Mysterious Stranger Manuscripts. And, of course, Jean Mercier is a type of the mysterious stranger. It should be noted further that Mercier, like Verne, is an important name in the history of science fiction. Louis-Sébastien Mercier is the author of *L'an deux mille quatre cent quarante* (1771), translated as *Memoirs of the Year Two Thousand Five Hundred* (1772), one of the earliest fully developed utopias.

A rational utopia, somewhat different from Louis-Sébastien Mercier's, may be the object of satire in "The Curious Republic of Gondour" (1875). In Gondour it was found desirable to expand the principle of universal suffrage. Everybody has the right to one vote but certain individuals are apportioned extra votes on the basis of education and wealth. In this way it is assured that only the right people hold power. It seems more than coincidental that an antithetical but equally curious utopian situation is presented in Vonnegut's "Harrison Bergeron."[14] The need for total equality in Vonnegut's future society has necessitated a leveling downward. People of more than average intelligence or beauty are provided with corresponding handicaps in the form of weights and disfiguring marks.

Mark Twain offers a skewed view of another supposedly desirable state (albeit a monarchical rather than a "republican" setup) in "Captain Stormfield's Visit to Heaven" (the first draft of which was written in 1873). This is a materialist heaven located in interstellar space. To get there, Stormfield sails through space with an increasing number of companions rather in the manner of the narrator in Olaf Stapledon's *Star Maker* (1937). At one point en route Stormfield races and overtakes a comet, a not unlikely invention for Mark Twain, whose birth and death coincided with the timetable of Halley's Comet. Throughout his life Mark Twain maintained that since he came in with the comet he expected to go out with it. To a contemporary he seemed "like some great being from another planet—never quite of this race or kind."[15] Perhaps with Stormfield in mind, in the prospectus for interplanetary and interstellar travel by means of a chartered comet—the piece entitled "A Curious Pleasure Excursion" (1874)—Mark Twain and P. T. Barnum "rigidly prohibit racing with other comets." In a fragment from the 1880s, "A Letter from the Comet," the comet concerned, which passes Earth once every seventy-one years (Halley's Comet comes around every seventy-five years), writes of his distress at failing to see Adam on his fourteenth swing by. On the other hand, in spite of the vast size of Sirius, the comet had "not missed a friendly face there in thirty million years."[16]

As one would expect, Mark Twain's interest in incredible astronomical distances is particularly prominent in "Captain Stormfield's Visit to Heaven." Hyatt H. Waggoner notes that Samuel G. Bayne's *Pith of Astronomy* (1896) was one of many books on the subject that Mark Twain is known to have read.[17] Also not surprisingly, he seems to have been particularly fascinated by the stars during his days as a riverboat pilot.

A parallel interest in vast temporal perspectives and geological ages is most conspicuous in the pieces that constitute Mark Twain's down-home version of the Genesis story, including his practical speculation concerning the daily lives of Adam and Eve in "Papers from the Adam Family" (written in the 1870s but not published until 1962), and "Letters from the Earth" (written in 1909 but again not published until 1962).[18] A considerably darkened sense of time and cyclical history informs a related later work, "The Secret History of Eddypus, the World-Empire" (written in 1901 and 1902 but not published until 1972). In this grim version of the future a thousand years hence, Mrs. Mary Baker Eddy's Christian Science rules the world.[19]

Other instances where Mark Twain presents glimpses of the future should be mentioned. For example, a letter addressed to Mark Twain's wife Olivia dated 16 November 1935, but actually written in 1874 and intended for William Dean Howells, purports to emanate from a Boston of the future. Foregoing modern methods of communication, the one-hundred-year-old author prefers the old-fashioned method of writing: "it is sixty years since I was here before," he notes in this letter that concerns encounters with his old and now visibly tottering acquaintances, including Howells. In one futuristic passage, Mark Twain writes that "my air ship was delayed by a collision with a fellow from

China. . . . As a result of the collision by the goodness of God thirteen of the missionaries were crippled and several killed."[20]

In 1877, while he was writing about the past in *A Connecticut Yankee*, Mark Twain made some notes for a vision of the future (including television) a century later.[21] And, on the occasion of Walt Whitman's seventieth birthday in 1889, Mark Twain offered this remarkably utopian view: "Wait thirty years and then look out over the earth. You shall see marvel upon marvels, added to those whose nativity you have witnessed; and conspicuous above them you shall see their formidable result—Man at almost his full stature at last!—and still growing, visibly growing, while you look."[22] Twelve years later, however, Mark Twain was at work on the bleak world of "Eddypus" and on a "translation," for which Albert Bigelow Paine has supplied the title "History 1,000 Years from Now," that is included in this collection as appendix E. This brief synopsis of the overthrow of democracy in America in favor of a monarchical system is clearly related to, and perhaps the germinal statement of, "Eddypus."

Mark Twain lived ten years into the twentieth century. To a greater or lesser extent all of his temporal scenarios reflect the fin de siècle experience of a man who spent much of his creative life anticipating the demise of one century and the advent of a very different one. In this regard Mark Twain's situation parallels our own. And his doubts about the brave new world of the twentieth century, which found expression not just in dire visions of the future but also in extreme epistemological and metaphysical speculations about microscopic worlds and dream realities, were every bit as intense as ours are concerning the twenty-first century.

III

Given this fascination with time and history, it is not surprising that Mark Twain's best and most influential work of science fiction, *A Connecticut Yankee in King Arthur's Court* (1889), should be concerned with time travel. Along with Bellamy's *Looking Backward* (1888), a case can be made for *A Connecticut Yankee* as one of the first genuine time-travel stories.[23] A case has also been made for its being an early parallel-world(s) story (whether by accident or design). In a paper entitled "Hank Morgan in the Garden of Forking Paths: Paradox in Mark Twain's *A Connecticut Yankee in King Arthur's Court*," delivered on 20 March 1981 at Florida Atlantic University's second International Conference on the Fantastic in the Arts, William J. Collins argued that, since King Arthur belongs to myth or folk history rather than to actual history, the sixth-century Britain that the Yankee, Hank Morgan, finds himself in must be part of a world parallel to our own. Furthermore, the fact that the guide in Warwick Castle refers to a suit of armor as belonging to one of King Arthur's knights means that the nineteenth-century present of the novel belongs to the same (?) parallel world. Is there an explanation here for the spatial displacement (from the U.S.A. to Britain) that accompanies Hank's first time-travel experience? Particularly significant here is the epistemological unease implicit in the development from a historical fiction to what Hank finally perceives as only a dream reality. But rather than concern himself overtly with the temporal paradoxes and forking parallel universes that appear in more recent time-travel tales, Mark Twain disposes of the anachronism issue by ensuring that all of the nineteenth-century innovations that Hank introduces to Arthurian Britain are obliterated in a concluding cataclysmic battle. All that remains is a bullethole in a suit of armor.

The "transcendent" scientist, Sir Wissenschaft (the name means "science"), in chapter 17 of *A Tramp Abroad* (1879), who routs a dragon with a fire extinguisher of his own invention, prefigures Hank, who also triumphs over superstition with his technological know-how. Hank's achievement, in turn, seems to have established the pattern for that power-fantasy species of science fiction, predominantly American, in which the hero, more or less single-handedly, affects the destiny of an entire world or universe. An example is L. Sprague de Camp's *Lest Darkness Fall* (1939), a novel that borrows quite directly from *A*

Connecticut Yankee: a modern archaeologist travels back in time to ancient Rome, where, thanks to his twentieth-century knowledge, he is able to prevent the collapse of civilization.

Perhaps the most spectacular "effect" in *A Connecticut Yankee* is that provided by the solar eclipse that Hank purports to bring about, thereby gaining his powerful position in the superstitious world of King Arthur. Elsewhere I have argued that Mark Twain presents the eclipse or displacement of one heavenly body by another as symbolically analogous, first, to the transposition of epochs that Hank experiences, and, second, to Hank's dawning apocalyptic realization that reality itself, whether that of the sixth century or the nineteenth, is an illusion, a dream.[24] The concluding "Battle of the Sand-Belt" chapter, which I have excerpted for this collection, includes a number of astronomically related details (the fifty-two boys corresponding to the number of weeks in the solar year, the Copernican setup of Hank's twelve encircling electrified wire fences, the semantic equation between the surrounding mined sand-belt and the zodiacal belt with its twelve constellations, and the phrasing of Hank's proclamation: "So long as the planets shall continue to move in their orbits, the BATTLE OF THE SAND-BELT will not perish out of the memories of men"), all suggesting that the battle should be viewed in comparably analogous terms as both a conflation of sixth- and nineteenth-century cosmologies and as a reenactment of the import of the solar eclipse.

Striking corroboration for the importance of the solar eclipse in *A Connecticut Yankee* (and the related emphasis on fiery destruction) is provided by "Eddypus." Again one epoch is being contrasted with another and again Mark Twain proposes the analogy of a solar eclipse:

At noonday we have seen the sun blazing in the zenith and lighting up every detail of the visible world with an intense and rejoicing brightness. Presently a thin black line shows like a mourning-border upon one edge of the shining disk, and begins to spread slowly inward, blotting out the light as it goes; while we watch, holding our breath, the blackness moves on-

ward and still onward; a dimness gathers over the earth, next a solemn twilight; the twilight deepens, night settles steadily down, a chill dampness in-
vades the air, there is a mouldy smell, the winds moan and sigh, the fowls
go to roost—the eclipse is accomplished, the sun's face is ink-black, all
things are swallowed up and lost to sight in a rayless gloom.

Christian Science did not create this eclipse unaided; it had abundant
help—from natural and unavoidable evolutionary developments of the disease called Civilization.

What may be only inferred in *A Connecticut Yankee* is here fully
spelled out.

As it happens, Halley's Comet made one of its rare but regular appearances during the ten or so years of Hank's stay in King Arthur's
England. Calculation indicates that it would have reached perihelion
on 5 September 530 A.D. However, there is no mention of Hank, who
arrived in 528 A.D., exploiting this astronomical spectacle.

Once established in King Arthur's court, Hank sets about "inventing" all manner of nineteenth-century marvels. His inventions reap
him great success and profit. In this respect Mark Twain himself, patent office habitué, was somewhat like his Promethean hero. His inventions include three which were patented—an "Improvement in Adjust-
able and Detachable Straps for Garments," a self-pasting scrapbook
(which Justin Kaplan notes was his most profitable book for the year
1877), and a board game for teaching history, played with pins and
cards—as well as a "perpetual calendar" and a "bed clamp" to prevent
children from kicking off their sheets and blankets. He also took an intense interest in the projects of a Polish inventor, Jan Szczepanik,
owned a four-fifths interest in "Kaolotype" (a process for making
printing plates), and invested heavily in a high-protein food concentrate called Plasmon, at the same time as he extolled the benefits of the
new science of osteopathy.[25] A play entitled *Colonel Sellers as a Scientist* (1883), on which Mark Twain collaborated with Howells, reflects
the importance he attached to such enthusiasms.[26]

Further evidence of Mark Twain's interest in new inventions is noted by Edward Wagenknecht. He was one of the first men in the world to install a telephone in his private residence, he was the first author of distinction to use the typewriter, and he initiated the practice of double-spacing manuscripts. It is therefore only characteristic of Mark Twain that he incorporated the new technique of fingerprinting in *Pudd'nhead Wilson* (1894).[27] In fact, given his reading preferences ("I like history, biography, travels, curious facts and strange happenings, and science") and his interest in the pseudosciences (particularly palmistry and phrenology), it is perhaps not really so surprising that, on occasion, he would write the kind of material collected in this volume.[28]

Of all the projects in which Mark Twain invested and lost money, none was as personally catastrophic as the typesetting machine invented by James W. Paige. The substance of *A Connecticut Yankee* and this abortive venture are intimately linked; while Mark Twain was writing the one he was sinking his fortune in the other.[29] This is perhaps the major reason why *A Connecticut Yankee*, with its sour attitude towards progress, is the transitional work between the light and the dark in Mark Twain's corpus. Many of the gloomy quasi-Darwinist ideas explored in the philosophical dialogue *What Is Man?* (1906) and the Mysterious Stranger Manuscripts—the notion that man is a machine, that everything is determined, and that reality is all a dream anyway— figure prominently in *A Connecticut Yankee*. There is little question, of course, that Mark Twain's scientific reading contributed to (if it did not itself determine) his deterministic philosophy.[30]

Some attention should be paid to the Mysterious Stranger Manuscripts in any consideration of Mark Twain as a science-fiction writer. This is not to say that these materials should be classified as science fiction. I prefer to locate them in the broad category of "apocalyptic" literature. But elements of science fiction abound in these writings. In "Young Satan" (Sholom J. Kahn's suggested title) or "Eseldorf" (Bernard DeVoto's suggested title), written in 1897 and 1898, the disquisition on determinism includes material that Jan Pinkerton has related to the parallel world/alternative universe class of science fiction.[31] Representative titles would be Ward Moore's *Bring the Jubilee* (1953), in which the South wins the Civil War, and Philip K. Dick's *The Man in the High Castle* (1962), in which the Nazis win World War II. Inspired perhaps by an episode in Voltaire's *Zadig* (1748), young Satan demonstrates how the course of events can be radically altered by very small changes in the chain of causality: "If at any time—say in boyhood— Columbus had skipped the triflingest little link in the chain of acts projected and made inevitable by his first childish act, it would have changed his whole subsequent life and he would have become a priest and died obscure in an Italian village, and America would not have been discovered for two centuries afterward. I know this. To skip any one of the billion acts in Columbus' chain would have wholly changed his life. I have examined his billion of possible careers, and in only one of them occurs the discovery of America."[32] Philip José Farmer has recounted one of those billion-less-one careers in "Sail On, Sail On" (1952)—Columbus sails off the edge of a flat world. The leap from *A Connecticut Yankee* to this kind of speculation is, of course, relatively obvious. What would have happened to the course of English history if Hank had won the Battle of the Sand-Belt?

The most science-fictional Mysterious Stranger fragment is the one written between 1902 and 1904 and entitled "Print Shop" by DeVoto. According to Kahn this version, with its conclusion that all reality is a dream, is "the only true text of *The Mysterious Stranger.*"[33] In the course of an exhaustive treatment of this text, which he prefers to call "No. 44, The Mysterious Stranger," Kahn spotlights the science-fiction details. In chapter 29, for example, "What might be called the science fiction element (present throughout our text in other aspects and this time in that of interplanetary travel) comes to the fore." A reference to "excursionists from Sirius"[34] may be an echo of Voltaire's *Micromégas*, long recognized as one of Mark Twain's sources. This space voyage, as Kahn observes, is comparable to that in "Captain Stormfield's Visit to Heaven."[35]

Unlike the young Satan of the "Eseldorf" version, Forty-four is a genuine alien (we do not know who or what he is); like Vonnegut's Tralfamadorians, he can "foresee everything that is going to happen."[36] At one point Forty-four engineers an eclipse. The reader may be reminded of the eclipse in *A Connecticut Yankee*, although Forty-four's is "not a real one but an artificial one that nobody but Simon Newcomb could tell from the original Jacobs."[37] Kahn notes that a reference to the astronomer Newcomb also occurs in Wells's *The Time Machine* (1895), a major work of science fiction published some years before "No. 44" was written that also makes use of an eclipse. At the same time, again as Kahn points out, the time-hopping "Duplicates" live in a "'science fiction' world."[38] In their travels they pick up phrases that "come from countries where none of the conditions resembled the conditions I had been used to; some from comets where nothing was solid, and nobody had legs; some from our sun, where nobody was comfortable except when white-hot."[39]

The penultimate chapter in which Forty-four presents August with a panorama of human history by turning time backwards (again *The Time Machine* may have been an influence) includes a science-fiction synthesis of Genesis and Darwin. In this vision of prehistory, "The skeletons of Adam's predecessors outnumbered the later representatives of our race by myriads, and they rode upon undreamt-of monsters of the most extraordinary bulk and aspect."[40] We are also treated to a description of the "Missing Link." It should further be observed that in an earlier incarnation—in the "Schoolhouse Hill" (Kahn's title) or "Hannibal" (DeVoto's title) version—Forty-four, in retelling the story of the Fall, points out that "No Adam in any of the millions of other planets (created previous to Earth) had ever disobeyed and eaten of the forbidden fruit."[41]

Young Satan's father is met with in an effective, relatively light-hearted sketch that does qualify as science fiction. "Sold to Satan," which includes much scientific talk about radium, was written in January 1904 (the year after Madame Curie and her husband Pierre had shared the Nobel Prize for physics) but not published until 1923 in *Europe and Elsewhere*. This green-colored, modern Satan is made of radium encased in a protective polonium skin without which his presence would destroy the world. Like Forty-four, Satan is a science-fiction figure who has the power to make a vacancy of objective reality. Satan informs a gullible Mark Twain that the light of the firefly and the glowworm is produced by a radium electron imprisoned in the Cordilleras that consists of pure radium. When Madame Curie succeeds in isolating polonium Mark Twain, clothed in a skin of same, can take possession of this immense energy source. If Mark Twain is duped here, so are those people who respond to the invitation to invest in his radium stock.

Many of the ideas present in *A Connecticut Yankee* and more fully expounded in *What Is Man?* and the Mysterious Stranger Manuscripts pervade Mark Twain's explorations in more or less microcosmic worlds in two important but unfinished works of science fiction. "The Great Dark" (DeVoto's title), written in 1898 but not published until 1962, is about an apocalyptic voyage in a drop of water. A similar microcosmic world, it may be noted, had been projected earlier by Fitz-James O'Brien in "The Diamond Lens" (1858). In "3,000 Years Among the Microbes," written in 1905 but not published until 1967, the narrator, reduced to microscopic size by a wizard, inhabits the world-body constituted by a diseased tramp. Not surprisingly, given the influence of Swift on fictional speculation concerning relativity of size, one of the denizens of this world is called Lemuel Gulliver. By means of this acknowledgment Mark Twain links his story to the grand tradition of "science fiction" that may be encapsulated in this formula adapted from Suvin: *Utopia* is to *Gulliver's Travels* as *Gulliver's Travels* is to Wells as Wells is to modern science fiction.[42] The implication is that the universe we inhabit is actually God's diseased body. The idea for this tale appears to go back to a notebook entry written on 12 August 1884: "I think we are only the microscopic trichina <[——]> concealed in the blood of some vast creatures veins, & that it is that vast creature whom God concerns himself about, & not us."[43]

A notebook entry outlining a story (included as appendix C) written shortly before the "microscopic trichina" idea hinges on a similar microcosm/macrocosm relationship. This outline is of extraordinary importance to the history of science fiction. It is the first recorded instance of a concept alluded to frequently in science-fiction circles as involving a "generation starship." Tom Shippey argues convincingly that this concept provides a structural or generic paradigm of the nature of science fiction itself.[44] Basically, what happens depends upon a group of people surviving for generations within an enclosed space (such as a starship). All manner of myths arise to account for the nature of this enclosed world, myths that are dramatically exploded when one of the more venturesome members of the community breaks through to the much larger encompassing reality. The best known examples of this plot are Heinlein's *Orphans of the Sky* (1963), originally serialized in 1941 as "Universe" and "Common Sense," and Aldiss's *Starship*, originally published in Britain as *Non-Stop* (1958).

The enclosed-world situation is, it will be recognized, the one that I have already mentioned as exhibited in "A Murder, a Mystery, and a Marriage" (it is also implicit in "The Great Dark" and "3,000 Years Among the Microbes"). But only in the outline for a story set in the enclosed world constituted by the interior of a drifting iceberg does this concept (to which the lost-world theme popularized by Conan Doyle, Rider Haggard, and Edgar Rice Burroughs is related) reveal its true science-fiction character. As in the "generation starship," the descendants of the original shipwrecked crew and passengers, knowing nothing of reality outside the iceberg, are provided with myths to account for the features of their environment. It seems appropriate, therefore, to entitle Mark Twain's story outline "The Generation Iceberg."

IV

In *A Connecticut Yankee* and the microscopic-world stories the transference from one time to another and from one spatial dimension to another occurs as an instantaneous experience. The nature of such an experience would be extraordinary from many points of view. In particular, if travel or long-distance communication could be managed instantaneously, it seems both likely and logical that some loss of faith in the physicality of existence might occur, augmenting Mark Twain's notion that reality is insubstantial, a vagrant thought, a dream. And, in fact, Mark Twain did have some experience of long-distance instantaneous communications. As I have noted, he was the proud possessor of a telephone.

It would, in fact, be hard to overestimate the importance of the telephone to life in general (as Stephen Kern makes very plain in *The Culture of Time and Space, 1880-1918* [1983]) or to the increasingly science-fiction and apocalyptic cast of Mark Twain's thought. Nevertheless, it is little appreciated that he may have written the first story to make use of the telephone as the central plot element. "The Loves of Alonzo Fitz Clarence and Rosannah Ethelton" was published in 1878, the year after the telephone became practically available. Not only does Mark Twain project the existence of a telephone line spanning the American continent (something not accomplished until 1915) and the confusing consequences of being able to communicate instantaneously across such a distance, but he also anticipates the technology of wiretapping. However, what particularly appealed to Mark Twain's artistic imagination was the lack of physical presence made possible by the telephone. Such is the very peculiarity to which he returned in the brief piece entitled "A Telephone Conversation" (1880).

In this connection two essays, "Mental Telegraphy" (1891) and "Mental Telegraphy Again" (1895), the first largely written in 1878, the year the Alonzo and Rosannah telephone story was published, assume an unexpected importance. In spite of their supposedly "nonfictional" nature I have included these essays in the body of my collection instead of relegating them to an appendix because of their direct bearing on the theme of instantaneous communication. At the same time, of course, these pieces provide evidence of Mark Twain's concern with psychic possibilities, doubles, and the whirligig of schizophrenia. His life-long interest in ESP and "mental telegraphy" (what we would today call telepathy, "coincidentally" a term coined by the Englishman F. W. H. Myers in 1882 four years after Mark Twain had written a first, shorter version of "Mental Telegraphy") was no doubt abetted by the knowledge that a mind healer named Dr. Newton apparently cured his wife Olivia of a partial paralysis she suffered for two years.[45] This concern with extrasensory phenomena frequently took the form of a fascination with spiritualism. In 1879, in spite of his skepticism, Mark Twain made an attempt to communicate with his brother Henry through a medium named Mansfield and, after his daughter Susy died, he had recourse to various other mediums.[46] In "Mental Telegraphy" the connection between telepathy and spiritualism is made by the reference to the English Society for Psychical Research.

Writing about mental telegraphy to R. W. Gilder, editor of *Century*, on 13 November 1898, Mark Twain observed "I have had 21 years of experience of it and have written a novel with that as *motif* (don't be alarmed—I burned it) and I know considerable about it."[47] He also claimed that mental telegraphy was the source of a rejected but superior story entitled "My Platonic Sweetheart," written in 1898. On the basis of this pseudoscientific explanation and Mark Twain's belief in the existence of a dream reality, I have included this apparent fantasy as a further example of his science fiction.

In "Mental Telegraphy" it is posited that something called a "phrenophone" might communicate thoughts instantaneously, just as the telephone communicates the spoken word. In "From the 'London Times' of 1904," published in 1898, another futuristic invention, a visual telephone called the "telelectroscope," is used to seemingly disprove a murder. In the future legalistic circumstances posited by Mark Twain's piece, the man "wrongly" convicted of the murder must nevertheless be executed. But since it is precisely the divorce between, and subsequent confusion of, image and reality, fact and fiction, afforded by telelectroscopic instantaneous communication that causes ontological anxiety, there is something appropriate about the apparent act of injustice. Who can unequivocally state that the man convicted of the murder is not in fact the murderer?

Something like the basic plot of "From the 'London Times' of 1904" (and, to a lesser extent, of "A Murder, a Mystery, and a Marriage") is recycled by Mark Twain in a scenario for a science-fiction play entitled "Shackleford's Ghost." This account of the antics of an Invisible Man, published here for the first time (see appendix D), was probably written about the same time as the "London Times" report, that is to say in the year following the publication of Wells's *The Invisible Man* (1897). Mark Twain certainly knew of the book since in *What Is Man?* (the first draft of which was also written in 1898) there is a reference to "Mr. Wells's man who invented a drug that made him invisible."[48] In "Shackleford's Ghost" a man named Benson, who was experimenting with ways to make people invisible, disappears after successfully rendering a stranger invisible. When an innocent man is about to be hanged for the supposed murder of Benson, the Invisible Man (who in the meantime has worked for a fraudulent medium named Shackleford) shouts that he is the spirit of Benson, who committed suicide. At this moment, Benson, very much alive, appears with an invisibility antidote. In this version, then, the naturalistic action works to dispel any ambiguity about the nature of reality.

But striking confirmation of the relationship between means of instantaneous communication and doubt about the substance of reality is provided by *A Connecticut Yankee in King Arthur's Court*. Among the nineteenth-century technological marvels that Hank establishes in King Arthur's Britain is a telephone system. As an indication of the importance that he attaches to this system, he names his daughter by Sandy, Hello-Central. The most tangible manifestation of this marriage between a nineteenth-century man and a sixth-century woman is addressed by the words of an often used telephone communication. Like Edison at the time of his death, Hank and Mark Twain were in search of a telephone connection between worlds.[49] At the end of the novel, Hank, unable to distinguish between dream and reality, indeed doubtful of the existence of anything that can be called reality as opposed to a dream, believes that he hears his child and calls to her: "Hello-Central! . . . She doesn't answer. Asleep, perhaps?" He addresses a dream vision of Sandy: "Bring her when she wakes, and let me touch her hands, her face, her hair, and tell her good-bye." But that is exactly the kind of tangible confirmation that is forever denied.

V

Just how important a figure is Mark Twain in the history of science fiction? *A Connecticut Yankee* is certainly a landmark work in the development of the time-travel theme. I have already indicated some of the ways in which Mark Twain might be viewed as a precursor of Kurt Vonnegut and the tradition of humorous science fiction. But it is another author, Philip José Farmer who, more than any other writer of science fiction, most clearly acknowledges the debt that science fiction owes to Mark Twain. In what may be taken as an act of tribute, Farmer makes Mark Twain the central character in *The Fabulous Riverboat* (1971), the second novel in his Riverworld series.

There are many series in science fiction, but the Riverworld series, although artistically flawed, is one of the most successful. This is owing largely to its central concept, a mysterious "afterlife" world traversed by an immense river where all the generations of Earth find themselves resurrected in twenty-five-year-old bodies and living anachronistically alongside one another. In various ways this setup reflects Mark Twain's science-fiction concerns, although the central feature of the environment may well have been inspired not by his science fiction but by *Huckleberry Finn*. Farmer has science-fictionalized Mark Twain's masterpiece (having done much the same thing, albeit less successfully, for *Moby-Dick* with *The Wind Whales of Ishmael* [1970]). Like Mark Twain's Mississippi, Farmer's "magical" river is a means of rebirth. In *Huckleberry Finn*, episodes involving various kinds of death alternate with periods of rebirth on the river. In the Riverworld series, ultimate death seems to be an impossibility. Whoever dies finds herself or himself reborn at some different point in the river's course.

To some extent the Riverworld is a science-fiction "heaven" and thus belongs in a tradition which may be traced back at least to "Captain Stormfield's Visit to Heaven." A scheme for electrically resurrecting or "materializing" the dead figures in Mark Twain's and Howells's abortive play, *Colonel Sellers as a Scientist*. The indiscriminate mixing of people, including historical personages from different ages, finds a parallel in the Assembly of the Dead episode in the "Print Shop" or the "No. 44" Mysterious Stranger manuscript. The concern with the nature of Riverworld reality is very similar to Mark Twain's concern with the nature of reality in the Mysterious Stranger Manuscripts and elsewhere. The business of instantaneous communication or translation that I have emphasized in Mark Twain's work applies equally to the Riverworld. For those resurrected, whether they find themselves reborn for the first or the five-hundredth time, the translation to a new environment certainly seems instantaneous.

In succeeding volumes of Farmer's Riverworld series, *The Dark Design* (1977) and *The Magic Labyrinth* (1980), Mark Twain becomes one of a company of major figures in search of the secret meaning of the Riverworld. Mark Twain is not then *the* hero of Riverworld; he shares that honor with the famous explorer Sir Richard Francis Burton and others. Mark Twain's status as a science-fiction writer may be evaluated similarly. A giant of world literature, he is also not an insignificant figure in the history of science fiction. However the matter of relative importance might be resolved, he belongs in the company of such seminal authors as Sir Thomas More, Swift, Mary Shelley, Poe, Verne, Wells, and Stapledon.[50] More particularly it should be noted that the temporal span of his career places Mark Twain alongside Verne and Wells, writers generally credited as marking the turning point in the development of science fiction. Their fame in this regard has eclipsed unfairly Mark Twain's importance. He is, nevertheless, the Halley's Comet of the genre, a feature of the science-fiction universe that cannot long be ignored.

Notes

1. Brian W. Aldiss, *Billion Year Spree: The True History of Science Fiction* (New York: Doubleday & Company, Inc., 1973).

2. Darko Suvin, *Metamorphoses of Science Fiction: On the Poetics and History of a Literary Genre* (New Haven: Yale University Press, 1979), 200-1.

3. "By 'scientification,'" Gernsback wrote, "I mean the Jules Verne, H. G. Wells, and Edgar Allan Poe type of story—a charming romance intermingled with scientific fact and prophetic vision." See the editorial to the first issue of *Amazing Stories* (April 1926). It was discovered recently, however, that the term "science fiction" seems to have been used first in William Wilson's *A Little Earnest Book Upon a Great Old Subject* (i.e., poetry) published in 1851. See Brian Stableford, "William Wilson's Prospectus for Science Fiction: 1851," *Foundation*, no. 10 (June 1976), 6-12; and Brian W. Aldiss, "On the Age of the Term 'Science Fiction,'" *Science-Fiction Studies* 3 (July 1976), 213. Aldiss mistakenly refers to the author of *A Little Earnest Book* as "William Watson."

4. C. S. Lewis, *An Experiment in Criticism* (Cambridge at the University Press, 1961), 109; Robert M. Philmus, "Science Fiction: From Its Beginning to 1870," in *Anatomy of Wonder: Science Fiction*, ed. Neil Barron (New York: Bowker Company, 1976), 3-16 (this is one of the best attempts at definition to date). For a "heterogeneous" approach which may be related to that of Philmus, see Robert Scholes, "Educating for Future Realism," *Alternative Futures* 1 (Fall 1978), 91-95.

5. See David Ketterer, "Take-Off to Cosmic Irony: Science-Fiction Humor and the Absurd", in *Comic Relief: Humor in Contemporary American Literature*, ed. Sarah Blacher Cohen (Urbana: University of Illinois Press, 1978), 70-86.

6. Pascal Covici, Jr., *Mark Twain's Humor: The Image of a World* (Dallas: Southern Methodist University Press, 1962), passim. On the hoax form and science fiction, see the "Biographical Perspective" to *The Crystal Man: Landmark Science Fiction by Edward Page Mitchell*, ed. Sam Moskowitz (New York: Doubleday & Company, 1973), xi-xvi; David Ketterer, "Science Fiction and Allied Literature," *Science-Fiction Studies* 3 (March 1976), 70; and Ketterer, "Take-Off to Cosmic Irony," 75-76.

7. Kurt Vonnegut, Jr., *Cat's Cradle* (1963; reprint, New York: Dell Publishing Co. Inc., 1970), 191; Harold Bloom, *The Anxiety of Influence: A Theory of Poetry* (New York: Oxford University Press, 1973), passim.

8. See H. Bruce Franklin, *Future Perfect: American Science Fiction in the Nine-*

teenth Century, rev. ed. (New York: Oxford University Press, 1978), 375. In *Metamorphoses of Science Fiction*, Suvin goes so far as to claim that Mark Twain's Siamese couple are "progenitors of the mutant twins that recur from Heinlein to Dick" (p. 201).

9. See Robert A. Wiggins, "The Original of Mark Twain's *Those Extraordinary Twins*," *American Literature* 23 (March 1952), 355-57.

10. See Edward Wagenknecht, *Mark Twain: The Man and His Work*, 3rd ed. (Norman: University of Oklahoma Press, 1967), 105; and Robert A. Rees, "Mark Twain and Lucius Fairchild," *Wisconsin Academy Review* 15 (1968), 8-9.

11. My sources of information regarding "A Murder, a Mystery, and a Marriage" are *Mark Twain's Letters*, ed. Albert Bigelow Paine (New York: Harper & Brothers, 1917), 275-76, 278-79, 284, 288; "News from the Rare Book Sellers," *Publisher's Weekly* 148 (18 August 1945), 620-21; and *The New Yorker* 25 (29 January 1949), 15-16.

12. Mark Twain, *A Murder, a Mystery, and a Marriage* (New York: Manuscript House, 1945), 9.

13. For this special use of the term "apocalyptic" (as distinct from the "mimetic" and the "fantastic"), see David Ketterer, *New Worlds for Old: The Apocalyptic Imagination, Science Fiction, and American Literature* (New York: Doubleday Anchor Press; and Bloomington: Indiana University Press, 1974), passim.

14. This story is included in Kurt Vonnegut, Jr., *Welcome to the Monkey House* (New York: Dell Publishing Co., Inc., 1970), 7-13.

15. Quoted in Albert Bigelow Paine, *Mark Twain: A Biography*, vol. 1, (New York: Harper and Brothers, 1912), 12.

16. *Mark Twain's Fables of Man*, ed. John S. Tuckey (Berkeley: University of California Press, 1972), 439.

17. Hyatt Howe Waggoner, "Science in the Thought of Mark Twain," *American Literature* 8 (January 1937), 360.

18. See Mark Twain, *Letters from the Earth*, ed. Bernard DeVoto (New York: Harper & Row, 1962), 1-134. His first reference to Darwin occurs in *Roughing It* (1872), ed. Paul Baender (Berkeley: University of California Press, 1972), 145.

19. See *Mark Twain's Fables of Man*, 315-85. "Eddypus" is the major source of "the image of a future dictatorship" establishing "a central theme for SF" to which Suvin somewhat misleadingly claims Mark Twain "returned frequently in his fragmentary sketches." See *Metamorphoses of Science Fiction*, 201; and n. 4 to "Eddypus." But the idea does crop up in this 1883 note: "For a play: America in 1985. The Pope here & an Inquisition. The age of darkness back again. Pope is temporal despot, *too*. A titled eccles aristocracy & primogeniture. No Europe is *republican* & full of science & invention—none allowed here." See *Mark Twain's Notebooks & Journals, Vol. III (1883-1891)*, ed. Frederick Anderson, Robert Pack Browning, Michael B. Frank, and Lin Salamo (Berkeley: University of California Press, 1979), 45.

20. *Mark Twain-Howells Letters: The Correspondence of Samuel L. Clemens and William Dean Howells*, ed. Henry Nash Smith and William M. Gibson, vol. 1 (Cambridge, Mass.: The Belknap Press of Harvard University Press, 1960), 38.

21. *Mark Twain's Notebooks & Journals*, vol. 3, 346-47.

22. *Camden's Compliment to Walt Whitman*, ed. Horace L. Traubel (Philadelphia: D. McKay, 1889), 64-65.

23. See, for example, Philip Klass, "An Innocent in Time: Mark Twain in King Arthur's Court," *Extrapolation* 16 (December 1974), 30. Mark Twain read *Looking Backward* in November 1889, that is, just before the publication of *A Connecticut Yankee*. See *Mark Twain's Notebooks & Journals*, vol. 3, 526. However, the next notebook entry, "The Curious Repub of Gondomar" (p. 527) indicates that he most immediately associated Bellamy's utopia not with *A Connecticut Yankee* but with his own early utopian sketch. In a piece published in the New York *World* (12 January 1890), 14, Mark Twain disavows (without naming) another possible influence: Max Adeler's (pseudonym of Charles Heber Clark) *The Fortunate Island and Other Stories* (Boston: Shepherd, 1882). However, the particular story that Mark Twain denies (again without naming) having read before 1889, "An Old Fogy," in which an old man returns in a dream to the world of his childhood, while relevant to the theme of time travel in *A Connecticut Yankee*, is not the story from which, according to Adeler, Mark Twain had plagiarized. That was the lead story which Mark Twain pointedly avoids mentioning in his somewhat bullying account of how (in the company of a witness, William Dean Howells) he acquired a copy of Adeler's book in late 1889 or early 1890. "The Fortunate Island" is about a scientifically knowledgeable American who is shipwrecked on an island that broke off from England during King Arthur's time. The similarities between this story and *A Connecticut Yankee* (names, numerous incidents and the humorous contrast of epochs) are very striking.

24. See Ketterer, "Epoch-Eclipse and Apocalypse: Special 'Effects' in *A Connecticut Yankee*," in *New Worlds for Old*, 213-32. An eclipse that Mark Twain witnessed on 7 August 1869 is described comically in a piece entitled "The Eclipse" which he wrote four days later for the Buffalo *Express*. See *The Forgotten Writings of Mark Twain*, ed. Henry Duskis (New York: Philosophical Library, 1963), 51-54.

25. See P. J. Federico, "The Facts in the Case of Mark Twain's Vest Strap," *Journal of the Patent Office Society* (21 March 1939), 223-32; reprinted as "Mark Twain's Inventions and Patents," *Twainian* 26 (November-December 1957), 1-4; and Justin Kaplan, *Mr. Clemens and Mark Twain: A Biography* (New York: Simon and Schuster, 1966), 150, 200, 215-53, 257, 351-52, 360.

26. For a text of the play (there are several versions in manuscript and typescript), see *The Complete Plays of W. D. Howells*, ed. Walter J. Meserve (New York: New York University Press, 1960), 209-41.

27. See *Mark Twain: The Man and His Work*, 105; and Anne P. Wigger, "The Source of the Fingerprint Material in Mark Twain's *Pudd'nhead Wilson and Those Extraordinary Twins*," *American Literature* 28 (January 1957), 517-20.

28. Quoted in Paine, *Mark Twain*, vol. 1, 512; see also, on palmistry, Joseph O. Baylen, "Mark Twain, W. T. Stead and 'The Tell-Tale Hands,'" *American Quarterly* 16 (Winter 1964), 606-12; and, on phrenology, Madeline B. Stern, "Mark Twain Had His Head Examined," *American Literature* 41 (May 1969), 207-18; Alan Gribben, "Mark Twain, Phrenology and the 'Temperaments': A Study of Pseudo-scientific Influences," *American Quarterly* 24 (March 1972), 44-68; and James D. Wilson, "'The Monumental Sarcasm of the Ages': Science and Pseudoscience in the Thought of Mark Twain," *South Atlantic Bulletin* 40 (May 1975), 72-82.

29. See Tom Burnham, "Mark Twain and the Paige Typesetter: A Background for Despair," *Western Humanities Review* 6 (Winter 1951), 29-36; James M. Cox, *Mark Twain: The Fate of Humor* (Princeton, N.J.: Princeton University Press, 1966), 198-221; and chapter 14, "The Yankee and the Machine," in Kaplan, *Mr. Clemens and Mark Twain*, 280-311.

30. See Sherwood Cummings, "Mark Twain's Social Darwinism," *Huntington Library Quarterly* 20 (February 1975), 163-75; and Cummings, "Science and Mark Twain's Theory of Fiction," *Philological Quarterly* 37 (January 1958), 26-33.

31. Jan Pinkerton, "Backward Time Travel, Alternate Universes, and Edward Everett Hale," *Extrapolation* 20 (Summer 1979), 172.

32. *Mark Twain's Mysterious Stranger Manuscripts*, ed. William M. Gibson (Berkeley: University of California Press, 1969), 117. See also John S. Tuckey, *Mark Twain and Little Satan: The Writing of "The Mysterious Stranger"* (West Lafayette, Ind.: Purdue University Press, 1963); *Mark Twain's "The Mysterious Stranger" and the Critics*, ed. John S. Tuckey (Belmont, Calif: Wadsworth, 1968); "Introduction" and apparatus to *Mark Twain's Mysterious Stranger Manuscripts*, 1-34, 409-606; and Sholom J. Kahn, *Mark Twain's Mysterious Stranger: A Study of the Manuscript Texts* (Columbia: University of Missouri Press, 1978).

33. Kahn, *Mark Twain's Mysterious Stranger*, xiii.

34. Ibid., 236; Gibson, ed., *Mark Twain's Mysterious Stranger Manuscripts*, 376.

35. Kahn, *Mark Twain's Mysterious Stranger*, 168.

36. Gibson, ed., *Mark Twain's Mysterious Stranger Manuscripts*, 386.

37. Ibid., 388.

38. Kahn, *Mark Twain's Mysterious Stranger*, 236, 177.

39. Gibson, ed., *Mark Twain's Mysterious Stranger Manuscripts*, 377.

40. Ibid., 403.

41. Ibid., 215.

42. Suvin, *Metamorphoses of Science Fiction*, 242.

43. *Mark Twain's Notebooks & Journals*, vol. 3, 56. ([——]) indicates cancelled illegible letters.

44. Tom Shippey, "A Modern View of Science Fiction" in *Beyond This Horizon: An Anthology of Science Fiction and Science Fact* (Sunderland, Durham: Ceolfrith Press, 1973), 8-9. Shippey sees the "generation starship" as providing the most familiar setting for what he calls the "deculturation" story. In my terms, this kind of story provides a paradigmatic example of one philosophical aspect of the "apocalyptic" nature of science fiction: works that, directly or indirectly, present the world we know in other terms, specifically in terms of a radically new definition of reality (as opposed to a radically new definition of man or the identification of a previously unsuspected outside manipulator). See Ketterer, *New Worlds for Old*, especially part 3, "The Present World in Other Terms," 159-333. The basic sense of Shippey's "deculturation" and my "philosophical apocalypse" is conveyed by the term "conceptual breakthrough" in *The Encyclopedia of Science Fiction*, ed. Peter Nicholls (London: Granada Publishing Limited, 1979), 134-36.

45. Kaplan, *Mr. Clemens and Mark Twain*, 77-78. On 4 October 1884, Clemens accepted an invitation to become a member of the Society for Psychical Research. He re-

mained a member until 1902. See *Mark Twain's Notebooks & Journals*, vol. 3, 260-61, n. 111.

46. Kaplan, *Mr. Clemens and Mark Twain*, 203. See also chapter 7, "'Sperits Couldn't a Done Better': Mark Twain and Spiritualism," in Howard Kerr, *Mediums, and Spirit-Rappers, and Roaring Radicals: Spiritualism in American Literature, 1850-1900* (Urbana: University of Illinois Press, 1972), 155-89.

47. Quoted in Kaplan, *Mr. Clemens and Mark Twain*, 343. Possibly related to telepathy is the perhaps occult, perhaps undeveloped natural talent of precognition that is displayed by the protagonist of the fragment "Clairvoyant" (1883-84?). See *Mark Twain's Hannibal, Huck & Tom*, ed. Walter Blair (Berkeley: University of California Press, 1969), 61-66. Young Satan will combine telepathic and precognitive powers. Blair notes (p. 59) the existence of an additional piece on mental telegraphy, "an unpublished article of seven hundred words, written in November 1907 and now in the Mark Twain Papers (DV254)."

48. *What is Man? and Other Philosophical Writings*, ed. Paul Baender (Berkeley: University of California Press, 1973), 179.

49. Many science-fiction plots would collapse without the existence of some form of instantaneous communication between interstellar locations. Thus James Blish gives us his Dirac Communicator in "Beep" (1954) and elsewhere, and Ursula K. Le Guin gives us her "ansible": "It will be a device that will permit communication without any time travel between two points in space. . . . So we will be able to use it to talk between worlds, without the long waiting for the message to go and the reply to return that electromagnetic impulses require. It is really a very simple matter. Like a kind of telephone." See *The Dispossessed* (New York: Harper & Row, 1974), 303. E.T., in the film of that name (1982), concocts something comparable, so that he can "phone home."

50. In addition to Swift, Verne, and Wells, Mark Twain was also familiar with Mary Shelley. A notebook entry written in 1884 directs "Write a burlesque Frankenstein—(Freestone)." He goes on in this and a subsequent entry to elaborate plot possibilities. See *Mark Twain's Notebooks & Journals*, vol. 3, 49, 50. *Frankenstein* is first mentioned in chapter 48 of *Life on the Mississippi* (1883).

Mark Twain and the Tradition of Literary Domesticity_____

Michael J. Kiskis

When I ask students what they know about Mark Twain, they invariably respond with a host of established images—white suit, white hair, frontier born and raised, westerner, southerner, the river. Many have read either *The Adventures of Tom Sawyer* or *Adventures of Huckleberry Finn*; few have moved beyond the party line of Twain as American classic. Fewer still know him as the author of *The Prince and the Pauper* or *Personal Recollections of Joan of Arc*; some have been touched by the controversy of race and have come to see the debate over racism in his works as the only issue worthy of attention or scorn; all tend to think that he emerged fully formed amid Mississippi sandbars and small towns constrained by solid family and community values. All are surprised by his attachment to his family.

For a good long time, Twain scholars, like my students, have been operating within exclusionary readings and tightly wrapped and carefully marketed icons. When I was introduced to Mark Twain's writing in 1981 during my first semester of doctoral study, the theme of the seminar was Mark Twain as Artist (emphasis, in fact, on failed artist). That focus on and interpretation of Twain were clearly tied to the debate begun more than sixty years earlier by Van Wyck Brooks and Bernard DeVoto: the two camps divide over Twain as frustrated and failed artist (Brooks) or Twain as essential proponent of American individualism and of the innate power of the vernacular and folk mind (DeVoto). Twain studies is still held hostage to that debate.

The relative ease of an interpretation based in such dualism has created a cottage industry in Twain studies. We continue to squeeze and mold Twain into prepackaged notions of who and what he was or should be—we apply current theoretical approaches and constructs to his works in a display of intellectual gymnastics rather than a concentrated and open-minded exploration. We do not often admit that the prism through which we read Twain conjures specific images and interpretations. Though we make noises about understanding the affect of interpretive paradigms on our work, we do not always view those paradigms with a skepticism that allows entry to opposing views or that allows us to appreciate a more (or less) complex understanding of Twain's humanity. It is a classic case of what Annette Kolodny describes as the challenge facing feminist scholars: "Insofar as we are taught how to read, what we engage are not texts but paradigms."[1] My point is that for too long we have kept to one interpretive paradigm when reading the works of Mark Twain. We have focused mainly on his supposedly unambiguous support for individual—even iconoclastic—freedom.

In her introduction to *Domestic Individualism: Imagining Self in Nineteenth-Century America*, Gillian Brown argues that we need to complicate our reading of American literature by blending the mythic criticism that focuses on the growth of a peculiarly American individualism (which takes explicit form with Emerson) with an understanding of nineteenth-century American women writers' focus on domestic images and experiences of home and hearth that they used both to challenge a market controlled by male writers and to build their own literary tradition:

> Individualism and domesticity have both long figured as thematics of nineteenth-century American culture, but as distinct and oppositional trajectories. Thus two disparate literary movements seem to emerge in the 1850s: on the one hand the American Renaissance, represented by the "classic works" of Emerson, Whitman, Hawthorne, Melville, and Poe; and on the other hand the Other American Renaissance, inscribed in the works of Stowe and such writers as Susan Warner, Fanny Fern, Harriet Wilson, and Elizabeth Stuart Phelps.
>
> This gender division has persisted with remarkable neatness and clarity throughout American literary criticism. Recall how myths of the origins of American culture describe second-generation Adamic and oedipal stories:

new Edens, sons in exile, estrangement from women. . . . In this andro-
centric, if not misogynistic, account of American culture, literature records
the battle between the masculine desire for freedom and the feminine will
toward civilization: the runaway Huck Finn versus the "sivilizing" Widow
Douglas. The paradigm of the dreamer's flight from the shrew defines the
domestic as a pole from which the individual must escape in order to establish and preserve his identity. Huck lights out for the territory in order to
avoid what Ann Douglas calls "the feminization of American culture," to
flee from the widow's sentimental values that epitomize, in Henry Nash
Smith's words, "an ethos of conformity."[2]

Brown begins a useful reappraisal of the validity of parallel literary
movements. She also points to a way to set Mark Twain and his literary
creations within a much broader and, I think, more accurate tradition
in American letters. Taking Brown's comments as my lead, I intend
to examine Twain's tie to the "Other American tradition" of literary
domesticity—to the definition of home, the boundaries of home, and
the freedom to be gained by belonging. Mark Twain never wanted to escape the "domestic"; in fact, his identity depended heavily upon values
embedded in home and hearth. For evidence, I will look to *Adventures
of Huckleberry Finn*, "The Death of Jean," and the *Autobiography.*

My experience as a reader of *Adventures of Huckleberry Finn* during the past fifteen years has introduced me to a variety of critical judgments ranging from the complaints against Huck's obstinate ignorance
to a celebration of his archetypal quest for freedom, to applause for his
ability to transcend both religious and racial prejudice, to disappoint-
ment with the final third of his story, to a sophisticated response to the
final adventures that argues for the unified whole. It fascinates me that
each of these approaches is still in play; none has been effectively
calmed. I now have a sense that we have recently turned a critical corner and face still another—and compelling—approach: the next interpretive battle may be over Huck's influence on how we see and understand family relationships.

This places *Adventures of Huckleberry Finn* at the center of the swirl over domestic concerns in the mid- to late nineteenth century. Huck's runaway status, his being essentially an orphan, places him at the side of young Ellen Montgomery of Susan Warner's *Wide, Wide World* (1850), Sylvy of Sarah Orne Jewett's "White Heron" (1886), or, later, even young Lily of Mary Wilkins Freeman's "Old Woman Magoun" (1891). These writers place their characters in a struggle for moral action—most often within households and communities shaped, perhaps exclusively, by women. In our own time, Huck is placed within the drive by social conservatives to highlight William Bennett's praise for supposedly conservative-owned virtues—Self-discipline, Compassion, Responsibility, Friendship, Work, Courage, Perseverance, Honesty, Loyalty, and Faith—and for stories that speak "without hesitation, without embarrassment, to the inner part of the individual, to the moral sense."[3]

Twain, I think, would be ambivalent. He saw the moral sense as no key to appropriate behavior; it is too easily shaped by external authority, too quickly transformed from an interest in compassion into the slave of a conscience like that which Twain's narrator battles in "The Recent Carnival of Crime in Connecticut," or like that which Huck battles as he runs for his life. Yet, issues of morality are deeply embedded in Twain's domestic fiction, especially the question of how to teach morality—by the voice of authority or by the resilience of tradition. In *Adventures of Huckleberry Finn* the debate is manifest in the conflict between the narrow blasts of Miss Watson and Pap on one side and the steady perseverance of the Widow Douglas and Jim on the other.

Twain insisted that the arena for this consideration of morality is the home. I recently taught a graduate class called "Mark Twain and Social Justice." Our discussion of the constellation of social issues in *Adventures of Huckleberry Finn* quickly focused on the profound absence of the "traditional" family and social networks within the tale. As we worked through Twain's writings, one student became more apprehensive: finally, looking very uncomfortable, he announced that he felt that he would have substantial problems bringing *Adventures of Huckleberry Finn* to his students. The questions of aesthetics were not the problem, nor did he feel the questions of race insurmountable. His prime concern became how to introduce a story about an abused child of an alcoholic parent to a group of students whose home lives were so much a mirror image of Huck's. "This story," he said, "is too close to their real lives." Twain's consideration of home—or absence of home—fostered his uncanny ability to look into the dark corners of human life and paint a picture that may, in fact, be more accurate in 2000 than it was in 1886 or 1846.

Clearly, just as the increased consciousness of civil rights since the 1950s inspired readers to consider the role that race plays in *Adventures of Huckleberry Finn*, our contemporary concerns ignite questions related to family issues, social and legal protections, and values. Consider that the new judge brought in to rule on the matter of Huck's custody (a battle between Pap and Judge Thatcher and the Widow Douglas) decides in Pap's favor based on an assumption that biology trumps compassion and overrides legal protection: "[H]e said courts mustn't interfere and separate families if they could help it; said he'd druther not take a child away from its father. So Judge Thatcher and the widow had to quit the business."[4] Four paragraphs later, however, that new judge is full of regrets after Pap's short-lived reform and "reckoned a body could reform the old man with a shot-gun, maybe, but he didn't know no other way" (*Case*, 49). The whole next chapter (chapter 6) presents a haunting picture of an abduction, frequent cowhidings and beatings ("But by-and-by pap got too handy with his hick'ry, and I couldn't stand it. I was all over welts"), psychological abuse, and, most troubling of all, attempted murder and Huck's contemplation of patricide:

By-and-by he rolled out an jumped up on his feet looking wild, and he see me and went for me. He chased me round and round the place, with a clasp-knife, calling me the Angel of Death and saying he would kill me and then I couldn't come for him no more. I begged and told him I was only Huck, and he laughed *such* a screechy laugh, and roared and cussed, and kept on chasing me up. Once when I turned short and dodged under his arm he made a grab and got me by the jacket between my shoulders, and I thought I was gone; but I slid out of the jacket quick as lightning, and saved myself. Pretty soon he was all tired out, and dropped down with his back against the door, and said he would rest a minute and then kill me. He put his knife under him, and said he would sleep and get strong, and then he would see who was who.

So he dozed off, pretty soon. By-and-by I got the old split-bottom chair and clumb up, as easy as I could, not to make any noise, and got down the gun. I slipped the ramrod down it to make sure it was loaded, and then I laid it across the turnip barrel, pointing towards pap, and set down behind it to wait for him to stir. And how slow and still the time did drag along. (*Case*, 54-55)

The choreography and pacing of the scene inspire terror. The experience itself motivates Huck to get the hell away. The disagreeable idea of being dragged from place to place by Pap to avoid another custody battle is replaced with a deliberate choice of homelessness and wandering and, what is worse for Huck, loneliness.

All of this takes place prior to Huck's coming upon Jim on Jackson's Island. Whether that reunion is part of Twain's initial plan or not (Vic Doyno has suggested that it was *not* part of Twain's early intention), the first seven chapters offer troubling images of an adolescent struggling at the furthest margins of small-town life. Huck's character is set. His actions and reactions for the rest of the tale remain consistent with what we know from these first episodes. We know that Huck, as the child of an alcoholic, as a young boy torn between loyalty and fear, as a student of violence and loneliness, will do what he can to survive, to get along. He will be reactive, not proactive. He will allow others to set the agenda (even his stories take their cue from the individuals he meets) and will choose to remain quiet: his refrain, whether to Miss

Watson's complaints or to the later felonies of the Duke and King, is to keep still; speaking up "would only make trouble, and wouldn't do no good" (*Case*, 33). Huck's behavior in the final section of the tale is consistent, which, in fact, helps to resolve at least part of the critical discomfort generated by Huck's reluctance to challenge Tom Sawyer's crazy actions toward Jim.

What, then, *does* the story offer if its teller's primary consistency is expedient behavior and reactions sparked by fear? At its heart, *Adventures of Huckleberry Finn* is the story of two survivors, each of whom is reluctant to act alone or to speak out: both Huck and Jim, though for different reasons, are robbed of their options and of their voices by the social system that reigns over them. Only when they are separated from that system are they able to consider choices and offer even tentative commentary on their lives; only when they loosen themselves from the constraints are they able to talk. And it takes a good deal of time before they can talk to each other on a human level rather than through the disguises they inherit from their social caste. (Compare, for example, Huck's attempt to explain the French language [chapter 14] to Jim to the later exchange after their separation in the fog when Huck is shamed into apologizing to Jim [chapter 15] or, still later, Jim's story about his deaf daughter [chapter 23].) Their increasingly intimate talk reinforces both their alienation from the society at large and, perhaps more important, their exile from any semblance of family.

And where does that lead us? If the whole of Huck's story is about the disintegration of human bonds and the eventual breakdown of even the most tentative of human connections, we will have grave problems making a case for its value as a moral tale. *Adventures of Huckleberry Finn* presents us with nagging questions: How do we deal with the dizzying array of possible—and very often ambiguous—lessons that push through the narrative? Do we pick and choose to make the text more palatable as moral instruction? Do we, for example, opt for an optimistic interpretation in order to demonstrate that Huck, in the end, has managed to grow into a critical but loyal member of the society? Do we present his rejection of society—all society—at the end of the novel when he decides to "light out for the Territory *ahead of the rest*" in order to escape the community to which he has recently returned as a positive step? Is self-exile an option to be applauded? Has his experience made him more or less suspicious of allegiances—not to mention relationships—with other individuals or groups? After all, staying very much in character, Huck decides to turn and run rather than confront the demands of community membership. He runs from the possibility of family. He turns to irresponsibility with relish and anticipation. That is not a moral lesson.

I would like to make a different argument. The key to the immorality of Huck's tale is not in *his* slouching toward irresponsibility and expediency but in *our* own ease in ignoring the whole of Huck's life or (worse) cheapening it with a condescending chuckle and a quickened step so that we push him from our view. Perhaps we decide that he gains sensitivity because it is safer for us if he does so. Huck, after all, is the homeless child on the street. The immigrant shut out from our schools. The child who, because of a self-destructive belief in his own corruption and worthlessness, grows up to be his pap. Mark Twain's moral lesson is *not* that Huck gains a sense of his own humanity by transcending the constraints and stereotypes placed on him and on Jim by the authority of school and church and home but that Huck fails. The stout heart does not win over the deformed conscience. Huck's failure is our lesson. Midpoint in the composing process, Mark Twain added the admonishment that "persons attempting to find a moral . . . will be banished" (*Case*, 27). Huck tried. And he was banished. Huck—and Mark Twain, and Samuel Clemens—left a story to us steeped in domestic concerns in the hopes that we would come to understand the primacy of home and the value of compassion.

Compassion is, however, a difficult emotion to pin on Mark Twain. At least it has been that way within our established interpretive paradigm. After our look at Twain's building a case for compassion in *Adventures of Huckleberry Finn*, let's turn now to his autobiographical writing to consider an even more profound description of the value of human relation.

In December 1909, Mark Twain penned what he called "the final chapter of my autobiography." The essay, published posthumously in 1911 as "The Death of Jean," has received only quick mention by biographers and has been passed off as highly sentimentalized, yet it is one of the more affective pieces in Twain's canon (frankly, I have found no piece so likely to destroy conventional notions of Mark Twain). Critics have been content to slip the piece among those works considered extraordinary not because it hints at a genuine domestic foundation in Twain's emotional life (though this *is* a valuable and neglected aspect of Twain's life and writing) but because it does not conform to established, comfortable ideas of Twain as misanthropic social philosopher. It challenges the established paradigm and is, therefore, relegated to the ash heap of sentimentalism. Mark Twain, it seems, is not allowed to express real and troubling emotion. And we, as critics, are made uncomfortable by that emotion and must look away before we admit that Twain had (and maybe that we have) an emotional life.

Some biographical background may be helpful here. In the summer of 1909, Jean Clemens, Twain's youngest daughter, arrived in Redding, Connecticut, to rejoin the Clemens household (to reconstitute that household may be a more accurate description since Clara would marry in October and later move to Europe). The aging Twain, who by this time had watched the procession of the dead as a genuinely interested bystander, was pleased with the potential for reconnecting with Jean, who had been shuttled back and forth between a maze of sanatoriums and cures since her diagnosis with epilepsy in the 1890s. Their relationship had been a difficult one. And while all Twain's relationships were difficult, none bore so tragic a tint as those with his children.

With a potential reconciliation in sight, Jean dies on the morning of Christmas Eve. She seems to have suffered a seizure and drowned in her bath. She is found by the household's servant, Katy Leary. Twain begins:

Jean is dead!

Has anyone ever tried to put upon paper all the little happenings connected with a dear one—happenings of the twenty-four hours preceding the sudden and unexpected death of that dear one? Would a book contain them? Would two books contain them? I think not. They pour into the mind in a flood. They are little things that have been always happening every day, and were always so unimportant and easily forgettable before—but now! Now, how different! how precious they are, how dear, how unforgettable, how pathetic, how sacred, how clothed with dignity! (*Autobiography* [henceforth *AU*], 245-46)

Twain's calm is extremely affective here. Throughout his career he was haunted by a tendency to burlesque and melodramatic pathos at moments of personal stress; however, here there are no histrionics, no melodramatic expression of grief. The grief is there. And it is deep. But it is present not in the specific experience of Jean's death but in the catalog of deaths that Twain creates as he replays his past:

In England thirteen years ago, my wife and I were stabbed to the heart with a cablegram which said, "Susy was mercifully released today." I had to send a like shock to Clara, in Berlin, this morning. . . .

I lost Susy thirteen years ago; I lost her mother—her incomparable mother!—five and a half years ago; Clara has gone away to life in Europe; and now I have lost Jean. How poor I am, who was once so rich! Seven months ago Mr. Rogers died—one of the best friends I ever had, and the nearest perfect, as a man and a gentleman, I have ever yet met among my race; within the last six weeks Gilder has passed away, and Laffan—old, old friends of mine. Jean lies yonder, I sit here; we are strangers under our own roof; we kissed hands goodbye at the door last night—and it was forever, we never suspecting it. She lies there, and I sit here—writing, busying myself, to keep my heart from breaking. How dazzling the sunshine is flooding the hills around! It is like a mockery. (*AU*, 246-47)

Twain's narrative distance is deceiving, and it is troubling. He mentions his losses to build to the climactic conflict between the glory of the world that surrounds an abundance of death. Most fascinating is his willingness to chronicle not only the names of his blessed but also the process that he uses to calm his hurt: writing acts as a restorative, as a balm that allows him to sit as a companion to Jean though her death is the final reminder of his own mortality. The contrast between her death and his life is too obvious. The final mockery may not be the shining sun, but his being alive to notice it and to gain some aesthetic thrill at the spectacle. The bitterness that supposedly wraps his thoughts and impressions is here nowhere to be found. Instead we have a sadness and a profound expression of emotional numbness and the dull recognition that longevity is more a cure than a blessing: "Would I bring her back if I could do it? I would not. If a word would do it, I would beg for the strength to withhold the word. And I would have the strength; I am sure of it. In her loss I am almost bankrupt, and my life is a bitterness, but I am content; for she has been enriched with the most precious of all gifts—that gift which makes all the other gifts mean and poor—death" (*AU*, 249). Twain echoes the message to which he returned so often in his fiction—the gift of death. It is, after all, the feigned death that allows Huck to escape an abusive and homicidal father; it is the release for Joan of Arc; it is the gift that Satan brings in "The Mysterious Stranger." Death prompts Twain to rejoice in the destruction of Eden in the diaries of Adam and Eve; it is the last, the most potent, of "The Five Boons of Life"; and it is the final release that he has evaded for so long.

Twain finally faces the image of his own death as he transports himself to the site of Jean's arrival and burial in Elmira. He did not make the funeral journey, but he imagines the scene:

2:30 P.M.—It is the time appointed. The funeral has begun. Four hundred miles away, but I can see it all, just as if I were there. The scene is the library, in the Langdon homestead. Jean's coffin stands where her mother and I stood, forty years ago, and were married; and where Susy's coffin stood thirteen years ago; where her mother's stood, five years and a half ago; and where mine will stand, after a little time. (*AU*, 252)

The deadpan voice that Twain used so expertly in his humor is here translated into a mechanism to relate emotional fullness and the exhaustion that is companion to grief. There is resignation and, as he has said earlier, contentment in the realization of his coming participation in the family pageant. Bitterness, anger, frustration have been put aside so that he can focus on reclaiming family attachment. Four months later Twain died of congestive heart failure. His coffin did stand in that same room.

But how does this evaluation of Twain's emotional tie to family enter into the established critical tradition within Twain studies? It doesn't. At this point, Twain is, by most accounts, bitter, cynical, railing against God and the universe, and taking every opportunity available to hoot and toss epithets at the possibility of human redemption. Critics, biographers, and scholars have taken an odd form (a perverse form?) of delight in perpetuating this sour image of Mark Twain. Yes, his comments carried strong indictments of human foolishness and folly. Yes, he saw the worst in humans, and especially saw the worst in himself. But there is much more to Twain than that, and this is not particularly good news to those still embedded in the Brooks-DeVoto argument or those who insist on Twain's exclusive title as definer of American individualism. The duality that resides in the opposing images of the writer who after Emerson is seen as most responsible for defining the character of American self-reliance and the carping, vituperative, and godless philosophical gadfly is too convenient. It is time we moved past that. But toward what?

Since most of my time is spent rummaging around in the attic that is Mark Twain's autobiographical dictations and writings, let me start there. The autobiography is very much a domestic tale. Looking especially at the portion of material that Twain published during his lifetime (principally in the *North American Review* in 1906 and 1907), we face a Mark Twain who is deeply involved in the tradition of literary domesticity. His concerns are with hearth and home. With family. With the absence of family and the need to locate and develop emotional ties within an extended community of friends and acquaintances. In scenes that echo the writings of Caroline Kirkland, Mary E. Wilkins Freeman, Sarah Orne Jewett, and, later, Willa Cather, Twain offers haunting descriptions of basic domestic life:

> I can see the farm yet, with perfect clearness. I can see all its belongings, all its details; the family room of the house, with a "trundle" bed in one corner and a spinning-wheel in another—a wheel whose rising and falling wail, heard from a distance, was the mournfulest of all sounds to me, and made me homesick and low-spirited, and filled my atmosphere with the wandering spirits of the dead; the vast fireplace, piled high, on winter nights, with flaming hickory logs from whose ends a sugary sap bubbled out but did not go to waste, for we scraped it off and ate it; the lazy cat spread out on the rough hearthstones, the drowsy dogs braced against the jambs and blinking; my aunt in one chimney-corner knitting, my uncle in the other smoking his corn-cob pipe; the slick and carpetless oak floor faintly mirroring the dancing flame-tongues and freckled with black indentations where fire-coals had popped out and died a leisurely death; half a dozen children romping in the background twilight; "split"-bottomed chairs here and there, some with rockers; *a cradle—out of service, but waiting, with confidence*; in the early cold mornings a snuggle of children, in shirts and chemises, occupying the hearthstone and procrastinating—they could not bear to leave that comfortable place and go out on the wind-swept floorspace between the house and kitchen where the general tin basin stood, and wash. (*AU*, 116-17; emphasis added)

In the background we hear the voice of Huck Finn—it resonates with deep emotional upset and loneliness. The forlorn cry of the spinning wheel, the uneasy spirits abroad in the night. And we have the signal image of home—the patient, confident cradle.

Embedded in this passage is, I think, a new understanding of Mark Twain. His interest in domestic life was neither shallow nor fleeting. It resonates throughout his major and minor works. Yet, we continue to skid past domesticity on the way to other topics and concerns. We consider Tom Sawyer's home life only to introduce the ironies of community leadership and values; we look at the dilemma of the prince and the pauper and see criticism of the arbitrary nature of royalty; we proclaim Huck's aloneness as a path to reinventing a moral consciousness; we watch Hank Morgan destroy Camelot and tie his actions to the failure of American imperialism or American reconstruction. Each of these readings furthers the agenda of the icon builders. Icons limit our appreciation of complexity. They limit our choices.

Clearly, then, I am arguing for a more complex reading of Mark Twain's work and an acknowledgment of and an appreciation for his connection to literary domesticity. Tom Sawyer, Huck Finn, Hank Morgan, Joan of Arc, Roxy, and Adam and Eve: all suffer the most domestic of ills—the inability to negotiate human relationships. And no matter how we turn away from this to find more seductive, more broadly political, more socially sophisticated readings, we still must face the reality at the heart of Twain's stories—that pain is at the center of home and grows out of the search for home.

At the end of *The Adventures of Tom Sawyer*, Twain offers an exchange between Huck and Tom that epitomizes that pain. Huck is considering escape from his newly assigned place in the home of Widow Douglas. Tom, however, will have none of that:

". . . Huck, we can't let you in the gang if you ain't respectable, you know."

Huck's joy was quenched.

"Can't let me in, Tom? Didn't you let me go for a pirate?"

"Yes, but that's different. A robber is more high-toned than what a pirate is—as a general thing. In most countries they're awful high up in the nobility—dukes and such."

"Now Tom, hain't you always been friendly to me? You wouldn't shet me out, would you, Tom? You wouldn't do that, now, would you, Tom?"

"Huck, I wouldn't want to, and I don't want to—but what would people say? Why they'd say, 'Mph! Tom Sawyer's Gang! pretty low characters in it!' *They'd mean you, Huck.* You wouldn't like that, and I wouldn't."[5]

Of course, Huck caves in to this pressure. Despite Tom's condescension, despite what we might, I think rightly, interpret as Tom's deep ambivalence (I am tempted to say hatred) toward the desperate boy, Huck gives in. He needs to belong. To someone. To something. And so does Twain. Once more to the end of "The Death of Jean":

It is all over.

When Clara went away two weeks ago to live in Europe, it was hard, but I could bear it, for I had Jean left. I said we would be a family. We said we would be close comrades and happy—just we two. That fair dream was in my mind when Jean met me at the steamer last Monday; it was in my mind when she received me at the door last Tuesday evening. We were together; we were a family! The dream had come true—oh, preciously true, contentedly true, satisfyingly true! and remained true two whole days.

And now? Now Jean is in her grave!

In the grave—if I can believe it. God rest her sweet spirit! (*AU*, 252)

Ultimately, Twain's work recounts the struggle of the human heart to find a place in this world, to find peace, to find a place to lie comfortably content with our mortality. To find a home. To hear the whine of the spinning wheel and think not of the mournfulest sound but of the peace of your own bed.

Mark Twain eventually left behind the hoax, joke, and tall tale for the more powerful images of community and home. In fact, he sought out the dilemmas of personal relationships as the basis for his storytelling. Whereas power, the lust for it and the failure to achieve it, is a focal point in many of Mark Twain's tales, he is at his best in those pieces that focus on domestic relationships: the childhood bluster at the opening to *The Adventures of Tom Sawyer*; the raft episodes in *Adventures of Huckleberry Finn*; the memories of an old and disappointed lover in *Personal Recollections of Joan of Arc*; the domestic fiction in the McWilliams short stories, the animal tales, the stories of the good and bad boys; and the anecdotes that creep into his speeches and his autobiography. This argues for complexity; however, we often continue to focus on "The Notorious Jumping Frog of Calaveras County," "Grandfather's Old Ram," "Dick Baker's Cat," along with a host of tales that fit our expectation of Twain's frontier roots, even those in *Innocents Abroad*. There is much more to Twain. Two of his more notable stories, "The Facts Behind the Recent Carnival of Crime in Connecticut" and "The Man That Corrupted Hadleyburg," center their deep irony within a domestic environment. We have rarely—and then barely—dipped into the outrageous diary entries of Adam and Eve or the quirkiness of Captain Stormfield's visit to heaven, each of which depends on the conflicts that inhabit domestic scenes lighted by parochial attitudes that underscore contrasts between expectations and reality. And Twain's "Chapters from My Autobiography" is best seen as an examination of domestic relationships in an extended family.

Gillian Brown's notion of combining the two now parallel traditions will help us understand Mark Twain, for in the end, his strength is demonstrated in his ability to incorporate the broader focus and social irony that comes through his literary mothers. Twain scholars would now do well to see that the humor of the old Southwest is only one of the influences and, perhaps, not a dominant influence after all. The frontier boast was an effective tool for Twain. But he had a good deal more success when he set aside the wool and furs of the frontier for the homespun and silk of the household.

Notes

1. Kolodny, "Dancing through the Minefield: Some Observations on the Theory, Practice, and Politics of a Feminist Literary Criticism," 280.
2. Brown, *Domestic Individualism*, 5. Hereafter referred to as *DI*.
3. Bennett, ed., *The Book of Virtues: A Treasury of Moral Stories*, 14.
4. Twain, *"Adventures of Huckleberry Finn": A Case Study in Critical Controversy*, 48. Hereafter referred to as *Case*.
5. Twain, *Adventures of Tom Sawyer*, 235.

Works Cited

Bennett, William J., ed. *The Book of Virtues: A Treasury of Moral Stories*. New York: Simon and Schuster, 1993.

Brown, Gillian. *Domestic Individualism: Imagining Self in Nineteenth-Century America*. Berkeley and Los Angeles: University of California Press, 1990.

Kolodny, Annette. "Dancing through the Minefield: Some Observations on the Theory, Practice, and Politics of a Feminist Literary Criticism." In *Falling into Theory: Conflicting Views on Reading and Literature*, ed. David H. Richter, 278-85. Boston: St. Martin's Press, 1994.

Twain, Mark. *"Adventures of Huckleberry Finn": A Case Study in Critical Controversy*. Ed. Gerald Graff and James Phelan. Boston: Bedford Books, 1995.

——————. *The Adventures of Tom Sawyer*. Foreword and notes by John C. Gerber. Berkeley and Los Angeles: University of California Press, 1980.

——————. *Mark Twain's Own Autobiography: The Chapters from the "North American Review."* Ed. Michael J. Kiskis. Madison: University of Wisconsin Press, 1990.

RESOURCES

1835	Samuel Langhorne Clemens is born in Florida, Missouri, on November 30 to John M. and Jane L. Clemens.
1839	The Clemens family moves to Hannibal, Missouri.
1847	John M. Clemens dies.
1848	Twain apprentices to a local printer, beginning his newspaper career.
1850	Twain works for his older brother, Orion Clemens, on his newspaper, the Hannibal *Western Union*.
1851	Twain publishes his first sketches in the Philadelphia *Saturday Evening Post* and the *Western Union*. He will continue publishing in some form every year for the rest of his life.
1853-1856	Twain leaves Hannibal for St. Louis and spends several years traveling around the Midwest and the East and working as a printer.
1857-1861	Twain becomes a steamboat pilot and travels up and down the Lower Mississippi River.
1861	The Civil War interrupts river traffic, cutting short Twain's piloting career. He briefly serves in a Missouri state militia before traveling to Nevada with Orion, who has been appointed secretary to the new territorial government.
1862	Twain unsuccessfully prospects for gold and silver before returning to journalism with the *Virginia City Territorial Enterprise*.
1863	The name "Mark Twain" appears for the first time on one of his stories on February 3.
1864	Twain moves to San Francisco, where he writes for the *Morning Call* newspaper.
1865	Twain's first nationally successful story, "Jim Smiley and His Jumping Frog," is published in the *New York Saturday Press*.

1866	Twain travels to Hawaii as a correspondent for the *Sacramento Union*, lectures in California and Nevada, and sails for New York.
1867	Twain travels to the Mediterranean and Middle East, where he writes the travel letters for the *Alta California* that will later be revised into *The Innocents Abroad*. He meets Olivia Langdon, who will become his wife, when he returns to New York. *The Celebrated Jumping Frog of Calaveras County, and Other Sketches* is published.
1869	*The Innocents Abroad* is published.
1870	Twain and Olivia Langdon marry on February 2. Their first child, Langdon, is born on November 7.
1872	*Roughing It* is published. Twain's daughter Susy is born, and Langdon dies. Twain travels to England.
1873	*The Gilded Age* is published. Twain buys a house in Hartford, Connecticut, which, after renovations are completed in 1874, will be the Twain family permanent residence until 1891. Twain returns to England, where he delivers lectures and meets other writers in London.
1874	Twain's daughter Clara is born.
1876	*The Adventures of Tom Sawyer* is published.
1878-1879	Twain travels in Europe and England with his family, then returns to Hartford.
1880	*A Tramp Abroad* is published. Twain's daughter Jean is born.
1881	*The Prince and the Pauper* is published.
1883	*Life on the Mississippi* is published.
1884	Twain founds the publishing firm Charles L. Webster & Co. with his sister's son-in-law. English and Canadian editions of *Adventures of Huckleberry Finn* are published.
1885	*Adventures of Huckleberry Finn* is Webster & Co.'s first publication.

1889	*A Connecticut Yankee in King Arthur's Court* is published.
1890	Twain is saddled with a large debt because of his unsuccessful investment in the development of a typesetting machine.
1891	Debts and household expenses motivate Twain to close the Hartford house and move to Europe.
1894	*Tom Sawyer Abroad* and *Pudd'nhead Wilson* are published. Webster & Co. declares bankruptcy and folds.
1895	Twain embarks on a worldwide lecture tour to pay off debts.
1896	*Personal Recollections of Joan of Arc* and *Tom Sawyer, Detective* are published. Twain's daughter Susy dies.
1897	*Following the Equator*, an account of Twain's 1895-1896 lecture tour, is published.
1898	Twain finishes paying off his debts and begins two years of travel in Europe and England.
1900	Twain returns to the United States and settles in New York City.
1902	Twain sells the family's Hartford house.
1903	Twain and his family move to Italy.
1904	Olivia dies in Italy on June 5. Twain returns to the United States and makes New York City his permanent residence.
1906	*What Is Man?* is published.
1908	Twain moves to newly built house in Redding, Connecticut.
1909	Twain's daughter Clara marries Russian musician Ossip Gabrilowitsch on October 6 and moves to Europe; daughter Jean dies on December 24. Twain is left alone in Connecticut.
1910	Mark Twain dies on April 21, shortly after returning to his Redding home from Bermuda.

Works by Mark Twain

Long Fiction

The Gilded Age, 1873 (with Charles Dudley Warner)
The Adventures of Tom Sawyer, 1876
The Prince and the Pauper, 1881
Adventures of Huckleberry Finn, 1884
A Connecticut Yankee in King Arthur's Court, 1889
The American Claimant, 1892
Tom Sawyer Abroad, 1894
The Tragedy of Pudd'nhead Wilson, 1894
Personal Recollections of Joan of Arc, 1896
Tom Sawyer, Detective, 1896
A Double-Barrelled Detective Story, 1902
A Dog's Tale, 1904
Extracts from Adam's Diary, 1904
Eve's Diary, Translated from the Original Ms, 1906
A Horse's Tale, 1906
Extract from Captain Stormfield's Visit to Heaven, 1909
Report from Paradise, 1952 (Dixon Wecter, editor)
Simon Wheeler, Detective, 1963 (Franklin R. Rogers, editor)
Mark Twain's Mysterious Stranger Manuscripts, 1969 (William M. Gibson, editor)

Short Fiction

The Celebrated Jumping Frog of Calaveras County, and Other Sketches, 1867
Mark Twain's (Burlesque) Autobiography and First Romance, 1871
Mark Twain's Sketches: New and Old, 1875
Punch, Brothers, Punch!, and Other Sketches, 1878
The Stolen White Elephant, and Other Stories, 1882
Merry Tales, 1892
The £1,000,000 Bank-Note, and Other New Stories, 1893
The Man That Corrupted Hadleyburg, and Other Stories and Essays, 1900
King Leopold's Soliloquy: A Defense of His Congo Rule, 1905
The $30,000 Bequest, and Other Stories, 1906
The Curious Republic of Gondour, and Other Whimsical Sketches, 1919
Letters from the Earth, 1962 (Bernard DeVoto, editor)
Mark Twain's Satires and Burlesques, 1967 (Franklin R. Rogers, editor)
Mark Twain's Which Was the Dream?, and Other Symbolic Writings of the Later Years,
    1967 (John S. Tuckey, editor)

Mark Twain's Hannibal, Huck and Tom, 1969 (Walter Blair, editor)

Mark Twain's Fables of Man, 1972 (John S. Tuckey, editor)

Life as I Find It, 1977 (Charles Neider, editor)

Early Tales and Sketches, 1979-1981 (2 volumes; Edgar Marquess Branch and Robert H. Hirst, editors)

A Murder, a Mystery, and a Marriage, 2001 (Roy Blount, Jr., editor)

Drama

Colonel Sellers, pr., pb. 1874 (adaptation of his novel *The Gilded Age*)

Ah Sin, pr. 1877 (with Bret Harte)

Is He Dead? A Comedy in Three Acts, pb. 2003, pr. 2007 (Shelley Fisher Fishkin, editor)

Nonfiction

The Innocents Abroad, 1869

Roughing It, 1872

A Tramp Abroad, 1880

Life on the Mississippi, 1883

How to Tell a Story, and Other Essays, 1897

Following the Equator, 1897 (published in England as *More Tramps Abroad*)

My Début as a Literary Person, 1903

What Is Man?, 1906

Christian Science, 1907

Is Shakespeare Dead?, 1909

Mark Twain's Speeches, 1910 (Albert Bigelow Paine, editor)

Europe and Elsewhere, 1923 (Albert Bigelow Paine, editor)

Mark Twain's Autobiography, 1924 (2 volumes; Albert Bigelow Paine, editor)

Mark Twain's Notebook, 1935 (Albert Bigelow Paine, editor)

Letters from the Sandwich Islands, Written for the "Sacramento Union," 1937 (G. Ezra Dane, editor)

Mark Twain in Eruption, 1940 (Bernard DeVoto, editor)

Mark Twain's Travels with Mr. Brown, 1940 (Franklin Walker and G. Ezra Dane, editors)

The Love Letters of Mark Twain, 1949 (Dixon Wecter, editor)

Mark Twain to Mrs. Fairbanks, 1949 (Dixon Wecter, editor)

Mark Twain of the "Enterprise": Newspaper Articles and Other Documents, 1862-1864, 1957 (Henry Nash Smith and Frederick Anderson, editors)

Traveling with the Innocents Abroad: Mark Twain's Original Reports from Europe and the Holy Land, 1958 (Daniel Morley McKeithan, editor)

Mark Twain-Howells Letters: The Correspondence of Samuel L. Clemens and William D. Howells, 1872-1910, 1960 (Henry Nash Smith and William M. Gibson, editors)

The Autobiography of Mark Twain, 1961 (Charles Neider, editor)
Mark Twain's Letters to His Publishers, 1867-1894, 1967 (Hamlin Hill, editor)
Clemens of the "Call": Mark Twain in San Francisco, 1969 (Edgar M. Branch, editor)
Mark Twain's Correspondence with Henry Huttleston Rogers, 1893-1909, 1969 (Lewis Leary, editor)
A Pen Warmed-Up in Hell: Mark Twain in Protest, 1972 (Frederick Anderson, editor)
Mark Twain's Notebooks and Journals, 1975-1979 (3 volumes; Frederick Anderson et al., editors)
Mark Twain Speaking, 1976 (Paul Fatout, editor)
Mark Twain Speaks for Himself, 1978 (Paul Fatout, editor)
Mark Twain's Letters, 1988-2002 (6 volumes; Edgar M. Branch et al., editors)
Mark Twain's Own Autobiography: The Chapters from the "North American Review," 1990 (Michael J. Kiskis, editor)
Mark Twain's Aquarium: The Samuel Clemens Angelfish Correspondence, 1905-1910, 1991 (John Cooley, editor)
The Bible According to Mark Twain: Writings on Heaven, Eden, and the Flood, 1995 (Howard G. Baetzhold and Joseph B. McCullough, editors)
Mark Twain: The Complete Interviews, 2006 (Gary Scharnhorst, editor)

Miscellaneous
The Portable Mark Twain, 1946 (Bernard DeVoto, editor)
Collected Tales, Sketches, Speeches, and Essays, 1853-1891, 1992 (Louis J. Budd, editor)
Collected Tales, Sketches, Speeches, and Essays, 1891-1910, 1992 (Louis J. Budd, editor)
Who Is Mark Twain?, 2009 (Robert H. Hirst, editor)

Bibliography

Baldanza, Frank. *Mark Twain: An Introduction and Interpretation.* New York: Barnes & Noble, 1961.

Blair, Walter. "Mark Twain." *Native American Humor, 1800-1900.* New York: American Book Company, 1937.

Bloom, Harold, ed. *Mark Twain.* New York: Chelsea House, 1986.

Budd, Louis J., ed. *Mark Twain: The Contemporary Reviews.* New York: Cambridge University Press, 1999.

Camfield, Gregg. *The Oxford Companion to Mark Twain.* New York: Oxford University Press, 2003.

Cox, James M. *Mark Twain: The Fate of Humor.* Princeton, NJ: Princeton University Press, 1966.

Dempsey, Terrell. *Searching for Jim: Slavery in Sam Clemens's World.* Columbia: University of Missouri Press, 2003.

Emerson, Everett. *Mark Twain: A Literary Life.* Philadelphia: University of Pennsylvania Press, 2000.

Fishkin, Shelley Fisher, ed. *A Historical Guide to Mark Twain.* New York: Oxford University Press, 2002.

_____. *Lighting Out for the Territory: Reflections on Mark Twain and American Culture.* New York: Oxford University Press, 1996.

Gerber, John C. *Mark Twain.* Boston: Twayne, 1988.

Gibson, William M. *The Art of Mark Twain.* New York: Oxford University Press, 1976.

Horn, Jason Gary. *Mark Twain: A Descriptive Guide to Biographical Sources.* Lanham, MD: Scarecrow Press, 1999.

Howells, William Dean. *My Mark Twain: Reminiscences and Criticisms.* 1910. Mineola, NY: Dover, 1997.

Kaplan, Justin. *Mr. Clemens and Mark Twain.* New York: Simon & Schuster, 1966.

Ketterer, David, ed. *The Science Fiction of Mark Twain.* Hamden, CT: Archon, 1984.

Lauber, John. *The Inventions of Mark Twain.* New York: Hill & Wang, 1990.

_____. *The Making of Mark Twain: A Biography.* New York: American Heritage Press, 1985.

LeMaster, J. R., and James D. Wilson, eds. *The Mark Twain Encyclopedia.* New York: Garland, 1993.

Leonard, James S., ed. *Making Mark Twain Work in the Classroom.* Durham, NC: Duke University Press, 1999.

Messent, Peter. *Mark Twain.* New York: St. Martin's Press, 1997.

_____. *The Short Works of Mark Twain: A Critical Study.* Philadelphia: University of Pennsylvania Press, 2001.

Messent, Peter, and Louis J. Budd, eds. *A Companion to Mark Twain*. Malden, MA: Blackwell, 2005.

Michelson, Bruce. *Mark Twain on the Loose: A Comic Writer and the American Self.* Amherst: University of Massachusetts Press, 1995.

Miller, Robert Keith. *Mark Twain*. New York: Frederick Ungar, 1983.

Paine, Albert Bigelow. *Mark Twain: A Biography—The Personal and Literary Life of Samuel Langhorne Clemens*. 3 vols. 1912. Philadelphia: Chelsea House, 1997.

Powers, Ron. *Mark Twain: A Life*. New York: Free Press, 2005.

Quirk, Tom, ed. *Coming to Grips with "Huckleberry Finn": Essays on a Book, a Boy, and a Man*. Columbia: University of Missouri Press, 1993.

_____. *Mark Twain: A Study of the Short Fiction*. Upper Saddle River, NJ: Prentice Hall, 1997.

Railton, Stephen. *Mark Twain: A Short Introduction*. Malden, MA: Blackwell, 2004.

Rasmussen, R. Kent. *Bloom's How to Write about Mark Twain*. New York: Bloom's Literary Criticism, 2008.

_____. *Critical Companion to Mark Twain: A Literary Reference to His Life and Work*. 2 vols. New York: Facts On File, 2007.

_____, ed. *The Quotable Mark Twain: His Essential Aphorisms, Witticisms, and Concise Opinions*. Chicago: Contemporary Books, 1997.

Robinson, Forrest G., ed. *The Cambridge Companion to Mark Twain*. New York: Cambridge University Press, 1995.

Sloane, David E. E. *Student Companion to Mark Twain*. New York: Greenwood Press, 2001.

_____, ed. *Mark Twain's Humor: Critical Essays*. New York: Garland, 1993.

Smith, Henry Nash. *Mark Twain: The Development of a Writer*. Cambridge, MA: Harvard University Press, 1962.

_____, ed. *Mark Twain: A Collection of Critical Essays*. Englewood Cliffs, NJ: Prentice-Hall, 1963.

Trombley, Laura E. Skandera, and Michael J. Kiskis, eds. *Constructing Mark Twain: New Directions in Scholarship*. Columbia: University of Missouri Press, 2001.

Wagenknecht, Edward. *Mark Twain: The Man and His Work*. 3d ed. Norman: University of Oklahoma Press, 1967.

Ward, Geoffrey C., and Dayton Duncan. *Mark Twain: An Illustrated Biography*. New York: Alfred A. Knopf, 2001.

Wilson, James D. *A Reader's Guide to the Short Stories of Mark Twain*. Boston: G. K. Hall, 1987.

Wonham, Henry B. *Mark Twain and the Art of the Tall Tale*. New York: Oxford University Press, 1993.

CRITICAL
INSIGHTS

About the Editor

R. Kent Rasmussen, now a reference book editor in Southern California, holds a doctorate in history from the University of California, Los Angeles, where he briefly taught history and later served as associate editor of the Marcus Garvey Papers. In addition to planning, organizing, and editing multivolume reference works on history, literature, government and politics, and other subjects, he has published hundreds of articles and reviews in scholarly journals, reference books, and other books and serial publications. The half dozen volumes on history he has written include two reference works on Africa that have gone through multiple editions. In 1995, he entered the field of Mark Twain studies with the publication of *Mark Twain A to Z: The Essential Reference to His Life and Writings*, which won an American Library Association RUSA award for outstanding adult reference books and became a standard authority within its field. Twelve years later, he published the two-volume *Critical Companion to Mark Twain: A Literary Reference to His Life and Work* (2007), an updated, vastly expanded, and completely reorganized edition of *Mark Twain A to Z*. His other books on Twain include *Mark Twain's Book for Bad Boys and Girls* (1996), *The Quotable Mark Twain: His Essential Aphorisms, Witticisms, and Concise Opinions* (1997; also published as *Mark Twain: His Words,Wit, and Wisdom*, 2001), *Mark Twain for Kids* (2004), and *Bloom's How to Write About Mark Twain* (2008). His other publications on literature include Salem Press's three-volume *Cyclopedia of Literary Places* (2003). He is currently working on a collection of letters to Mark Twain from his readers that the University of California Press will publish as *Dear Mark Twain*.

About *The Paris Review*

The Paris Review is America's preeminent literary quarterly, dedicated to discovering and publishing the best new voices in fiction, nonfiction, and poetry. The magazine was founded in Paris in 1953 by the young American writers Peter Matthiessen and Doc Humes, and edited there and in New York for its first fifty years by George Plimpton. Over the decades, the *Review* has introduced readers to the earliest writings of Jack Kerouac, Philip Roth, T. C. Boyle, V. S. Naipaul, Ha Jin, Ann Patchett, Jay McInerney, Mona Simpson, and Edward P. Jones, and published numerous now classic works, including Roth's *Goodbye, Columbus*, Donald Barthelme's *Alice*, Jim Carroll's *Basketball Diaries*, and selections from Samuel Beckett's *Molloy* (his first publication in English). The first chapter of Jeffrey Eugenides's *The Virgin Suicides* appeared in the *Review*'s pages, as well as stories by Rick Moody, David Foster Wallace, Denis Johnson, Jim Crace, Lorrie Moore, and Jeanette Winterson.

The Paris Review's renowned Writers at Work series of interviews, whose early installments include legendary conversations with E. M. Forster, William Faulkner, and Ernest Hemingway, is one of the landmarks of world literature. The interviews received a George Polk Award and were nominated for a Pulitzer Prize. Among the more than three hundred interviewees are Robert Frost, Marianne Moore, W. H. Auden, Elizabeth Bishop, Susan Sontag, and Toni Morrison. Recent issues feature conversations with Salman Rushdie, Joan Didion, Norman Mailer, Kazuo Ishiguro, Marilynne Robinson, Umberto Eco, Annie Proulx, and Gay Talese. In November 2009, Picador published the final volume of a four-volume series of anthologies of *Paris Review* interviews. *The New York Times* called the Writers at Work series "the most remarkable and extensive interviewing project we possess."

The Paris Review is edited by Philip Gourevitch, who was named to the post in 2005, following the death of George Plimpton two years earlier. A new editorial team has published fiction by André Aciman, Colum McCann, Damon Galgut, Mohsin Hamid, Uzodinma Iweala, Gish Jen, Stephen King, James Lasdun, Padgett Powell, Richard Price, and Sam Shepard. Poetry editors Charles Simic, Meghan O'Rourke, and Dan Chiasson have selected works by John Ashbery, Kay Ryan, Billy Collins, Tomaž Šalamun, Mary Jo Bang, Sharon Olds, Charles Wright, and Mary Karr. Writing published in the magazine has been anthologized in *Best American Short Stories* (2006, 2007, and 2008), *Best American Poetry, Best Creative Non-Fiction*, the Pushcart Prize anthology, and *O. Henry Prize Stories*.

The magazine presents two annual awards. The Hadada Award for lifelong contribution to literature has recently been given to Joan Didion, Norman Mailer, Peter Matthiessen, and, in 2009, John Ashbery. The Plimpton Prize for Fiction, awarded to a debut or emerging writer brought to national attention in the pages of *The Paris Review*, was presented in 2007 to Benjamin Percy, to Jesse Ball in 2008, and to Alistair Morgan in 2009.

The Paris Review was a finalist for the 2008 and 2009 National Magazine Awards in fiction, and it won the 2007 National Magazine Award in photojournalism. The *Los Angeles Times* recently called *The Paris Review* "an American treasure with true international reach."

Since 1999 *The Paris Review* has been published by The Paris Review Foundation, Inc., a not-for-profit 501(c)(3) organization.

The Paris Review is available in digital form to libraries worldwide in selected academic databases exclusively from EBSCO Publishing. Libraries can contact EBSCO at 1-800-653-2726 for details. For more information on *The Paris Review* or to subscribe, please visit: www.theparisreview.org.

Contributors

R. Kent Rasmussen is best known as the author of *Mark Twain A to Z: The Essential Reference to His Life and Writings* (1995), which has become such a standard reference source in its field that Dayton Duncan and Ken Burns called it their "bible" when they produced their four-hour documentary on Mark Twain for Public Television in 2001. Rasmussen's many other books on Mark Twain include *Critical Companion to Mark Twain: A Literary Reference to His Life and Work* (2007), a greatly expanded and substantially reorganized edition of *Mark Twain A to Z*.

Sasha Weiss is a writer living in Brooklyn. She is on the editorial staff of the *New York Review of Books*.

Stephen Railton teaches American literature at the University of Virginia. He is the author of books on Fenimore Cooper, the American Renaissance, and Mark Twain. He has edited four volumes as well, including *Connecticut Yankee* for Barnes & Noble (2005) and the forthcoming *Huckleberry Finn* for Broadview Press. His work in virtual reality includes *Mark Twain: An Electronic Archive* and *"Uncle Tom's Cabin" and American Culture: A Multi-Media Archive*.

Alan Gribben has been nationally recognized with an honorary lifetime membership in the Mark Twain Circle of America and other awards. Best known as the author of the two-volume *Mark Twain's Library: A Reconstruction* (1980), which he is currently updating and expanding, he is coeditor of *Mark Twain on the Move: A Travel Reader* (2009) and author of the biography of a major library builder, *Harry Hunt Ransom: Intellect in Motion* (2008). Since 1991 he has served as head of the Department of English and Philosophy at Auburn University at Montgomery, where he received the Dr. Guinevera A. Nance Alumni Professorship in 2006.

Hilton Obenzinger is a critic, poet, novelist, and historian, and the recipient of the American Book Award. He is the author of *American Palestine: Melville, Twain, and the Holy Land Mania* (1999) as well as articles in scholarly journals on American Holy Land travel, Mark Twain, Herman Melville, and American cultural interactions with the Middle East. His most recent book is the autobiographical novel *Busy Dying* (2008). He teaches writing and American literature at Stanford University.

Lawrence I. Berkove is Emeritus Professor of English at the University of Michigan-Dearborn and specializes in late-nineteenth- and early-twentieth-century American literature. He wrote his dissertation on Ambrose Bierce and has published articles on him ever since as well as the book *A Prescription for Adversity: The Moral Art of Ambrose Bierce* (2002). A former president of the Mark Twain Circle, he has published frequently on Twain since 1967. In 2004, he edited the Modern Library *Best Short Stories of Mark Twain*. With Joseph Csicsila, he is the coauthor of *Heretical Fictions: Religion in the Literature of Mark Twain* (2010).

Larzer Ziff is the Caroline Donovan Professor of English Emeritus and Research

Professor at Johns Hopkins University. As the first person appointed to the English faculty of Oxford University to teach American literature, he has contributed greatly to the study of American literary culture. His publications include *The Portable Benjamin Franklin* (2006), *Writing in the New Nation: Prose, Print, and Politics in the Early United States* (1991), and *The Literature of America: Colonial Period* (1970).

Cynthia Griffin Wolff is the Class of 1922 Professor of Literature, Emerita, at the Massachusetts Institute of Technology. Her books include *A Feast of Words: The Triumph of Edith Wharton* (1995) and *Samuel Richardson and the Eighteenth-Century Puritan Character* (1972). She has also served as editor of such literary works as *Classic American Women Writers* (1980).

Tom Quirk is Professor of English at the University of Missouri. His lectures focus on American literature and culture, specifically the works of Joyce Carol Oates, Willa Cather, Edgar Allan Poe, and Nathaniel Hawthorne. He has authored, edited, or coedited dozens of literary works, including Mark Twain's *The Innocents Abroad* (2002), *The Portable American Realism Reader* (1997), *Mark Twain: A Study of the Short Fiction* (1997), and *Romanticism: Critical Essays in American Literature* (1982). He is also the editor of the scholarly book series Mark Twain and His Circle.

Everett Carter was Emeritus Professor of English at the University of California, Davis. He is the editor of *The Damnation of Theron Ware* (1996) and author of *Howells and the Age of Realism* (1954), which was awarded the Commonwealth Gold Medal for nonfiction.

David L. Smith is the John W. Chandler, Francis Christopher Oakley Third Century Professor of English at Williams College in Massachusetts. He specializes in the Black Arts movement, Mark Twain, and Wendell Berry, and is the editor of *The Encyclopedia of African American Culture and History* (1995) and the author of several essays, including "Huck, Jim, and American Racial Discourse" and "The Black Arts Movement and Its Critics."

David Ketterer is Emeritus Professor of English at Concordia University in Montreal and Honorary Research Fellow in English at the University of Liverpool. He is the author of *Imprisoned in a Tesseract: The Life and Work of James Blish* (1987), *The Science Fiction of Mark Twain* (1984), and *The Rationale of Deception in Poe* (1979). He is currently on the editorial board of *The Edgar Allan Poe Review* and is working on a biography of John Wyndham.

Michael J. Kiskis is Leonard Tydings Grant Professor of American Literature at Elmira College in New York. He has served as president of the Mark Twain Circle of America and of the Northeast Modern Language Association. He is coeditor (with Laura E. Skandera Trombley) of *Constructing Mark Twain: New Directions in Scholarship* (2001) and editor of *Mark Twain's Own Autobiography: The Chapters from the "North American Review"* (1990).

Acknowledgments _____

"The *Paris Review* Perspective" by Sasha Weiss. Copyright ©2011 by Sasha Weiss. Special appreciation goes to Christopher Cox, Nathaniel Rich, and David Wallace-Wells, editors at *The Paris Review.*

Excerpts from "Mark Twain" by Larzer Ziff. From *Return Passages: Great American Travel Writing, 1780-1910* (2000), pp. 171-180, 183-185, 187-200. Copyright © 2000 by the Yale University Press. Reprinted with permission of the Yale University Press.

"*The Adventures of Tom Sawyer*: A Nightmare Vision of American Boyhood" by Cynthia Griffin Wolff. From *The Massachusetts Review* 21, no. 4 (1980): 93-105. Copyright © 1980 by *The Massachusetts Review.* Reprinted by permission from *The Massachusetts Review.*

"The Realism of *Huckleberry Finn*" by Tom Quirk. From *Coming to Grips with "Huckleberry Finn": Essays on a Book, a Boy, and a Man* (1993), pp. 83-105. Copyright © 1993 by the Curators of the University of Missouri. Reprinted with permission of the University of Missouri Press.

"'Huckleberry Fun'" by Everett Carter. From *Making Mark Twain Work in the Classroom*, edited by James S. Leonard (1999), pp. 131-139. Copyright © 1999 by Duke University Press. All rights reserved. Reprinted with permission of Duke University Press.

"Huck, Jim, and American Racial Discourse" by David L. Smith. From *Mark Twain Journal* 22, no. 2 (1984): 4-12. Copyright © 1984 by the *Mark Twain Journal.* Reprinted with permission of the *Mark Twain Journal.*

"*Connecticut Yankee*: Twain's Other Masterpiece" by Lawrence I. Berkove. From *Making Mark Twain Work in the Classroom*, edited by James S. Leonard (1999), pp. 88-109. Copyright © 1999 by Duke University Press. All rights reserved. Reprinted with permission of Duke University Press.

"Introduction" by David Ketterer. From *The Science Fiction of Mark Twain* (1984), pp. xiii-xxxiii. Copyright © 1977 by David Ketterer. Reprinted with permission of the author.

"Mark Twain and the Tradition of Literary Domesticity" by Michael J. Kiskis. From *Constructing Mark Twain: New Directions in Scholarship*, edited by Laura E. Skandera Trombley and Michael J. Kiskis (2001), pp. 13-27. Copyright © 2001 by the Curators of the University of Missouri. Reprinted with permission of the University of Missouri Press.

Civil War, 112-114, 116, 126, 129; military training of, 112; and Mark Twain, 114-115
Bixby, Horace, 18
Blaine, Jim (*Roughing It*), 159-160
Blair, Walter, 78, 132, 194, 288
Bliss, Elisha, 23, 25-27, 156
Bloom, Harold, 264
Boer War. *See* South African War
Boggs (*Huckleberry Finn*), 94, 97, 182, 193, 200; daughter of, 197; death of, 187
Bohemia, 34
"Boy books," 8, 32, 71; and *Huckleberry Finn*, 67
Boyesen, H. H., 73
Bridgman, Richard, 81
Bring the Jubilee (Moore), 275
Brooks, Van Wyck, 62-63, 92, 289, 300
Brown, Gillian, 290-291, 304
Brown, John, 28
Brown, Mr. (travel letters), 145
Browning, Robert, 28
Budd, Louis J., 8, 68, 78, 80
Buffalo, New York, 26-27
Buffalo Express, 26-27
Bunker, Chang and Eng, 34
Burns, Ken, 63, 321
Burroughs, Edgar Rice, 278
Bush, Harold K., Jr., 83
Buzzard, James, 155

Cable, George Washington, 224
Cacography, 7, 70
California, 21-22, 24-25, 83, 113-114, 117, 132, 142; and Ambrose Bierce, 114, 120, 131; Calaveras County, 21; corrupt justice system, 122; gold rush, 21, 141; and *Roughing It*, 55, 70, 156

Calvinism, 123, 235, 237, 259-260
Camelot, 56, 59, 74, 242, 256, 302
Camfield, Gregg, 82
Canada, 36; pirate publishers, 31
"Cannibalism in the Cars" (Twain), 118
"Captain Stormfield's Visit to Heaven." See *Extract from Captain Stormfield's Visit to Heaven*
Carlyle, Thomas, 77
Carnegie, Andrew, 60
Carroll, Lewis, 28
Carson City, Nevada, 20
Cather, Willa, 301
Cat's Cradle (Vonnegut), 264
Cave (*Tom Sawyer*), 71, 176-178
"Celebrated Jumping Frog of Calaveras County, The" (Twain). *See* Jumping frog story
Celebrated Jumping Frog of Calaveras County, and Other Sketches, The (Twain), 29
Censorship, 53, 57, 60, 92, 215
Central America, 22
Cervantes, Miguel de, 189, 238
Chadwick-Joshua, Jocelyn, 80, 103
Champion, Laurie, 80
Charles L. Webster & Co., 33, 35, 116
Chatto & Windus, 116, 133
Chérie (Goncourt), 201
Chesnutt, Charles, 60
Children, 100, 120, 165, 167, 170, 213, 297
Chinese, 122, 129, 161-162
Chivalry, 59, 250, 259
Christian Science, 269, 273
Christian Science (Twain), 38
"Chronicle of Young Satan, The" (Twain), 128
Cincinnati, Ohio, 17
Civil War; and Ambrose Bierce, 112-114, 116, 126, 129; outbreak, 18-19,

112; in science fiction, 275; and the South, 218; and steamboat traffic, 18-19, 141, 152; and Mark Twain, 19, 49, 112-113, 140

Clarence (*Connecticut Yankee*), 240, 242, 253, 256

Clark, Charles Heber, 117, 286

Clemens, Clara, 36-38, 298, 303; birth of, 28; daughter of, 39; marriage of, 39, 297

Clemens, Henry, 13-14, 17, 280

Clemens, Jane Lampton, 12, 17

Clemens, Jean, 36-38, 297, 299, 303; birth of, 28; burial of, 299; death of, 39, 297-298

Clemens, John Marshall, 11-12, 14, 28; Tennessee land, 29

Clemens, Langdon, 27-28

Clemens, Livy, 25, 35, 37; death of, 38; health, 38, 280; influence on Mark Twain, 79; inheritance, 115

Clemens, Orion, 12, 14, 17, 113, 141; daughter of, 28; fictional characters modeled on, 13, 29, 31; and Abraham Lincoln, 20; Tennessee land, 30

Clemens, Pamela. *See* Moffett, Pamela Clemens

Clemens, Samuel Langhorne. *See* Twain, Mark

Clemens, Susy, 28, 36-37; death of, 37, 280, 298

Code Duello, 90, 95, 105

Collins, Wilkie, 28

Collins, William J., 271

Colonel Sellers (Twain), 30

Colonel Sellers as a Scientist (Twain and Howells), 273, 283

Columbus, Christopher, 275

Congo Free State, 57

Congress, U.S., 24, 58

Connecticut Yankee in King Arthur's

Court, A (Twain), 9, 33, 59, 93, 107, 235-260, 276-277; and American imperialism, 55; hoaxes in, 236, 238, 241; humor in, 238, 243, 245, 258; inartistry of, 67, 238; irony in, 56; narrative voices, 240-242; and Paige compositor, 274; plagiarism and, 286; and religion, 126; reviews of, 56, 60, 74; science fiction of, 270-273, 278, 281-282; slavery in, 15, 57, 98, 250; solar eclipse, 272; structure of, 243, 258; travel in, 50; violence in, 9, 99, 244-245; and war, 128, 244

Conscience, 105, 169, 187, 211-212, 237, 296; and Huck Finn, 212, 225-227; and Tom Sawyer, 226

Constantinople, 54, 149, 155

Cooper, James Fenimore, 161

Copyright, 31, 35, 266

Coulombe, Joseph L., 83

Courage, 89, 292; and Huck Finn, 104, 208; moral, 107

Covici, Pascal, 236, 243, 263

Cox, James M., 78

Coyotes, 157-158

Crane, Stephen, 52, 129, 258

Crane, Susan, 27

Crusoe, Robinson, 248

Csicsila, Joseph, 81

Cummings, Sherwood, 82

"Curious Republic of Gondour, The" (Twain), 122, 265, 268

Cynicism, 121, 124

Daisy Miller (James), 54

"Dandy Frightening the Squatter, The" (Twain), 236

Daniel, Uncle, 16

Dante's hell, 256-258

Darwin, Charles, 276

Darwinism, 274

of Crime in Connecticut, The"
(Twain), 292, 304
Farmer, Philip José, 275, 282-283
Feldner, August (*No. 44, The Mysterious
Stranger*), 126
Fern, Fanny, 290
Feuds, 200; in *Huckleberry Finn*, 89,
94, 96, 181, 207, 212, 225
Fiedler, Leslie A., 93
Fingerprinting, 97, 274
Finn, Huck (*Huckleberry Finn*), 43; and
food, 112; heroism of, 164;
humorlessness, 190; and Jim, 105,
217, 225-226; lying, 60, 74, 104; as
narrator, 8, 83, 181-191; realism of,
183; as a writer, 195-197
Finn, Pap (*Huckleberry Finn*), 200,
205-206, 212, 223, 292-294; on
"borrowing," 189; death of, 103,
198; drunken tirade, 210, 213, 218-
219; Huck's description of, 189-
190; manhood of, 89, 101
First Families of Virginia, 95
Fishkin, Shelley Fisher, 5, 80, 92
"Five Boons of Life, The" (Twain), 299
Flexner, Stuart Berg, 219
Florida, Missouri, 11, 14, 16, 110
Following the Equator (Twain), 36-37,
56-57; critical studies of, 82;
Pudd'nhead Wilson maxims, 76,
119; reviews of, 76-77
Fortunate Island and Other Stories, The
(Adeler), 286
Forty-four (*No. 44, The Mysterious
Stranger*), 276-277
France, 23, 29, 34, 148, 155; medieval,
50
Franklin, Benjamin, 75
Franklin, H. Bruce, 265
Freeman, Mary Wilkins, 292, 301
Freud, Sigmund, 59

"From the 'London Times' of 1904"
(Twain), 281
Frontier humor, 6, 63, 132, 263, 304;
stereotypes, 219
Fun, 115, 118, 120

Gabrilowitsch, Clara. *See* Clemens,
Clara
Gabrilowitsch, Nina, 39
Gabrilowitsch, Ossip, 39
Galaxy, 27, 122
Gale, Robert L., 121
Gender studies, 83, 92, 101, 290
Genres, 71, 122; humor, 118; local
colorism, 52; picaresques, 189;
science fiction, 261-285, 287; travel
books, 139
Genteel tradition, 59-60, 174, 178
Germany, 29, 31-32; student dueling,
191
Gernsback, Hugo, 261
Gibson, William, 194
Gilded Age, The (Twain and Warner), 29,
49, 71; autobiographical chapters, 12;
as a subscription book, 30
Gilder, Richard Watson, 280, 298
Gillis, Steve, 21
Gillman, Susan, 81
Goldsmith, Oliver, 121-122
Goncourt, Edmond de, 201
Goodman, Joseph, 20, 123, 132
Goshute Indians, 55
Grangerford family (*Huckleberry Finn*),
191-192, 226, 229; house, 181, 196,
207
Grangerford, Buck (*Huckleberry Finn*),
187, 197
Grangerford, Colonel (*Huckleberry
Finn*); manhood of, 89, 94-95
Grangerford, Emmeline (*Huckleberry
Finn*), 191-192, 197

Grant, Ulysses S., 32; memoirs, 33
"Great Dark, The" (Twain), 263, 277-278
Greece, 23, 155
Grenander, M. E., 116, 118, 133
Gribben, Alan, 8, 82
Gulliver's Travels (Swift), 122, 245, 277

Haggard, H. Rider, 278
Hall, Frederick J., 34
Hall, G. Stanley, 100
Halley's comet, 64, 273, 284
Hank Morgan. *See* Morgan, Hank
Hannibal, Missouri, 14, 16, 19; cave, 52, 263; slavery in, 15, 80; and Twain's fiction, 111; Twain's last visit, 38
Harkness, Buck (*Huckleberry Finn*), 197
Harper & Brothers, 35
Harper's Magazine, 36, 38, 60
Harper's Monthly, 66, 75
Harper's Weekly, 120
Harris, Joel Chandler, 15, 73
Harris, Mr. (*A Tramp Abroad*), 22
Harris, Susan K., 79, 92
Harte, Bret, 24, 131
Hartford, Connecticut, 28; Clemens house, 28, 34, 66; Colt Arms Factory, 99, 244, 254
Hawaii, 21, 36, 56, 113, 142; and *Roughing It*, 55, 70
Hawaiian letters (Twain), 21, 142-144, 146, 148
Hawkins, Si (*The Gilded Age*), 12, 29
Hawkins, Washington (*The Gilded Age*), 29, 31
Hawthorne, Nathaniel, 144, 202, 290
Hearn, Lafcadio, 73
Heaven, 22, 118, 124, 268
Heinlein, Robert, 278

Hemings, Sally, 231
Hemingway, Ernest, 58, 60, 63
Henrickson, Gary P., 80
Heredity, 244
Higginson, Thomas Wentworth, 219
Hill, Hamlin, 79-80
Hill, Richard, 80
Historiography, fictional, 261
Hoaxes, 20, 122, 243, 265-266; in *Connecticut Yankee*, 236-238, 241; and frontier humor, 90, 263; in *Huckleberry Finn*, 97, 200
Holmes, Oliver Wendell, 59
Holy Land, 22-23, 53-54, 146, 148, 150-151
Homer, 238
Honorary degrees, 38, 60
Hornet (ship), 21
Horse's Tale, A (Twain), 38
Howells, William Dean, 15, 37, 144, 194, 202, 269, 286; and *Atlantic Monthly*, 31; and *Mark Twain's Library of Humor*, 117; playwriting, 30, 273, 283; reviewing Twain's books, 31, 66, 69-71, 75
Huck Finn. *See* Finn, Huck
Huckleberry Finn (Twain); African Americans in, 214-232; classic status of, 3; composition of, 31; controversies surrounding, 53, 83-84; critical studies of, 80; episodic nature of, 182, 193-194, 200-201, 282; "evasion" episode, 99, 102, 106, 193, 199-200, 224; humor in, 204-213; introductory apparatus, 196; irony in, 103, 107, 180, 210-213; and literary domesticity, 292, 294-295; murder in, 187; narrative structure, 8; as a picaresque] novel, 189; plotting of, 196-198, 201; racism of, 53, 215, 218; realism of, 181-202, 211;

reviews of, 74; Royal Nonesuch episode, 97; slavery in, 83, 102, 104, 212, 216, 223, 225-226, 228

Humor; Ambrose Bierce on, 119; and science fiction, 263

Huxley, Aldous, 261

Illustrations; *Connecticut Yankee*, 257; *Huckleberry Finn*, 195; *Roughing It*, 71, 156; subscription books, 143

Imperialism, 42, 55-56, 130, 302

India, 36, 56

Indians. *See* Native Americans

Injun Joe (*Tom Sawyer*), 52, 55, 167, 173-174, 176-178; manhood of, 89, 102

Innocents Abroad, The (Twain), 24, 59, 148, 152, 155, 161, 304; composition of, 24, 147, 156; corpses, 263; fictional elements of, 29; humor in, 54, 158; narrative voice, 54; reviews of, 31, 68-69, 145; success of, 25, 27, 49, 53

Interviews, 82

Inventions, 5-6, 31, 50, 273, 280; Paige compositor, 33-35, 274; Twain's, 32

Invisible Man, The (Wells), 281

Iowa, 17

Italy, 23, 29, 34, 38, 54, 149, 153, 155

Jackson's Island (*Huckleberry Finn*), 200, 294

James, Henry, 54, 181, 183, 238; "The Art of Fiction," 201

Jeffers, Robinson, 188

Jefferson, Thomas, 153, 214, 216, 222, 230; and Sally Hemings, 231

Jewett, Sarah Orne, 292, 301

Jim (*Huckleberry Finn*), 198, 217, 219-220, 222, 226-229; as buffoon, 206, 220, 225; compassion of, 216, 228;

dignity of, 211; and Huck Finn, 105, 217, 225-226; intelligence of, 216, 221, 224; manhood of, 89, 101-103, 105; model for, 16; as a "nigger," 217, 229; pranks played on, 207, 220-221, 227, 229; and Tom Sawyer, 99-100, 106; superstitions of, 216, 220-222; worldview, 223

Jim (*Tom Sawyer*), 15

"Jim Smiley and His Jumping Frog" (Twain). *See* Jumping frog story

Joan of Arc, 299, 302

Joan of Arc (Twain), 35, 50, 107-108, 289, 304

Joe. *See* Injun Joe (*Tom Sawyer*)

Johnson, Samuel, 267

Jonson, Ben, 238

Josh (pen name), 20

Jumping frog story (Twain), 21, 42-43, 49, 204, 304; mysterious stranger character, 259

Kaolotype, 273

Kaplan, Justin, 78, 143, 167, 273

Kemble, Edward Windsor, 195

Keokuk, Iowa, 17

Kern, Stephen, 279

King (*Huckleberry Finn*), 186-187, 190, 197, 201, 208, 295; manhood of, 96

King Leopold's Soliloquy (Twain), 38, 57

Kirkland, Caroline, 301

Kolb, Harold H., Jr., 187

Kolodny, Annette, 290

Krause, Sydney J., 83

Krauth, Leland, 83

Kruse, Horst H., 81

Lancelot, Sir (*Connecticut Yankee*), 255

Langdon, Jervis, 27, 115

Lecturing, 21-22, 142-143; in England,

28; in Nevada, 25; round-the-world
tour, 56; tours, 26, 28-29, 36, 49
LeMaster, J. R., 82
Leonard, James S., 80, 84
Leonardo da Vinci, 54
Leopold II, 57
Lest Darkness Fall (de Camp), 271
"Letters from the Earth" (Twain), 127,
226, 236, 269
Lewis, C. S., 261
Life on the Mississippi (Twain), 19, 32,
50, 165, 183; corpses, 263; critical
studies of, 81; reviews of, 73
Lincoln, Abraham, 20
Linotype, 33, 35
"Little Bessie" (Twain), 120
Litwack, Leon, 214
Local colorism, 52
Logomachies, 103
London, 37, 115
Long, E. Hudson, 82
Longfellow, Henry Wadsworth, 59
Looking Backward (Bellamy), 271
"Loves of Alonzo Fitz Clarence and
Rosannah Ethelton, The" (Twain),
279
"Luck" (Twain), 117
Lying, 7, 100; Huck Finn, 60, 74, 104
Lynching, 57, 90, 96, 182, 197, 199,
228; in *Huckleberry Finn*, 89, 96,
182, 197, 228
Lyon, Isabel, 39
Lystra, Karen, 79

Mabie, Hamilton W., 52
McKinley, William, 57, 130
Macnaughton, William R., 79
McWilliams, Carey, 111, 114-115, 117,
123, 126
Magic; in *Connecticut Yankee*, 247; in
Huckleberry Finn, 210

Male friendship, 53, 103, 106, 198-199
Malory, Thomas, 241
Man-factory (*Connecticut Yankee*), 98-
99, 251
Man in the High Castle, The (Dick),
275
"Man That Corrupted Hadleyville, The"
(Twain), 16, 111, 121, 304
Manhood, 89-108, 169-170, 175, 291
Manifest Destiny, 55
"Mark Twain" (pen name), 20, 42, 49,
261
Mark Twain Papers, 39, 79, 266
Mark Twain's America (DeVoto), 63
Mark Twain's Library of Humor,
116-117
Mark Twain's Travels with Mr. Brown,
22
Marx, Leo, 164, 187
Mary (*Tom Sawyer*), 13
Masculinity. *See* Manhood
Massacre hoax, 118
Maxims. *See* "Pudd'nhead Wilson's
Calendar"
Melodrama, 53, 75, 161, 298
Melton, Jeffrey Alan, 81
Melville, Herman, 4, 181-182, 202, 215,
224, 258, 290
"Mental Telegraphy" (Twain), 279-280
Mercier, Louis-Sébastien, 268
Mergenthaler, Ottmar, 33
Merlin (*Connecticut Yankee*), 99, 244,
247-248
Messent, Peter, 80-81
Michelangelo, 54, 59
Mickey Mouse, 4
Mississippi River, 14, 42; in *Huckleberry
Finn*, 43, 183, 185, 200, 207; and *Life
on the Mississippi*, 32; steamboats on,
18-19, 112, 141; in *Tom Sawyer*, 176;
Twain's last visit, 38

Missouri, 11, 14, 16-17, 19, 50, 52, 110; and Civil War, 19, 141; in fiction, 32, 34, 266; slavery, 15, 80; Twain's last visit, 38; violence in, 95
Missouri River, 20
Moby Dick (Melville), 4, 164, 202, 282; and *Huckleberry Finn*, 181-182, 188
Model boys, 169, 178
Moffett, Pamela Clemens, 13-14, 17, 33
"Monument to Adam, A" (Bierce), 121
"Monument to Adam, A" (Twain), 120
Moore, Ward, 275
Moral sense, 99, 292
More Tramps Abroad (Twain), 76
More, Thomas, 283
Morgan le Fay, 246, 257
Morgan, Hank (*Connecticut Yankee*), 55-56, 59, 62, 239-259; inventions of, 248, 273; manhood of, 89, 93, 107; as a mysterious stranger, 64; name of, 246; as narrator, 240-241; and Theodore Roosevelt, 101; as self-made man, 98-99
Morris, Linda A., 83
Morte d'Arthur (Malory), 75, 241
Mufferson, Willie (*Tom Sawyer*), 169
Murder, 129, 280; in *Huckleberry Finn*, 94, 97, 182, 187, 190, 200, 207, 212, 229; in "A Murder, a Mystery, and a Marriage," 267; in *Pudd'nhead Wilson*, 34, 97; in *Tom Sawyer*, 75, 102, 173
"Murder, A Mystery, and a Marriage, A" (Twain), 265-267, 278, 281
Muscatine, Iowa, 17
"My Debut as a Literary Person" (Twain), 263
"My Platonic Sweetheart" (Twain), 280
Myers, F. W. H., 280

"Mysterious stranger" themes, 18, 64, 67, 81, 126, 236, 262-263, 266-267, 274-275, 277, 283; and *A Connecticut Yankee in King Arthur's Court*, 246; in jumping frog story, 259

Native Americans; in *Roughing It*, 161; in *Tom Sawyer*, 55
Nevada, 21, 24, 83, 117, 140, 142; lecture tours in, 21, 25; and *Roughing It*, 55, 70, 156; Sagebrush School, 122; silver mining, 141; territorial government, 20, 113
New Orleans, Louisiana, 18-19, 32, 73, 112
New York City, 17, 22, 25, 38, 113
New Zealand, 36, 56
"Nigger," 83, 217, 220; in *Huckleberry Finn*, 216-219, 229
North Africa, 148
North American Review, 300
"Notorious Jumping Frog of Calaveras County, The" (Twain). *See* Jumping frog story
No. 44, The Mysterious Stranger (Twain), 18, 111, 126, 275
Nye, Emmy, 27

"Occurrence at Owl Creek Bridge, An" (Bierce), 123, 132
"Old Fogy, An" (Adeler), 286
"Old Masters," 54, 153
"Old Times on the Mississippi" (Twain), 18, 31-32, 50
Ordeal of Mark Twain, The (Brooks), 62
Orwell, George, 261
Osgood, James, 32
Overland Monthly, 21, 70, 116
Oxford University, 38, 60

Paige, James W., 33, 274
Paige compositor, 33-35, 274
Paine, Albert Bigelow, 39, 78, 270;
    Mark Twain biography, 217
Palestine, 23
Pap Finn. *See* Finn, Pap
Paris, 54, 153; balloon ascension,
    265
Parker, Edwin Pond, 73
Peck's Bad Boy and His Pa, 100
Personal Recollections of Joan of Arc.
    See *Joan of Arc*
"Petrified Man" (Twain), 263-267
Phelps, Elizabeth Stuart, 290
Phelps, Roswell H., 32
Phelps, Sally (*Huckleberry Finn*), 99,
    106, 186, 213, 217, 229; character
    of, 182
Phelps, Silas (*Huckleberry Finn*), 197,
    208
Philadelphia, 17
Philippines, 51, 57, 91, 130
Philmus, Robert M., 261
Photography, 6, 49
Pinkerton, Jan, 274
Plasmon, 273
Playwriting, 30, 273, 283
Poe, Edgar Allan, 123, 131, 261, 265,
    267, 283, 290
Polly, Aunt (*Huckleberry Finn*), 100
Polly, Aunt (*Tom Sawyer*), 12, 14, 52,
    168-172
Pond, James B., 36
Potter, Muff (*Tom Sawyer*), 166-167
Pound, Ezra, 63
Powers, Ron, 79
Practical jokes, 100, 141, 237; and
    hoaxes, 236
Prince and the Pauper, The (Twain),
    32, 55, 289; classic status of, 3;
    reviews of, 73; slavery in, 15

"Private History of a Campaign That
    Failed, The" (Twain), 19, 128
Pudd'nhead Wilson (Twain), 34;
    fingerprinting in, 97, 274; reviews of,
    75-76; slavery in, 34, 83, 95, 97
"Pudd'nhead Wilson's Calendar," 58,
    118-119

Quaker City (ship), 22-23, 25, 32, 53,
    146, 155; itinerary, 23, 155
Quarles, John, 16, 27
Quarry Farm, 27, 36
Quirk, Tom, 81

Race, 52, 97; and identity, 34;
    stereotypes, 219-220
Racism, 53, 97, 224, 289; and
    Huckleberry Finn, 53, 103, 215-216,
    228-229; and slavery, 80
Railroads, 5, 155, 266
Railton, Stephen, 5
Rasmussen, R. Kent, 82, 119
Rasselas (Johnson), 267
Reconstruction, 114, 216, 218, 226; and
    Huckleberry Finn, 218
Redding, Connecticut, 39, 297
Reference works, 82
Religion, 83, 123-127, 226, 236, 243,
    260; in *Connecticut Yankee*, 249,
    252-253
Riis, Jacob, 52
Riverworld series (Farmer), 282-283
Robinson, Forrest G., 78, 81
Rogers, Henry Huttleston, 35, 298
Rohman, Chad, 81
Roman Catholic Church, 249
Rome, 154-155, 162
Roosevelt, Theodore, 60, 91; and Tom
    Sawyer, 101
Rotundo, E. Anthony, 90
Roughing It (Twain), 20, 27, 55, 113,

125, 141, 158-159, 162; fictional elements of, 29; and Hawaiian letters, 142; Indians in, 161; publication of, 156; reviews of, 70; structure of, 156; success of, 25

Roxana (*Pudd'nhead Wilson*), 34, 75, 92, 95, 97, 302

Royal Nonesuch, 97

Ruskin, John, 155

Russia, 23, 155

Sacramento Union, 21, 142

Sagramor le Desirous, Sir (*Connecticut Yankee*), 244, 255

St. Louis, Missouri, 17, 19, 22, 32, 73, 112

Saint Nicholas Magazine, 35

St. Petersburg (*Tom Sawyer*), 51-53, 99, 105, 112, 132, 164-165, 167, 173; and Hannibal, 14, 16

San Francisco, 21, 24, 142-143, 145; and Ambrose Bierce, 114, 121, 124

Sand-Belt, Battle of the. *See* Battle of the Sand-Belt

Sandwich Islands. *See* Hawaii

Satan ("The Chronicle of Young Satan"), 263, 275-276

Sawyer, Sid (*Tom Sawyer*), 13

Sawyer, Tom (*Huckleberry Finn*), 99, 209; devotion to sentimental literature, 209-210; and Huck Finn, 192; and Jim, 220-221, 225, 227-228; as role model, 105

Sawyer, Tom (*Tom Sawyer*), 164, 169-170, 172, 178; death wishes, 175-176; fantasies of, 99, 173-174; future of, 99, 167, 177; heroism of, 176; and manhood, 170; and other children, 170; as a rebel, 169; role models for, 168, 170-171, 175; and violence, 172

Scharnhorst, Gary, 82

Schmidt, Barbara, 64

Schmitz, Neil, 190

Science fiction, 261-285, 287

Scott, Walter, viii, 131

"Secret History of Eddypus, the World-Empire, The" (Twain), 269-270, 272, 285

Self-pasting scrapbook, 32, 273

Sellers, Colonel (*The Gilded Age*), 30-31

Sentimentalism, 52, 59, 92, 108, 207, 209, 297

Sexuality, 60, 95, 174, 203

"Shackleford's Ghost" (Twain), 281

Shakespeare, William, 60, 97, 238

Shelden, Michael, 79

Shelley, Mary, 283, 288

Sherburn, Colonel (*Huckleberry Finn*), 182, 197, 202; manhood of, 89, 93-94, 96, 99, 102, 107

Sherman, William T., 23, 147

"Siamese twins," 34, 64, 265

Sid. *See* Sawyer, Sid (*Tom Sawyer*)

Slavery, 105, 214, 259; in *Connecticut Yankee*, 15, 57, 98, 250, 258; critical studies of, 83; in *Huckleberry Finn*, 102, 104, 212, 216, 223, 225-226, 228; Missouri, 15-16, 80; in *The Prince and the Pauper*, 15; in *Pudd'nhead Wilson*, 34, 95, 97; in *Tom Sawyer*, 52

Sloane, David E. E., 78

Slote, Daniel, 32

Smiley, Jim (jumping frog story), 21, 43

Smith, Henry Nash, 78, 194, 199, 291

Smith, John, 162

Snodgrass, Thomas Jefferson (pen name), 17

Social criticism, 128, 258, 292

Twichell, Joseph, 26
Typesetter, automatic. *See* Paige compositor
Typewriters, 5, 50, 274

Uncle Tom's Cabin (Stowe), 84, 227
"United States of Lyncherdom, The" (Twain), 57
Utopia (More), 277

Verne, Jules, 261, 265-267, 283
Violence, 90-91; in *Connecticut Yankee*, 9, 99, 244-245; in *Joan of Arc*, 107; and racism, 231; in *Roughing It*, 159; in *Tom Sawyer*, 102, 171-173; in *A Tramp Abroad*, 191
Virginia City Territorial Enterprise, 20-21, 142, 263
Virginia City, Nevada, 20-21, 143
Voltaire, 275
Vonnegut, Kurt, 263-265, 268, 276, 282
Voorsanger, Jacob, 124

Wagenknecht, Edward, 274
Wakeman, Ned, 22
Walter Scott (steamboat), 187, 200, 207
War, 91, 107, 130, 244, 251; and Ambrose Bierce, 114, 129-130; and Mark Twain, 128. *See also* Civil War
"War Prayer, The" (Twain), 57, 128
Ward, Artemus, 7-8, 42
Warner, Charles Dudley, 12, 30, 71
Warner, Susan, 290, 292

Washington, D.C., 17, 24
Wasp, 111, 117, 119, 121, 127
Watson, Miss (*Huckleberry Finn*), 190, 205, 292, 294; death of, 209; and Jim, 192, 198, 206, 212
Webster, Charles L., 33-34. *See also* Charles L. Webster & Co.
Wells, H. G., 261, 267, 276-277, 281, 283
West Point (*Connecticut Yankee*), 245
What Is Man? (Twain), 38, 61, 62, 236, 274, 277, 281
Wheeler, Simon (jumping frog story), 43
Whitman, Walt, 152, 186, 195, 270, 290
Whittier, John Greenleaf, 32, 59-60
Wilks, Mary Jane (*Huckleberry Finn*), 195, 208
Wilks sisters (*Huckleberry Finn*), 190, 198
Wilson, David (*Pudd'nhead Wilson*); manhood of, 90, 97, 101, 104, 107
Wilson, Harriet, 290
Wilson, James D., 82
Wilson, John Lyde, 90
Wissenschaft, Sir (*A Tramp Abroad*), 271
Wit, 59, 118-119, 133; in *Huckleberry Finn*, 208
Wolff, Cynthia Griffin, 8
Women, 92, 143, 168, 179

Zadig (Voltaire), 275
Ziff, Larzer, 83